Tony Tales
An Anthological Journey

Rev. R. Tony Ricard, M.Th., M.Div.
A Priest of the Archdiocese of New Orleans
and An Extremely Grateful Soul

Two Knights Publishing Company
25 Christopher Court
New Orleans, Louisiana 70128

First Edition 2016

Tony Tales

Request for permission must be addressed in writing to:

Two Knights Publishing Co.
25 Christopher Court
New Orleans, Louisiana 70128

Printed in the United States of America

For more information about Two Knights Publishing Co. or KnightTime Ministries, please visit

www.**FatherTony**.com

All Scriptural quotations are from the New American Bible.

Book edited by Rev. R. Tony Ricard, M.Th., M.Div.

Contributing Photographer - Paula Burch-Celentano

ISBN-13:   978-0-9793157-6-3
ISBN-10:   0-9793157-6-X

**With a truly Grateful Soul,
I am honored to dedicate this book to
those who have helped me keep our Eaglets in Catholic Schools:**

The Los Angeles Religious Education Congress Family
Especially my "Congress Fans"
Ms. Sheryl Lange, Archdiocese of Los Angeles
Mr. James "Jim" Murphy
Mrs. Rosa Gallardo and The DBS Krewe
Jonathan, Erin and Charlie Avila

Mrs. Frances Ramirez (My #1 Stalker in Heaven)

Holy Name of Jesus Catholic Church, Los Angeles, CA

The African-American Catholic Center for Evangelization

The Father Tony Documentary
Cynthia Capen, Producer
Bjorn Madrid, Graphic Artrist

All of my Canadian Friends and Family
Especially Mr. Larry Elliott (in Heaven)

The National Catholic Youth Conference
Dioceses and Youth from all Across our Nation

My Personal Family
Kevin Ricard and Deidra Lopez
Corey, Andrew, Shanna,Albert & Kristen
Paul Florez and all the Florezes
My Boys: Dernattel, Steve, Cedric, Chris, Denzel,
Justin-Juggy, Brandon & ,Tavis
The Grand Kids: Jada, Lil Dee, Chortni, Landon and Zahri
My Best Friends: Cathy Allain and Glenn Chenier
Uncle Glenn and Aunt Susan Ricard

Much Love to All of Y'all!

Introduction

I give thanks to my God through Jesus Christ for all of you,
because your faith is heralded throughout the world.[1]

During the summer of 2004, Chris Quest and I spent weeks working a a prayer booklet for St. Augustine High School. Back then, Chris had just finished his sophomore year of high school and I had been named as the new Campus Minister of my Alma Mater. Our vision was to create a booklet the teachers and students could use in the classroom and at home.

Because we wanted our booklet to look official, we decided to create our own publishing company. It was in that summer that the Two Knights Publishing Company was born. We called ourselves Two Knights Publishing because we were two Purple Knights from St. Augustine High School.

Who could believe that our little company would evolve into a very successful ministry? *KnightTime Ministries* is the offshoot of Two Knights Publishing Co. Through *KnightTime Minsitries*, we have helped to keep dozens of students in Catholic Schools. The past decade of book sales has allowed us to donate more than $100, 000 in financial assistance to several schools in the Archdiocese of New Orleans. To God be the Glory!

In 2006, following the aftermath of Hurricane Katrina, we work with the students of the MAX Satellite School to publish our first "official" book. *MAXimum Faith: Prayers and iby Young Katrina Survivors* is a great collection of faith and history. Through it, you can connect with the hearts of our youth as they triumphed over the greatest disaster in our nation's history.

Our second book, *I Still Believe: A Testimony of Faith After the Storm*, is filled with reflections by me on Faith-filled endurance. Our third publication, *Don't Be Stupid: Lessons You should Already Know*, brings together awesome lessons from Jesus, my Momma and me.

Through our fourth book *I Don't Make them Up: Reflections, Stories and Jokes from a Faithful Fool*, we shared almost all of the major stories that I use during my presentations. Our fifth book, *Keepin' It Real: Reflections on Faith, Hope and Forgiveness,* has spiritual reflections in both English and Spanish.

---

[1]Romans 1:8

Our sixth book, *The Eagle Story*, is a children's book that focuses on our being chosen by God to soar on Eagles' Wings. It was illustrated by Anthony Jones, a 16 year old artist from St. Augustine High School. It also tells The Eagle Story in Spanish.

In our seventh book, *Diary of an Unapologetic Roman Catholic Priest*, I stepped out in faith to "tell it like it is." This book is filled with 52 letter that each teach valuable lessons on faith and our relationship with God.

To create our eight book, *A New Purple Heart: Reflections and Poems by Young Purple Knights*, we worked with Mr. Chad Smith and the 6th and 7th Grade Students from st. Augustine High School. It is a awe-inspiring collection of faith and courage by our young soldiers on the Battlefield for Our Lord.

Our ninth book, *The Gumbo Pot*, was dedicated to my Nanny. Like her delicious Gumbo, the book is filled with stories of Faith, Love and Forgiveness.

With the publication of *Tony Tales: An Anthological Journey,* we have officially reached out tenth book. This book is a collection of the "greatest hits" from our previous nine publications. It is filled with many of the "Sold out" stories and jokes that everyone has been waiting to have.

This book takes you on my journey from devastation to jubilation. It is a true example of what God will do for those who love Him.

This book is also a testimony of thanksgiving. I know that it is because of the people of God that we have been able to help so many of God's children.

I pray that God will bless you in great abundance for the many ways you have blessed me, my church, my family and my students. By purchasing our books and products, you are helping us to continue spreading the Love of God to people around the world.

It is because of you that I continue to give thanks to God!

Be blessed!

Rev. R. Tony Ricard, M.Th., M.Div.
A Priest of the Archdiocese of New Orleans
and An Extremely Grateful Soul

Table of Contents

Book One

MAXimum Faith

Prayers and Reflections
by
Young Katrina Survivors

edited with an introduction and prayers by

**Rev. R. Tony Ricard, M.Th., M.Div.
and Mr. Chris A. Quest, II**

 Published in 2006

Introduction to MAXimum Faith

The American Heritage Dictionary of the English Language defines "Maximum" as "the time or period during which the highest point or degree is attained."

It defines "Faith" as "The theological virtue defined as secure belief in God and a trusting acceptance of God's will."

As Men and Women of *MAXimum Faith*, we use our time here on Earth to attain the highest degrees of success by relying on God's Love and Grace.

Hurricane Katrina rocked the City of New Orleans and the Gulf Coast Region on August 29, 2005. Never could we have imagined the great destruction this storm would cause. Never could we have imagined the pain and heartache that we would have to endure. Yet, somehow, we are surviving. Somehow, we are making it. We know that it is through God's Grace that we have been able to make it this far. Our Faith is what has strengthened us for the Battle of Recovery.

The MAX Satellite School of New Orleans was a direct result of Hurricane Katrina and the *MAXimum Faith* of three Historically Black Catholic High Schools. Back in September of 2005, the leaders of St. Mary's Academy, St. Augustine High School and Xavier University Preparatory High Schools banded together to provide a combined institution for our particular students. The MAX School proved to be one of the greatest blessings to come out of the Katrina Recovery efforts. The MAX became a major piece in this most crucial period in the history of our great nation. We were truly blessed to be able to write our piece in that history.

In this Post-Katrina Era, we truly understand that success should not be measured solely in economic or material achievements. (*Katrina has help us understand that quite clearly.*) True Success is measured by our relationship with God and how much we have grown to Know Him, Love Him and Serve Him. If we attain True Success on Earth, we will attain the highest point of human existence as we join God and all the Saints in the Kingdom of Heaven.

This book was comprised of prayers, poems and narratives that were written by the Truly Successful members of the MAX family. It is a collection of our heartfelt communication with God. It is also our way of sharing our true faith with our nation.

We commit ourselves to God through the prayers of our Ancestors in Faith:
Mary, St. Joseph, St. Augustine of Hippo, St. Katherine Drexel, SBS, Venerable Mother Henriette Delille, SSF - a Servant of God, and **St. Elizabeth Ann Seton, SC**.

Rev. R. Tony Ricard, M.Th., M.Div.
St. Augustine Class of 1982

Chris A. Quest, II
St. Augustine Class of 2006

Basic Katrina Statistics

★   Hurricane Katrina made landfall in Louisiana on The Morning of August 29, 2005

★   80% of the City of New Orleans was flooded

★   The Water levels reached as deep as 20 feet

★   90,000 miles covered by official national disaster declaration

★   Estimated cost of damages to the region: more than $200 Billion

★   An estimated 2/3 of the City of New Orleans' population was displaced by the Storm

★   As of January 18, 2006, 3200 people were still declared missing

★   More than 1,000,000 residents evacuated from the affected areas

★   Catholic Charities' Second Harvest Food Bank of Greater New Orleans and Acadiana has distributed more than 40 million pounds of food

★   As of March 9, 2006, the Official Louisiana Death toll stands at 1418 people - 1,833 lives were lost during and after the storm

MAXimum Belief: The Editors

"Taking It To The Max"

Rams, Cougars Jackets and Knights:
banding together to put up a fight.

All four groups were battered.
Their hearts were all torn.
For, Katrina tried to destroy
the place they were born.

She hit them really hard.
She knocked down their walls.
She even closed the doors
of their honored school halls.

Somehow, Katrina thought that
she'd win this fight.
But that girl wasn't ready
For Rams, Cougars Jackets and Knights.

They banded together to form one accord.
They showed their allegiance to our Savior and Lord.

And, with Jesus to guide them,
they fought back with pride.
Knowing that the Lord
was right by their side.

Young Black and Gifted:
Young Strong and Brave,
together they'd send Katrina
to her watery grave.

They are weathering the storm.
They are enduring the attacks.
With Jesus close by
they're *Taking it to the MAX*.

Rev. R. Tony Ricard, Campus Minister

A Dream From the Past, Present, and Future

As I walked in to my house, today
I was greeted by my son, who had plenty to say

He began on what he had learned in class
And while listening I couldn't help but to think of how time had past

He looked up, into my face
And saw a slight smile, and a stare into space

He looked and said, " Dad, not again,
another story? These never end."

I laughed and said, " Come sit down son, right here next to me.
I'm going to give you a lesson in History.

When I was growing up I met this girl.
This girl who had come to change my world.

She swept in faster than a speeding car.
I then said, but may I ask, who it is that you are?

She replied, You'll never meet anyone meaner.
For my name is Katrina!!!
And, I have come to make this dirty place cleaner.

I said, look around, everybody's down,
people are without homes on each side of town.

She said, young man you should see this as a gift.
I said, and why is that whose spirits did you uplift?

She said, my boy, these were not just idol attacks.
For this is your chance to take it to the MAX.

I said, what is this *talk that you talk*?
She said, in January down the halls of the MAX you will walk.

Rams, Jackets, Cougars, and Knights
In a confused way, I replied, Nah that ain't right.

Oh, but it is together you'll be
As one big, happy family.

And until the day that you finish the race
There will be those who doubt that it should ever take place.

But you'll move along, and at a positive rate
For you are now one, and your bonded by faith.

She continued by saying,
I leave you now with a boggled brain,
but you now also know what you must obtain

I sat there for a while dazed and confused
And I didn't understand until my first day of school.

I then realized that this was a gift from above
Three schools in one that are filled with God's love.

With everyone's perseverance and strength
The MAX was an awesome experience."

After completing my story, I looked at my son
On his face was disbelief, with him seeming outdone

He said, " Who would have ever thought,
that my father fought a war that had to be fought.

I laughed and said, " Son, this is something that had to be.
I was a part of the MAX, and that its History."

Then the alarm clock rang and my eyes opened up.
For this was all a dream, and I had just woken up.

Then I got all dressed and ready, and to school I went.
For this was the place, where my most valuable time is spent.

I learned that all knowledge is mine for the taking,
and that I'm at the MAX and this is history in the making.

Chris A. Quest, II, 12th Grade

"Reading the Restless Heart"

Can anyone pierce his armor
    in order to read his heart?

He is the Knight.
    Strong, Fearless, Victorious.

He is the Purple Knight. . . .
    My brother....my friend.

For decades he has worked to build his Castle
    and protect His Center of Love.

Yet not even his armor could not prevent his pain.

The storm roared.
    The winds battered.
        The sea rose like none had ever seen before.

Yet, the Knight stood his watch.

Striving to protect his Castle....
    Working to protect his Heart.

Now he stands battered and worn.

His armor has taken a beating,
    the walls of his Castle destroyed.

But, his Faith is unyielding
    and his Heart is still strong.

He is a Knight: a Purple Knight.

He is the Champion of the Restless Heart.

How blessed am I to have the privilege of reading his Restless Heart.

Rev. R. Tony Ricard, Campus Minister

Blessed Assurance is our Blessed Insurance

Bak in October of 2005, I went to New Orleans to begin the process of sorting through all of my stuff in the Rectory. I assure you, it was not an easy task. Trying to decide what to keep and what to throw-out means trying to decide what memories are more precious than others. Some things are worth the fight of cleaning while other things, well, "You Just Gotta Let It Go!"

In the Archdiocese of New Orleans, we have had several churches that were devastated by the Storm. Churches like St. Maria Goretti, St. Raphael and St. Philip are going to have a tough time putting everything back in order. Many of our places saw their pews tossed like toothpicks by the flood waters. Others saw rectories and offices decimated by the winds. There will be a lot of Precious Memories to sort through in our Churches.

One of the great tasks, following a storm, is writing a list of items that were lost in the storm. When you meet with the insurance adjusters, they are looking for lists of things that need to be replaced or repaired. Creating these lists is also a tough task.

In doing the list, you have to really think about all that has been lost. In the city, we have received reports of folks committing suicide as a result of thinking about what they lost. (May God have mercy on their souls.)

One of the great lessons that Hurricane Katrina has taught us is the fact that you can accumulate an awful lot of stuff but in the end, "You can't take it with you." Material things are material things. Only your Spiritual Treasures will be with you when you reach your final destination: our home in Heaven. (Remember: You have never seen a Hearse pulling a U-Haul - YOU Can't take it with you!)

In the Gospel of Matthew, Jesus said,
> "You shall love the Lord, your God,
> with all your heart, with all your soul, and with all your mind.
> This is the greatest and the first commandment.
> The second is like it: You shall love your neighbor as yourself."
> Matthew 22:37-39

In this, Jesus tells us just what is most important in life: Love for God, Love for our Neighbors and love for Ourselves.

The inventory that will really matter most in life is our Inventory of Love. Our acts of love will be the treasure that we will store up in Heaven.

As nice as a 52 inch Plasma TV may be, as nice as a PT Cruiser may be, as nice as 200 plus DVD's of your favorite movies may be, loving God, loving our Neighbors and loving Ourselves will be more valuable in the long haul.

8

Hurricane Katrina brought a lot of work for us to do. And, it really isn't easy. When we meet with our insurance adjusters, they really are taking account of all that we have, all that we have done in life and all that we have achieved. It really is tough trying to put all of that down on paper.

Well, soon, we are going to have to meet with the Big Adjuster in the sky. Instead of meeting with men from State Farm, All State or Geico, we will have to meet with the MAN from GOD-CO (The only Insurance Company that truly matters).

Soon, Jesus, the Great Adjuster, will come to collect and inspect our Inventories of Love. And, those inventories will determine just how nice our lives will be when we get to our New House in Heaven.

Almost 2000 years ago, he purchased our Eternal Life Insurance Policy when he paid the ultimate price on a Hill called Calvary. Each Sunday, when we come to the Eucharist, Jesus pays our home owner's insurance premium with the ultimate payment deal: His Body and His Blood.

His Blessed Assurance is our Blessed Insurance.

In the Blessed Sacrament, Our Blessed Insurance is presented to us by our Insurance Adjuster. And that really is our Blessed Assurance!

May God continue to Bless all of us on this Journey!

Written on October 25, 2005

Rev. R. Tony Ricard, Campus Minister

The Soldiers in Your Army

Dear Lord,

The dealings with Hurricane Katrina have been devastating.

Yet, you never cease to amaze.

I am blessed to be able to realize all that you do for me, my family, and my friends.

I pray strongly for those who have lost faith in you,
     and also for those who don't seem to understand you.

Lord, use me as a vocal instrument, to help people realize that
     the good in this out weighs the bad.

Lord help me so that I may continue to find the positive
     in things that seem to be totally negative.

Help me Lord, to be strong for all those who may cross my path,
     in their times of weakness.

Lord, give those who are impatient, patience;
     Those who at times lose sight of you,
     the vision to see that you have our best in mind and at heart.

Lord, we realize that this was always in the plan
     and that we will never have to bear more than we can handle.

So use us the soldiers in your army,
     to fulfill all goals that you have in store for us.

Allow them to come back and have better attitudes, get better jobs,
     and build their homes better than ever before.

Amen.

Chris A. Quest, II, 12th Grade

Don't Forget the Children

Lord, as we try to get our lives back on track,
please help us to remember the children.

Unlike us, Lord,
they are not yet at a level of faith that they can simply say,
"It was God's Will" or "Thy will be done."

Thy are children:
preciously innocent and still quite naive.

Too many grown folks expect them to somehow "just understand."

But, Lord,
how can we expect them to understand
when we are grappling with trying to understand all of this ourselves.

So, Lord,
please don't forget the children.

Help them to use this time to grow in faith.
Help them to use this time to grow in hope.
Help them to use this time to grow in love.
And Lord,
Help them to use this time to grow in maturity.

But, Lord,
most of all. . . when all is said and done,
please help them to still be children.

We need the children to still be children:
preciously innocent and still quite naive.

'Cause when the children are children,
we realize that we have to be the grown folks:
called to protect Your children.

So, Lord, please don't forget the children.

Rev. R. Tony Ricard, Campus Minister

Stirred but Not Shaken!

Here in New Orleans, during the holiday season, one of our local television channels runs a series called "Twelve for the Road." During the Twelve Days of Christmas, they ask local celebrities to offer personal recipes for non-alcoholic drinks that folks could fix during the holidays.

Some of our local greats like Aaron Neville, Anne Rice, and Pete Fountain have all participated in this wonderful series. Some of you may know that my father, Rodney J. Ricard, is a recovering alcoholic. On November 18, 2005, he celebrated his 26th year of Sobriety! Having an alcoholic father makes me truly appreciate News Programs that offer non-alcoholic alternatives for celebrations.

I thought about that news series this morning because today, Thanksgiving Day, is the official beginning of the Holiday Season. For those of us who live in New Orleans, this season lasts until the Easter Season. We journey from Thanksgiving Day through Advent, Christmas, New Years, Twelfth Night, Mardi Gras, Lent and into Easter. Beginning on Thanksgiving Day, there is usually a lot of partying going-on in the Big Easy.

In the aftermath of Hurricane Katrina, some folks will be in "I don't wanna party" moods. It is tough to get into the Holiday Spirit when your home is still cover in mold and your insurance company is dragging its "you-know-what" in getting your insurance settlements completed. Yet, when we think about it, we do have reasons to celebrate.

In my personal family, we did not lose anyone's life during the storm. All of my relatives are alive and well. Though we collectively lost more than 1,000,000 dollars in properties, what is most precious to us is still with us.

My church families are also going to be OK. St. Philip the Apostle Parish was devastated by the storm. The interior of the church was pretty much destroyed. More than 8 feet of water ravaged the interior of the facilities. The Altar, the pews and the organs were all strewn about. It looks like a giant came by and played "pick-up sticks" with our church. There is even a pew sitting on top of our pulpit. How it got there, only God knows. Yet, the Tabernacle remained on its stand and the Crucifix that is suspended in the center of the Sanctuary still hangs there, untouched by the devastation.

Our Lady Star of the Sea will hopefully be up and running for Christmas Day. Inside this church, we only had about six inches of water. The church sits about five feet above the ground. Thus, the ravaging waters that rose outside were not high enough to do extensive damage inside. Though we did lose the boiler and the air conditioners, we have been told that once the electrical stuff is checked and the boiler is replaced, we should be able to "Have Church," again.

My rectory is in the process of being cleaned-out. The same goes for the houses of my parents and the rest of my family. I am guessing that we will be able to at least use a portion of the rectory in a few months.

In the great aftermath of Hurricane Katrina, we are in the full swing of restoration!

That is why I thought about the "Twelve for the Road" news series. You see, quite often when a celebrity is making a special concoction for the viewing audience to try, they will tell you to put all of the ingredients in a mixing bowl and stir the mixture up. Some may tell you to put the ingredients in a drink shaker and "shake it up." One way or another, you have to mix it up to really make it work well.

Well, I think that's what has happened to my city, my family and my churches. Hurricane Katrina blew into our city and truly mixed-us-up. But, rather than leaving a confusing path of devastation, I now see a faith-filled path of revitalization. I fully believe that God is using the aftermath of Hurricane Katrina to create a "New" New Orleans that will be a special concoction filled with the ingredients of love, care and determination.

In the Aftermath of Katrina, I have come to realize that the City of New Orleans has been "stirred but not shaken!"

What is emerging in our City is a Spirit of Community, a Love for the Common Good and a True Concern for the Welfare of All. In a place that was once known as the "Murder Capital of the World," we are now becoming the "New Life Capital of the World." We are truly seeing the creation of a better New Orleans.

Everything we know has changed. Life as we know it may never be the same. However, we are determined to persevere and make our city a better place than it was when Katrina stirred us up on August 29, 2005.

Because we know that God is with us on our mixed-up journey of restoration, we can truly say that we have been "stirred but not shaken!"

Thanksgiving Day, November 24, 2005

Rev. R. Tony Ricard, Campus Minister

13

MAXimum Potential: The Seventh Grade

Thinking about the Days

I think of the time when I was at home,
Maybe with someone or even alone.

Thinking about the days or the time that has past,
since Hurricane Katrina came with Wrath.

Sometimes you want to scream or shout in pain,
because people were lost in water like rain.

Even tear drops fall from your eye
when You've found out a family member has died.

But don't keep crying you are not alone.

Other people have suffered, they feel your pain.
I know things won't be the same.
But soon we will rebuild and you can go home again

Glenn Gilyot, 7th Grade

Night Time Prayer

Now I lay down to sleep on 8/29/05 I weep.
I prayed the Lord my soul to keep.

Before I woke the water rose like a lake.
I prayed the Lord my soul to take.

Katrina was here but now she's gone.
New Orleans is left all alone.

I prayed to the Lord and now I'm back at home.

Russell Cornin, 7th Grade

14

MAXimum Strength: The Eighth Grade

You've Done So Much for Me

Lord, You've done so much for me
That all I can say is thank you
Even though there were hard times
You still brought us through

Thank you for keeping my friends
And family in your hands.
Thank you for showing that protecting us
Was always in your plans.

There were even some times
When I doubted your power
But every time I needed you
You were with me every hour.

I pray that my family
My friends and myself
Always have you when
We need some help?

I know all of my blessings
Come from you up above
And I'm glad to know
They come from you with love.

Amen

Brittany Stepter , 8th Grade

I Thought It Was A Dream

Lord help me through these hard times
and make me understand that this was a part of your glory. . .

What the storm had done and what it could have done.

Lord when this happened,
I thought it was a dream,
but it turned out a nightmare.

The only thing that helped me was your praise.

My mother, dad, grandma, grandpa, and my siblings needed you
and you were there.

I knew you were there
and that you helped us.

For that, I am eternally thankful.

Bradley Chapman, 8th Grade

Home

What are you going to do when you go home and realize that your home is gone?

When you step into the room that was once yours
      and you come to realize that it is no more?

When you think about all the people that died, and it really makes you want to cry.

People were moved to the Superdome, then to the Astrodome,
      and some still wander looking for a place to call home.

When the path you take seems almost unbearable
      if you trust in God it's never impossible.

When you want to keep going but it seems too hard,
      just believe that God will help you and you will go far.

From the people standing on top of their home,
      to the people living in the Superdome, everyone can use the help of God,
      the power of the most high.

      So I ask again:

What are you going to do when you go and realize that you're HOME IS GONE?

Janquil Poret, 8th Grade

The Death of a City

There was no way out
> There was no hope
Imagine your life
> Depending on your neighbor's boat

It wasn't just for clothes and shoes
> They had to loot for H2O and food

So it wasn't stupid antics
> What if the water was up to your attic?

What about safety on the streets?
> No peace because of no police

What happened to the President
> No trace of him no evidence
he's hiding
> Hiding in his residence

My people we need to better our self
> So next hurricane we can fend for our self
And that putting power to self

The more you know
> the more you grow

Knowledge is wealth
> Be optimistic don't feel hurt

The death of the city just means a rebirth

Rodja Fields, 9th Grade

17

After the Pain

After all the pain and all the rain
will it be the same?

If you could turn back the hands of time
would you?

Or would you rather see it go down in the history books?

All the tears
All your fears
happened all in one day.

Watched as the water
filled up our precious houses
and took all of our memories away.

After all the pain and all the rain
will it be the same?

Sometimes I wonder
whether or not
the city will be halfway the unique city it once was.

If you had to deal with this,
what would you do?

Everyday we have to live our lives
as if it was our last day alive.

Because now its clear in my mind
what a storm like this could do.

So now let me ask you

After all the pain and all the rain
will it be the same?

Will it be New Orleans?

Lindsey Hubbard, 9th Grade

A Positive and A Negative Experience

For me, the Katrina experience was both a positive and a negative experience. Within my short life, I will always wonder why I had to go through this experience. But, I guess it had to come for a reason. It gave me more faith in God and most of all it helped me get closer to Him. It helped me to build a sense of security within my family by appreciating them more. It also helped me to learn more about how people react to a situation of this kind.

Katrina was a negative experience for me in three ways: death, destruction, and relocation. Katrina killed three people who I will no longer be able to see. My best friend Edward and his parents drowned during this hurricane. Edward was only thirteen years old and was looking forward to attending high school this fall. All of his dreams were thrown away when his parents decided to say in New Orleans instead of evacuating for the hurricane. Secondly, Katrina destroyed my grandmother's home. This was her first home and it was also a home for our family. Third, Katrina made my family move to Natchez, Mississippi, and then to Baton Rouge. This made it hard for me to go to school when my parents got transferred, because as soon as I got used to one school I had to go to another. In both of the schools, I had a negative experience. In Natchez, the students fought with us because we came from a Catholic school. In Baton Rouge, the Catholic school put us all in a class where we had to take classes that weren't challenging because they thought we could not be challenged academically. These were just a few negative assets I had to face during the hurricane.

The positive asset of Katrina was that it let me get closer to the Lord, brought me closer to my family, and made me appreciate my surroundings. Though Katrina may have made me question my faith, it also helped me to build up my prayer power with God. It made me realize how awesome the Lord can be. In one day He can destroy a whole coast line if He has to. Secondly, it helped me realize how much my family means to me, even though we had to stay together for a whole month, all sixteen of us. Throughout this time, I learned to be a peacemaker and a listener to among my cousins. Third, it made me aware of the fact that we can survive without material things such as a television, phone and even video games. For eleven days in Natchez, we were without electricity and in Baton Rouge we didn't have electricity for three days. This made us learn how to talk and play games with each other. To tell you the truth, this was exciting for all of us.

In conclusion, the experience of Katrina was said by others, to be a depressing time, but to my family and me, it was a building up period. When we thought that we lost love, yet we met people who needed to be loved. When we thought we were going to lose our faith, we found out that our faith in God grew even more. When we thought our financial stability was going to be destroyed we found out that, with God, we can build up to better financial goals. This experience taught me to appreciate what I have and enjoy life because you never know when it could be taken from you.

Raymond J. Brown, II, 9th Grade

19

MAXimum Courage: The Tenth Grade

Katrina and Cancer, Enough Already!

Back on February 23, 2005 at 5:30 PM, I got the news from the doctors at Children's Hospital in New Orleans that I had Hodgkin's Lymphoma, a form of Cancer. For the past several months, I have been going through all kinds treatments to help clear the cancerous cells from my body.

When the doctors told my family and me that I had cancer, everybody in the room was crying. But, I told them to stop because I wasn't planning on dying. I know that they were scared, but I was like "don't worry 'bout it." "I am gonna be alright."

The first thing I had to do after I was diagnosed was to have a port-a-cath placed in my chest. This was so that I could be hooked up to the chemotherapy treatments. I was afraid that once it was in my chest, I could be hit and really hurt. For the first few weeks, I was really really protective of my chest.

Going to get the chemo treatments wasn't as bad as I thought it would be. There were people in the hospital who look really sick. You could tell that they were suffering from something. But, I didn't look sick. For a while, I felt guilty because I looked too healthy.

For the next few months of treatments, I was doing fine. I never lost my hair and I looked pretty healthy. I was grateful that I wasn't looking as sick as I could have been looking. Everything was going well.

Just as I was supposed to be completing my last two treatments, Hurricane Katrina came. If having Cancer wasn't enough, now I had to deal with having cancer and running from a hurricane.

On Sunday, August 28, 2005 at 10:00 AM, my family evacuated to Jackson, Mississippi. We were able to find shelter in a local hotel. While we were having breakfast at a local waffle place, the first wave of winds from the hurricane hit Jackson. Signs were blowing everywhere. We went back to the hotel to take cover. By nightfall, the hurricane arrived and all the light went off.

Here we were, in Jackson, trying to run away from the storm, and it found us!

All I could think was "Enough Already!"

After the storm, we headed to Atlanta, Georgia. In Atlanta, we had to find a place for me to receive my Chemo Treatments. We looked in the phonebook and found the Scottish Rights Children's Hospital. There, I was able to meet a lot of great people and have my treatments taken care of.

While in Atlanta, I was enrolled at Lithia Springs High School. The folks at the school were very nice. And, the girls were as fine as fine could be (for adults that means they really looked good). And, they thought that I was cute, too. In fact, on the very first day that I was there, the captain of the cheerleading team asked for my phone number because she really wanted to be my friend (if you know what I mean).

The people in Atlanta were very nice to us. When one of the local churches heard that I was sick, they sent us food, clothes and money. But, when they came to meet me and saw how well I looked, they didn't believe I had cancer and even called me a liar. Later, they probably felt bad when they found out that I really was sick.

I finally was able to return to the New Orleans area on October 16, 2005. I couldn't come into the city because they were afraid that I would get sick. So, we stayed at my Paw Paw's house in Lacombe, LA. I enrolled at nearby Fontainebleau High School in Mandeville, LA. I had to go back and forth from Lacombe to Children's Hospital in New Orleans to continue my treatments.

Driving through the empty city wasn't easy. It was totally devastated by the storm. I wondered if the city would ever be the same. I also wondered if my friends would ever return from where they had evacuated.

Now, I am living in New Orleans at the house of my Momma's friend. We go back and forth from New Orleans to Lacombe to spend time with my Paw Paw.

Dealing with Katrina and Cancer at the same time has been a true learning experience. Although we are still dealing with aftermaths of the storm, we realize that we have gained a lot even as we access what we have lost.

Now, I am attending The MAX Satellite School of New Orleans. It is a school that has been formed by the three leading High Schools for African-American students in New Orleans. St. Mary's Academy, Xavier University Preparatory High and St. Augustine High (my school) have created a school that has made it possible for my friends and me to come back home. This is a history making experience. And, I am a major part of that history!

I am now finishing my radiation treatments. The treatments have caused my hair to thin but at least I haven't lost it. (I still look pretty good!) I realize now that both Katrina and Cancer can be hard to deal with. But, through it all, I have come to truly appreciate life and all that goes with it.

When you deal with having Cancer, you learn to appreciate the little things in life. I love just doing normal stuff. I especially love goofing off with my friends and family. I have never asked nor expected to be treated differently from any other person. (Even though, it is nice to be spoiled!!!)

I am thankful for everything that God has shown me through this tough path. I hope that I can one day inspire others to deal with the stuff in their lives as well as I have dealt with the stuff of my life.

If people can learn just one thing from my experiences, I hope that they learn to just be grateful for everything. Life is short so "live it up, ya dig."

Katrina and Cancer, what a pair?

But, with God on my side, I know that even a hurricane or a disease can't hurt me.

Cause, I am Blair K. McDonald a Soul Survivor! (And, I'm Real!)

Blair McDonald, 10th Grade

(A Note from Fr. Tony about Blair: I thank God for the gift of Mr. Blair McDonald. Watching him battle Cancer has been such a great source of strength for me and the rest of the St. Augustine High School community. Blair has shown us how we need to deal with the adversities of our lives.

Throughout our time of Katrina Exile, I stayed in contact with Blair and his step-mom, Juana Villavasso. Both are very strong persons. *You have to be strong if you are going to deal with Cancer and Katrina.* They are examples to us of how we should deal with all the troubles of life.

Their simple technique is this: ***Just Deal With It!*** And, in dealing with it, rely on the Love of God and the support of others to bring you through the heartaches and pain.

We continue to pray for Blair's victory over Cancer. But, since we have already claimed his Healing Miracle - In Jesus' Name - we only need to anticipate its arrival! We know that his complete healing is already on its way. Thank you, God, for Blair!)

2016 Update: Blair is now a three-times - Cancer Survivor! He is one of the strongest men that I am privileged to know. To God be the Glory!

When I Did Cry

I didn't cry when Katrina came nor when my house went under.

I didn't cry when I saw New Orleans my birthplace, my residence,
      and all I know of get destroyed..

I didn't cry when I knew we couldn't go back.

But, I did cry when my grandpa was missing for about two and half weeks.

The thought of not seeing him again was something I couldn't bare.
      I couldn't take it! It was as if something from my spirit wasn't there.

See he kept me alive, going, and energized.
Without him it's like being locked in a closet with no lights, no food, and no water.

So I prayed and prayed, and prayed, until one day I saw him on TV in a boat,
      holding my dog close to his chest.

After seeing him, we called all over and we finally received a call back.

It was my grandpa saying that he was fine.

      He said, "Don't worry. I will be there in time."

See that's when the storm was over for me.
      I was okay and no longer had to live in misery.

And, I cried, again.

Jazlyn Robertson, 10th Grade

Heart Be Still

God, may you grant me the power to settle my Restless Heart.
      For, the obstacles in my way tears me apart.
Through your mercy my mind will be made clear
      and my worries become just a memory.
I turn to you, now, for the power to go on here this day
      and the next following your ministry.

This day I turn to you to start,
      the rebirth of my Restless Heart.

Alacia Honora, 10th Grade

"Heavenly Father Will There Be A Tomorrow"

Oh Lord, as the water rose,
> We looked up to the heaven and asked,
> please spare us from this pending danger.

As we wondered what would come ashore,
> we prayed to You,
> please help us along with all of our little children.

Occasionally, we began to feel as though there would not even be a tomorrow.

Oh Father, we implore Your grace and many blessings
> for deliverance from this tragedy.

We heard many cries for help through the night;
> we held each other and cried out to our Blessed Mother, Mary.

Lead, guide, and strengthen us
> and help us deal with our plight
> by day and night. Amen!

Tayari Porche, 10th Grade

How Could I Look Back?

How could I look back to see that my city was destroyed?
How could I look back to see that it would hit so hard?
How could I look back to see that my people had suffered and died?
How could I look back to see that my world can be coming to an end?

How could I look back and wonder why?

How could I look back to see that my life had been turned all around?
How could I look back to see if there would be a new life?

How could I look back and question Jesus Christ?

How could I look back to see that New Orleans was over?
How could I look back and see that Jesus wanted us to be better?

How could I look back, sometimes never.

Michael Barnes, 10th Grade

MAXimum Praise: The Eleventh Grade

Give Us the Faith to Keep Going

Lord, give us the faith to keep going.

When the world seems over and all is lost, help us to keep going.
At the times when all we own is gone and all we have is faith, make us keep going.

In these trying times, when our world is crumbling to pieces, and we almost give up the little hope we have left, lead us to keep going. There will always be a time when we fall, give up the hope we have, and give in. Lord, force us to keep going. Pick us up and dust us off. Let us know that all is not lost and tomorrow is another day.

Remind us that You don't put us through anything we can't handle, and that we are blessed to be alive, because so many others don't have that. When we become ungrateful and take for granted all You have given us force us to realize that You are a merciful God and will give us all we need. When a blessing is all we seem to have reassure us that more is on the way. I know that some things that seem like curses are really blessings. We just have to find them.

Let all things be done by Your will. In Your Son Jesus' name I pray.

Amen.

Kia Turner, 11th Grade

In God We Trust

Dear God,

Thank You for bringing us through the storm.
        You kept us safe in your warm loving arms.

You brought my family and friends out of harm way.
        Thank you, God, is all I can say.

Bless every family and all whom we lost.
        Help us to rebuild no matter the cost.

Help us to praise You
        and to remember we must
never forget that in "God We Trust."

Amen.
Courtney Carr, 11th Grade

A Blessing in Disguise

Ever heard of the phrase " a blessing in disguise."

Those are really hard to realize especially with mass chaos going on all the time.

So many people complain and moan about their problems
       that they don't see the good in things.

KATRINA

      Mention that and you'll get a story out of anyone,
          but listen carefully as to what they say.

You'll hear how people traveled
      and were uprooted to places they never thought they'd go.

How they got help from both friendly and unfriendly faces,
      got a food stoop card or a FEMA check.

Then some might mention the heartache they felt when they came home and found out that they lost everything that they worked so hard for.

How there was traffic no matter where you want to go whether it was to Wal-Mart or to go to the neighborhood corner store or to go shopping because places closed early.

But how many will tell you they are thankful that she came;
      That she was their "Blessing in Disguise."

If you don't believe me just compare pre-Katrina to post-Katrina.
      The murder and crime rates are down.
      The job rate is higher than its been in a while.
      People are working together rather than against each other.

Sure people get frustrated and angry but most just deal with it and pray.
Because they know that tomorrow will be a better day.

There is always a helping hand out there.
      This school is an example of that hand.

Schools were damaged and students needed a place a little closer to home to go to.
Now we have The MAX where we are history in the making.

So Katrina turned out to be a "blessing in disguise."
Some may not think so, but I do…

Kirbye Sullivan, 11[h] Grade

MAXimum Success: The Twelfth Grade

Normal Times

My life was drastically changed on August 29, 2005. This was the day that Hurricane Katrina devastated the whole Gulf Coast. During the storm, we lost an awful lot of things. Some people miss their material possessions like games and clothes. I really don't miss these things as much as I miss the special moments my mom and I shared together.

One of the many special moments I really miss happened almost everyday before the storm. Each day, when I got home after a long day of practice, I used to grab a *Gatorade*, get on the Internet, watch *Recess* on the Disney Channel, and just relax.

Almost like clock work,
> my mom use to come into my room about 8:30 PM every night and say,
> "Korey, you can't do all of those things at one time…
> > turn off the computer or the T.V., right now!"

> I use to just move into the kitchen and watch *Recess*.
> Now my mom and I just laugh about this cherished moment.
> We both miss those "normal times."

When the youth of Katrina look back at our days before the storm, I'd bet that we all have those special moments we miss; especially the moments we share with our parents and/or our friends.

Korey Jones, 12th Grade

Lord, I Do Not Understand

Dear God,

I know that you are mighty and that all things happen for a reason, but this Lord I do not understand. Why did my city, my home, and my family have to suffer. As many hurricanes that have come and gone, Lord, why did You choose this one? It was the beginning of my senior year and I lost that. Lord, I know You work in mysterious ways, but Lord this mystery is just to hard to figure out.

Lord can You please help me? Can You bring my family back together and bring my friend back home? My Lord, can You help me get back all of the days of school I missed? My Savior can You give me back my home and my city? Lord, can You give me back my life?

Love,   A Troubled Soul

Courtney Duplessis, 12th Grade

Everything Happens for a Reason

Dear God,

You make everything happen for a reason. Although I've lost my home, my belongings, and most of all my senior year, I still have all of my family, and we are closer than ever. It was through You that we stuck together, during Katrina and Rita. It was because of You, we went our separate ways in the end. It was because of You, we were reunited of the eve of Your Son's birth. And it is because of You, that my fellow classmates and myself can still graduate from THE AUG. It is said that everything happens for a reason. And one day in the near future, I will figure out that reason.

In your name I pray, Amen.

Marcus Alston, 12th Grade

Questions?

O, Lord, the thunders are crying,
-What shall I do?
-Where shall I go?

People are crying and dying before my eyes,
-Is Katrina really a cleansing of my city?
-Why is there trash everywhere?
-Why is sin still going on in my city?

The rain has stopped showering, the wind has stopped blowing,
-Why is the water rising?

-Why are so many people crying?

-Why are so many people dying before my eyes?

Lord, this is my country,
-Why do they call us refugees?
-Why do they call us looters?

And the Lord said, "Just have faith and everything will be alright."

Johnathan Cummings, 12th Grade

"Senior Memories"

Senior memories is what this year was all about,
feelin' as if you run your high school,
because you've paid your dues out.
Placing pictures in a scrap book that enshrines
all those emotional moments of your last year.
In our minds, "doing it real big"
as we hold hands that last day shedding tears.
We had plans for homecoming,
and the limo's we would ride in.
Dates already set and couples carefully paired
not knowing in our naive minds
in 2 weeks where our journey's would really begin.
We were buying outfits for St. Aug's Jamboree,
and begging mama to let us see the car.
Knowing us, we could never show up in anything
less than the best when perpetrating our frauds.
The news began to broadcast
the need for everyone to go ahead and get out.
So we packed up our bags
laughing at how we would be back next week
eatin' pancakes and actin' like clowns at school.
We were having fun going to the mall
with clothes that we couldn't wait to show off.
But to our surprise the TV gave us teary eyes,
because we were now faced with a situation we didn't know to solve.
3 weeks later we were enrolled in schools that we knew nothing of.
In our new uniforms we walked down the halls through crowds of students
who didn't care to show us any love.
The conversations became more distant,
because we were now displaced.
Our future didn't seem so bright anymore,
because all we could talk about
was the Red Cross and FEMA problem that we began to embrace.
Our senior memories are now pictures
of our destroyed homes and FEMA trailers.
Our journals are testimonies of shattered
dreams that the world might views as failures.
But what the news didn't report was our strength,
and the tears we wept for the other unfortunate few.
Senior memories is what for this year was all about,
they're not for senior trips and back to school dances,
they're of the city we once had and the people we once knew.
Our senior memories are constant remainders of our struggle.
Our pain and our lives.

Whitley Mercadel, 12th Grade

Book Two

I Still Believe!
A Testimony of Faith After the Storm!

Rev. R. Tony Ricard, M.Th., M.Div.

 Published in 2007

Introduction to *I Still Believe*

On August 29, 2005, life as I knew it was changed forever. It was on this date that Hurricane Katrina, the costliest storm in the history of the United States, struck the Gulf Coast. Never could I have imagined the great destruction this storm would cause. Never could I have imagined the pain and heartache that we, the *Katrina Survivors*, would have to endure.

Yet, somehow, we are surviving.
Somehow, we are making it.
And, somehow, *We Still Believe!*

We know that it is through God's Grace that we have been able to make it this far. Our faith is what has strengthened us for the *Battle of Recovery*.

As I look back on my post-Katrina journey, I realize now, more than ever, how much God loves us. This is my testimony to that faith.

The reflections in this book speak about keeping the faith in tough times. It is my hope that the People of God will find strength and encouragement in these words.

As the old folks would say,
> *"As long as there is a God in Heaven,*
> *I know that I am going to be all right!"*

That is why. . .
> I Still Believe!
> I Still Believe in Jesus Christ, the Son of the Living God!
> I Still Believe That You Can't Let the Devil Steal Your Joy!
> I Still Believe That Mary, Jesus' Momma, Can Help Us!
> I Still Believe That We All Have a Call!
> I Still Believe that Everybody Deserves A Little Lagniappe!"

With this faith, now offered to you is My Testimony of Faith After the Storm!

In Christ,
Rev. R. Tony Ricard, M.Th., M.Div.
A Priest of the Archdiocese of New Orleans
and a Hurricane Katrina Survivor

Part One
"I Still Believe!"

Our Lady Star of the Sea Church
September 13, 2005

Two weeks after Hurricane Katrina

"I Still Believe!"

Oh, how quickly the Year 2006 has passed. How quickly my life has been changed. How quickly life as I know it will never be the same. Looking back on all that I have had to endure in the Post-Katrina Era, I think that I can truly testify to the fact that God will never put more on me than I can bear.

Hurricane Katrina has forever changed life as I know it: my parishes, my family and my priesthood.

Before the storm, I was the Pastor of Our Lady Star of the Sea and St. Philip the Apostle Parishes in New Orleans. My parents, brother and sister were all doing well; living happily in their respective homes with their families.

On August 29, 2005, Hurricane Katrina flooded all of our buildings in Our Lady Star of the Sea Parish. In the rectory, there was at least 3 and a half feet of flood waters. We lost everything that was on the first floor. This included the offices, den, kitchen, meeting room and work room. Everything was destroyed and needed to be replaced.

In our School building, there was approximately six feet of flood waters. The cafeteria and reception hall were completely destroyed. Along with those two great rooms, the School of Religion's office and two classrooms were also lost. The school's roof was so damaged that the entire covering needed to be replaced. This means that the second floor rooms of the school were also severely damaged.

In our Church, we ended up being pretty lucky. We only endured 2 inches of water inside the church because it was built five feet off of the ground. Though the floors of the church were pretty nasty, we only needed to have them cleaned in order to begin our preparations for re-opening. We did have a great deal of electrical wiring that needed to be redone. We also had major repairs that needed to be done to the roof.

The major loss to our church building was with our heating and cooling system. It has cost us well over $100,000 to have the system repaired.

At St. Philip the Apostle Parish, our rectory, office buildings, school and church have been considered a total loss by the Archdiocese of New Orleans. As a result of Hurricane Katrina and its aftermath, the Archdiocese has decided to permanently close and suppress the parish.

My family has also lost a great deal. My parents' home was flooded by five feet of water. The home of my brother, Kevin, and his family was almost completely covered. There was about ten feet of water was in their neighborhood. The home of my Sister, Deidra, and her family withstood at least five feet of Katrina's floods.

Indeed it has been a journey.
     A journey that has forever changed our lives.

In this past year, we have been through more than we could have ever expected. And, yet, we are still here!

We are still here, praising God and thanking Him for His goodness!

How is that possible?

How is it possible that after all we have been through,
     we are still here?

How is possible that after all we have had to endure,
     we are still able to praise the Lord?

How can we continue to "Thank the Lord,"
     even though most of us are still in our greatest point of need?

I assure you that when people look at all that has transpired in our lives, since Hurricane Katrina, most would agree that we have had the right to give up a long time ago and just say, "to Heck with it. I quit!"

Who could have blamed us if we did?

But, some how, we are still here.

We are still here!

As I travel around the nation and the world, using the gifts that God has given me to "preach the Word to all nations," many have asked me, how is it possible that we can still be rolling like we are rolling, in the face of all that we have been through?

Many just can't understand why I am still here.

Well, for me, the answer is really simple:
I am still doing what I have to do because,

I Still Believe!

I Still Believe!
And, that's why I am still here!

I believe that the God who set the Earth in motion is still God today!

I believe that the God who called Abraham, Isaac and Jacob to found a nation
that he could claim as his own, is still God today!

I believe that the God who humbled Himself to share in our Humanity
so that we might one day share in His divinity, is still God today!

You see, I am still here, because I believe with all the fibers in my being that
the God who knit me in my mother's womb is still the one who is in control of
my church, my nation and my life.

I am still here because God is still here, too!

And, I know now, more than I have ever known before that
He'll never put more on me than I can bear!

I know that because in this past year,
I have had to bear more than even I thought that I could.

And, yet, I am still here!

People of God,
Throughout all of human history, God has promised that he would be with us.
He has not only promised it, he has also shown it through the lives of the
prophets and believers.

When we look back in Sacred Scripture,
we can see instances of this great promise.

In the seventh chapter of the Book of Daniel, the prophet tells us that from the
very beginning of time, people have believed that God's dominion over the Earth
is everlasting; it cannot be destroyed. In this, Daniel reminds us that the God who
made the Heavens and the Earth will be God forever and ever.

"His kingship shall not be destroyed!"[2] Amen!

As we deal with the aftermath of the storm, this is so important for us to hear. Because, Lord knows, in this past year, we have had time when other elements of this world have led themselves to believe that their ways were greater than God's ways. In many ways, we were being called to follow the will of Man and disregard how God calls us to live our lives.

St. Luke in his Book of Revelation reminds us that regardless of what we face on earth, we must continue to be faithful witnesses to the Lord.

Just as our Lord, Jesus Christ, did not allow the ways of this world to deter him from being faithful to His Heavenly Father, we cannot allow the fires, flood or lightning of our lives to cause us to deter from our service of God and one another.

If we falter, if we fail, our witness of faith becomes nothing more than empty vessels which will never be filled up by God.

Through the Book of Revelation, God tells us that "(He is) the Alpha and the Omega, the One who is and who was and who is to come, the almighty!"[3]

In other words, the God who was the God in the Beginning is God now and will be God when all is done!

And, that's why I am still here!

In the Gospel of John, Jesus Christ, the Son of the Living God, bore witness to God still being God when he stood in the praetorium before Pontius Pilate and courageously told the earthly leader of the region that "His kingdom was not of this world."[4]

In this, Jesus was telling Pilate that He was in a sense a King, but not a king like Pilate understood a king to be. He was a King on a level that was greater than anything we could have imagined. He was King of both Heaven and Earth!

---

[2]Daniel 7:13-14

[3]Revelations1:5-8

[4]John 18:33-37

36

And, that is why Pilate handed Him over to be crucified. Pilate could not understand just who Jesus truly was and still is!

Jesus was not afraid to stand firm in the face of death. He was not afraid to bear witness to His Heavenly Father, even though He knew that He was going to suffer severely and eventually die.

Knowing that the outcome of His "trial" would eventually end in an earthly death, Jesus said to Pilate, *"For this I was born and for this I came into the world, to testify to the truth. Everyone who belongs to the truth listens to My voice."*

Wow, talk about strength!

Talk about courage!

Talk about a true King!

When I look at all that I have been through in this past year, it would have been easy for me to give up. In fact, most thought that by now, I would have given up.

But, how little must their faith be if they thought that going through the fire and the floods of this world could somehow defeat a people that God has chosen as his own.

Today, I stand firm in a similar faith that,
        if I name it and claim it, God will bring it to fruition.

Today, I stand firm and believe that the Will of God
        is far greater than the will of man or woman.

Today, I have the courage necessary to look Evil in its eyes and say,
        "The Alpha and the Omega is the Lord of my life and you can't have it!"

I am still here because in Jesus Christ,

"I Still Believe!"

Today, I say to you, as Jesus said to Pilate,
        *"For this I was born and for this I came into the world,
        to testify to the truth."*

And this is the truth:

I believe that Jesus Christ is my personal Lord and Savior.

Do you believe the same?

I openly and happily receive the gifts and protection that Christ Jesus has promised me because He is the true Lord of my life.

Do you receive the same?

I claim the healing that I need in my heart, in my life and in my church parish, because I believe that I have received the power of God in my life.

Do you claim the same?

Today, through the power of the Holy Spirit,
I declare that Jesus, who is the Alpha and the Omega,
the Beginning and the End,
the one who has come into the world to set us free,
is indeed the one to whom I dedicate my life
and the one to whom I vow
I will never allow the ways of this world to conquer my heart.

Can you say the same?

Today, may the strength of Daniel give you the courage to stand firm in the Lions' dens of this earth.

May the visions of Luke, help you to realize that this ain't all we get, the best is yet to come.

And, may the power of our Lord Jesus Christ, help you to change your lives and live for Him and Him alone.

The Word of God promises us that He won't give you more than you can bear.

May you believe it, receive it and claim it for yourselves.

I stand as a tried and tested witness before God and before you I can honestly testify to the fact that I am a better man today because

"I Still Believe!"

My Katrina Journey

In the closing week of August 2005, I, my family and much of the Gulf Coast Region were monitoring the news and weather reports about the reported storm that had been building strength in the coastal waters.

Hurricane Katrina, as the storm would be later called, first formed over the Bahamas on August 23, 2005. On that date it quickly grew into a minor hurricane and passed over the edge of Florida on August 25, 2005. By the time it reached Florida it had reached a Category 1 status for a storm.

After passing over Florida and causing some deaths and a great deal of flooding, it entered the Gulf of Mexico. Though it had weakened as it passed over landfall, it soon began to grow as it stretched into the warm waters of the Gulf.

Before the week's end, it reportedly had grown to the strength of a Category 5 Hurricane. This means that the top wind-gusts speeds in the storm were well over 155 mile per hour with sustained winds of at least 70 miles per hour. On August 28, Katrina reportedly was pushing maximum sustained winds of well over 175 miles per hour.

In the few days before Katrina, Mr. C. Ray Nagin, the Mayor of New Orleans, began the call for a voluntary evacuation of the City of New Orleans. After receiving the reports from the weather bureaus, the mayor consulted with Governor Kathleen Blanco and President George Bush and called for a mandatory evacuation of the City of New Orleans on August 28, 2005.

You should know that throughout the history of the City New Orleans, we have seen our share of major storms. Year after year, we deal with the possible threat of storms passing through our town. So, as Hurricane Katrina began to head our way, I really was not in a panicking mode. It was going to be just "another hurricane. "

During the week of August 23, as I watched the news about Hurricane Katrina, I made plans and preparations to do what I usually do for a storm. I had already gone out and purchased our regular storm supplies: batteries for flashlights and radios, can goods and non-perishable foods, gas for the generator, and stuff like that. I was ready to ride this one out just like I have ridden out storms in the past.

As usual, my family was going to probably join me at the rectory and together we would laugh and pray as the storm passed over. We knew that the rectory at Our Lady Star of the Sea was old enough to have withstood several storms. So, we were confident that it would be a good place to stay as the storm came our way.

But, on the morning of August 28, 2005, our confidence and our plans changed.

At about 5 o'clock in the morning, Cedric, one of the persons who was going to be staying with us for the storm, arrived at the rectory. Cedric is a cab driver and was coming over to the rectory directly from his late night shift. When he came in, he asked me if I had been watching the news. I told him that I was just getting up and had not yet turned on the television.

Once I turned on the TV, my whole outlook of the storm shifted. On the news, the reporter was talking about the strength of the storm and the fact that it had now reached the level of a Category 5 Hurricane.

The reporter said that all of the major weather bureaus were certain that the storm was heading directly for the Mouth of the Mississippi River. This meant that the City of New Orleans was in line for a direct hit from the greatest storm in recent history.

As I watch the reports, I still was not ready to call for an evacuation of my own family. I still was prepared for us to hunker down inside of the rectory. Then one of the commentators on the news said, "Too many people are out there believe that they will be able to survive this storm. Well, they may survive the storm but they may not survive the aftermath." He went on to explain that the city was definitely going to have massive flooding with nasty infested waters. He also explained that it was quite possible that dead animals would be floating by.

Listening to him, I still was under the impression that we could ride out this storm. However, as the commentator continued talking, he finally said something that woke me up. He said, "Not only will dead animals be floating by, you don't know *who* might come floating by." It was at that point that I realized we had to go!

Water, I can handle.
Dead animals, I can handle.
Dead bodies, no can do!

So, at about 6 o'clock in the morning, I called my father and my friend, Diane, and told them to tell anyone who was coming to the rectory that were getting the "*you know what*" out of Dodge!

Being the diligent priest that I am, I did not want to skip saying Mass on that morning, so I still opened the Church and celebrated the 8 o'clock morning Mass. But, I assure you that it was the shortest Sunday Morning Mass that I have ever said in my entire priesthood!

At about 11:00 a.m., we gathered together our caravan and headed out of the city. In our group of nine cars were had a total of 22 people and two dogs. One of the dogs was the girl of my life, my Rottweiler, Pepper Louise.

We all headed to the Louisiana Lions Camp in Anacoco, Louisiana. Anacoco is near Leesville, La., and Fort Polk. Lions Camp is the host site for the two camps that I do each summer: Camp Pelican and Camp Challenge. It normally takes four and a half hours to drive from New Orleans to Leesville. But, because of the evacuation traffic and the number of folks in our group, it took us more than sixteen hours to make the trip.

Of course, it would have been a much shorter trip if we did not have to make three bathroom stops that each averaged forty-five minutes. And, of course, every time we stopped, Pepper needed to get out and walk around, sniff a few new smells and do her business.

We arrived at the Louisiana Lions Camp at about four in the morning on August. 29, 2005. By the time we got everyone settled into the bunk house, Hurricane Katrina was making landfall. The storm officially reached land at 6:10 AM.

Almost all of the 500,000 residents of the city of New Orleans evacuated. More than 1,000,000 folks had to leave the area. Some who were not lucky enough to get out in time, headed to the shelters of last resort. The Louisiana Superdome, some of the hospitals and some of the hotels became places of emergency refuge.

By the end of the storm and in the wake of its aftermath, hundreds of thousands of homes flooded. Well over 80% of the city was under water. And, there were at least three different points at which the levees broke. (You should know that the levees were build to help protect the city from the flood waters of the Mississippi River.)

As the light of morning dawned, none of us knew what were should do next. We stopped to thank God that we were safe. But, at the same time we were left lost and confused. As the new began to reach camp about the aftermath of Katrina, all of us realized that life as we knew it would never be the same.

Here we were, miles from home and not knowing when (if ever), we would get to go back home. Most of us evacuated with enough clothes to last a few days. Like Jesus, we thought that we would all be back home in three days!

But, we were definitely wrong. Although some of those who lived in the suburbs were able to go home after two weeks, it would be 77 days before I was able to move back to the New Orleans area.

All of my family members' homes endured some level of destruction. Collectively, we lost more than a million dollars in property. But, I thank God that my personal family did not lose any lives as a direct result of the storm.

On the second morning after the storm, I sat with my father, discussing the storm and our future plans. I asked him what did he think that we should do next. His reply was simply, "We are going to do whatever you tell us to do."

That was not the response that I was looking for. I did not know what to do. I had never been through anything like this. I wanted him, my Daddy, to tell me what we were supposed to do. Like Jesus in the Garden of Gethsemane, I was looking to my father for help at my darkest hour. What I did not realize was the fact that my Daddy was also in the Garden, too, looking for help.

When my father said to me, "We are going to do whatever you tell us to do," it was at that point that I realized how much confidence my father had in me. It was at that point that I realized that I was not only an adult in his eyes, I was also his pastor. And, I needed to pastor him and our flock back home to New Orleans.

Most of my family lost everything in the storm. We live in the regions of the city that flooded the most. Houses were lost. Cars were lost. And, some pets were lost, too. But, again, we thank God that we did not have to bury anyone in our family as a direct result of the storm.

We lived in Anacoco, La., for 77 days. Our time together was indeed a blessing in disguise. This was the most time that our family spent together since we were children. It really was a fun time being with my folks.

We are forever grateful to the citizens of Leesville, La., and the Village of Anacoco. The entire region welcomed us with open arms and did whatever they could to help us feel at home. We are also very grateful to Mr. Ray Cecil, Executive Director of Lions Camp, and his family for the love and hospitality that was shown to us. The Louisiana Lions Clubs, Lions Clubs International and the Cecil family are the primary reasons why we were able to survive the storm.

Though our journey is not over, our journey is blessed!

My First Trip Home

Some of you may know that I snuck into the City of New Orleans on Tuesday, September 13, 2005. Though the city was still closed to all residents, I devised a plan that would get me back to my rectory so that I could see what had happened to my home.

I know that as I drove along, I would encounter military road blocks. So, at each road block, I decided to tell them that I was heading to a church in a region of the Archdiocese that was open to its residents. As I drove further, I would eventually have to tell the truth. But, by that time, I would be close enough to convince the military to let me continue on. (The plan worked! It will probably cost me three Hail Mary's and Two Our Father's.)

You see, I really wanted to make sure that my two churches were secure. I knew from watching the news that the military and police had opened the doors of all the buildings in the city to go in and check for humans beings.

There were also a few things that I needed to retrieve from the house. First, I needed to find and secure the parish Sacramental Records. When a pastor evacuates from the rectory, he is supposed to make sure that the records are safe from harm or in his physical possession. Our records were in the safes at Our Lady Star of the Sea and at St. Philip the Apostle Parishes. Second, I wanted to find my personal chalice. To a priest, the chalice that he uses to celebrate his first Eucharist is similar to a wedding dress or wedding ring. It is a concrete symbol of his big day before God and his family. It was very important to me to make sure that the parish records and my chalice had survived the storm.

The ride from Anacoco, LA, was a long ride. Luckily, I was not riding alone. Two of the young men that I have mentored, Steve and Cedric, were on the journey with me. Having them with me not only gave me company for the ride, it also made me feel a bit safer with them in the car.

As we drove into the city, the first thing that struck us was the fact that everything looked gray. There was a film of mud/sludge that covered almost everything. The streets, the bushes, small trees and even the large oak trees were all covered with this coat of dried mud.

Most of the small plants, grass and stuff like that were all dead. The City of New Orleans looked like one of those old Ghost Towns that you see in western movies. At any moment, I expected a tumble weed to come rolling across the street.

The Louisiana Superdome had large gaping holes in the roof and most of the buildings that surround the Dome were severely damaged. Broken glass and flooded out cars were everywhere.

As to my two parishes, St. Philip the Apostle Church was still under water on September 13th. I was not able to get close enough to survey the damages or retrieve the parish's Sacramental Records. (We would later discover that the records were severely damaged by the flood waters.)

Our Lady Star of the Sea Church was in pretty good condition. Because it was built up pretty high, I would guess that only about 2 INCHES of water got inside the church. That meant that only the wood floors were messed up. The pews, the altar area, the new chapel and the sacristy all faired pretty well. (Thank God!)

There was a small hole in one of the stain glass windows that can be repaired. In the sacristy, one of the large windows was broken. Also, it was apparent that the military broke into the sacristy doors to check for people (dead or alive) that may have gone into the church to escape the rising water.

The inside of Our Lady Star of the Sea's rectory was another story. It took on about three feet of water. The first floor was pretty messed up. Almost everything down stairs had to go (I hated that den's sofa, anyway!). Mud was everywhere. But, it was not as bad as I feared. It could be cleaned up.

The Sacramental records of Our Lady Star of the Sea Parish were fine. I was able to get them out of the safe and bring them back to Anacoco, LA, with me. I was also able to salvage the hard drives from the computers and some of my cherished family heirlooms.

Once I was sure that the parish records were safe, I began to look for my chalice. I knew that I had left it in the den, so I went there to begin my search. Nothing on the first floor of the rectory was where we had left it. The force of the flood waters moved everything around. Sofas, chairs, tables desks were all thrown about during the storm. The place was a mess!

As I entered the den, I immediately went to the spot where I had placed my chalice before we evacuated. However, I did not see my chalice in that spot. After moving a few things around, I realized that it was not in that room.

As a sense of panic began to overcome me, Cedric came into the den carrying a mold covered square box and ask, "Father, what is this?" As you can guess, my heart jumped wen I realized that it was the case for my chalice.

I immediately asked him to open it up. When the case was opened, there inside was my chalice - bone dry, untouched by the flood waters. Even, the paper towel that was in the box was dry.

When I asked him where he found the box, I had to laugh when I got his reply. "It was in the bathroom," he said, "right next to the toilet." (Those were his exact words.) I though to myself, either God is trying to tell me where my priesthood is heading or he is letting me know that everything is going to be all right!

The upstairs of the rectory was untouched by the storm. It looked just like I had left it: No broken windows, no water or wind damage. (God is good!)

Overall, the city looked like a war zone. Military Hummers and National Guard troops were everywhere. I could not drive more than three blocks at a time without seeing some form of police or military presence down the streets. As weird as it may sound, I felt very safe in our city!

We were at the rectory for about an hour and a half. On five different occasions, the police or military pulled-up on us to see why were there. They were really patrolling and watching all the houses.

Each time they drove up and approached us, it was usually about five men with their rifles drawn and pointed directly at us. But, each time, I showed my St. Aug ID (I had on a black, roman collar - priest shirt in the picture) and my driver's license to proved that I lived there.

Once I proved that this was my home and church, they told us that were really not supposed to be there and that we should hurry up and do what we had to do. It was scarey. I have never had to stare down the barrel of a gun before this.

Steve and Cedric were also shaken up by the military and the guns. Neither of the two had ever had these kind of experiences. As scary as it was, on a smaller level, it felt good to know that our homes were indeed being protected by our police and military forces.

Though it was painful to see some of the neighboring houses, back on September 13, 2005, I left New Orleans knowing that one day we would be able to return home and resurrect our Church, our city and our homes.

It was then that I fully believed that *We Would Survive!*

Quiet! Be Still!

Back in September of 2005, just days after Hurricane Katrina, whenever you turned on the TV, all you saw was Hurricane coverage.

Scenes from our flooded city flooded the airwaves. All you saw was the devastation. All you saw was the pain. All you saw was trapped people trying to get out of their houses (days upon days after the storm.)

For most of us, it was hard to watch TV. But, we had to watch. We needed to watch. We couldn't help but watch as the news reported the devastation of our city.

On many of the news programs, they immediately began to talk about what New Orleans needed to begin doing to recover from this disaster.

They talked about rebuilding the houses. They talked about rebuilding the infrastructure. They talked about reopening the French Quarters.

Indeed, they talked about a lot of things that the Government, the Churches and the Citizens needed to do to rebuild the city that we love.

But, not everyone was talking about rebuilding our city. In fact, some were talking about what it would take to *close down* an entire metropolitan region. They actually talked about not reopening New Orleans, Louisiana.

They even went as far as asking, why should we rebuild New Orleans?
Why would anyone want to go back there?

As tough as it was to see pictures of the devastation on the News, I think listening to all of these experts talk about the possibility of not rebuilding our city, was even tougher.

How dare they even question whether or not we should rebuild?!
How dare they even question whether or not we should come home?!

New Orleans, Louisiana is our home.
And, no one has the right to tell us that we shouldn't be here.

When folks asked me should we go back, I did not hesitate to tell them that I couldn't wait to get home. No matter how bad it is: Home is Home!

It may not be Home *SWEET* Home! But, by God, it is still *HOME*!

Even if we have to deal with more hurricanes, I still want to be at home.

When you think about it, just as we have to deal with hurricanes, no matter where you may live in our nation, there will be some form of natural disaster or storm that you may have to deal with.

In California, they deal with earthquakes. In the Mid-West, they deal with tornados. In the North, they deal with snow storms and freezing winters. Time and time again, people throughout our nation and our world have been called to weather the natural storms which arise in our varying climates.

It doesn't matter where you live on the face of the Earth, there is always some form of natural disaster, some type of storm, some form of destructive power that can threaten your life.

Everyone deals with storms in their lives. Some natural and some unnatural, emotional or even spiritual.

The good thing is the fact that God is right there with us as we deal with those storms.

Whenever a storm arises,
        The Father sends the Holy Spirit to help us deal with them.

This is made quite evident in the Book of Job, St. Paul's Second Letter to the Corinthians, and the Gospel of Mark. Each of these great works tell us that no storm, no destructive power on earth can ever be compared to the power that our God possesses.

But, they also tell us to be ready because, Bad Things will happen to Good people. It is just a fact of life.

In particular, the *Book of Job* calls us to deal with the timeless question of
        "Why do Bad Things happen to Good People?"

As we all know, Job was a good and upright man. He faithfully followed the commands of God and did what was right before the Lord. Yet, despite his being a just man, he was suffering through many hardships. His property had been destroyed in a storm, his children and his wife were killed, and he was being accused by his friends of being a sinner.

There were many destructive storms raging in his life.

47

Much of the Book of Job is a discourse between Job and three of his friends as they all pondered his suffering and tried to figure out an answer to the question, *"Why do Bad Things happen to Good People?"*

Though their discourse wanders through almost 37 chapters, they never really come up with an answer. Near the end of the book, one of Job's friends encourages him to turn to God for an answer. Maybe God would explain why this "just man" was being hit by so many destructive storms.

In Chapter 38, God intervenes to help Job sort out some of his thoughts and feelings. From the midst of a storm, God lets Job know that He is God, the Creator of the Heavens and the Earth. Thus, He possesses the Divine Power to control all things.

At His commands every force on earth can be stilled. Every storm can be stopped. For, God and God alone possesses the ability to end all forms of earthly suffering.

Yet, in the *Book of Job,* God never really does answer the question, *"Why do Bad Things happen to Good People?"*

The only valid answer is that there is no valid answer.

People suffer because people suffer.

In the time that the *Book of Job* was written, the Believers in God did not have the insight that we now possess through Christ Jesus.

Job and his companions could only surmise that people suffer because they or someone in their family offended God. They believed that people suffered because they or their parents we sinners.

But, this was not the case with Job. He nor his family members did anything wrong. He was a *Just Man* in the Eyes of God. Yet, Job was being devastated by the powers of the world. There really was no valid answer as to why he was suffering.

Luckily, in our day and age, we don't have to live with the Old Testament's understanding of why people have to suffer. Through Jesus Christ, we have been given a new view on the destructive storms and devastating powers of our world.

In his *Second Letter to the Corinthians*, St. Paul tells us that, in Jesus, the old order of confusion has passed away. In this, Paul reminds us that our earthly suffering immediately connects us to the ultimate sacrifice, the Suffering and Death of Jesus on the Cross.

There could never be a more unjust form of suffering than one *innocent* and *without sin,* to be put to death for the sake of others.

When we see our suffering as our sharing in the Suffering and Death of Jesus, our Christ, we are given a new vision into the destructive storms in our lives.

For through Jesus, we are elevated above this devastating world and become a new creation. *"The old order (old things) have indeed passed away."*[5]

We no longer suffer alone. In a very real way, when we face the storms of our lives, our God faces them with us.

In the *Gospel of Mark,* we have a vivid reminder that Jesus is with us through the storms of our lives. Mark 4:35-41 says,

> *On that day, as evening drew on, Jesus said to them, "Let us cross to the other side." Leaving the crowd, they took Him with them in the boat just as He was. And other boats were with Him. A violent squall came up and waves were breaking over the boat, so that it was already filling up.*
>
> *Jesus was in the stern, asleep on a cushion. They woke Him and said to Him, "Teacher, do you not care that we are perishing?" He woke up, rebuked the wind, and said to the sea, "Quiet! Be still!"*
>
> *The wind ceased and there was great calm.*
>
> *Then He asked them, "Why are you terrified? Do you not yet have faith?" They were filled with great awe and said to one another, "Who then is this Whom even wind and sea obey?"*[6]

The storm that arose over the Sea of Galilee, caused the disciples to panic. Rather than realizing that with Jesus aboard the boat with them, they would never perish, they began to lose faith. Fearing for their lives they woke Jesus and asked Him, *"Teacher, do You not care that we are perishing?"*

---

[5] 2 Corinthians 5:17

[6] Mark 4:35-41

Seeing their fear, Jesus rebuked the winds and said to the sea: *"Quiet! Be still!"*

In three simple words, Jesus demonstrated His mastery over all of the elements of this world. *"Quiet! Be still!"*

Upon experiencing Jesus as He unleashed his Divine Power,
      the disciples were filled with awe and said to one another,
      "Who then is this whom the wind and sea obey?"

Jesus' words to the winds and the seas, *"Quiet! Be still!,"* were also His words to His disciples. *"Quiet! Be still!"*

Had they not calmed down enough to realize that Jesus was with them in that boat, they would have never been able to fully experience the Divine Power of our Lord.

Had they not calmed down, they may have been overcome by the destruction that overwhelming storms can cause.

Well, just as Jesus challenged the disciples to have faith in the midst of that storm, Jesus challenges us to have similar faith in the midst of our storms (especially in the aftermath of Katrina).

If He could control the winds and the seas,
if He could be resurrected after being crucified,
if He could raise the dead, heal the lame, and give sight to the blind,
surely He could handle the storms in our lives.

But, are we willing to let him handle them? Are we willing to be *"Quiet!"*?
Are we willing to *"Be still!"* and let God handle it?

In faith, we know the answer to the disciples' question of
"Who then is this. . . . . ?"

For, through the Holy Spirit, we have come to fully believe that He is Jesus, the Emmanuel, *"God with us."*

In faith, we know that Jesus not only calms the storms that rage around us,
He rides in the boat with us.

Faith that Jesus is in the boat with us brings about a calm in our lives that cannot be compared to any other feeling.

Yes, the storms will continue to rage. The winds will continue to blow and the breakers will continue to dash. So, do be misled to believe that with *Faith in Jesus Christ we will no longer have to face earthly storms.*

But, what it does mean is that we do not have to face them alone.

In Baptism, the Holy Spirit takes up a dwelling within us. In the Eucharist, Jesus comes to nourish our souls and become one with our bodies.

In the Eucharist, Jesus comes to give us strength and courage to face the raging winds and storms of life.

Though we may sometimes feel overwhelmed by our earthly suffering, faith that Jesus is with us in the boat, rescues us from the despair that life often brings.

Back in September of 2005, folks asked,
      "Why should we return to New Orleans?"

      "Why should we rebuild our city?"

I immediately began to ask, "Why shouldn't we return and rebuild?"

This is home.   This is *our home.*

And, no one has the right to tell us that we can't go home!

Plus, by evidence of all the lives that were saved,
by evidence of all the folks who have come to help rebuild,
by evidence of the fact that the Archdiocese of New Orleans is rebuilding,
we know that Jesus was not only watching over us,
He was riding in those rescue boats,
He is helping to hammer in the new nails,
He is ever present in the Eucharist as we gather in His name.

So, in the words of Jesus, to all who question whether or not we should be here, I say to you, "Quiet! Be Still!"

This is home. And, the last time I checked, Jesus is still here!

My Pre-K Graduation

Usually around the age of three or four years old, a young person begins their journey into the real world by being enrolled in either a Pre-Kindergarten program or by participating in the programs at the neighborhood daycare center. For the child, this is an exciting and yet a very scary time.

It is exciting because the world of knowledge is laid open right before their eyes. There is so much to learn. In Pre-K, you have to learn how to recognize all of those primary colors like blue, red and green. You also have to begin learning about numbers and shapes and letters. Man, it is an exciting time.

It is also scary because this is usually the first time that you are asked to venture out into the world without the comfort of having your mommy or daddy by your side. As nice as it is to be independent, there is something to the security that you have at home when you are wrapped in the arms of a parent.

At the end of the Pre-Kindergarten years, it has become the usual custom to celebrate your leaving for "big school" with a graduation celebration that could rival the graduation ceremonies of most major institutions of higher learning.

In these modern times, a Pre-K Graduation can be as involved as a graduation from college or medical school. The graduation ceremonies usually will involve a great deal of music, some poetic readings, the proclamation of a few Scripture passages and, of course, speeches by the class valedictorian and class president. (I guess that the valedictorian and the salutatorian are chosen from those who have successfully learned all of their colors and has demonstrated the ability to traverse the complicated steps of using the bathroom on their own.)

Graduation from Pre-K has really become a "big ta-do." (And, so it should be.)

Now, once you've graduated from Pre-K, it is time for you to be a Big Boy or a Big Girl. When you enter big school, you are expected to be just like the older kids. That means that you have to put childish things away (except for the occasional binky or pacifier that your Maw Maw hides for you in your SpongeBob SquarePants book bag).

After you graduate from Pre-K, you have to grow-up!

In the thirteenth chapter of St. Paul's First Letter to the Corinthians, St. Paul sounds like a man who is giving a speech to group of Pre-K graduates. First, Paul speaks about being people of true love.

He tells everyone that if you do not speak with love in your hearts, you are nothing more than a clashing cymbal.[7]

Being a man of love, he then writes words which basically say to us, now is the time for us to graduate and become the "Big Boys and Big Girls" that God has called us to be.

In First Corinthians 13:11, Paul says,
"When I was a child, I used to talk as a child, think as a child, reason as a child; when I became a man, I put aside childish things."[8]

Wow, what a great message for a Pre-K Graduation speech.
Once you have graduated from Pre-K, it is time to put away childish things.
It is time to be a Big Boy or Big Girl!

On August 29, 2005, Hurricane Katrina hit New Orleans and the Gulf South and forever changed the landscape of our region and our lives. For me, August 29th, was really the day that I finally graduated from Pre-K (That's Pre-Katrina). And, I assure you that it has been both exciting and scary at the same time.

Before Hurricane Katrina struck landfall, I really was in a *"Pre-K"* state of mind. As I look back to my Pre-Katrina (my *Pre-K"*) years, I realize now just how naive I really was. You see, I was a young priest who really did see the world through rose-colored glasses.

In my eyes, I thought that everyone really did have my best interest at heart. I thought that everyone really did want to see others grow and prosper. I thought that if anything bad (like a devastating hurricane) would happen, we would all pull together and work as one for the common good. Indeed, I truly believed that the world was filled with wonderful people who only wanted the best for everyone.

Well, since graduating from Pre-K, I have come to realize that the world isn't how I thought it was. Though the overwhelming number of folks in the world really are men and women of love, there are some people in this world who really are not good people. There are some folks in this world who will only be out to help themselves and not the rest of the community.

---

[7] 1 Corinthians 13:1

[8] 1 Corinthians 13:11

Back in February of 2006, I really was going through a tough time. It was at that time that the aftermath of Hurricane Katrina was finally hitting my little portion of the world. I was being informed that one of my parishes was being closed and the other was going to be clustered with a neighboring parish. It would not open again until enough families had returned to New Orleans to justify reopening its doors. In my family, not everyone was doing well with their recovery phase. Many were dealing with real issues of post-traumatic stress. Katrina had taken away our jobs, our homes and our friends. Our lives were being changed forever.

In the depths of my struggles, I began to write my thoughts and prayers. The following is what came to my heart.

> *I want my life back.*

> *Once upon a time, I used to be in control of me.*
> *Now, I am feeling less and less in control.*
> *In fact, I am afraid that I am losing it.*

> *Nothing is the same anymore.*

> *My rectory is in shambles.*
> *My churches are hurting, too.*
> *Everything seems to be blowing up.*

> *Those I love seem to betray me at the drop of a hat.*
> *I can't figure out how you can love folks as much as I do*
> *and yet they can still hurt you.*

> *This is not the life I had.*

> *Or maybe it was.*
> *Maybe it was like this and I just couldn't see it.*

> *Where is the life I dreamed of?*

> *I want my life back!*
> *Or at least the life I thought I had.*

The six months or so that followed Hurricane Katrina, were, in a very real way, the darkest months of my life. I was so confused after the storm. Nothing seemed to be going right and no one seemed to be noticing that I was about to lose it. (But, I was.)

Luckily, Archbishop Alfred Hughes was at least paying attention to my cries for help. On a few occasions, he called my cellular phone to see how I was doing and to make sure that I knew that he was keeping me in his prayers. I don't know if he realized then, how important those phone calls were to me. In a very real way, my spiritual shepherd was reaching across the pastures of Louisiana and guiding this little lamb to safety.

Even when he knew that I was not in agreement with some of the proposed plans for my parishes, he showed concern and respect for me by calling to inform me of any major changes that were being planned for the communities that were under my pastoral care. His phone calls definitely helped to relieve some of the post-Katrina stress that was beginning to weigh me down.

Just when I thought that I was about to lose it, God let me know that it was time for me to be a Big Boy. He let me know that it was time for me to let go of the "Pre-K Tony" and be the man that He has made me to be. It was time for the "Grown-Up Tony" to hit the world. *Pre-K* is over. It is time to go to Big School!

The "post-Katrina Tony" is indeed a man who has had to grow up "quick, fast and in a hurry." My *Pre-K* Graduation ceremony did not last very long. There was no time for a post-graduation party with ice cream and cake. I had to be a Big Boy. There really was no time to play around.

In this post-Katrina world, I have had to demonstrate before God and His people I that I am willing face even the "Fires of Hell" on their behalf. Where I used to get away with being naive, those days are now gone. And, in a very real way, that's a good thing.

Once you remove the rose-colored glasses, you can see folks for who they really are. You can see who will love and support you through all times. And, you can see who will be kicking you at your lowest moments. But, regardless, you know who is real and who isn't. That's a big part of being a grown-up.

Pre-K is over for me. I have graduated from the world of a child and now I must be the Man of God that I am called to be. So, look out world, I'm a Big Boy, now! Oh, I still may be a little naive, but I assure you that I ain't as blind as I used to be. As Paul said, "When I was a child, I used to talk as a child, think as a child, reason as a child; when I became a man, I put aside childish things."

I have finally gotten my life back!

(And, I like it without the *Binky*!)

Post-Katrina Stress!

Up until I took my great world adventure, I have to admit to ya'll that a brother had been getting tired. Since Katrina, like everyone else, I have had to deal with a great deal of heartaches and headaches.

From working with the Archdiocese of New Orleans to keep the doors of Our Lady Star of the Sea Parish open, to worrying about the future of my family and trying to get my parents' New Orleans East home back in shape, I have had to deal with more than I really have wanted to deal with. And, all truth be told, it was wearing me down.

It ain't no secret that as a direct result of the stress from the storm, I have lost more weight than I needed to lose. At last count, I have dropped about 25 pounds all from the stress and worry that came from all the post Katrina stuff that I have had to bear.

It really was getting to me.

And, like many, I wasn't paying attention to the signs.

Oh, I kept telling folks that I was about to lose it.

But, nobody was paying attention to what I was saying.

The stress of pastoring a community that was counting on me was really getting to me.

As much as the waters destroyed our homes, I have come to realize that the post-traumatic stress that has resulted from the storm can destroy stuff that is even more precious than our homes.

It can destroy our very lives.

Once you start allowing the stress to get to you,
        you begin to lose sight of what is truly important.

You lose sight of the needs of your family.

You lose sight of the needs of your community.

You can even lose sight of the needs of your Church.

Stress and worrying can zap you of the necessary energy to do what you gotta do. And, when that happens, you'll have more to recover from than just wind and water damage.

Believe it or not, stress is not just a modern phenomenon. Stress has been a part of the human existence since the moment Adam and Eve decided to disobey God and do things their own way.

If we look into the Bible, we can see that the Prophet Elijah, the Apostle Paul and even Jesus had to deal with real stressful lives.

The demands of their lives, the demands on their time, the demands on their energy and even the demands for immediate miracles (immediately taking care of the needs of many) brought major issues of stress into their lives.

As we all know, the Prophet Elijah was a very, very successful prophet. He was a great success preaching all across the land. He was great at working miracles wherever he went. He was indeed a very powerful servant of God.

Yet, if we look at The First Book of Kings, Chapter 19, verses 4 through 8, we can find a moment in his life where he was feeling as if nothing he was doing was working. The stress of being a prophet of God was apparently getting to him.

At one point, Elijah was so overwhelmed by the demands on his life that he sat underneath a broom tree and began to pray for death. Looking to Heaven, Elijah prayed, "This is enough, O LORD! Take my life, for I am no better than my fathers."[9]

Even though he had defeated more that 400 prophets of the false god Ba'al back on Mount Carmel, Elijah was beginning to wonder if being a prophet was worth all the stress.

Though he had helped many, some of the very folks that he had helped were beginning to forget all he did for them in the name of God and were beginning to hate him. Some were even beginning to threaten his very life.

That is why he felt as if he were no better than his predecessors.

Instead of bringing him glory,
        his deep devotion to God was bringing threats against his life.

---

[9] 1 Kings 19:4

Talk about stress!

Yet, just when Elijah was at his lowest point, God sent an angel to care for him. Bearing a hearth cake and a jug of water, the angel wakes Elijah and tells him, "Get up and eat, else the journey will be too long for you!"[10]

In his Letter to the Ephesians, St. Paul talks about some of the stress that was resulting from his life of ministry. Like Elijah, Paul was recognized by many as a great disciple of the Lord.

Yet, Paul worried that when he was gone, folks would not live as he had instructed them to live.

Paul worried that folks would fall back into the traps of the Devil as soon as he was physically gone from their town.

Talk about ministerial stress.

In writing to them, Paul told the Church of Ephesus that he was worried about their future. He told them to look into their hearts and make sure that they are not carrying anything in their hearts that would bring grief to the Holy Spirit.[11]

He tells them that they needed to remove all bitterness, fury, anger, shouting, reviling and malice that might exist within them.

Carrying all of these forms of hatred in your heart brings grief to the Holy Spirit Who "by virtue of the waters of Baptism," lies deep within you.

Paul tells us to "be kind to one another; forgiving one another as God has forgiven (us) in Christ."[12]

Forgiveness in the Name of Jesus Christ is indeed a great stress reliever.

Like Elijah and Paul, Jesus also had to deal with stress that others can put upon you; especially when folks do not understand what you are truly about.

---

[10] 1 Kings 19:7

[11] Ephesians 4:30-32

[12] Ephesians 4:32

A good example of this can be found in the Gospel of John, Chapter 6, verses 41-51. In this episode from Sacred Scripture, we join Jesus as He tells the people that He was "The Bread that came down from Heaven."

While giving this great discourse on the Angelic Bread, He could hear the people behind Him murmuring with one another. They were literally "talking behind His back."

As he spoke to the crowd, He could hear His own people saying, "Is this not Jesus, the son of Joseph? Do we not know His father and mother? Then how can He say, 'I have come down from Heaven'?"[13]

Once again, here is a Man of God, wait here is God, Himself, standing before them and they couldn't see Him for who He was.

Though He had taken care of all of their needs, though He had already fed more than 5000 men, women and children, , though He had already heal the blind and gave new legs to the lame, though He had already brought a couple of folks back to life, they still were questioning who He was and whether He was truly some one who had come down from Heaven.

Man, talk about stress!

Jesus, Paul and Elijah all had to deal with it!

Looking at the life of our Savior and the lives of these two great men, we can see that even though the stress was getting to them, God the Father knew how to help them deal with it. You see, Jesus, Elijah and Paul essentially used the same method to help them make it through their tough times. They used the same technique to get over the troubles that seemed to weigh them down.

Just in the nick of time, God showed each of them, in their own time and space, what they needed to do to persevere through the storms of their lives.

And, what is crazy is the fact that the stress solver that God showed to Elijah, Paul and Jesus is the very same solution that God shows us in our modern days.

And, it all can be found in the words of King David in the 34th Psalm.

You see, the solution to dealing with stress in your life is to simply,

---

[13]John 6:41-43

"Taste and See the Goodness of the Lord."

Or as the New American Bible puts it,
"Learn to savor how good the Lord is!"[14]

That is the solution to stress!

"Taste and See the Goodness of the Lord."

When the stress of life is getting to you,
"Taste and See the Goodness of the Lord."

When the battles of rebuilding is weighing you down,
"Taste and See the Goodness of the Lord."

When it seems as if no one understands why you do what you do,
"Taste and See the Goodness of the Lord."

For, the Goodness of the Lord that we can taste today is the same goodness that Elijah had. It is the same goodness that Paul had. It is definitely the same goodness that Jesus had, because for us, the Goodness of the Lord is Jesus.

Stress can wear you down when the burdens of life seem to overcome the blessings that God has already sent you and the additional blessings that God is now trying to send you.

In this Post-Katrina life, we have to be able to see that we are still Blest in the Midst of the Mess.

If not, the stress will get the best of our lives.

I can tell you that, like everyone else, there have been times since we got back from the storm that I have wanted to sit under a tree like Elijah and just quit.

It ain't easy to do what I do.

But, every time one of those moments hits me, God simply says to me,
"Taste and See."

"Taste and See the Goodness of the Lord."

---

[14]Psalm 34:9

60

People of God, I know that for most of us, life has been tough.

I know that we have all had times when we have stopped and said,
    "It shouldn't be this hard to get by."

I know what it is like to just want to give up and say,
    "to hell (I mean heck) with it."

I know it because I have had those moments, too.

Lord, knows that I have had those moments, too.

That's why I wanted to share with you,
    just what has been helping me make it through.

I have learned to savor how good the Lord is.

I have been able to repeatedly
    "Taste and See the Goodness of the Lord."

Savoring the goodness of the Lord worked for Elijah.
    Tasting and seeing God's love worked for Paul.
    Remembering that His Father was with Him worked for Jesus.

And, it will work for you, too.

God is continually blessing us with Bread that has come down from Heaven.

In our Daily Bread and in the Eucharist,
    God invites us to come to His Banquet Table and receive the very thing
    that can help you get through the stress of recovery
    and the ordinary stress of life.

May God allow you to simply,
    "Taste and See the Goodness of the Lord."

Amen.

Part Two
"I Believe in Jesus Christ, the Son of the Living God!"

**The Flood Damaged Tabernacle of
St. Philip the Apostle Catholic Church**

November 11, 2005

Who Do You Say I Am?

As you well know, because I am who I am, I get the chance to travel the nation and the world preaching the Good News and spreading the Mission of the Church to thousands upon thousands of folks.

I have preached to arenas across America, packed with as many as 12 thousand adults and as many as 14 thousand teenagers. Indeed, I have been blessed to be able to do what I do, in the name of the Lord.

For every big conference, every revival and even every retreat I do, there usually is someone who is responsible for introducing me to the crowd. More times than not, the person introducing me has heard me speak before and is usually HONORED to be the person that was selected to present me to the group.

Now, when they introduce me, they often read something like this:

"Fr. R. Tony Ricard is proud to be on fire with the Power of the Holy Spirit. As is evident in his faith-filled presentations, Fr. Tony is committed to a steadfast journey to God's Kingdom. While sharing his faith, he invites others to join him on this journey.

His joy and excitement in being a Christian and a member of the Roman Catholic Church are quite contagious. Through the power of the Holy Spirit, his enthusiasm spreads like wildfire.

Rev. R. Tony Ricard is a Priest for the Archdiocese of New Orleans and is the Pastor of Our Lady Star of the Sea Parish in New Orleans. He is also one of the Core Instructors of Church Doctrine for the Institute for Black Catholic Studies at Xavier University.

He is the co-author and editor with Mr. Chris Quest, II, of the book, "MAXimum Faith: Prayers and Reflections by Young Katrina Survivors."

He also is the Camp Director for LA Lions-L.P.D.C.I.-Camp Pelican, a camp for Children with Cystic Fibrosis, Chronic Asthma and other pulmonary disorders. He has been a part of Camp Pelican since 1984. He became the Camp Director in 1985.

He is the Assistant Camp Director for Camp Challenge, a camp for children with (and survivors of) Cancer, Sickle Cell Anemia and other Hemotology-Oncology Diseases. He has been a part of Camp Challenge since 1993.

Fr. Tony is a Past-President of the National Black Catholic Seminarians Association and has held positions on several diocesan and national boards.

He has given keynote addresses, retreats, revivals, and youth talks across the nation. At last count, Fr. Tony has visited and preached in 18 different countries.

He is a native of New Orleans and a proud graduate of Our Lady of Lourdes Elementary School and St. Augustine High School. He is a former New Orleans Public School Teacher who holds a Bachelor of Science degree in Elementary Education from Loyola University, a Master of Theology degree from Xavier University and a Master of Divinity degree from Notre Dame Seminary."

After that intro, folks usually add stuff like: "You have heard about his ministry. You have heard about his zeal. Now, you have a chance to hear *him*, yourself.

We have a chance to feel his Spirit. It is my privilege to present to you, the world-renown Preacher, the Gifted Teacher, the one and only, *Fr. Tony."*

Well, I can tell you after all that, I have to be good!

"Who do people say that I am?"

Well, since I usually write my own introductions, I usually know who most folk will say I am!

But, back in Jesus' day, they didn't introduce Him with the kinds of introductions that the big speakers of today get.

So, I would guess that on many occasions Jesus wondered if people really knew who he was.

In the Gospels of our Brothers Matthew and Mark, there is a story of Jesus trying to find out what folks were saying about him.

In Matthew, we read:

> *Jesus went into the region of Caesarea Philippi and He asked His disciples, "Who do people say that the Son of Man is?"*
>
> *They replied, "Some say John the Baptist, others Elijah, still others Jeremiah or one of the prophets."*
>
> *He said to them, "But who do you say that I am?"*

*Simon Peter said in reply, "You are the Christ, the Son of the
Living God."*[15]

In this passage, we find Jesus and the disciples walking on a journey to villages near Caesarea Philippi. As they walked along the road, Jesus decided to ask them what were people saying about Him. He was curious to know whether or not the people to whom He was preaching, actually knew who He was.

This is why He asked His disciples, *"Who do people say that the Son of Man is?"*

When Jesus asked, "Who do people say that I am?" Their first reply was "John the Baptist."

Why would some think he was John the Baptist?

Well, John was a very charismatic leader. Folks would travel for miles and miles to hear John preach and to be baptized by him in the Jordan. John's reputation, as we know, spread into many regions of Asia Minor and North Africa.

Like John, Jesus also had developed a great reputation and a large group of followers. Many thought he could possibly be the same man as the Baptizer.

But, we know that John came only to prepare the way for the coming of the Lamb of God. He was not *THE* Lamb of God. This is why Jesus went to John to be baptized. It was a sign that the reign of God was at hand. Clearly, Jesus was not John the Baptist.

Their second reply was "Elijah."

Why would some think that Jesus was the Prophet Elijah?

We know that Elijah was a great prophet. Like the Baptizer, Elijah also had a large following. He was known for his preaching, the many miracles God had worked through him, as well as the fiery chariot that swung low to carry him into the presence of God.

Elijah was one of the strongest defenders of the covenant made by God with Abraham and Moses. Thus, Jesus could possibly be this prophet because Jesus also defended the Covenant between God and our Fathers in Faith.

---

[15]Matthew 16:13-16

There was also a strong Jewish belief that before the Messiah returned, Elijah would return to prepare the way. Therefore, in their hearts and minds, many wanted to believe that Jesus was this Prophet and that the Messiah would soon be coming. But, all truths be told, Jesus was not Elijah.

Their third reply was "Jeremiah."

Why would some think that Jesus was the Prophet Jeremiah?

Well, Jeremiah was a young itinerant preacher just as Jesus was a young Rabbi. Jeremiah would travel the regions preaching about repentance and acceptance of God's law. Jesus echoed much of what Jeremiah proclaimed, for both spoke the Word of God.

In his time, Jeremiah experienced rejection and suffering and he prophesied that the Messiah would experience the same. Jesus was also experiencing rejection and suffering. Thus, it was possible that Jesus was the Prophet Jeremiah and that the Messiah would soon come. But, we know that Jesus was not the Prophet Jeremiah.

Their fourth reply to the question, *"Who do people say that the Son of Man is?"* was "One of the prophets."

If Jesus wasn't Elijah and He wasn't Jeremiah, He could have possibly been one of the other prophets. Maybe He was Elisha, Jeremiah, Isaiah, Deborah, Esther, or even Moses. Or maybe, Jesus, the Nazarean, son of Mary and Joseph, was a new prophet: sent by God to declare a new day. With all that He had done and all that He was saying, it was possible that Jesus was a new prophet of the Lord.

But we know that He was not a mere prophet.

Turning again to the disciples, Jesus asked: *"But who do you say that I am?"*

Simon Peter's answer to this powerful question was:
"You are the Christ, the Son of the Living God."

In the Latin translation, Peter's response is "You are the Messiah!"

The word Christ or Messiah literally means "Anointed."

There are many occurrences in the Old Testament that point to individuals who were deemed to be anointed. More often than not, those who were declared as *"Anointed"* were the Kings.

King David and King Solomon were both honored as the anointed ones of God.

For Peter to openly say that Jesus was the Messiah, the Anointed, was a risky statement. For during the time Jesus walked on earth, the word Messiah or Christ was reserved for referring to Israel's Future Leader: one who was to come triumphantly into the land to save the Chosen People of God.

What was risky about declaring that Jesus was the Messiah was the connected belief that the future leader would wage a battle against the Romans and all else who oppressed the Israelites.

Thus, saying that Jesus was the Messiah or the Christ could mean death to the believer. Therefore, "Messiah or Christ" was not a popular identification used to describe Jesus during the time He was here on earth.

Following Peter's courageous answer, Jesus blesses Peter and tells him that it will be through his courage that the Church will be instituted.[16]

Jesus also gave a prediction of His upcoming passion and resurrection.

And, He tells the disciples, that to be one of his followers, they must deny themselves, take up their cross and follow in his foot steps.

This was hard for them to understand because they as of yet, did not fully know how Jesus would be glorified.

They only believed that one day He would reign with God as their leader and king.

I think that as we look at this passage from the Gospel of Matthew, the question for us today is that same question that Jesus asked Peter: "And you, who do you say I am?"

Whatever our role is in life, whatever our role is in the Church, our starting point is the same as that of Peter and the disciples. We have to answer the same question that Jesus put to them: Who do you say Jesus is?

If your reply is "You are Jesus the Christ, the Messiah, the Anointed One, the one sent to save the world," then, you have to follow that question up with another question: "Knowing that Jesus is the Messiah and has redeemed the world, what

---

[16]Matthew 16:17-20

67

are you going to do?"

Or as the young folks back in the 1990's would say, "How you gonna act?"

Just as in the time when Jesus walked on earth, there are serious implications to saying Jesus is Lord. For, if you truly believe that Jesus the Christ has Died, Jesus the Christ is Risen and that Jesus the Christ will Come Again, then you must profess this belief through your actions.

You cannot simply profess your faith and believe that is all you need to do to be saved. Such a faith is a Dead Faith. We are called to profess a Living Faith: a faith that is evident in our actions, in our business transactions and in our daily happenings. If Jesus is not present in every aspect of your life, then can you really say to Him, *"You are the Christ, the Messiah, the Son of the Living God?"*

It is not always easy to live lives that show our Faith in Jesus as the Messiah. As sinners, we often fail to live up to our callings. We often fail to show we are Christians by our love.

But, through the Blood of Jesus, and His obedience to the Father, we have been washed clean of our failures and brought into the light of a new covenant.

As those who have been saved by the Messiah, we have been made ready to enter the Kingdom of God.

However, if we are not living out our faith as the Father, Son, and Spirit calls us to live, then can we expect to reap the glorious harvest of the Heavenly Kingdom.

As Roman Catholics, we profess that same faith professed by Peter, by the disciples and by our Early Church founders. We profess a faith that was begun with Abraham and sealed at the Day of Pentecost. We profess a faith which irrefutably declares that Jesus, the Nazarean, the Son of Mary, the only Son of God, eternally begotten of the Father, is the Christ, the Messiah, the Anointed One.

After coming to this deep rooted stance in faith, we are called to share this knowledge with others.

In the sacrifice of the Holy Eucharist, Jesus Christ comes to us in a very special way.

He looks into each of our hearts and asks, "And *you*, who do you say I am?"

He also looks into our lives, to the way we live as Church among the people of the world, to find our answers to His question:

For, I was hungry, and you gave me food,

> *I was thirsty, and you gave me something to drink,*
>
> *I was a stranger, and you welcomed me,*
>
> *I was naked and you gave me clothing,*
>
> *I was sick and you took care of me,*
>
> *I was in prison and you visited me.*[17]

And, they'll know we are Christians by our love.

"And you, who do you say, I am?"

People of God,
On this day, let us stand before the throne of Grace,
look Jesus directly in His eyes
and emphatically declare to Him
and to the entire world:

"You are the Christ, the Messiah, the Son of the Living God."

---

[17]Matthew 25:35-36

Jesus Is With Us Through All Things

Some of my most favorite times of the year are the times when we either give or receive gifts. Special days like Birthdays, Christmas, Easter, Anniversaries, and even receiving good report cards are great days for gifts.

Whenever I look back on my childhood, I can remember many special gift giving days. However, one special time really stands out in my mind.

It is the memory of the beautiful Christmas day, when I was about ten years old. On that day, I received a gift that I have never forgotten. It was a gift that I have come to cherish - not for its monetary value, but for the message that came with it.

For as long as I can remember, my parents' house was always the place where the entire family gathered for Christmas Dinner and to give each other gifts. Every Christmas, my aunts and uncles and their families would all assemble at our house for 2:00 p.m.

One particular aunt, Auntie Susie, my Dad's brother's wife, was very well loved and was quite famous (at least among the children) for the wonderful load of gifts she would bring to us on Christmas Day.

Aunt Susie loved to give presents (especially to children) and to watch the family's reactions when they opened their gifts.

Christmas Day, when I was about ten years old, was no different from any other Christmas. Like clock work, Auntie Susie appeared at our front door at 2:00 p.m., arms loaded with boxes and boxes of gifts.

As always, the young folk's excitement grew because Aunt (Auntie) Susie, second only to Santa Claus, always brought the best gifts.

As she handed out her presents to the kids, I dreamed of what would be in the Box she had for me.

Was it a G. I. Joe figure with the Kung-Fu Grip?

Was it an Official NFL Junior Duke Football?

Was it Rock'em Sock'em Robots that I had always wanted?

Only God, and Aunt (Auntie) Susie, knew what she had gotten me that year.

Well, when she handed me that box, I ripped off the Christmas wrapping, like a Catholic in a candle factory.

And when I open the box, there to my surprise was a brand new, still in the plastic bag, six pack of tube socks. And not just any kind of tube socks, they were the kind that had those big colored stripes, the kind that no one *who knew anything about style* would be caught dead wearing.

Well, as you could guess, I, like any ten-year-old, was somewhat disappointed with her gift. But, when I looked up at her and into her love-filled eyes, I did just as Momma had always taught me to do, I said, *"Thank you."* And being the sweet little kid that I was, I added, *"It's just what I always wanted."*

You know, almost all people have to deal with some form of disappointment at early stages of their lives. Disappointment comes when unexpected events or actions dash the hopes and dreams that are essential to healthy life.

The greater the hope, the wilder the dream, the greater the disappointment and disillusion when the hope is dashed.

With each successive disappointment, it becomes a little harder to believe that the good will come true, that God will see you through the tough times.

Our world can be shaped by the disappointment we feel, as we struggle to hope again: thus, blinding us from the hopeful reality that surrounds us.

A great illustration of real disappointment can be found in Luke 24:13-35. In this episode from the work of our brother Luke, we hear the story commonly know as "The Road to Emmaus."

In this story, the two disciples, who walked along the road to Emmaus, could not hide the fact that they were disappointed with the outcome of the events that had transpired in Jerusalem. That is why they were not slow in explaining their gloom to the stranger who was walking with them on their journey.

You see, Jesus, their friend and trusted teacher, had been crucified. *"We were hoping,"* they said, *"that he was would be the one to redeem Israel."*[18]

This had been their hope. This had been their disappointment.

---

[18]Luke 24:21

They felt that the death of Jesus had left them without the gift they longed for and had been promised for many generations. In Jesus, they hoped to receive the gift of freedom, a gift of emancipation. Their hope in Jesus was immense. Thus, their disappointment was just as severe.

Jesus' response to them is interesting to note. First, He takes the initiative, prompting them to tell of their disappointment: to just talk it out.

Listening to their story, He responds by opening up the *Word of God* to them, showing how it was foretold that the Christ should suffer and so enter into His glory.

When Jesus sat with them for supper and led them in the breaking of the bread, they immediately recognized Him, realizing that all along they had sensed His presence.[19]

The story ends by telling us that from the table where they broke bread with the Risen Lord, they went out to proclaim the Good News that He had risen from the dead.

In speaking frankly with the Divine Stranger and in celebrating the Eucharist with their Heavenly Companion, the two disciples came to know Jesus though their hearts were overflowing with disappointment.

The Emmaus story is a clear model of how you can be like the disciples and come to know my Jesus. For, the Jesus I have come to know and love walks with us just as He walked with the two disciples on that road to Emmaus.

However, unlike the journey of those two disciples, our journey will not end in a Middle Eastern town. For, the journey we travel hopefully ends at the heavenly banquet table of our Creator.

By the Grace of God, we are given the opportunity to meet and speak with our Jesus each and every day. Through the power of prayer, we can bring our everyday experiences, our hopes and our disappointments before our God. By pouring out our hearts to our Heavenly Companion, we ask Him to walk with us until we are together with our Father.

Through reading the Sacred Scriptures and celebrating the Eucharist, we stand in the presence of the Risen Christ.

---

[19]Luke 24:30-31

72

I don't know about you, but whenever I open my Bible or participate in the Mass, something stirs within me; something causes my heart to burn with hope for our future. That something is the sense that Christ is truly present with me and with all who share my belief that Jesus is our Lord and Savior.

Like the disciples, we must invite Christ, our Risen Lord, to stay with us: not only as we gather within the walls of our churches, but also as we walk along the hope-filled but sometimes disappointing roads of our lives.

My Brothers and Sisters in Christ,

"Were not our hearts burning (within us)
while he spoke to us on the way
and opened the scriptures to us?"[20]

"Were not our hearts burning as they came to know Him
in the Breaking of the Bread?"

It is in this burning that we must come to recognize the presence of our God.

I thank God that he has allowed me to realize His presences within my heart and within the hearts of others.

I can honestly say that I know and love my Blessed Savior, for, I have met Him in both my hopes and my disappointments.

And, I realize that it is through those hopes and disappointments that He is making me ready for the glory that is on the other side of the cross.

Together, as we walk this road, may our hearts burn from within as we realize that Jesus is on this journey with us.

---

[20]Luke 24:32

"Do Not Be Afraid"

When I was young boy, I always looked forward to the big kiddie days. You know, days like Christmas and birthdays, Easter and the Fourth of July. Days when it was just a joy to be a kid. I especially loved Halloween. As you could guess, I loved it because of all of the free candy you could get from your neighbors.

Like most kids, I just couldn't wait until it got dark enough on Halloween night, so that we could go out on the streets of our neighborhood and go from house to house collecting all kind of yummy stuff.

Halloween was one of the best days to be a kid. In our old uptown-neighborhood, you could spend hours walking up and down the street visiting neighbors, laughing at each others home made costumes, and sizing-up who had the most candy in their bags.

Yep, Halloween was a great day to be a kid.

One very special Halloween Day that I can remember happened back around 1975. This was the Halloween when my Uncle Cyril[21] decided to scare the neighbors as they passed along the street "Trick or Treating."

On that night, he dressed in a make-shift costume, put on a very scarey mask and hid in an old garage next to the *haunted house*[22] of our neighborhood. Now, the mask was that of a white monkey-looking creature and his costume was nothing more than an old overcoat.

As he sat in the garage behind an old abandoned car, he would wait until unsuspecting Trick-or-Treaters would pass, then he'd jump out of the garage at them.

Talk about scary.

---

[21]My Uncle Cyril is Mrs. Felicie Coulon's husband. He moved to Heaven on October 5, 2004. Felicie Coulon is my god-mother/my Nanny. Though my Uncle Cyril was not officially my god-father, for much of my life, he did all the things with me and foe me that a god-father should do.

[22]This was an abandoned house in our uptown neighborhood.

When he jumped out and yelled, "Booga-Booga-Boo," some folks screamed, some ran across the street, and some just froze in their places.

We laughed and laughed and laughed as we watched him scare the daylights out of hundreds of passers-by. Oh, those were the days.

You know, almost every one who passed by that old garage was sacred. Old and young alike.

However, there were a few kids who seemed to not be afraid when they saw him. No matter how far he jumped out, no matter how loud he yelled, "Booga-Booga-Boo," they just weren't scared at all.

Now as a young child, it didn't take much to scare me and send me running to the protection of my momma or daddy's arms. All you had to say is "Boo," not even the whole "Booga-Booga-Boo," to scare the lights out of me. So, when I saw other kids being scared by my Uncle Cyril, I understood their fears. It was the ones who weren't scared by him, that I just couldn't figure out.

What made them so strong?

What was it that gave them the courage not to be afraid of something or someone that was scaring almost everyone else?

How could they stand so strong in the face of the great "Booga-Booga-Boo?"

Only God knows why they were not afraid. But, at the time, I was scared of the "Booga-Booga-Boo Man," even though I knew it was my Uncle Cyril.

It would be many years before I had the strength to stand up and face my fears like those boys stood up and faced that spooky garage and the Booga-Booga-Boo Man of Uptown New Orleans

You know, the Books of the Bible talk a lot about facing our fears. We can gain courage over our fears through the faith of Daniel as he stood unharmed in the lions' den.[23] We can inspiration from Shadrach, Meshach, and Abednego as the walked around inside the fires of King Nebuchadnezzar singing songs of praise to our God.[24]

---

[23]Daniel 6:17-24

[24]Daniel 3:1-100

In a very real way, much of Sacred Scripture challenges us to face our fears with the same courage that those kids had back on that Halloween night.

In their writings, St. Peter, King David and St. Matthew all give us reasons why we should not be afraid.

In the First Letter of St. Peter, we are told not to be afraid of things that others fear.[25] When this letter was written, the Christian faithful were facing possible persecution because of the allegiance to Christ. St. Peter says that with Christ in our hearts, we can bear any hardship that may come our way. Nothing of this world should scare us, for with the Lord on our side, we will be protected from true harm.

In the 27th Psalm, King David proclaims,
> "The LORD is my light and my salvation; whom do I fear?
> The LORD is my life's refuge; of whom am I afraid?"[26]

I assure you that the darkness of this world cannot harm us, because Jesus, the Light of the World came to illuminate the pathway to Heaven.

Thus, nothing that can jump out of the dark and abandoned garages of the Earth can harm us.

For, Christ takes what is done in the scary darkness and brings it into the secure light. Thus, of whom should we be afraid?

In the Gospel of our Brother Matthew, we can read about a time when Jesus sent the apostles out to fish in the sea of Galilee.[27] In the story it is apparent that they had been fishing for quite a while because at about three in the morning, they looked up and thought that they were seeing things.

As the boat was being tossed back and forth by the early morning waves, they saw this figure walking toward them on the water. Crying out in fear, the disciples exclaimed, "It is a ghost!"[28]

---

[25] 1 Peter 3:14-17

[26] Psalm 27:1

[27] Matthew 14:22-36

[28] Matthew 14:26

Now, I don't know about you, but, if I were fishing on the Lake Pontchartrain[29] and saw someone walking toward me, I'd probably think it was a ghost, too. But, unlike the disciples, I wouldn't be around to find out who it was.

When Jesus sensed their fear, He yelled to them,
"Take courage. It is I - Do not be afraid."[30]

In other words, he was saying to them, "Gentlemen, get a hold of yourselves!"

Now when St. Peter recognized the Lord, he was so excited that he asked Jesus if he could walk to Him on the water. And the Lord said, O.K.

Initially, Peter did pretty well, walking on top of the lake. But, then, he got distracted by the waves and took His eyes off the Lord.

When he started paying attention to the winds and the waves, he began to sink. He cried out, "Lord, Save me!" Jesus immediately stretched out His hand and caught him. After he got Peter safely in the boat, He asked Peter, *"O' you of little faith, why did you doubt?"*[31]

I would bet you, that it was years before Peter fully understood why he faltered.

You know Halloween Night could be a scary night, if you allowed it to be. In fact, every night could be a scary night if you allowed them to be.

When you think about all the stuff that's going on in our world, ghosts and the *Boogie Man* are the last things that we need to fear. In the light of Christ, they are not scary at all.

Now, I can tell you about some stuff that's truly scary!

The ruthless business man who puts making money before caring for his wife and children - now that's scary.

The emotionless doctor who has no problems with aborting babies - now that's scary.

------

[29]Lake Pontchartrain is the large lake that forms the northern border of the City of New Orleans.

[30]Matthew 14:27

[31]Matthew 14:31

77

The racist politician who passes laws which defeat all of the advances our society has made over the past few decades - now that's scary.

The young black man who has no value for his own life, thus holds no value for the lives of others - now that's scary.

Yes, on Halloween Night, there is a lot that can scare us. And, ghosts and the *Boogie Man* are the least of them.

But, Children of God, as we sail along through this often scary world, Jesus the Christ yells to us just as he yelled to the disciples, "Take courage. It is I - Do not be afraid." or put more simply, "Get a hold of yourselves and do not be afraid."

Part of the message that we must convey to one another is that with Christ in our hearts, we can bear any hardship that may come our way.

This ills of this society can be scary when your heart is not rooted in the Lord.

Part of the reason why St. Peter began to sink in the water was because he took his eyes off the Lord and began to fear that the elements of the world were stronger than the protection that Jesus was offering him.

Peter sank because he took his eyes off the prize.

For, as long as his eyes were fixed on Jesus, he was able to do the impossible.

He could walk on water.

Today, as we face the fears of our lives, I say to you, "Do not be afraid."

Fear not.

For, Jesus is walking towards us across the Jordan.

Jesus is walking towards us and summoning us to leave the comfort of our boats, to step out onto the treacherous seas and to draw near to Him.

Do not be afraid.

You know, when I look back to that Halloween of 1975, I especially remember those few children who were not scared by my Uncle Cyril.

Watching them made me less afraid of him, too.

Through their standing firm, others began to realize that whatever it was that was jumping out of the darkness would not harm them.

In their defiant essence, those courageous children were like little Saints of God.

Just like those children, the Saints stand firm in the face of known adversities and unknown dangers.

When others might ordinarily run and hide, the Saints march on, doing the work of the Lord. That's why we honor them and recall their heroic deeds.

Through their examples, and their constant prayers, we too are made firm; able to face what ever lurks in the dark corners of our world.

Today is the day to stand up, look into the darkness of our lives and say, "I am not afraid."

(If you are afraid, do like St. Peter did and simply hold out your hand and let Jesus guide you safely back into His boat of comfort!)

Part Three
"I Believe That You Can't Let the Devil Steal Your Joy!"

**The Mangled Bleachers from
Harold Sampson- St. Roch Playground.**
This playground in located directly across the street
from Our Lady Star of the Sea Church and Rectory.
October 17, 2005

Who Invited the Devil?

As many people already know, I love being a Roman Catholic Priest. From the celebration of the Sacraments to leading pilgrimages to more than eighteen different countries, I can't really begin to tell you how much fun I have been having, serving the people of God as a Priest.

Like the Gospel song says, *"I know I've been blessed."*

Now, celebrating the Sacraments and leading trips abroad are indeed some of the great perks of being a priest. They are probably the most visible of the perks we get. But, there are some subtle perks that folks don't often know about. Perks that are given to priests simply because they decided to dedicate their lives to God.

Like when you go to the grocery store and you see one of your parishioners in line. If you are in a rush, one of the perks is that they will usually let you skip the line and you can skirt right out of the door.

One of the special perks that I enjoyed before Hurricane Katrina struck was something that I used to do every Sunday Morning. You see, every Sunday, I would go over to the #1 Po-Boy and Donut Shop on Elysian Fields and Claiborne Avenues to get a dozen of Donuts.

On the first time that I visited that shop, I was greeted by Rochelle, the cashier and Miss Kim, the Vietnamese owner. I promptly ordered a dozen of donuts and waited for them to be prepared. While waiting I told them that I was the new Pastor at Our Lady Star of the Sea Church and that I would probably be seeing them almost every Sunday.

When they handed my the box of donuts, I reached into my wallet to pay them and Miss Kim looked up and said, *"Oh no..... You don't pay....you pray!"*

And from that Sunday on until the Hurricane, I received a complementary dozen Donuts from my most favorite Po-Boy and Donut Shop.

Back then, I would usually go there around 6:15 a.m. on a Sunday Morning. At that time, I was usually greeted by a variety of "city folks" who were on their way in from a night on the town.

You can only imagine the types of folks that will greet you at that time of the morning in a breakfast place.

From drunken, Mardi Gras revelers to other folks who think that Mardi Gras lasts all year long, indeed, there was usually a real cast of characters to meet and greet when I would get there.

One morning, I had the joy of encountering a group of women who were heading in from a big night on the town. Now, this group was a very unique group indeed. They were a group of about five African-American women, whom each were teetering at some degree on a level of sleepiness mixed with a level of intoxication.

One of the ladies, approached me and said, *"Hey father. I've got a problem."* So, I looked at her and asked, "And, just what is that problem?" (Thinking to myself, I probably can't solve some of her problems.)

She went on to say, "You see, the Devil just keeps coming by me, time and time again. No matter what I do. No matter what I say. I can't seem to get the Devil away from me."

As she was talking to me, I was looking at her friends as they giggled behind her back. So, I decided that even though it was 6:15 a.m., now was as good a time than ever to give a sermon. So, I promptly jumped on to my spiritual soap box and began to preach. I said, "My Sisters, I see that you have a problem with the Devil. You say that the devil keeps coming by your house. The Devil just don't want to leave you alone. And, you seem ready to invite the Devil out. Well, I have a solution for you."

The way to keep the Devil from visiting your house is simply this: Stop visiting the Devil's house.

Cause, if you don't pay the Devil a visit, he won't visit you.

You can't go sit down at the Devil's Table and think that he won't wanna come and sit at your table. Remember, the Devil is just neighborly. If you visit him, he thinks that he is supposed to come and visit you. So, if you don't visit the Devil, the Devil will stop visiting you."

Well, she looked at her friends, as they giggled even louder and said, "You know, Father you are right. I gotta leave these devils alone!"

You know, you never know when a good sermon will come to you. Right there at Miss Kim's #1 Po-Boy and Donut Shop, I realized that if you don't visit the Devil's house, he won't feel like he is supposed to visit you.

In the Book of Job, we hear the story of a man who was visited quite often by Satan, the Adversary, the Devil.

Job was a good man; a very good man. And yet, some how God allowed the Devil to test Job to the point in which all of his family and his property were taken away. Though Job had done nothing wrong, it seemed that his troubles were so insurmountable that a weaker man would have indeed cursed God.

But, Job refused to give up. He refused to allow Satan to win. Though he did not know why he was testing him or where the devil came from, Job stood firm and eventually had everything restored in his life 100 fold.

Jesus also fought the test of the Devil. When Jesus was in the Desert, in the midst of his 40 day Retreat with God, the Devil came to Him and began to test Him; tempting Jesus to turn away from God and use His Divine Gifts for His own good and for the sake of the Devil.

Jesus was in that desert to commune with God - to spend 40 days in prayer and fasting. He wanted to be alone. Yet, Satan did not let Jesus have this time by Himself. Satan had to stick his nose in *God's business*.

I would bet that in the midst of His prayer and fasting, Jesus, upon seeing Satan coming near Him, looked up to Heaven and asked, *"Who Invited the Devil?"*

Well, just like Job and just like Jesus, we all are faced with times in our lives when it seems that the Devil is all around us. It is amazing how the Devil can weasel his way into our most intimate and secure places, and become our uninvited Guest!

Somehow he can get into our relationships with our spouses and our children. He can get into our relationships with our parents and our teachers. He can get into our relationships with ourselves and appear to get into our relationships with even God. Somehow, the Devil can mess up so much stuff that we all want to scream, "Just who in [the] *Hell* invited the Devil?" (The word, "*Hell,*" here refers to the Devil's domain.)

Well, part of the key in finding out *who invited the Devil* is first asking yourself are *you the one* who delivered the invitation?

Are you the one who stopped by Satan's Sensual Palace and dropped off an invitation to the Devil to come and visit you anytime he felt like it?

Are you leaving your home, going to the places where sin is *"in"* and then somehow wondering why the Devil, the Prince of Sin, seems to always follow you home?

Well, if you keep going to his house, then you can't blame him for wanting to come to yours.

Remember, the Devil is just neighborly!

Now is the time to stop visiting the Devil.
And then, invite Him to stop coming by you.

Now is the time to rebuke Satan, like Job did in the Old Testament; to Reject his temptations, like Jesus did during His 40 day Retreat in the desert; to walk in the valley of darkness, fearing no evil and rebuking the Devil with God's Rod and Staff giving you courage.

Yes,
now is the time to renew your first three Baptism Promises and live for God.

But, first, you've got to stop visiting the Devil!

And so, if these are your promises,
I want you to respond loudly and clearly by saying, *"I do."*

Do you reject Satan?
"I do."

And all his works?
"I do."

And all his empty promises?
"I do.".

People of God,
I don't know about you. But, as for me and my House,
we're gonna serve the Lord. So, I say loudly and clearly,

"Together, in the Name of Jesus, we rebuke thee Satan."
"I don't know who invited you. But, Devil, it is time for you to go!"

84

"You Can't Let the Devil Steal Your Joy!"

Back in August of 2002, I began a new priestly ministry, one that I thoroughly enjoyed. You see, it was then that I began a four year tenure of teaching at my Alma Mater, St. Augustine High School in New Orleans.

I never could have imagined how much fun I would have as a teacher at St. Aug. Each day for four years, I got to go over to a place I love, and teach my young African-American brothers about the God I love and serve. And, the great thing about it was the fact that they loved when I got there and hated to see me leave. (Of course, who could blame them? I would have loved to have *me* as a teacher, too.)

In the four years that I taught at St. Aug, including the one semester I taught for the MAX School,[32] I was able to teach on all of the high school grade levels, 8th through 12th grades. I was also able to bring the Word of God to the students and faculty in a unique manner as the school's Campus Minister.

Quite often, the students would tell me how much they loved having me there and how much fun our classes were.

At first, I wondered whether or not they were saying all that flattering stuff because they though that it would help their grades. Later, I realized that they really were sincere in their compliments. (Even though, it did not hurt their grades to continuously flatter the teacher!)

I think that the greatest compliment that I have ever received from a student was when one of the students looked up at the end of our hour and a half of class time and said, "Class is over, already?" You know that you really love what you are doing when you look up and are amazed at just how fast the time has flown.

As a teacher, I was paid to impart my great gift of wisdom upon the poor, ignorant children to whom I have been sent.

---

[32]The MAX Satellite School of New Orleans was a school formed out of the three historically Black and Catholic High Schools in New Orleans. Two all girls schools, Xavier University Preparatory High School and St. Mary's Academy, and one all boy school, St. Augustine High School, combined to allow our students affected by Hurricane Katrina the chance to return home and continue their education.

It was my job to educate the masses. But, I have to admit something to you. I believe that as much as I was teaching them, they were also teaching me. We were truly learning together.

Back in the Fall of 2002, during my first semester teaching at the Aug, I learned a lesson from one of my students that I will never forget.

In my class was a young man named Ja'mal. Now, Ja'mal was one of those kids that you truly love to teach. Ja'mal was eager to learn and eager to achieve in class. He always did his homework and usually did pretty well on the tests. He was truly a joy to teach.

One of things that all of his teachers noticed about Ja'mal was the fact that he always seemed to be happy. No matter what happened to him or happened around him, Ja'mal always seemed to have a smile on his face.

You could be yelling and screaming at him, reading him his pedigree (as my Momma would call it) and Ja'mal would still look at you with a big grin on his face. (Do you know how hard it is to fuss at somebody who has a big grin on their face?)

Well one day, I decided to ask Ja'mal about his contagious smile. I asked him, just how was it that he always would smile and seem to be happy no matter what went on around him or was happening to him. And his answer was quite simple.

He said, *"Father, you can't let the Devil steal your joy."*

"You can't let the Devil steal your joy!"

You know, right there in that classroom, that happy-go-lucky thirteen-year-old, summed up all of life for me, "You can't let the Devil steal your joy." (Period)

No matter how hard the Devil tries to mess up your life and get in your business, don't let him steal your joy!

All you have to do is rebuke him and tell him to get on his way.

One of the things that I have come to realize in this past year is the fact that the closer you are to God the harder the Devil will work to get at you. If you are walking as a child of God, the Devil will see you as a very valuable prize to win. So, he is going to do all that he can to get you to turn away from the Lord and turn to him.

86

He will try to use the people that you love the most to be the instrument through which he turns you away from the Lord. That is why you have to stand firm just as Jesus did when the Devil was trying to use St. Peter to get Jesus to walk away from the tasks that God had assigned Him.

The Devil doesn't want you to have a great relationship with God. Of course He doesn't want to have a great relationship with you, either. He just wants to mess up the good thing you got going on with God.

That is why we have to be like Ja'mal.

Every time the Devil seems to be trying to get in your business, you have to look up and say, "I can't let the Devil steal my joy!"

You see, if you know what I know and believe what I believe, the Devil really can't get at your joy if your joy is true. Because, if *Jesus is the center of your Joy*, there is nothing that the Devil can do to take it away.

Unlike the people of old times, we are strangers and sojourners no more. We are those who have been called to walk humbly with God and to love our brothers and sisters.

God has called us to his side and has promised through His Holy Spirit to be with us always. That is why we can't allow the Devil to somehow take it away.

So, when that messy person on your job seems to be trying to mess up your good thing, you've gotta look up and say, *"Devil, you can't steal my joy."*

When that disrespectful classmate seems to always be trying to distract you from learning, you've gotta look up and say, *"Devil, you can't steal my joy."*

When that no good husband or quarrelsome wife seems to be sowing dissension in your home, you've gotta look up and say, *"Devil, you can't steal my joy."*

No matter what may come your way, be it good or be it bad, you have to adopt the Spirit of Ja'mal and with a bold conviction and an unwavering heart say: *"Devil, you can't steal my joy."*

I know from my own experiences that it really is easy to be happy most of the time. In fact, many folks ask me like I asked Ja'mal, "How can a person be so happy everyday of his life?" And, in the words of Ja'mal, I find it to be quite simple, "You can't let the Devil steal your joy." *(Out of the mouth of babes!)*

"Devil Get Your Hands Off My Child!"

Anyone who knows me, knows that I was raised in a pretty good home. The bulk of my childhood was spent living in a double shotgun house on Jena Street in Uptown New Orleans.

I loved living in that house. On one side of that shotgun house was my family, which included my mom and dad, my maternal grandmother and my brother, sister and me. On the other side was my Aunt Fell (my nanny), my Uncle Cyril and their three children.

It really was a blessed place to live. Our two families really lived as one. That's why I often tell folks that in our family we had five parents and six children.

Do you know how spoiled a person can be when he has five parents to beg before he has to give up on something?

Now, the central part of our family was indeed my Grandmother, Anestasia Honore. We called her Momma Stasia.

Momma Stasia was a mother to everyone in those houses. Her daughters, her sons-in-law and her grandchildren all considered her to be their mother. She was a matriarch in the truest sense of the term. She was a real Momma to us all.

And, it is no secret that I was the apple of her eye. I was her baby.

It is partially because of her love and devotion to God and her family that I am the priest that I am today. She was and *spiritually is* my Saint and my Heavenly Guide.

Momma Stasia was indeed a matriarch and a protector (especially of her baby). I remember one time my Dad was coming after me to "fuss at me for something I did wrong." (Can you image that?) So, I ran into her room and she got up out of her recliner chair. I immediately jumped into her chair and she sat down on top of me.

When my Daddy finally made it to her room, he looked at me sitting under her and leaned over to grab me. Momma Stasia simply sat back in the chair (on top) and said, *"I know you are not gonna hurt the baby."*

Indeed, God is Good. And, my tail lived on to see another day.

My grandmother was indeed a very protective lady. She wasn't gonna let anything or anyone hurt the baby. I have to admit to you that not only was she protective of me but she was very protective of her entire family.

Like a momma pit bull, I believe that my grandmother would have fought anyone who tried to hurt any of her family members.

She saw all of us as gifts from God and she wasn't gonna let anything hurt her gifts.

My Grandmother moved to Heaven on November 4, 1989. Though she has been living in Heaven for more than a decade, I believe that she is still quite active in our lives, praying for us and still protecting us, with the help of the Saints and our Guardian Angels. (Although she may never be canonized on earth and formally named as a Saint, I believe that she has already made it into Heaven!)

Even death, itself, cannot deter her from her role as protectress of our family.

When my grandmother died, I had the joy of packing-up her altar and her many sacred items. While packing her statues, I found a folded napkin under a statue of St. Jude. On the napkin, my grandmother had written the name of her oldest child, My Aunt Grace.

Inside the napkin were two dollar bills that were meant for my aunt. You see, my aunt was struggling at the time with diabetes, an alcoholic husband and six sons who often drove her crazy.

So, though she was a grown woman and a grandmother, in her own right, she was still my Grandmother's Child, and so, my grandmother would do whatever she could to help her.

Written inside the napkin was a note that I have never forgotten. It was, indeed, a prayer from my grandmother's heart; a prayer about her daughter from a woman who would fight anything and anyone for the sake of her children.

Inside the napkin she boldly wrote, *"Devil, Get Your Hands Off My Child!"*

Wow, what a strong woman. My little bitty, 4' 11" grandmother was willing to take on even the Devil to protect her children. (You think Muhammad Ali was the greatest fighter of all times. Mess with a woman's child and you'll find out just who the greatest is.)

And, I know that the Devil didn't want to take her on. (She was no Joe Frazier. She wasn't gonna get beat!)

I assure you that the Devil could have never won that battle.

People of God,
How often have we had to pray like my grandmother;
    Pray with the conviction of a momma
    who would shake the gates of Hell to save their children?

Many mothers and fathers go to church to pray like my grandmother prayed.
They pray for their children who are addicted to drugs.
They pray for their children who are living on the streets.
They pray for their children who are caught up in relationships
    that are based on sin and seem to be doomed.

Indeed, many parents come to God asking God to help them and help their children.

Maybe, as part of your prayer, you ought to use the words of my Grandmother.
Just boldly in faith, say from the depths of your being,
"Devil, Get Your Hands Off My Child!"

Your children are gifts to you from God. So, don't let the Devil steal your gifts. Tell him that in the Name of Jesus you reclaim the gifts that God has given you and you refuse to let go.

From the depths of your being, cry out, *"Devil, Get Your Hands Off My Child!"*

Sometimes, we are too proud to let folks know that our children are falling into the traps of the Devil. That is in and of itself a Trap of the Devil.

When we become too embarrassed to say that our children have fallen into the traps of sin, we prevent the community of believers from being able to join us in our prayer.

We prevent the people we love from being able to join us in our fight against the Devil.

That is why we have to be able to face the trials of our lives and the lives of our children with bold faith and with real conviction.

It is time for us to put our pride aside and build up our courage.

It is time for us to reclaim our children and tell the Devil to step off.

Like my grandmother, I am extremely protective of the gifts that God has sent me. And, I refuse to let the Devil take them away.

I pray extremely hard for the children that God has sent into my care.

And, I am willing to go down and shake the Gates of Hell, if I have to, in order to make sure that the Devil doesn't claim any of them.

St. Paul, in his *Letter to the Romans*, wrote about the great anguish he had in his heart: Anguish like the anguish that a parent feels when they see their child fall into the addictive traps of sin.

That is why we have to pray like Paul. We have to pray like my grandmother. We have to pray like grandmothers and grandfathers have prayed for centuries.

"Devil, Get Your Hands Off My Child!"

"Devil, Get Your Hands Off Our Children!"

People of God,
There is no trap that God cannot get our children out of.

There is no trap that God cannot get you out of.

All we have to do is have the faith and conviction that indeed God is getting us out of the traps we are in.

Today, let us call on the name of Jesus to help us and to help our children.

Today, let us claim those who belong to us and in the words of my grandmother, look the Devil straight in the eye and boldly say,

"Devil, Get Your Hands Off My Child!"

Part Four
"I Believe That Mary, Jesus' Momma, Can Help Us!"

**This Statue of the Blessed Mother
belongs to my Momma. It was salvaged
from the back yard of our Family Home.**

December 12, 2005

Don't You Remember?

I once heard a story about a Sunday School Teacher who gave his class a very unique assignment for Easter.

One Sunday he told his class that they were going to have a Scavenger Hunt. He handed each of the children a large plastic egg (like those Red Goose, Golden Eggs from long ago).

He told them to go out and find something that they thought represented Easter and New Life and to put it in their egg.

Within a short time, the excited children returned to the classroom with everything from Spring flowers and green grass to birds' eggshells and butterfly cocoons.

Only one child came back with an empty egg container. His name was Philip and he had Down's Syndrome, he was usually referred to as being "slow."

When the teacher opened Philip's egg, and everyone saw that there was nothing inside, all of the children began to laugh at Philip, the "slow kid."

Everyone began to say that , once again,
     Philip had done it wrong because his egg was empty.

The teacher asked Philip, "Did you understand that I wanted you to find something that represented Easter and then put it in your egg?"

"Yep," Philip replied, "And I did."

"But there is nothing in here." responded the teacher.

And looking up, Philip said, *"And there was nothing in the tomb!"*

In John 20:1-9, we hear the words of St. John as he recounted for us that great getting-up morning (when, St. Mary Magdalene, St. Simon Peter and "the other disciple," all experienced the joy of finding an empty tomb).

Though only "the other disciple" immediately believed that Jesus had Risen from the Dead, all three shared in some level of excitement because there was nothing in the grave.

93

I would bet that when Mary Magdalene, Peter and "the other disciple" got back to the Upper Room and began to recount what they had just experienced, the disciples who were hiding out in the Upper Room, were probably a little shaken by the news.

I would guess that it wasn't just Thomas who was doubting whether or not Jesus had risen from the dead. Just by the very nature of the fact that they were hiding out, I believe that some probably began to wonder who could have taken the body.

Remember, they were in the upper room, not because they were waiting for Jesus to come back, but because they were afraid that the Jews would killed them, too.[33]

But, at some point, I can't help but believe that as they huddled in fear , *Mary the Mother of Jesus* stepped into the center of the room and began to speak to them.

I believe that Mary was in that room with them simply because I can't imagine them leaving her all alone during one of the darkest moments of her life.

Can't you just see Mary, standing there in the middle of those men, a woman wracked with grief over the death of her son, but yet standing firm in faith and trying to comfort others?

I can imagine Mary yelling at the disciples and saying,
   "Young men, get a hold of yourselves."

"I can assure you that this will not end in death. This will not end in death.

   Don't you remember when He turned that water into wine?

   Don't you remember when He fed the five thousand?

   Don't you remember when He gave sight to the blind?

   Don't you remember when He made the lame walk?

   Don't you remember when He called Lazarus out of the tomb?

---

[33]John 20:19

94

*Don't you remember when He healed the woman
who had been hemorrhaging for 12 years?*

*Don't you remember when He raised Jairus' daughter from the dead
by simply touching her hand and saying,
"Talitha Cum - Little Girl, get up!"?*

Don't you remember?

Don't you remember?!!!"

And in the midst of her recalling all that Jesus had done with them, through them and for them, in His ministry, I can see the door frame shaking and Jesus coming through the locked door and saying to them,

"Shalom - Peace be with you."

(Now, I don't know about you.)

But, I can't help but imagine Mary's reaction
to seeing Jesus coming through that door.

I fully believe that at the moment the Blessed Mother saw her Son come through that door, she broke through the boys, grabbed her child and began to shout,

"My Baby's Back! My Baby's Back!"

"I told you that this would not end in death."

In that Upper Room, before Jesus appeared to them, I can't help but believe that Mary, the Mother of Jesus, was the stabling Force of Faith for the disciples.

As the men huddled in fear, this middle-aged woman held them together.

She believed all that angel told her at the Annunciation.
She remembered all that Her Baby had done.
She wasn't afraid, because she had first hand experiences of
the power of God and she wasn't sacred to talk about them.

When I think about the role that the Blessed Mother probably played in that upper room, once again, I am drawn to how much she can do and does do for those who believe in her Son.

95

For many Christians, Mary is the stabling force when their faith is being rocked by the deadly horrors of this modern age. *Like the disciples*, many Christians, when faced with hardships, run off and begin to hide in the Upper Rooms of this world.

But, in a very real way, the Blessed Mother intercedes on our behalf, like she probably did in the Upper Room, and assists us through her prayers to remember all the things that her Baby has done.

What a better world this would be, if more folks would turn to Our Blessed Mother instead of running to the Upper Room.

What a better world this would be, if more folks would turn to Our Blessed Mother when they find themselves beginning to forget
"Just How Good the Lord Has Been to Us."

There ain't nothing better than talking to someone's Momma when you want to know more about them and to learn how good they can be for you.

Indeed Mary can tell us all we need to know about the Savior 'cause She's His Momma and that's her job.

My Brothers and Sisters,
I assure you that when you find yourself huddling in the upper room, wondering where the Lord is in your life, all you've gotta do is go ask "Big Momma."

The Virgin Mary, the Big Momma of the Kingdom of Heaven, will indeed intercede for us whenever we call on her.

For the past 2000 years, Mary has been fulfilling her role as a primary care-giver for God 's Children.

Just like the Big Momma in most families, Mary understands what we need and is willing to ask her Son, Jesus, to give it to us.

That is why, whenever we think about all that Mary has done for us through her prayers, we shouldn't hesitate to look up to Heaven and say,

"We love you, Big Momma."

Mary, A Very Proud Momma

Over the course of the past twelve years or so, I have had the joy of traveling around the world, proclaiming the Good News. As most of you know, I have lead different groups on Religious Pilgrimages to various parts of the world.

In just twelve years of being a priest, I have been privileged to visit and preach in the countries of Jordan, Israel, Egypt, The Netherlands, Germany, Croatia, Bosnia-Herzegovina, Portugal, Spain, France, Italy, Senegal, Russia, China, Korea, Japan, Canada and Mexico.

I have been given these privileges simply because I, like the Blessed Mother, decided to say, *"Totally Yes,"* to God by answering The Call.

Each time that I've traveled abroad, I have truly been blessed by God with an overwhelming sense of His Divine Presence.

In the Holy Land, I stood in the Church of the Holy Sepulcher, completely blown away as I climbed Mount Calvary. There pilgrims are able to place their hands in the hole where it is believed that the Cross of Christ once stood and to entered the Tomb that once held the Body of the Savior.

In Western Europe, I visited two of the great shrines that have been built on sites where the Blessed Mother has appeared.

In Portugal, I visited the Shrine of Our Lady of Fatima. It was there that Mary appeared to Blessed Francisco, Blessed Jacinta and to Sr. Lucia. (As a side note, I also said Mass in the Chapel of the convent where Sr. Lucia lived.)

In France, I visited the Shrine of Our Lady of Lourdes. There I had the chance to drink directly from the Miraculous Stream of Lourdes and to wash in the waters just as St. Bernadette drank and washed from the stream.

There at the Grotto in Lourdes, I felt the presence of God as I reflected on the words of Mary. When asked by St. Bernadette, "Who are you?," Mary replied, "I am the Immaculate Conception."

In Bosnia-Herzegovina, I had the joy of visiting Medjugorje. This is the site where it is believed that Mary is still appearing to six visionaries.

In Medjugorje, I also had some very profound experiences of God's Presence. It is my experiences in Medjugorje that I want to tell you a little more about.

On our way to Medjugorje we flew into Zagreb, Croatia. From there, our group traveled by bus for three hours down a narrow mountainside road that was alongside the Asiatic Sea into Bosnia-Herzegovina.

This was a very beautiful ride. Croatia and Bosnia-Herzegovina are both beautiful countries. From the mountainside, you could see the sea and the coast of Italy. You could also see that there was no guard rail to stop the bus from tumbling over the side of the mountain.

Unfortunately (or should I say fortunately), I slept for most of the journey to Medjugorje. So, I did not get to see much of the scenery. Now, I did not sleep because I was tired. I went to sleep because I was too sacred to open my eyes and look over the side of the mountain!

Once in Medjugorje, we visited the various places that are associated with the reported apparitions.

We celebrated Mass in St. James Church, which is the site of the on-going apparitions. We climbed up *Apparition Hill*, the site where the reported apparitions first began. And we visited the homes of several of the visionaries. We even had the chance to visit with a fireman from Slidell, Louisiana, who was living in Medjugorje. He was there helping the community to build a retreat center for priests, deacons, religious brothers and religious women.

We also had the chance to hear talks by many of the folks who are directly associated with the apparitions of the Blessed Mother. We heard talks by Vitca and Ivan, two of the visionaries. And, we also heard a talk by Fr. Yozo, a Franciscan Priest, who was the pastor of St. James during the time of the first apparitions.

In Medjugorje, I was privileged to experience a couple of powerful moments that showed me the Power of God and the role of the Blessed Mother in our faith life.

On one blessed occasion, we were going to climb up Apparition Hill when suddenly, a quick rain storm began to fall. You should know that Apparition Hill has a very rocky terrain. On an ordinary day, it is tough to climb up that hill. With the rain falling as it was, not many of our group would have been able to make the climb.

While we were standing under a shelter at the bottom of the Hill, one of the ladies in our group suggested that we say a decade of the Rosary - asking the Blessed Mother to work on getting the rain to stop.

98

Now, I have got to tell you, I have always believed that Mary could get the Lord to do special things for us, but stopping the rain was not on my list of things that I thought that she would ask the Lord to do.

But, not wanting to be the skeptic, I "played along" with the group and joined them as they began to say the Rosary.

Well, would you believe that immediately after we finished that decade of the Rosary, the rain stopped? (Needless to say, I have no doubt that Mary could handle any request.)

In Medjugorje, I was present on the Hill for an Apparition. I was truly overwhelmed by a feeling of peace that came over the crowd during the time of that Apparition was taking place. I remember looking into the sky and seeing the most peaceful display of stars. I had no doubt that something powerful was happening at that moment.

On the night before we left Medjugorje, I concelebrated in St. James Church at the Vigil Mass for the Feast of the Ascension of our Lord. At that Mass, I had one of the most profound religious experiences of my life.

First, this Mass was celebrated in Croatian, which meant that other than the parts of the Mass that I recognized, I hadn't the slightest idea what the priest was talking about..... (kind of like how some folks feel during one of my sermons).

On that night, the Church was extremely packed. The folks were literally wall-to-wall. People were sitting and standing in every open space there was in the Church. They were even sitting on the first step of the Sanctuary.

There was also a very large overflow crowd that gathered outside on all sides of the Church. Speakers were provided in the courtyards so that those who could not get inside the church could at least listen to the Mass as it was being celebrated.

The celebration of the Eucharist went on as usual, with the readings and sermon being said in Croatian, and me sitting there wondering what they were talking about.

But, during the Eucharistic Prayer, during the Cconsecration, I knew what was going on, because no matter what language it is being said in, the *Consecration* is the *Consecration*. And, Jesus, the Christ, was being made present to us through the Breaking of the Bread.

Throughout the Mass, I was literally being blown away at the devotion to Jesus that was being shown by the people of Medjugorje. The folks at that Mass seemed to have a very profound awareness of the Lord's Presence.

During the distribution of Communion, I had an experience that has stuck with me and indeed is the highlight of the entire trip.

At Communion time, the priests were given bowls of Consecrated Hosts and directed to different stations, to distribute the Body of Christ. I was given a bowl and sent to offer Communion at the rear of the church, near the big, front doors.

When I reached the back of the church, the crowd was so thick that they could not form a line for Communion. So, they literally began to push and shove through each other in order to get to where I was standing.

As they pushed and shoved for Communion, I saw hands coming at me from every direction.

That special moment reminded me of those scenes that are on the world news when United Nations trucks enter a starving nation and distribute food to the hungry. You know, the scene where the truck is driving through the town and folks are running along the side of the truck - reaching our vigorously - hoping to get hand full of rice.

That is what I experienced while giving out Communion in Medjugorje. It felt like people were starving for Jesus and I was sent by God to give Him to them.

When my ciborium was empty, all I could think about was that I had to go back and consecrate some more.

The people were starving for Jesus and I had to do something about it.

I can honestly tell you, that experience at Mass was a very profound moment for me. I left Medjugorje determined to do whatever I needed to do to get Jesus to His Starving People.

You know, in Fatima, in Lourdes and in Medjugorje, The Blessed Mother has delivered messages of peace and love. And, in all of her messages, she calls us to a stronger faith in her Son.

Part of the great messages of our Lady is that, in order to obtain peace, we must be willing to be like her and pray, pray, pray.

We must also come to know her Baby in a very intimate way.

As Roman Catholics, we are often challenged by other denominations because of our great love and devotion to the Blessed Mother. Most of the time, folk just understand what we believe.

In no way, shape or form, have we tried to make Mary anything more than a totally devoted Saint of God.

Never in any of her messages has Mary ever said, "Give me the glory and praise." She has always, always, given messages that point away from her honor and to the glory of her Son.

I fully believe that Mary only appears to us in order to point the way to her Son.

She is not seeking to become the fourth person of the Holy Trinity. She only wants to bring us to Christ.

Mary is simply a Loving Mother who wants everyone to know, love and serve her Baby.

And, like I experienced in Medjugorje and like the Disciples experienced on the Road to Emmaus, the greatest way that we can come to know Him and love Him in this world is through the breaking of the bread.

People of God,
It is my privilege to share with you my Faith in Jesus and how I have seen that faith grow and develop through the love I have for His Mother.

It is my fervent prayer for you that through the intercession of our Blessed Mother, you, too, will grow in your love for the Savior.

The Virgin Mary has time and time again, appeared to God's Children to direct their paths to her Son.

Together, let us follow her spirit-filled lead.

Part Five
"I Believe That We All Have A Call!"

**Bishop Dominic Carmon, SVD,
Auxiliary Bishop of New Orleans
and Fr. R. Tony Ricard**

This was taken on the day of
Fr. Tony's First Mass, May 28, 1995,
Our Lady of Lourdes Church in New Orleans

Behold, My Child!

*And you, child, will be called prophet of the Most High,
for you will go before the Lord to prepare His ways,
to give His people knowledge of salvation
through the forgiveness of their sins.*
(Luke 1:76-77)

These are the words of Zachariah as he thanked God for the gift of his son, John, and dedicated his child to the Lord. These are also the words that I chose to use for the prayer cards that were distributed on the weekend of my ordination to the priesthood. (May 27, 1995)

As a priest, like John the Baptist, I have been called by God to be both the one who has been dedicated to God as well as the one who dedicates others to the Lord. This is a call that I do not take lightly.

The image that you see above was created specifically for my ordination invitations by my seminary classmate, Fr. Herbert Kiff. Fr. Kiff used his artistic gifts to put in a concrete form a vision that I shared with him.

103

In my vision, I saw a priest standing on the banks of the Mississippi River, dedicating a child to the Lord. He was praying before God, just as Zachariah prayed, for the protection of the child in his hands and in thanksgiving for the blessing that this child would be to the world. In my vision, this dedication ceremony was taking place in the middle of the night.

As I shared my vision with Fr. Kiff, his creative thoughts began to flow. This artwork was the results of his gifts and talents. Fr. Kiff explained to me that he used a technique called *pointalism* to create this piece. In this form of art, the artist creates an image through the painstaking task of placing dots by dots on the paper. No lines are used to create this style of work: just dots. The shading was done by varying the number of dots in a given area. I was blown away at the details in Fr. Kiff's work.

In the picture, your eyes are immediately drawn to the priest and the child. You also realize that he is standing in the waters of the river. Fr. Kiff was able to represent the night by placing the moon in the background of the picture.

Believe it or not, I actually posed for this picture. We were in my seminary room and I was sharing with Fr. Kiff exactly how I saw the priest standing in my vision. So, he asked me to just stand still for a moment as he sketched the position of the priest and the child. Since we were in my room, we did not have vestments for me to wear which would allow Fr. Kiff to sketch how the material would fall and fold. So, Fr. Kiff improvised by taking a sheet off of my bed and draping it over my arms. With that, he was able to clearly see the vision that came to me. He returned about a week later with the art work in hand.

Many have asked who am I in this piece? Am I the priest or am I the baby who is being dedicated to God? My response to them has been simple, I am both.
For, I was dedicated to God at my Baptism and through the gift of Holy Orders. And, now, as a priest, I am called to dedicate others to the Lord in Jesus' Name.

However, to truly be the one who dedicates others to God, I must never forget that I first had to be chosen by God for my own moment of dedication.

"Before I formed you in the womb, I knew you, before you were born, I dedicated you, a prophet to the nations I appointed you."[34]

And God said, **"Behold, My Child."**

---

[34]Jeremiah 1:5

Book Three

don't be
stupid!

Lessons You Should Already Know

Rev. R. Tony Ricard, M.Th., M.Div.

Published in 2009

Introduction to *Don't Be Stupid*

During my formative years, I was blessed to attend some of the most outstanding schools in the City of New Orleans and to have been taught by some of the most outstanding teachers that have ever walked the face of this Earth.

My first *school* was in the home of my Aunt Grace, my Momma's oldest sister. Aunt Grace helped to teach my cousins and me the alphabet, our basic prayers and the difference between Coca-Cola and Pepsi. I am sure that I learned how to count by watching the globe spin around on *As The World Turns!* At Our Lady of Lourdes Elementary School, my most favorite teacher was my First Grade Teacher, Mrs. Herdine Scott. Her love for her students was always evident in her ministry. (After I became a public school teacher, Mrs. Scott visited my classroom to tell me how proud she was of me. I have never forgotten that day!)

Later at St. Augustine High School, I was blessed to be inspired by Mr. Edwin Hampton (Band Director), Fr. Howard Byrd, SSJ, (Theology), and Mrs. Anne Frenier Charbonnet (Algebra). They made me proud to be a Purple Knight! When I transferred from Tulane University to Loyola University, New Orleans, Mrs. Mary Fitzgerald, professor of Elementary Education, took me under her wing and into her heart. Mrs. Fitzgerald helped to refine my gift of teaching and fueled my love for the classroom.

At Notre Dame Seminary, Fr. Stan Klores and Fr. Frank Montalbano. OMI, were very inspiring teachers. Their love for Sacred Scripture, our Church's History and their priestly ministry were always evident in their faith-filled presentations. At Xavier University's Institute for Black Catholic Studies, Fr. Joseph Brown, SJ, and Sr. Patricia Haley, SCN, were not only great teachers but, also great role models. At the Institute, they helped me to fully see the blessings of my faith, my family and my rich cultural heritage.

Indeed, I have had some of the world's best teachers. But, of all my teachers, the greatest has always been my Momma. She taught me about life and unconditional love. My love for God, my love for my family and my love for myself flows from the love of my Momma. She is a no-nonsense, "straight from the hip" mother. Rather than complicating the concept, she just "tells it like it is." I am who I am today, because she answered the Call to be a Momma.

This book is a collection of spiritual lessons that I have learned from all of my teachers, especially my Momma and my Lord and Savior, Jesus Christ. I pray that this collection of lessons will be a blessing to you and all you love.

Rev. R. Tony Ricard, M.Th., M.Div.

SECTION ONE
Lessons from My Momma

Iva O'Rita Honore Ricard
Fr. Tony's Momma

Don't Be Stupid!

As I begin my reflection, I need to address a rumor that has been going around this country about me. It seems that some of you have been talking behind my back and thinking that I would never find out about it. Well, I did.

In fact, not long ago, one of my own fellow parishioners had the audacity, the unmitigated gall, to tell me to my face, something that ya'll have apparently been saying about me for years.

This supposed-lady of faith let me know that many of you are going around and telling other folks (whom I don't even know) that I am. . .
"A Momma's Boy."

Who me?

Today, I want to set the record straight. I am not a Momma's Boy.

I am not a Momma's Boy.

You see, I called my Momma, and, my Momma told me that I could tell you, that I am not a Momma's Boy! (I'm just very well kept!)

But, you know, when I think about it, being called a Momma's Boy might not be all that bad. First, if somebody messes with you, you ain't gotta be scared 'cause you know that you won't have to fight by yourself. You know that your momma will have your back.

In fact, I have told folks in other cities that if they mess with me, "my Momma will parachute down and hurt somebody!."

So, I'm not a Momma's Boy. I am just a fella who has been lucky enough to have a Momma who knows everything, can do anything and would whip anybody who messed with her baby. (I mean her grown-man son.)

Now, I can give you some examples of real Momma's Boys.

Have you ever heard of a fellow named, Bobby Boucher? He's the guy from "The Waterboy" movie. Now, that Boy was a real Momma's Boy. His Momma controlled almost everything about his life, everything about his world.

Everything that Bobby did somehow revolved around the will of his Momma.

Although his momma was a little crazy, even she had a little wisdom to share.

For example, when the young Bobby was talking to his Momma about girls, his momma said, "I don't ever want you associatin' with little girls." And when he asked, "Why not, Momma?" She replied, "Because little girls are the devil!" See, that's wisdom!

And when he asked her, "Momma, When Did Ben Franklin Invent Electricity?" She replied, "That's Nonsense." "I invented Electricity. Ben Franklin is the Devil!" (Once again, Wisdom!")

Another really famous Momma's boy has to be Forrest Gump.

That boy quoted his Momma all of the time. In fact, whenever Forrest wanted to sound wise, he always began his statements by saying, "Momma always said..." In the movie, "Forrest Gump," Forrest says, "Momma always had a way of explaining things so I could understand them."

One time, Forrest said, "Momma always said there's an awful lot you could tell about a person by their shoes. Where they're going. Where they've been. I've worn lots of shoes."

That's some deep stuff. Now, I really don't fully understand what it means. But, it's sounds deep!

And, we all remember, this one: "My momma always said, 'Life was like a box of chocolates. You never know what you're gonna get.'"

And, one of my most favorite Forrest Gump quotes came after his soon to be girlfriend, Jenny, asked him, "Are you stupid or something?" and Forrest replied by saying, "Momma says stupid is as stupid does."

So, being a Momma's Boy ain't that bad. Even though I ain't one.

Now, I do have to admit to you that I have been pretty successful, traveling around the world and living a life that is eerily similar to the lives of Bobby Boucher and Forrest Gump. You see, I've spent a lot of time quoting my Momma in front of thousands and thousands of folks.

Although I am not a Momma's Boy, I talk about my Momma in almost every city I visit and during most of the presentations I give. But, of course, if you had a Momma like I have, you would do it, too.

I think that I have probably made a lot of money by quoting lessons from my Momma. You see, like many Mommas, Iva O'Rita Theresa Ann Honore' Ricard had all of those usual quotes that most Momma's use.

For example, just after whipping your behind or fussing at you, she'd say something like "You had better hush up before I give you something to cry for!" To which you responded in your mind by saying, "I believe that you just did!"

Or when you were cutting up in a store, she'd say, "Oh, you can act a fool, now, but, just wait till we get home!" (Little did she know how much money I'd make acting a fool in front of thousands and thousands of folks.)

One of my most favorite stories that I love to tell about my Momma happened back in 1989, when my nephew Corey was only 4 years old.

One day, my Momma decided to take Corey with her to the grocery store. As she walked along the aisles, my precious little nephew decided that it was a good day for him to have a temper tantrum. Right there in the cereal aisle, my nephew laid down on the floor and began to kick and scream.

Kicking and screaming, screaming and kicking... in front of everyone!

Now, the one thing that we learned a long time ago was that you should never embarrass my Momma in public. I assure you that the results would always be ugly.

Now, don't get me wrong. He probably had a very good reason to "cut-up" in that store. You see, we had the kind of Momma who would pass up the *Captain Crunch with Crunchberries* and put those dry corn flakes in the basket.

Well, not to be embarrassed, my Momma looked down at the boy and went straight into action. Instead of trying to kill him, she began to call folks over to come and see him.

"Sir," she said. "Come see the boy." "Ma'am," she called, "Come see the child." Before you knew it, there was a crowd gather around my little nephew. And in unison, they all looked at him and began to applaud.

Without hesitation, my Momma leaned down to Corey and said, "You know, son, everyone who puts on a show in public will get a paycheck when the show is over. When we get home, I'm gonna sign your check!"

Needless to say, that was the last time Corey put on a show in public. In fact, to this day, my 30 year-old nephew is still afraid to go into a grocery store. I tell everyone that I'm scared that my nephew is going to be a serial killer. One day he's going to go into the store and shoot all the boxes! (A Cereal Killer!)

Indeed, my Momma has quite a few quotes that teach major lessons in just a few words. One of the quotes that I think that I have used the most, as I travel around the world, is something that she used to tell us (when we were little) as we left the house.

Just before we walked out of the door, she would say to us,

"Remember who you belong to and Don't Be Stupid."

Now, the "Remember who you belong to" part was pretty easy to understand. It meant that wherever we went and in whatever we did, we had better remember that we belong to her. Ass her children, we knew that regardless of what we did, we were going to show the world what kind of parents we had.

If we behaved well, we were showing that our parents were doing a great job in raising their kids. But, if we were bad, we were telling the world that our parents were not teaching us right from wrong. Be it good or bad, our actions would be a reflection on her and my daddy.

In fact, back in our old neighborhood, everyone knew who our Momma was. So, if we did something that was wrong, one of those nosey, no-good, always-up-in-your-business neighbors would call my Momma. Before we could make it back home, my Momma would already be waiting for us on the front porch of our house.

She would be standing there with her arms folded like Clint Eastwood.

In a deep voice, she would look at us and say, "Where have you been?" and "What have you done?" It would be at that moment that she would give us timeout.

Now for some of you, timeout is would be "Billy, you've been naughty. So, sit on the steps and I'll tell you when you can get up!"

But for us, timeout was (**BAM**). And, whatever time it took for you to get up off the ground and recover, that was your time-out! That is why we never wanted to face our Momma.

In our house, we were always "scared of my Momma." However, we were never scared of my daddy. In fact, in our home, you never heard my Momma say, "Just wait until your Father comes home!" In our house, you would hear my Daddy say, "I'm going tell your Momma!"

Back when I was in high school, I used to have to bribe my Daddy not to "rat on me" to my Momma. I think that I bought him lunch for every day of my 12th Grade year. We just never wanted to face our Momma. So, the "Remember who you belong to" part was easy to understand.

However, it's the "Don't Be Stupid" part that used to confuse our friends. When they would here our Momma say, "Don't be stupid!", they would immediately ask if our Momma had just called us stupid.

We would then explain that she didn't say, "You are stupid." She said, "Don't be Stupid!"

And this is why...

Early on in life, our Momma taught us that ignorance is when you don't know something. Stupidity is when you know it's wrong but you still do it.

Just a side note: Whenever I start talking about "Don't be stupid!", it is all but inevitable that some well-meaning adult will come up to me and say, "You know, Father, in our home, Stupid is a bad word." To which I always reply, "And that how you end up with some stupid kids. You are afraid to tell them what they need to hear in a way that they just might understand it."

Ignorance is when you don't know something.
Stupidity is when you know it's wrong but you still do it.
You ain't ignorant. You're just stupid.

Far too often, we spend a lot of time worrying about our children's feelings.

Rather than teaching them some "real" lessons about life, we want to make sure that they are always feeling good. Good parents know that sometimes you have to put their feelings aside and tell what they really need to hear. Stop worrying so much about their feelings and just "tell it like it is!" You can worry about their feelings at another time.

More often than not, all that our kids need to hear from us is "Remember who you belong to and Don't Be Stupid."

112

Over the span of my priestly studies, I have come to realize that my Momma was able to sum up for me all that Sacred Scripture and the Church have tried to teach us by simply saying, "Remember who you belong to and Don't Be Stupid."

If you think about it, you can see that all of the Hebrew Scriptures were written to remind us that we belong to God. From Genesis to Malachi, everything before the New Testament was recorded to help us remember that it was God who created us. Thus, we belong to him.

Each time we forgot that we belonged to God, we found ourselves in trouble. The first time we forgot, we ended up as slaves in Egypt. After being set free, we forgot again and ended up wandering in the desert for 40 years. After entering the Promised Land, we forgot again. That's why we had to endure the Babylonian exile.

Psalm 137:1 says, "By the rivers of Babylon, there we sat weeping when we remembered Zion." Of course we wept. Stupid people are supposed to cry! If only we had remember that we were the Children of God, maybe we wouldn't have ended up in slavery or in exile from our home land.

We have to always remember that we ultimately belong to God. From the moment he knit us in our Mother's wombs, He claimed us as His own. We are Co-heirs to the Kingdom! Thus, we should act like we are God's Children.

When thinking about the "Don't Be Stupid" part, we can definitely see where it connected to the Passion of Christ. In the New Testament, we realize that Jesus came to same some really "stupid people."

You see... if ignorance is when you don't know something and stupidity is when you know it's wrong but you still do it. Jesus definitely didn't come to save the ignorant. He came to save the stupid.

In our Church's teachings, we have a word that is equivalent to stupidity. We define it by saying, "It's a grave matter. You have full knowledge of what you are doing. And, you do it of your own free will." In the Church, we call that "Sin."

My Momma defined sin as "you know it's wrong but you still do it." Thus, when we sin, we can't plead ignorance. We just have to admit that we were stupid. It's amazing how my Momma was able to take something that seemed complicated to understand and simplify it in such a way that her children and her children's children would remember it.

113

"Remember who you belong to and Don't Be Stupid."

St. Paul in his Second Letter to St. Timothy says that we are to "bear our share of hardship for the gospel with the strength that comes from God."[35] In other words, "remember who you belong to...." Remember that even when it gets tough, you belong to God and must represent Him in good times and in bad times.

In this letter, Paul is telling us that we cannot be a part time lover of the Lord. We have to be full time Christians, even if it gets tough. Remember, it was God and not this world, that saved us!

So, "Remember who you belong to and Don't Be Stupid."

You know, in a Bobby Boucher's Momma and a Momma Gump kind of way, those few words basically summed up everything we need to know about life, about faith and about our relationship not only with our family but also with our God.

Thus, wherever we go, we ought to remember who we belong to!

I always tell teens that by 9th Grade, you already know everything you need to know about life.

You know about drugs. You know about pre-marital sex. You know about the dangers of drunk driving. So, if you go out and engage in any of those life altering and possibly life ending things, you can't say you didn't know. You can only say that you were stupid! How much better our lives would be if we just summed up all that God has been trying to teach us by saying, "Remember who you belong to and Don't Be Stupid." Today, I guess that I have to admit that at some level that I really am a Momma's Boy.

In fact, I have told folks that when I died, all that they need to put on my grave is simply this,

He Loved the Lord and the Lord loved Him....
and of course, he was his Momma's Baby!"

Today, I hope that you have learned a little bit from this Momma's Boy and from the wisdom of His Momma.

35

2 Timothy 1:8

114

Today, I say to you, in the name of Jesus,
"Remember who you belong to and Don't Be Stupid."

Wherever you go,
represent our God in the way He has called us to represent him.

And, if you are tempted to fall into the traps of the Devil, "Don't Be Stupid." - "Just Don't be Stupid."

And if by chance, you are doing something that you know is wrong, "Stop."

"That's all just stop!"

And, if you are doing something that you don't think that you can stop on your own, find someone who can help you stop.

Ignorance is when you don't know something and Stupidity is when you know it's wrong but you still do it. So, just don't be stupid! Because, "stupid is as stupid does." And, you don't need to be stupid anymore.

May God give us the strength to live a life worthy of His Name. May he bless us with His protection and grace.

And, may he give us the strength to not be Stupid any more.
People of God, using the words of my Momma and in the name of Jesus,
I say to you, whenever you go and in whatever you do,

"Remember who you belong to and Don't Be Stupid."

Shut Up and Just Listen!

A Message to My Teenage Brothers and Sisters.....and to the Grown Folks, too!

Alex Trebek the host of the TV game show, *Jeopardy,* once said,
"It's very important in life to know when to shut up!"

But, unfortunately, most people don't know when that point is!

In relationships, like with a girlfriend or boyfriend,
> sometimes you ought to *Shut Up and Just Listen!*

In relationships with your parents,
> sometimes you ought to *Shut Up and Just Listen!*

In relationships with yourself,
> sometimes you ought to *Shut Up and Just Listen!*

And most definitely in your relationship with God,
> sometimes you ought to *Shut Up and Just Listen!*

I assure you that at age 13, 14, 15 or even 18 years old, you do not know
everything that there is to know about life! You really don't know everything.
So, sometimes you need to *Shut Up and Just Listen* to what others have to say.

Shut Up right now and Just Listen!

Turn off the music.

Turn off the television.

Turn off the computer.

And close your mouth!

Right now, all you need to do is Shut Up right now and Just Listen!
('Cuz you just might learn something.)

Not only do you need to Shut Up. If there is someone in your life that is talking
so much that they are causing you to miss whatever it is that God is trying to tell
you, tell them to Shut Up, too.

My young brothers and sisters,

116

God indeed has a lot that He wants to say to us. But, first we have to be ready to listen. First, we have to be willing to tune our ears to the voice of God. We have to be ready to listen because God has some really cool things that He wants us to know.

From the very beginning of time, God has been trying to tell us stuff.

First of all, He wants to tell us how much He loves us and that He is willing to do anything that He can to make sure that we feel His love.

In the Book of Genesis, for example, God, himself, talked directly to us. Time and time again, God spoke directly to Adam and Eve. He told them how much He loved us by first, giving them dominion over the whole world. That means that everything on Earth was created for us to enjoy. *That's* how much God loves us. Everything that the eye can see was made for us. To God, we are the peak of Creation. We are His children.

God also loves us enough to give us a perfect gift: The gift of a free will. He loves us so much that He gave us the complete freedom to choose to do right or wrong.

We can freely choose to love God with our whole hearts, our whole minds and our whole souls. And, we can freely choose to love our neighbors as we love ourselves.

Talk about a message of True Love from God!

In the Hebrew Scriptures[36], God also talks to those He loves through His blessed messengers, the "visitors" or angels.

Angels bring us messages from the Lord. The visitors that stopped by to see Abraham were angels. The visitors that tended to the care of Isaiah, were angels, too. And, of course, the figures that Jacob saw ascending and descending on a ladder that reached up to Heaven, were messengers or angels from the Lord. From the very beginning of time, the Lord has been speaking to us and sending us Messages of Love.

Even when we are stupid and are choosing to do stuff that we know that *God did not want us to do*, God is still sending us Messages of Love.

---

[36]The Hebrew Scriptures is another name for The Old Testament.

The Ten Commandments[37] are perfect examples of Loving Messages that the Lord wanted to send us. Although some have seen the Ten Commandments as rule on what we should not do, they really are Messages from God that remind us just who we are to God and how He wants us to show His Love to the world.

The first parts of the Ten Commandments remind us that we should Love God above everything. The rest of the Commandments tell us that we should love everyone else and treat them right. But, we all know that even after we got the Commandments, we still wanted to do stuff our way. We didn't want to shut up and listen to God.

Humans have got to be the most *hard-head'est* creatures on the face of the Earth.[38] As free as we are, we still can't figure out how much God loves us and how we are supposed to respond to that love. Some even want to tell God how He is supposed to be God.

I think that there have been many times in our history that God has wanted to yell down from Heaven, "Shut Up and Just Listen to Me!"

But, nooooo, we don't want to do that.

Oh nooooo, Heaven forbid we Shut Up and Listen to the Lord!

But, that is exactly what God wants us to do.

He especially needs the young folks in our world to Shut Up and Just Listen. Because, we already have too many grown folks who are so set in their ways that they will never ever get to experience what God has in store for those who love Him. There are way too many grown folks who I believe think that they are God.

I can't wait to get to Heaven to see their faces when they get to the Judgment Seat and find out that not only are they not God, but, because they thought that they were, they will get to see where the Devil lives.

(Remember, Satan didn't want to listen to God because he thought that he was equal to God, too.)

---

[37]See Deuteronomy 5:1-21 and Exodus 20:1-17

[38]I don't know if *"hard-head'est"* is actually a word. If it isn't, it is now! So, the dictionary should give me credit for creating it.

That's why God needs you to pay attention to what He has to say.

You young people must realize, God really does need you!

In the Old Testament, God spoke to a good deal of young folks. And, was able to use them to bring His Word to the world. Through many young folks, God was made present to those He loves.

Shadrach, Meshach and Abednego are good examples of young guys that God used to send a message to the world. They were the three guys whom Nebuchadnezzar was trying to burn in a fire because they did not want to blaspheme against God, worship a false God and reject His love.

When they were put into the fire, the three of them began to pray to the Lord and testify to His goodness. As they prayed, the fire never harmed them. In fact, those who witnessed their defiant acts of love and prayer, saw what looked like an angel walking in the fires with them. As a result of their faith, their oppressors were changed and began to join the guys in praising the God of Abraham!

For those boys, praying in that fire was their way of telling their torturers, Shut Up and Just Listen!

Another young person that God used to bring His Messages to the world was the Prophet Jeremiah. Jeremiah was one of the youngest prophets ever called by the Lord to His service. Jeremiah was also very reluctant to listening to God and accepting His call to ministry.

When God called Jeremiah, this soon-to-be prophet tried to get out of it by using one of the lamest excuses that I have ever heard.

In Jeremiah 4:1-10, God speaks directly to Jeremiah, saying,

> *Before I formed you in the womb I knew you,*
> *before you were born I dedicated you,*
> *a prophet to the nations I appointed you.*
>
> *"Ah, Lord GOD!" I said,*
> *"I know not how to speak; I am too young."*
>
> *But the LORD answered me, Say not, "I am too young."*
> *To whomever I send you, you shall go;*
> *whatever I command you, you shall speak.*

Have no fear before them,
        because I am with you to deliver you, says the LORD.

Then the LORD extended his hand and touched my mouth,
saying,
        See, I place my words in your mouth!

This day I set you over nations and over kingdoms,
        To root up and to tear down, to destroy and to demolish,
        to build and to plant.

The word of the LORD came to me with the question:
        What do you see, Jeremiah?[39]

When God called Jeremiah to service, Jeremiah tried to get out of it by saying he was "too young" for God to use him. But, the Lord cut him off by yelling to him, *"Say not I am too young."*

Jeremiah was trying to tell God that he was not ready to do what the Lord needed him to do. But, the Lord told him that he was not going to accept that lame excuse of "I am too young." God need Jeremiah to be his prophet, to be his messenger. That is why I believe that when God say to Jerry, "Say not I am too young," God was basically saying to Jeremiah, "Shut Up and Just Listen!"

God, has always needed young folks like the three boys in the fire and Jeremiah to be His messengers to the world. He has always wanted to see the younger generation step up to the tasks of being *real* Disciples of God. The Lord loves us so much that He gave us this world and has prepared an even better world for us when we get to Heaven.

In the Gospels, we discover that God found an even better way to talk to us and to send us His Messages of Love. And, He used a young teenaged girl to make that way of talking to us possible.

When the Lord sent the Angel Gabriel to Mary to talk about love and to ask her to be the *one who would bear the purest form* of *love* into the world, God told Mary, "Girl, I need you to help me to do what I need to do for my children."

But, at first, Mary wasn't really ready to hear what God had to say. That is why

---

[39]Jeremiah 1:4-11a

her first response to God was, *"How can this be, since I have no relations with a man?"*[40]

To help her understand, Gabriel had to explain to Mary that the Holy Spirit was going make it happen. Because, with God, all things are possible.[41] When Gabriel said to Mary, "All things are possible," he was essentially saying to her, "Shut Up and Just Listen!"

Well, we all know the *rest of the story.*

Mary did indeed shut up. And through this young girl, God brought pure joy into the world. Through this teenaged girl, God brought Salvation to those *who were lost.* Through this young teenaged girl, God brought His only Begotten Son into the world to show us the way to the Kingdom of Heaven. All because, Mary, a young teenage girl, was willing to Shut Up and Just Listen!

As we look into the life of Mary's Baby Boy, Jesus, we can see that God wanted to talk to us so badly that He came down to Earth to do it directly. Since folks had stopped listening to Him through the ministry of the prophets, God knew that He needed to come down *HIMSELF* and bring His messages to us.

In Jesus, we have been given the greatest opportunity to hear what God has to say to us. Because, Jesus is indeed *God-Incarnate.* In Jesus, God says to us, I love you so much that I am willing to do whatever I have to do to help you make it home to me in Heaven. God the Father wanted the whole world to know just who Mary's Baby Boy is.

That is why at the Baptism of the Lord, Our Heavenly Father opened the Heavens, sent the Holy Spirit down in the form of a Dove and said to the world, *"This is My Beloved Son; with You, I am well pleased."*[42]

In a very real way, God was telling us and the whole world, that Jesus was His Baby Boy and is His greatest communication to the world. When you think about it, we are extremely blessed to be living in the time and era that we are now living. The life we have now is so much better than the life of the prophets of the Old Testament.

---

[40]Luke 1:34

[41]Luke 1:37 says, *"Nothing will be impossible for God."*

[42]Luke 3:22

First, we don't have to eat some of the stuff they ate, like locusts and wild honey.[43] Since I am a picky eater, and I don't like to eat green stuff like vegetables, I know that I would hate eating locusts and wild honey!

But, more importantly, we have something that they longed to have. We have something that they dreamed about. We have the presence of Jesus, the Messiah, in our lives.

As tough as it may be to understand, having Jesus in our lives makes our earthy lives far better than even the life that Moses lived! Although it might have been nice to be one of the Prophets from the Old Testament, I would never chose to trade places with them. There is no way that I would want to live a life in which I would still be longing for a Savior.

After Jesus grew up and was ministering in His land with the help of His boys, the Apostles, God the Father still wondered if folks were getting His Message of Love. He wondered if folks were listening to Him.

So, God the Father led Jesus, Peter, James and John up the mountain to talk a little bit about what He wanted us to do. In the blessed events of the Transfiguration of our Lord, Jesus was transfigured and transformed right before the eyes of His three boys.

And, as they gazed upon the Glorified and Radiant Lord, as He stood in the presence of the Prophets Moses and Elijah, they heard the voice of our Heavenly Father say to them and to us, *"This is My Beloved Son, Listen to Him."* [44]

In saying, *"This is My Beloved Son, Listen to Him,"* God the Father was basically saying to the Apostles and to us, *"Shut Up and Just Listen. Jesus Has Something to Say!"*

That is why we have to stop and pay attention to what Jesus has to tell us. He has, as Peter would put it, *"the words of eternal life."*[45]

Jesus' Words to us not only speak about life, they also can bring us back to life.

---

[43]Matthew 3:4

[44]Mark 9:2-13

[45]John 6:68

His words are words of healing.
His words are words of peace.
His words are words of love.

But, we can't get that healing, peace or love for our lives if we are not willing to *Shut Up and Just Listen* to Him!

Today, Jesus once again says to us, *"Ephphatha."*
He says to us, *"Talitha koum."*
He says to us, *"Eli, Eli, lema sabachthani?"*

"Ephphatha" means *"be opened."*
"Talitha koum" means *"Little girl, I say to you, arise!"*
"Eli, Eli, lema sabachthani?" which means, *"My God, my God, why have you forsaken me?"*

In His Words, we can find all that we need to know about His love for us and the love that we should have for Him.

When He touched the ears and mouth of a deaf and mute man, Jesus said to him, *"Ephphatha."*[46] With that simple touch and that simple word, the deaf man was healed was able to hear clearly the messages that Jesus came to bring.

When He walked into the room where Jairus' Daughter had died, He gently touched her and said, *"Talitha koum."*[47] And, the dead girl came back to life.

As He hung upon the tree, dying for our sins through no fault of His own, He screamed out, *"Eli, Eli, lema sabachthani?"*[48] In these words, Jesus was *telling us* and *showing us* how much He loved us. Through His words, we can see that Jesus was willing to die, even though He was afraid.

My young brothers and sisters,

If only we could be like Peter, James and John...
If only we would be like that deaf man or that dead girl...
If only we would just Shut up and Listen!

---

[46]Mark 7:34

[47]Mark 5:41

[48]Matthew 27:46

Can you even imagine what it would be like to see Jesus transfigured and transformed?

That's why we have to learn *how to be deaf* to some of the things in this world. We have to be deaf to some of the bad things that are influencing our lives, our thought patterns and our choices.

We have to turn off some of the music that is influencing us. We have to turn off some of the websites that are influencing us. We have to turn off the TV and even the voices of some of our *so-called* friends, if we truly want to be deaf enough to hear what Jesus as to say. We have to be deaf to this world in order to have Jesus come to us and say, *Ephphatha* - be opened! *We have to Shut Up and Just Listen to Him!*

We also have to choose to die to the things of this world, if we truly want to be His disciples. Like Jairus' Daughter, Jesus wants to touch us and say, *"Talitha koum"* means "Little girl, I say to you, arise!" But first, we really have to die: not die in a physical sense, but die in a spiritual sense to the ways of this world so that we can be *Born Again* in the Spirit.

We also have to be willing to stand at the foot of the cross and listen to the Lord as He cries out to His Father. We have to stand right next to Mary and the Beloved Disciple, as the Lord looks up to Heaven and cries out, *"Eli, Eli, lema sabachthani?"*

We have to be there because as He cries out, He is crying not only for Himself, but He cries out for us, too. First, He is praying that we, too, will not abandon Him. And second, He is asking the Father to never abandon us.

As he hung on that cross, Jesus was saying to all of us,

"Please, Please Shut Up! Please just listen to what I am saying to you! I love you! I love you! I love you so much that I am willing to take this pain so that you might have life and have it more abundantly.

I love you......So, Please Just Shut Up and Listen to Me!"

The greatest Message of Love that Jesus gave us was right there on Calvary.

By hanging on the cross, He was telling us *why* God made us and who we are called to be. In the Crucifixion, Jesus allowed His actions to say all that He needed to say. In the Crucifixion, we can truly see that *Actions Speak Louder than Words!*

Now, it is up to us to respond to His words and actions of love. Now, it is up to us to do what we have to do to return to Him the love that He has given to us. Now, we have to Shut Up and Just Listen as Jesus says to us,
"Ephphatha."
"Talitha koum."
"Eli, Eli, lema sabachthani?"

Now is the time for us to be still and know that God is still God.

Now is the time for us to be like the waves and the seas, and hear Jesus say to us, *"Quiet! Be still!"*[49]

Now is the time for us to have folks look at us just as the Disciples looked at the calm waters of that once storm driven sea and say, *"Who then is this whom even wind and sea obey?"*[50] They need to be looking at us and saying, *"Who then is this whom even* this Knuckle Head and that Knuckle Head obey?"

Today, we are all challenged by God to be like Shadrach, Meshach and Abednego. We are challenged to be like Isaiah and Jeremiah; to be like Peter, James and John and simply, *Shut up and Just Listen!*

In Jesus Christ, God, the Father, says to us,
"This is My Beloved Son, Listen to Him."

Young People, in the Name of Jesus I say to you,
"Shut Up and Just Listen. Jesus Has Something to Say!"

---

[49]Mark 4:39

[50]Mark 4:41

Feed the Children

While growing up in Uptown New Orleans, I spent most of my childhood years living in a shot-gun double house on Jena Street in the shadows of Our Lady of Lourdes Catholic Church. I always like to talk about where I come from. I know that much of who I am today is a direct result of where I come from and the folks who were responsible for making sure that I turned out alright!

Back then, I was blessed because I was raised in a house with five parents and six kids. You see, on one side of the shotgun house was my family consisting of my Momma, Daddy and Grand Momma plus my sister, brother and myself. On the other side of the shotgun house lived my Nanny, my Uncle Cyril and their three kids. We were all raised like one big happy family: five parents and six kids.

The two Daddies were hard laborers. My "Pops" was a welder who spent hours upon hours in the heat of New Orleans helping to provide security to homes and ornamental beauty to buildings. My Uncle Cyril was a painter. He worked hard brightening up the houses and businesses of our city.

My Momma was the Business Manager for Martin Wine Cellar. Her job was to make sure that the wine flowed freely and the employees got paid.

My Nanny and My Grand Momma both worked in the Catholic schools as Lunch Ladies. Each day, they headed to one of our elementary schools like Holy Ghost, St. Joan of Arc and St. Raymond, dressed like queens in their dazzling white uniforms, with their heads crowned with beautiful hairnets.

They were responsible for taking care of the children: feeding them, nursing them and loving them in ways that were often taken for granted because they were not the official "Teachers and Counselors" in the schools. But, just like the teachers, my Nanny and Grand Momma played vital roles not only in the kitchens of the Catholic schools, but also in the lives of all the children and their families.

Their job was to feed the hungry each and every day. More often than not, they spent days, proving some of the children with the only balanced meals that they would possibly see on those days.

If it were not for the breakfast and lunch programs that they labored to provide, many of the kids would have gone hungry and become malnourished. In a very real way, their roles as cooks and later for my Nanny as a Cafeteria Manager were more than just a job. It was their ministry. It was their Calling from God. It was their Vocation!

On raining days, they had to feed the kids.
On hot August mornings, they had to feed the kids.
On cold winter afternoons, they had to feed the children.

No matter what was happening at home, in the city or in the world, they knew that they had to be at school, often arriving before sunrise, to make sure that someone was there to feed the gifts of God who would walk through the doors.

It wasn't just their jobs, it was their ministry. It was their Vocation!

In the Gospel written by our Brother Matthew, we hear of a day when Jesus also had to feed the children.

> *When Jesus heard of it, he withdrew in a boat to a deserted place by himself. The crowds heard of this and followed him on foot from their towns. When he disembarked and saw the vast crowd, his heart was moved with pity for them, and he cured their sick.*
>
> *When it was evening, the disciples approached him and said, "This is a deserted place and it is already late; dismiss the crowds so that they can go to the villages and buy food for themselves."*
>
> *(Jesus) said to them, "There is no need for them to go away; give them some food yourselves."*
>
> *But they said to him, "Five loaves and two fish are all we have here."*
>
> *Then he said, "Bring them here to me," and he ordered the crowds to sit down on the grass. Taking the five loaves and the two fish, and looking up to heaven, he said the blessing, broke the loaves, and gave them to the disciples, who in turn gave them to the crowds.*
>
> *They all ate and were satisfied, and they picked up the fragments left over - - twelve wicker baskets full.*
>
> *Those who ate were about five thousand men, not counting women and children.*[51]

---

[51]Matthew 14:13-21

When I read this passage, I thought about all those mornings on which my Nanny and Grand Momma had to get up and head to a cafeteria to cook for their children.

No matter what might have been happening in their lives, no matter what the weather was like, they headed out each morning, religiously, to cook for and feed the children of God.

In this Gospel episode, Jesus and His disciples took time to feed the people of God. Although they had more in their natural cafeteria than my Nanny had at St. Raymond Catholic School, they basically had the same task to face. They had to feed the hungry and minister to the needy. And like those cold or rainy days, they had to do it on a day on which many would have decided to not go to work.

You see, on the day that Jesus and His disciples fed the multitudes, they had just found out that the great Prophet John the Baptist had been murdered by Herod's people.

Upon hearing the news that His cousin, John was dead, Jesus wanted to just get away from everybody and spend time in prayer and morning. So, He withdrew in a boat to a deserted place to be by Himself.

We can only imagine how heavy His heart had to be.

John was His cousin, His contemporary and His friend. John was the last of the great prophets. John was the one who announced to the world that The Reign of God was at Hand because the Lamb of God was walking in our midst.

John was Jesus' cousin; someone that Jesus loved like a brother.
And, now He was dead.

So, Jesus withdrew to spend time alone in prayer;
dealing with the death of His loved one.

But, the people of God followed Him, yearning to be filled by His love and His wisdom. They followed Him , not knowing about His grief and pain. They followed Him, not know about His families loss. They followed Him because they need Him to share with them *"words of everlasting life."*[52]

---

[52] John 6:68

128

Jesus understood that even though He was dealing with His own pain, He still needed to minister to His people. This was His Ministry. This was His Calling. This was His Vocation.

Although probably He wanted to take the day off, He knew that both His Heavenly Father and His Followers needed Him to still minister to the Faithful.

God the Father needed His only Begotten Son to be the instrument through which the words of the Prophet Isaiah could be fulfilled. The Father needed Jesus to be the provider for which Isaiah proclaimed,

> *"All you who are thirsty, come to the water!*
> *You who have no money, come, receive grain and eat;*
> *Come, without paying and without cost"*[53]

Although Jesus could have easily taken the day off, God the Father needed Him to be the Life-Giving Water that was promised by Isaiah. He needed Jesus to be the grain that was provided to the people of God, without cost.

Jesus couldn't take the day off, because, the Father needed Him to feed the babies that were knocking on God's Cafeteria Door.

Although Jesus was dealing with the death of his close family member, He did not walk away from His Vocation from God. He ministered to His people, even when He had a valid reason to stop for a while.

In his Letter to the Romans, St. Paul offers us the assurance that nothing can or will stop Christ from loving and providing for us.

In asking the question, *"What will separate us from the Love of Christ?,"*[54] Paul immediately gives the answer.

> *"Will anguish, or distress, or persecution, or famine, or*
> *nakedness, or peril, or the sword? . . .*
>
> *No, in all these things we conquer overwhelmingly through Him*
> *who loved us. For I am convinced that neither death, nor life,*
> *nor angels, nor principalities, nor present things, nor future*

---

[53] Isaiah 55:1

[54] Romans 8:35

things, nor powers, nor height, nor depth, nor any other creature
will be able to separate us from the love of God
in Christ Jesus our Lord."[55]

Nothing can separate us from the Love of God. Nothing can stop Jesus from loving us and wanting to feed us each and every day of our lives. That is why, even the death of His cousin, John, could not stop Jesus from ministering to those who needed Him most.

When the crowd followed Him to a distant place, Jesus put aside His own pain and continued to fulfill His calling from the Father. He and His disciples provided the wisdom and grace for which the people were longing. He not only provided the Wisdom and Grace in words. They also provided them in actions and deeds by miraculously feeding bread and fish to more than 5,000 men, women and children.

"Neither death, nor life, nor angels, nor principalities," could stop Jesus from providing what His people needed. Even when others might give up or walk away, Jesus will be there for us.

My brothers and sisters, with Christ as our Light and our Salvation,[56] there is nothing that we should fear! No one can truly harm the Children of God and the followers of the Savior.

In our time of need, Jesus will indeed protect and feed us just as He provided for the people of His day.

But, the miracle of feeding the 5,000 also tells us that in a very real way, Jesus needs all of us to help Him fulfill His Calling. He needs all of us to help Him feed the hungry and give refreshment to the thirsty. Although He is providing the wheat for the bread, He needs us to bake it and place it before His babies.

In the miracle of feeding the 5,000, Jesus provided the food first from the offering of just two fish and five loaves of bead that was presented by a little boy. From that small gift, all would be nourished. But, we need to realize that it was not Jesus who handed out the food. It was the disciples who physically gave to the people the food that the Lord had provided.

---

[55]Romans 53, 37-39

[56]Psalm 27:1

In a very real way, this tells us that we must be the ones through whom Jesus physically feeds the people of our day. We must provide the Wisdom of Christ to His Children. We must provide the Bread of Life to the masses. We must be the faucets through which the life giving waters now flow.

Like the disciples of old, Jesus needs us to provide to others, the very thing that has given us life, time and again. No matter what may be happening in our personal lives, we must provide His love to the World.

In the City of New Orleans, the People of God endured what we hope was our darkest hours. Hurricane Katrina was indeed one of the most devastating times of our lives. I know that for me, I can truly testify that neither anguish, nor distress, nor persecution, nor famine, nor nakedness, nor peril, nor the sword can conquer the Will of God.

Like many, I have experienced all of these things as a result of the aftermath of both natural and man made destruction from that deadly hurricane.

But, I can also testify to the fact that if you stay true to your Calling, God will handle all of the adversities that may come your way.

For, like Paul, *"I am convinced that neither death, nor life, nor angels, nor principalities, nor present things, nor future things, nor powers, nor height, nor depth, nor any other creature will be able to separate us from the love of God in Christ Jesus our Lord."*[57]

Now, more than ever, God needs us to be His Disciples.

God needs all of us, not just the Priests, Deacons, Seminarians, Religious Sisters and Religious Brothers, but everyone in the pews to be the one who carry the baskets of bread and fish to His starving people.

He needs us to carry the Baskets of Hope to the children.

He needs us to carry the Baskets of Gratitude to the elderly.

He needs us to carry the Baskets of Care to the sick.

He needs us to carry the Baskets of Comfort to the grieving.

---

[57]Romans 8:38-39

He needs us to carry the Baskets of Forgiveness to the sinners.

He needs us to carry the Baskets of Love to the forgotten.

God needs all of us to be the one who carry the baskets of care to all those who hunger and thirst for righteousness. Today, God calls all of us to be the bearers of His love just as the Angels and Saints have carried those very same baskets for us.

When my Nanny retired from the school system, I had the joy of "saying a few words" at the retirement dinner for all of the Food Services Workers who were bringing their school journey to a close. I thanked them for the ministry that they provided to our children for many decades of years. I also thanked them for the sacrifices that they made to make sure that no child went hungry or thirsty. In a very real way, they were and are the Disciples who carried the baskets of bread to the thousands who came to listen to the Lord and to be fed.

Today, may God allow you to see where He needs to take His Baskets of Love.

Your task is to take and bring what you receive from Jesus back into the world so that everyone will know that nothing can separate us from the Love of God!

May God bless you in Abundance for the Bread and Fish
that you provide to His Children.

Amen

(A Special Note to my Nanny, Mrs. Felicie Honore Coulon: Thank you for your ministry to the children back then. And, thank you for your ministry to me now as my House Keeper and Cook!)

SECTION TWO
Lessons from Jesus

The Crucifix
Our Lady Star of the Sea Church

Do You Love Me?

The Love Boat Theme

> Love, exciting and new
> Come aboard, we're expecting you.
> And, love, life's sweetest reward,
> Let it float, it floats back to you.
>
> The Love Boat soon will be making another run.
> The Love Boat promises something for everyone.
> Set a course for adventure,
> your mind on a new romance.
> And love won't hurt anymore.
> It's an open smile on a friendly shore.
>
> Welcome Aboard - It's Love..........
> The Love Boat.
> The Love Boat.
> It's love. It's love.[58]

In my younger days, I loved watching *The Love Boat* on television. That show seems to be a TV Show that will never go away. Most of us know that *The Love Boat* was an immediate hit back in 1977 when it debuted. The show featured a cast of regular characters that seemed to either fall in love with someone new every week or end up in some type of trouble every week.

From Gopher, the Yeoman-Purser, who was always cooking up stupid schemes to "get over" on the captain, to Isaac Washington, the Ship's Bartender, who always seems to know the answers to everyone's love problems. Although, he never had a regular girlfriend on the show.

Part of what made the Love Boat a great success was not only the antics of its regular crew, it was also the parade of major TV and Movie Stars that showed-up for the cruise each week. On the show, big stars like Gene Kelly, Tom Hanks, and Vanessa Williams all appeared. But, my favorite star who seemed to show up almost every year was Charo (the *Cuchie Cuchie* Girl) from the 1970's. Indeed, now that there is late night cable television, *The Love Boat* will sail on for many more years.

---

[58] *The Love Boat* theme song was sung by Jack Jones. The lyrics were written by Paul Williams with music by Charles Fox.

Just as *The Love Boat* helped the entire nation learn more about falling in love, the Bible helps the entire world understand how to better be people of love. In fact, The Bible really is a big Love Letter from God. In Sacred Scripture, God tells us just how much He loves us and how we should respond to that love.

That is why in summing up His messages to us, Jesus simply says, "This is my commandment: love one another as I love you. No one has greater love than this, to lay down one's life for one's friends."[59] Simply put, our expected response to God's offer of love is to share that love with all we meet.

In the First Letter of Saint John, we read, *"See what love the Father has bestowed on us that we may be called the Children of God."*[60] In this, we are called to remember that God loves us so much that He has not only claimed us as His subjects. He has bestowed upon us the title of *Children of God*. That means that in the Eyes of God, although we are created beings, we have been elevated by the love of Christ to a new level of creation and are destined to be with God in the New Eden that is the Kingdom of Heaven.

But, we cannot take our lofty positions for granted. Just because we have been promised a place at the Banquet Feast in Heaven doesn't mean that we can live our lives in any manner that we choose. We are called to give an active and obvious response to God's love.

> *"Beloved, let us love one another, because love is of God;*
> *everyone who loves is begotten by God and knows God. Whoever*
> *is without love does not know God, for God is love.*
> *In this way the love of God was revealed to us: God sent His*
> *only Son into the world so that we might have life through Him.*
>
> *In this is love: not that we have loved God, but that He loved us*
> *and sent His Son as expiation for our sins. Beloved, if God so*
> *loved us, we also must love one another.*
>
> *No one has ever seen God. Yet, if we love one another, God*
> *remains in us, and His love is brought to perfection in us."*[61]

---

[59] John 15:12-13

[60] 1 John 3:1

[61] 1 John 4:7-12

It is only when that love reaches perfection that we will get our chance to see God face to face.

One of my most favorite scripture passages is found in the Chapter 21 of the Gospel of John. In this particular passage, we get a glimpse of an earlier version of *The Love Boat*. But, rather than it being a boat filled with folks searching for "a love mate," it was a boat filled with men who were still trying to figure out how to continue loving and serving Jesus even though He had been crucified by the civil authorities. Chapter 21 is the final Chapter in the Gospel of John and describes the final appearance that the Risen Lord made to Apostles.

As the men of pure love fished, Jesus the Man of Divine Love appeared to them. In this, His third appearance to His beloved followers, Jesus first shared breakfast with them and then taught St. Peter the greatest lesson of love.

In this lesson, Jesus asked St. Peter a simple question, *"Do you love Me?"*

> *"Simon, son of John, do you love Me more than these?"*
> *He said to Him, "Yes, Lord, You know that I love You."*
> *He said to him, "Feed My lambs."*
>
> *He then said to him a second time, "Simon, son of John, do You love Me?" He said to Him, "Yes, Lord, You know that I love You." He said to him, "Tend My sheep."*
>
> *He said to him the third time, "Simon, son of John, do you love Me?" Peter was distressed that He had said to him a third time, "Do you love Me?" and he said to Him,*
> *"Lord, You know everything; You know that I love You."*
> *(Jesus) said to him, "Feed My sheep.*
>
> *Amen, amen, I say to you, when you were younger, you used to dress yourself and go where you wanted; but when you grow old, you will stretch out your hands, and someone else will dress you and lead you where you do not want to go."*
>
> *He said this signifying by what kind of death he would glorify God. And when He had said this, He said to him, "Follow Me."*[62]

---

[62]John 21:15-19

Some believe that this episode of love was Jesus' way of saying to Peter, "I forgive you for denying me." That's why Jesus asked three times, *"Do you love Me?"* Remember, Simon Peter had denied Him three times before the crucifixion.

What I loved about this interchange between Jesus and the First Pope, is the fact that every time Peter said, *"Yes, Lord, You know I love You,"* Jesus gave him a simple command.

"Feed My lambs." "Tend My sheep." "Feed My sheep."

In the end, Jesus simply says to Peter, *"Follow Me!"*

In other words, *"Respond to My Love by Loving others!"*

You know, when I was in elementary school, back when the Love Boat first came on television, we used to write little love letters to some of the girls in class. And at the end of the letter, we would do that old elementary thing in order to get a response from the girl. We would draw two boxes at the end and write, "Do you love me check yes; check no."

That was always the best way to find out if the girl would be your girlfriend. "Do you love me, check yes; check no." And of course, for me, they always checked, "yes." (Who could blame them?)

Well, I believe God, He too concluded *His Love Letter* to us in the same way we used to conclude our love letters in elementary school. You see, this episode between Jesus and Saint Peter, actually comes from the last chapter of the Fourth Book of the Gospel. Essentially, God ends His love-filled writings to us, by asking St. Peter and us, "Do we love Him?"

And like an elementary school boy, God is also is waiting for a response:

We either need to check "Yes" or check "No!"

You see, when he asks us "Do we love Him?" If we answer by saying yes, then we must be like Peter and respond by "Feeding His Lambs" and "Tending His Sheep."

That's how we will show God that we have indeed checked "Yes" as we respond to His love.

137

Like with St. Peter, God needs all who love Him to take care of the folks around us. That might mean, feeding the homeless, giving to the poor, or even laying down your life for Him by becoming a priest, a deacon, a Religious Sister or a Religious Brother.

But, it also goes farther than that. Checking "Yes" also means seeing your family and friends as God's Sheep. Taking care of your loved ones, your children, your parents and your friends, as God has called you to do.

Today, God asks each of us, "Do you love Me? Check yes; check no."

You know, I believe that the greatest gift that God has ever given us on Earth is the life of His Son. The next great gift He will give us is entrance into Heaven. But, to get in, He is going to be looking for how we responded to all that He has written in His *Love Letter* to us. He's going to check to see if we checked "Yes" or checked "No" by seeing if we loved one another as He has loved us.

You know, The Love Boat series ended in May of 1986. Though it may live on during late-night reruns, the Love Boat will never really sail, again. And, that's OK.

Because, the boat that we need to really be concentrating on is the boat that will cross the River of Death and take us to the Kingdom of Heaven. Oh, the Love Boat may have sailed to Cancun and the Bahamas, nice little paradises on Earth. But, the Boat that Captain Jesus drives will take us to a Paradise that will surpass anything we can ever experience here.

So, as one of the church's First Mates, in the name of Jesus I say, I say to you:

Love, exciting and new
    Come aboard, He's expecting you.
And, love, life's sweetest reward,
    Let it float, it floats back to you.

Our Savior soon will be making another run.
Our Savior promises salvation to everyone.
    Set a course for the Kingdom,
    your mind on a new romance.

Come and experience Love. . .   Amen

I Mean to Stay at Your House

As a teenager, I attended St. Augustine High School[63] in New Orleans, Louisiana. While as a student there, I actively participated in many school organizations. I was a class president, the yearbook editor, the City's high school representative on Mayor Ernest "Dutch" Morial's Mardi Gras Task Force, and an American Legion's delegate to Louisiana Boys State.

Along with many other activities, I also played Xylophone and Tympani in St. Augustine's concert band. However, the activity that I cherished most from my high school years, is my participation in the nationally known marching band, the St. Augustine's Marching 100.

During my years in St. Aug's Marching Band, we were honored to participate in many big events in New Orleans and throughout the South.

We played at many New Orleans Saints Games, performed for President Jimmy Carter (which shows how old I am), played for numerous downtown conventions, and marched in several Mardi Gras Parades.

We even performed at the *1980 Abbeyville Cattle Festival*. (O.K., So the Cattle Festival isn't that big of an event to folks around the nation. But, for the people in Abbeyville, LA, it is.)

Some of our more exciting experiences happened as we marched down the streets of New Orleans in the many major Mardi Gras Parades. No words can truly explain the feelings you have when marching in a parade as a member of the city's most popular high school band.

The excitement in the crowd reaches a fever pitch when St. Aug passes by during a parade. Even before St. Aug reaches your block, there seems to be an electricity that runs through the crowd. The band could be blocks away and yet people somehow know that the Marching 100 is coming.

It was not uncommon to see people holding up their children so that they might get a good look, as the *Best Band* in the city performed for them. Boyfriends often lifted their girlfriends onto their shoulders so that they might also see the sparkling helmets and those dancing shoes of the Purple Knights.

---

[63]In New Orleans, St. Augustine High School is affectionately known as "St. Aug."

Folks climbed trees and stood on trash cans. Ice-chests became step stools and the beds of pick-up trucks became dance floors. People did whatever they could to *see and hear* the Purple Pride of New Orleans.

No feelings in the world could replace the excitement that most band members had when we saw the joy that our music and performances brought to many on the streets of New Orleans.

For some, the excitement at seeing The Marching 100 was almost a religious experience!

In the Gospel according to our Brother Luke, we hear a similar story of excitement in a city's streets. But, the level of this excitement surpasses even that which accompanies the coming of *St. Augustine's Marching 100*.

In Luke 19:1-10, the excitement in the streets of Jericho was in anticipation of the coming of *Jesus the Nazarean*.

> *At that time, Jesus came to Jericho and intended to pass through the town. Now a man there named Zacchaeus, who was a chief tax collector and also a wealthy man, was seeking to see who Jesus was; but he could not see Him because of the crowd, for he was short in stature. So he ran ahead and climbed a sycamore tree in order to see Jesus, who was about to pass that way. When He reached the place, Jesus looked up and said to him, "Zacchaeus, come down quickly, for today I must stay at your house."*
>
> *And he came down quickly and received Him with joy.*
>
> *Then they all saw this, they began to grumble, saying, "He has gone to stay at the house of a sinner." But Zacchaeus stood there and said to the Lord, "Behold, half of my possessions, Lord, I shall give to the poor, and if I have extorted anything from anyone I shall repay it four times over."*
>
> *And Jesus said to him, "Today salvation has come to this house because this man too is a descendant of Abraham. For the Son of Man has come to seek and to save what was lost."*[64]

---

[64]Luke 19:1-10

In this beautiful story of love and forgiveness, we hear that when the town's folk had heard that Jesus was passing through, many of them lined the streets to catch a glimpse of the great healer and preacher about whom so many had been talking.

Zacchaeus, a respected member of the Jericho's upper class, also shared this excitement. Like people waiting to see St. Aug's Marching 100, he wanted to have a good view for seeing Jesus when the Lord passed-by in the streets.

First, he pushed his way to the front of the crowd and tried to get a good spot. But because he was not very tall, he found it hard to really see the Lord.

Spotting a Sycamore Tree along Jesus' route, Zacchaeus climbed up its branches so that he could see over the crowd. There, in the tree, he could see Jesus as He passed below. It was because Zacchaeus climbed that tree that Jesus noticed him and subsequently ate at his house and offered Zacchaeus the gift of salvation.

Though Zacchaeus was a known sinner, Jesus did not refuse to offer him the chance to be saved. For, Jesus was able to see the imperishable spirit which dwelled inside of Zacchaeus.[65] Although he was a sinner, Zacchaeus still had the opportunity to welcome Jesus into his home because of the blessed Spirit which was given to him at the moment of his conception.

In a very real way, Each of us is like Zacchaeus. The arrival of Jesus Christ in our midst breathes an air of hope and excitement into our lives. None of us would want to have our sight of Jesus blocked by a crowd or obstructed by people who do not really care that Jesus is alive.

Each of us wants to make sure that when Jesus returns we have the best seat in the grand stands. A seat where we might clearly see and hear the revelation of Christ's Second Coming.

However, in a very real way, many of us allow our sins to become the crowd that blocks our vision of Christ. Many allow the negative attitudes of others to impede their minds and block their understanding of Christ's ongoing revelations through Creation. Many allow their personal inhibitions to prevent them from doing all that is possible to assure that they will have a good view when Christ comes again.

---

[65] Wisdom 12:1 says, God's "imperishable spirit is in all things!"

Like Zacchaeus, we are all called to find a way to better see Christ in the midst of the crowds that block our paths to Him. Like that Sycamore Tree which grew along the streets of Jericho, there are many sacramental trees offered to us by God, through the Church, which help us to climb up and see over the crowds in our lives.

The Sacrament of Reconciliation, The Sacrament of the Anointing of the Sick, and The Sacrament of the Eucharist are three primary ways that God offers us a grace-filled boost to see over the crowd.

In the Sacrament of Reconciliation, the Sacrament of Penance, we are able to wipe away all of those things which have clouded our view of God's Love for us, God's Love for Others and God's Love for Creation. Through the forgiveness of our sins, we are offered a higher spot on the tree which allows us to see Christ in our midst.

In the Sacrament of the Anointing of the Sick, we are offered mental, spiritual and physical healing which are necessary for us to be able to climb the trees along Christ's route.

In paragraph 1532 of the Catechism of the Catholic Church, we read,

> "The special grace of the sacrament of the Anointing of the Sick has as its effects: the uniting of the sick person to the passion of Christ, for his own good and that of the whole Church; the strengthening, peace, and courage to endure in a Christian manner the sufferings of illness or old age; the forgiveness of sins, if the sick person was not able to obtain it through the sacrament of Penance; the restoration of health, if it is conducive to the salvation of his soul; the preparation for passing over to eternal life."[66]

This tells us that in the Anointing of the Sick, it is possible for our sins to also forgiven. Thus, we are boosted higher on the tree and above the crowd.

In the Sacrament of the Eucharist, we not only experience the arrival of Christ in this, our spiritual home, we have the opportunity to experience the arrival of Christ in our bodies.

---

[66]Catechism of the Catholic Church Section Two: Article Five Paragraph 1532

Zacchaeus not only welcomed Christ into his physical home. He welcomed Christ into his life. In this, he showed us that no crowd can prevent us from seeing and hearing what Jesus has to offer. For, through the Eucharist, Christ offers us a view from within; a view with not external obstructions.

From this interior viewpoint, the questions that we must all ask ourselves are: "Am I willing to be like Zacchaeus and climb a tree to see Jesus?"

"Am I willing to be like Zacchaeus and put aside my public position, to put aside my personal prestige and earthly success, in order to get a better view of the Christ in our midst?"

"Am I willing to do whatever it takes to let Jesus know that I want Him to honor me like He honored Zaccaeus by entering and reclining in my house?"

In a very real way, Jesus is looking at you and me on this very day and saying *"Come down quickly, for today, I must stay at your house."* Knowing that Jesus wants to come home with us today, we must also ask, "Are our houses ready for Jesus to come home with us? Do I need to do some house cleaning before Jesus comes in?"

During a momentary pause in Mardi Gras Parade, it was nothing for someone in the crowd to come up to a member of the Marching 100 and ask if he would mind being in a picture with them. From my four years of marching in St. Aug's band, I must be in hundreds of pictures taken during Mardi Gras Parades (which is good because every home should have at least one picture of me).

I can remember that most of the people taking pictures were tourists. They wanted to take a piece of New Orleans home with them. And what better piece to remember Mardi Gras than a picture with a member of St. Augustine Marching 100: especially a picture with this good-looking member of the band.

Well, in the Eucharist, we not only have the chance to take the memory of Christ back with us and into our homes. *We have the opportunity take Jesus Christ, Himself,* into our homes.

People of God, may we come to realize that in the Eucharist, Jesus is not only passing by on His Route to the heavenly Jerusalem. He is truly present in our midst. May we have the strength to do all that we have to do, to see over the crowds, and to join in the celebration of Christ's arrival: even if it means that we have to climb a sycamore tree to see Him. May we realize that Jesus wants to stay at our houses, today!

The Coffin Attack!

The other night, my Rottweiler, Pepper, and I were out on an evening stroll. As we walked a block from my rectory, we began to pass the entrance gates to the Historic St. Roch Cemetery. Now, normally, I won't walk past those gates at night. I am easily scared! But, for some reason, Pepper wanted to head in that direction.

As we passed the gates, we suddenly heard a noise coming from behind the walls of the graveyard. "Thump Thump.............Thump Thump............Thump Thump!"

As the noise got louder, I grew more scared and wondered what could be making the noise. "Thump Thump...............Thump Thump...................Thump Thump!"

However, Pepper was not as curious as I was. Once she heard the noise, she immediately took off running back to our rectory. Although she is supposed to be my protection, she wasn't going to be around to see from what I was going to need to be protected!
"Thump Thump.......................Thump Thump.........................Thump Thump!"

Once she took off running, I took off running, too.
"Thump Thump.......................Thump Thump.........................Thump Thump!"

When I look behind us, would believe that I saw a coffin coming out of the cemetery and heading towards us. It was standing on it's edge moving in our direction. "Thump Thump...................Thump Thump.................Thump Thump!"

The quicker we ran, the quicker the coffin began to follow us.
"Thump Thump...........Thump Thump............Thump Thump!"

Once we made it to the rectory, we ran inside and locked the doors.
"Thump Thump....Thump Thump....Thump Thump!"

And, the coffin smashed right through the wooden door.
"Thump Thump....Thump Thump!

So, we ran up the stairs.....
        And the coffin followed us.
           "Thump Thump!"

We ran into my bed room.....
        And the coffin followed us.
           "Thump Thump!"

We ran into the bathroom....
        And the coffin followed us.
           "Thump Thump!"

So, I opened the medicine cabinet,
   hoping to find something to throw at the coffin.
But all I could find was a bottle of Robitussin.
   "Thump Thump!"

So, in horror, I tossed the bottle at the coffin......
   "Thump!"

And, would you believe
   (just hold ya' breath for this one)

The Coffin Stopped!

Because.....Robitussin can always stop a "Coffin Attack!"[67]

When I look through Sacred Scripture, I assure you that there are several episodes that would not have been recorded if I were one of the Four Evangelists. We are all lucky that the quartet of Matthew, Mark , Luke and John were not dependant on Tony recording any of the events in the life of Jesus.

If they were waiting for me to help write the scriptures, we would have never been able to read about the raising of the Widow's Son in the City of Nain[68], the raising of Jairus' Daughter[69] or the raising of his friend Lazarus[70].

Because, if I see just a blade of grass move by somebody's grave, I'm not going to be there to find out what else is going to happen!

So, first we ought to thank God that the four Evangelists either saw for themselves or had wonderful sources that recorded these blessed events for themselves. In knowing that Jesus can raise the dead, we know that he can bring us through anything that we face.

In the raising of Lazarus, for example, we experience the power of Christ at one of the greatest peaks.

---

[67]It's OK to laugh out loud! Don't act like you didn't see that one coming!

[68]Luke 7:11-17

[69]Matthew 9:18-26; Mark 5:21-43; Luke 8:40-56

[70]John 11:1-44

*When Mary, the sister of Lazarus, came where Jesus was and
saw Him, she knelt at His feet and said to Him, "Lord, if you had
been here, my brother would not have died." When Jesus saw
her weeping, and the Jews who came with her also weeping, He
was greatly disturbed in spirit and deeply moved. He said,
"Where have you laid him?" They said to Him, "Lord, come and
see." Jesus began to weep. So the Jews said, "See how he loved
him!" But some of them said, "Could not he who opened the
eyes of the blind man have kept this man from dying?"*

*Then Jesus, again greatly disturbed, came to the tomb. It was a
cave, and a stone was lying against it. Jesus said, "Take away
the stone." Martha, the sister of the dead man, said to Him,
"Lord, already there is a stench because he has been dead four
days." Jesus said to her, "Did I not tell you that if you believed,
you would see the glory of God?" So they took away the stone.*

*And Jesus looked upward and said, "Father, I thank You for
having heard Me. I knew that You always hear Me, but I have
said this for the sake of the crowd standing here, so that they
may believe that You sent me."*

*When He had said this, He cried with a loud voice,
"Lazarus, come out!"*

*The dead man came out, his hands and feet bound with strips of
cloth, and his face wrapped in a cloth. Jesus said to them,
"Unbind him, and let him go." Many of the Jews therefore, who
had come with Mary and had seen what Jesus did, believed in
Him.*[71]

In this story, that comes from the Eleventh Chapter of the Gospel of our Brother
John, we hear a story that has many different meanings and messages.
Throughout it, we experience the many facets of Jesus' ministry, and the many
ways we have come to know and love the Lord.

In retelling this life-giving story, we meet the Jesus of Love and Compassion,
we meet the Jesus of Healing, and we meet the Jesus of Reconciliation and
Forgiveness.

---

[71]John 11:32-45

Through the story of Lazarus, we meet the Jesus that has come to call each of us out of our deadly tombs of Temptation and Sin and into the Born-Again world of Salvation.

My Brothers and Sisters, as we know from this gospel account, Lazarus was a very close friend of Jesus. So, when Jesus heard that His friend, Lazarus, was dying, he traveled from Jerusalem to Bethany to be with Lazarus' sisters, Mary and Martha, and to bring about a miracle that would bring many doubters to believe that He truly is the Son of God.

When He arrived in Bethany, Mary and Martha both greeted Him with the same statement: *"Lord if you had been there, my brother would never have died."* Jesus told both of them that their brother was not dead. For, indeed, he will rise again. He, then, asked them to take Him to Lazarus' Tomb.

At the tomb, Jesus instructed them to roll away the stone that was blocking the entrance to the grave. Now, you could only imagine the reactions of the people around them.

Lazarus had been dead for four days before Jesus even got to Bethany. Therefore, his body would have begun to decay. *"Lord, by now, there will be a stench."* Martha said. Let's just say that the smell inside the tomb was not going to be pleasant. But, Jesus insisted that the stone be rolled away.

When they did, Jesus looked up to heaven, gave thanks to God and called out with a loud and clear voice, *"Lazarus, come out!"*

At the command of Jesus, the Bread of Eternal Life, the dead man came out of the tomb. St. John tells us that as he came out his hands and his feet were still tied with the *traditional, Jewish,* burial bands. Seeing that Lazarus was now free from death, Jesus looked at the people and said, *"Untie him and let him go!"*

People of God, in a very real way, we are all like Lazarus. There are many aspects of our lives which lead us into the dark and damp tombs of temptation and sin.

Within these tombs, we find endless sickness, heart ache, and grief. Ultimately, our tombs can lead us away from life and to eternal death.

Just pause for a moment and look at world around us. Look at the many things that tempt us to turn our backs on God and on our fellow human beings. There are many things that lead or tempt each of us to fall into the traps of sin.

The hard part about these sinful temptations, these tombs of temptation, is that the things that really tempt us usually feel good. In fact, if it didn't feel good, it wouldn't really be tempting. That is why it is so difficult to resist temptation.

But like Lazarus, we have a choice. We can either cross the thresholds of our tombs of temptation and sin or we can remain among the dead in these tombs.

Part of our problem is that some of us have become so comfortable in our tombs that it has become difficult to hear the voice of Jesus calling us out. We have actually convinced ourselves that this is the way that it is supposed to be!

In fact, some of us have been in the tomb so long that we have fixed it up, and made it so comfortable, that we don't want to leave.

In our tombs of sin, we have gotten comfortable sitting on our stolen furniture, watching our illegal cable television and eating our scrumptious meals that were bought with a fake food stamp cards! And, yet we wonder why nothing around us seems to be coming to life. It is because we have chosen to make our homes among the dead!

Each of us deals with the deadly elements of temptation and sin on a daily basis. No one is immune to being tempted. Even Jesus, during His 40-day retreat in the desert, was tempted by the Devil. The key is you don't have to bow to temptation.

God, the Father of Mercy and Love, sent Jesus Christ to call each of us forth from our tombs, just as He called Lazarus. Through the Death and Resurrection of Christ, we have been saved from the sinfulness of humankind. However, to receive the full benefits of our salvation, we must respond to God's call. We must be willing to leave behind our tombs.

That is why Jesus Christ is standing at the door of our tombs and yelling to each of us, "Come Out!"

Each day, we must remember this call to salvation and eternal life. Once you respond to Christ's call, you then have a new role in helping to bring about the salvation of others. Remember in the Gospel, when Lazarus came out of the tomb, his hands and his feet were bound. Seeing this Jesus told the crowd to "Untie him and set him free."

The image that we have is of Lazarus, calmly walking out of the tomb. But, if I was in the tomb and I heard Jesus calling me, I would have been jumping out of that tomb, hand and feet still bound!

Those who already know the loving forgiveness of Jesus Christ are called to be the "untie-ers," the ones who do the untying. Once you have come to know and love Jesus, our Lord, you must be willing to bring others to that level of love.

Many people carry with them burdens from long ago. These burdens are the cloth burial strips that tie our hands and feet.

For some, it may be a sin that you have already confessed but can't bring yourself to a point of self-forgiveness. For others, you may have hurt someone but haven't been able to seek their forgiveness. While for others, you may have been hurt by someone else and have not been able to truly forgive them as God forgives you.

These are some of the burial bands that those who are called to salvation can bring with them. But, I assure you that you can't get across the doorway of Life, past the Gates of Heaven, if you are still bound with these burial bands.

Others are called to help untie those who are trapped in these bands. The Sacrament of Reconciliation or Penance is one of the ways that our Church can help to untie you and let you go free.

Unfortunately, not enough people are willing to take advantage of this Sacrament of Untying, the sacrament of release and freedom.

The Sacrament of Penance is a visible sign that you have stepped out of your tomb of Temptation and Sin.

Our God is truly a good God.
Our God is truly a loving and forgiving God.

As we know, nothing is impossible with God on your side.
No stone is too big for God to roll away.
No tomb is too old for God to call you out of.
No band is too tight for God, His people and the Church to untie.

All you need to do is Trust in God!
All you need to do is COME OUT OF THE TOMB!

Jesus Christ is standing at the door of our tombs and yelling to each of us, "Come Out!"

I have come to know my Jesus as "the Resurrection and the Life."

I have come to hear my Jesus call me out of the Tombs of Temptation and Sin.

I have heard His cry and exited the tomb.

Can you hear Him?

Today, may the God of Forgiveness and Grace call you out of your tombs of sin and temptation, untie your burial bands of sin and finally, yes finally, let you go free.

You know as good as Robitussin can be at stopping a coughing attack, only the Love of Jesus can stop a real coffin attack!

So, in the name of Jesus, don't let the tomb or the coffin catch you!

Wealth is useless on the day of wrath,

but virtue saves from death.

Proverbs 11:4

Protect the Children: From Womb to Tomb

Since May 27, 1995, I have been having a good time being a Roman Catholic Priest for the Archdiocese of New Orleans. In this role, I have had the opportunity to speak to many churches and gatherings (literally) around the world.

I have celebrated the Sacraments in almost every part of the Continental U.S. (North, South, East and West). I have anointed the sick in Los Angeles, celebrated the Eucharist on the shores of the Sea of Galilee and even rededicated people during a Baptism-like celebration in the River Jordan.

I have heard confessions in people's homes. I have celebrated the Rite of Confirmation as we welcomed a new parish member into full Communion with the Church, and I have presided at numerous weddings in my Archdiocese.

The only Sacrament that I have not had the opportunity to preside at is the ordination of a deacon or priests. You have to be a bishop to ordain someone.

God has surely blessed me with many great opportunities: opportunities to proclaim His loving commitment to His Chosen People through the liturgical life of the Church.

All of our Sacraments are filled with God's Blessings. Our Church comes alive when the people of God gathers to hear His Words and experience his compassion through liturgical celebrations.

Though I enjoy presiding for and celebrating all of the Sacraments, there is one of the Big Seven that I really enjoy celebrating. That is the Sacrament of Baptism. How blessed we are to welcome new members into our fold as they welcome the Holy Spirit into their lives. I particularly enjoy celebrating the baptism of a new baby.

There is something about the baptisms of new babies that lets us know that God is still moving and working in our lives. God knows that without babies continually coming into the Church, the Church would eventually grow old and literally die. Thus, new babies mean new life for a faith community.

Not only does the presence of the babies bring a message to us from God, but also the presence of the adults at the Baptismal Celebration. The presence of parents, families and God-Parents at baptisms lets us know that people are willing to take the responsibility of assuring the Church that the child will grow up knowing God through the Faith Practices of the Roman Catholic Church.

Baptisms also give adults an opportunity to renew not only their Baptismal Promises but also their commitment to sharing their faith through practicing it in a Roman Catholic Church.

One of the most popular scripture passages read at Baptisms is taken from the Gospel of Mark. In the Tenth Chapter of Mark we hear:

> *And people were bringing children to Him that He might touch them, but the disciples rebuked them. When Jesus saw this He became indignant and said to them, "Let the children come to Me; do not hinder them, for the kingdom of God belongs to such as these. Amen, I say to you, whoever does not accept the kingdom of God like a child will not enter it." Then He embraced them and blessed them, placing His hands on them.*[72]

In this passage, Jesus takes children in His arms, embraces them and blesses them. This is truly one of the most tender moments in Sacred Scripture. It shows the depth of God's concern for His little ones: His out-stretched arms, His loving embrace and His offering of love. What more could we ask?

In reading this passage, we can be so taken by this loving image that we can sometimes miss the stern warning that God gives the adults as a major part of this passage. Jesus says, *"Let the children come to Me; and do not hinder them."*

Sometimes people are so caught in the loving scene of Jesus welcoming the children that they miss the *"do not hinder them part."*

When I think about the plight of the unborn children in our nation, we know that there are many ways that adults can hinder children from growing up with a clear and sincere knowledge of God.

One way we as a society have hindered our children is through the legalization of abortions. How much more hindrance can there be than the willful removal of a developing baby from its mother's womb?

The baby growing inside of a mother's womb cannot defend itself from predators. It is at the mercy of the mother dependant on her for nourishment and protection. To not protect the child is to hinder him or her from growing up knowing that God is God and that all human beings are His people.

---

[72]Mark 10:13-16

Another way we can hinder them is by rearing them in homes where love that was once sacramentally-professed on the Altar of God is shattered by the sins of a mother or a father. Children, who experience divorce, experience the break down of a sacramental covenant. Sometimes they can be the forgotten victims of their fighting parents. They, too, are victims of the divorce and can be hindered from gaining a true knowledge of God whose covenant with us is unending and unbreakable.

Still another way that we hinder our children from coming to God is by allowing our society to pass laws which are contrary to the teachings of our faith. Any law which does not protect the dignity of the individual, the sanctity of marriage and the lives of those who cannot protect themselves is a law against the Laws of God.

Children who grow up in communities which do not protect a person's basic right to life are hindered from full knowledge of their inherent dignity and the love of the Creator who calls us to uphold that dignity.

People of God, as I travel around the globe proclaiming the Good News, I really do have a good time. Through the Grace of God, I have written and delivered some very powerful sermons in the Name of Christ Jesus.

I may even tell a good joke or two.

But, when it comes to the protection of life, *from Womb to Tomb*, I never joke.

There is nothing funny about the willful neglect or taking of a human life. There is nothing funny about the willful neglect or disregard for a person's inherent dignity as a Child of God. There is nothing funny about the harm that millions of children, born and unborn, face each and every day.

I may joke about a lot of things, but I will never joke about the willful destruction or harming of a Child of God.

Better for you to be hurt, defiled or defamed than to be *thrown into the fires of Gehenna* because you chose to hinder a child's sacred movement toward God.

My Family in Christ,
Today, I want you to sincerely ask yourself,
have I in anyway hindered a child from coming to Jesus?

Have I hindered their knowledge of God through my words or deeds?

Have I hindered a child from experiencing the dignity that is rightfully given to them by our Creator?

Have I hindered a Child of God, young our old, a child, physically able or disabled, a child, intelligent or mentally challenged, a child of my race or of another race, have I hindered a child of God in anyway as they tried to get to Jesus?

And if I have in any way, shape or form, hindered a child's path to Jesus, what must I now do to atone for my sins?

Jesus says, *"Let the children come to me; do not hinder them, for the kingdom of God belongs to such as these."*[73]

Better for you to be hurt, defiled or defamed than to be *thrown into the fires of Gehenna* because you chose to hinder a child's sacred movement toward God.

If you have hindered or are hindering a child, My fervent prayer for you is May God have mercy on your soul.

If a son ceases to hear instruction,

he wanders from words of knowledge.

Proverbs 19:27

---

[73]Mark 10:14

The Devil Made Me Do It

Back in the early 1970's, Comedian Flip Wilson was on top of the television market with his variety comedy show. Long before there was a Dave Chapelle or an Eddie Murphy, Flip Wilson was commanding the market as one of the funniest men on television.

On his variety show, he featured many special guests like Dean Martin, Redd Foxx, Paul McCartney, Gina Lollabrigida, and Muhhamad Ali. The "Flip Wilson Show" debuted in 1970, and was an instant hit.

Flip's comedy was the real focal point of the series. In various skits, he played a collection of regular characters, which included: The Reverend LeRoy of the *"Church of What's Happening Now,"* a gospel preacher who seemed to be slightly less than honest but was a pretty good fundraiser, Danny Danger, private detective, and Herbie, the Good Time Ice Cream Man, are just a few of the characters he played as parts of his act.

Of all of Flip Wilson's characters, the one that most folks remember was the glorious Miss Geraldine Jones. Now, just to jog your memory, Geraldine was Flip's female persona. To play her Flip would wear a blond wig, an extremely short skirt, and pair of high heels.

Geraldine was not the prettiest woman you could imagine. And, that's a good thing. Geraldine was a sassy, swinging, liberated woman with a very jealous boyfriend named "Killer." Even though we never ever saw "Killer," she kept telling folks that he was coming there.

Through his character, Geraldine, Flip Wilson has been credited with creating some of the biggest catch phrases in television history. Geraldine was the first to get on TV and say, *"When you're hot, you're hot; when you're not, you're not."*

Now, her most famous line is what came to my mind when I was thinking about this reflection, because every time, Miss Geraldine Jones found herself getting into trouble, she would look up and say, *"The Devil Made Me Do It."* Lord, who could ever forget, Geraldine and her very memorable line, *"The Devil Made Me Do It."*

You know, when I was a young child, I was really afraid of the Devil. From the way folks acted and the way some folks talked, the Devil seemed to always have the power to control everything.

155

When something went wrong in your life, it was because of the Devil. When you said a bad word, it was the Devil in you talking. When you committed a sin or did something that you knew was wrong, some how it was the Devil that made you do it.

You know, as a young child, growing up and hearing all this stuff that the Devil could control and make you do, I couldn't help but be afraid of the Devil.

What if the Devil tried to control me like he was apparently controlling others? What if the Devil visited my house and made everybody do what he commanded? What if the Devil took over not just my house but my family, my city, the world? The Devil must be a mighty powerful being if he could do all that folks claimed he could do.

Throughout Sacred Scripture, we hear about men and women who remained committed to the Will of God, even though it seem as if the Devil was trying to turn them away from the Lord. Time and time again, the great men and women of the Bible show us how the power of God will continually defeat the power of the Devil.

In the Book of Jeremiah, Chapter 20, the Prophet speaks as if the Devil himself was talking through him. He says to God,

> *"You duped me, O LORD, and I let myself be duped; You were too strong for me, and You triumphed. All the day I am an object of laughter; everyone mocks me."*[74]

Now, this can also be translated as, "You seduced me, Lord, and because I allowed myself to be seduced by you, people are making fun of me." Here, Jeremiah is saying that because he decided to follow God, to be His messenger, the world seems to be against him.

But, Jeremiah shows that the Love of God is far more powerful than the Devil when he says,
> *"I say to myself, I will not mention him, I will speak in his name no more. But then it becomes like fire burning in my heart, imprisoned in my bones; I grow weary holding it in, I cannot endure it."*[75]

---

[74] Jeremiah 20:7

[75] Jeremiah 20:9

In other words, knowing about God's Grace and Mercy is too much for him to hold in. He's got to proclaim it. Because when he doesn't proclaim God's Word, it becomes like a fire burning inside.

St. Paul also felt the internal pull between Good and Evil that Jeremiah spoke of in his book. In the 7th Chapter of Paul's Letter to the Romans, he speaks about how internally he knows what he is supposed to be doing, yet more often than not, he does what he's not supposed to do.

In this great letter, St. Paul says,
> *"For I do not do the good I want, but I do the evil I do not want. Now if (I) do what I do not want, it is no longer I who do it, but sin that dwells in me. So, then, I discover the principle that when I want to do right, evil is at hand."*[76]

That is why in Chapter 12 of this very same letter, Paul says to us,
> *"I urge you therefore, brothers, by the mercies of God, to offer your bodies as a living sacrifice, holy and pleasing to God, your spiritual worship."*[77]

In this, he is say to us, "Don't allow the ways of the world to become your God. Do what is good, be renewed in the Spirit and thus, you'll be pleasing in the eyes of the Lord." This means that we must be on guard to make sure that the Devil doesn't take control of our lives. We must take control of the Devil and let God lead the way. We can only do this if we work towards having a transformation of our hearts from hearts that listen to and are afraid of the Devil to hearts that focus only on the Love and the Will of God.

Even Jesus Christ had to be on guard against the powers of the Devil. In the 16th Chapter of the Gospel of Matthew, Jesus shows us how to deal with the Devil when The Prince of Evil tries to get in our way. In Verse 21, Jesus tells the disciples about the path God has chosen for Him to be glorified. He says,

> *"He must go to Jerusalem and suffer greatly from the elders, the chief priests, and the scribes, and be killed and on the third day be raised."*[78]

---

[76]Romans 7:19-21

[77]Romans 12:1

[78]Matthew 16:21

Now, when Peter heard this, he pulled Jesus aside, and said, *"God forbid, Lord! No such thing shall ever happen to You."*[79] In other words, "Jesus, don't let it end this way. It will be a disgrace to You and the Father and to us!"

In his "always say the wrong thing at the wrong time" way, Simon Peter shows us how the Devil can try to block the path of God, as God tries to communicate His Loving Plan to His Chosen People.

Jesus immediately recognized Peter's caution for what it was. It was the Devil speaking! And so Jesus responded with *"Get thee behind me, Satan."*[80]

Now, I don't think that Jesus thought that His best friend, Simon Peter, was actually the Devil. But, Jesus knew that it was something evil speaking in Peter that needed to immediately be rebuked. When Jesus said, *"Get thee behind me, Satan,"* He was saying, "I know the Will of God, I accept the Will of God, and I refuse to let you or anything else stop Me from doing the Will of God."

Children of God, when I was younger, I was truly afraid of the Devil. If the Devil was something or some kind of force that could cause folks to do the wrong thing, or say the wrong thing or even think the wrong thing, then I really needed to be afraid.

You see, when you analyze it, fear can be a good thing.

When you are afraid of something, you recoil back from the thing you fear and avoid going near it. If only others could be as afraid of the Devil as I was, what a better world this would be. For, rather than entering into a relationship with the personification of Evil, they would recoil or draw back from the very Force of Evil that causes mankind to do wrong.

You know, I have to admit that even today, I am still afraid of the Devil.

Oh, now don't get me wrong, I am not scared of some mythical horned-fellow with a pitch fork and a red face. No, I ain't scared of that Devil.

What I am afraid of is the great power of evil, the real Devil, that forces folks to do what they know they ought not do, that forces folks to fall, time and time again, into the traps of temptation and sin.

---

[79]Matthew 16:22

[80]Matthew 16:23

See that's the Devil that I am afraid of.

We, as God's Chosen People, ought to start rebuking that Devil just as Jesus rebuked Satan when he tried to impede the path to God's Glory.

You see, if more folks walked around saying, *"Get thee behind me, Satan,"* rather than saying, "The Devil made me do it," what a better world this would be.

We ought to look at those things that lead us into committing the Seven Capital Sins, the deadly Forces of Evil and say, *"Get thee behind me."*

To things that lead to Pride, the deadly sin which makes us want to be exalted above others and even above God, to the Sin of Pride, we ought to say, *"Get thee behind me."*

To things that lead to Gluttony, the sin that places a priority on physical satisfaction and mental gratification, rather than on the virtues of restraint and temperance, to the Sin of Gluttony, we ought to say, *"Get thee behind me."*

To things that lead us to Avarice or Greed, the sin that makes us want more than we really need, to the Sin of Greed, we ought to say, *"Get thee behind me."*

To things that lead us to Lust, the sin that makes us see other human beings as objects for our sexual gratification, objects of sexual indulgence, to the Sin of Lust, we ought to say, *"Get thee behind me."*

To things that lead us to Sloth, the sin that is best translated as just-plain-Laziness, you know, the temptation to do nothing constructive, to the Sin of Sloth, we ought to say, *"Get thee behind me."*

To things that lead us to Envy, the green-eyed sin that causes us to resent the good things other people have received or achieved. The sin that causes us to see the ability of other people, their talents, gifts, diligence, and energy as reasons to dislike both the person and their achievements. To things that lead us to the deadly Sin of Envy, we ought to say, *"Get thee behind me."*

And finally, to things that lead us to the Sin of Anger, the sin through which we encounter an expression or a feeling of resentment toward someone else. To the Sin of Anger, we ought to say, *"Get thee behind me."*

My brothers and sisters, to anything that leads us into the deadly sins of Pride, Gluttony, Greed, Lust, Sloth, Envy or Anger[81], we ought to say, *"Get Thee Behind Me."*

I fully believe that through the waters of Baptism, God's Holy Spirit moved in and took up dwelling in my soul. And, it is from my soul and through God's Spirit that I now have the power to control all things and the people that might tempt me to stray off the path that God has chosen for me.

There is no power within us or around us that is more powerful than the Love and Providence of Our God. Thus, to say, the Devil made you do, you've got to lie. To say, it was the Devil talking, you've got to lie. For, if you have been Baptized, if you have accepted Jesus Christ as your personal Lord and Savior, if you have come to know and feel the love of God in your lives, then you can't keep blaming your sins on this mythical character known as the Devil.

You have to take control of yourself, and know that with God's Spirit within you, nothing will be able to defeat your desire to do God's Will.

On this day, let us firmly say,
"Get thee behind me, Satan, 'cause I am going to see my Lord."
"Get thee behind me, Satan, 'cause I know that the Lord is Good."
"Get thee behind me, Satan, 'cause I know my Redeemer lives."

"Satan get your hands off me."
"Satan get your hands off my child."
"Satan get your hands off my world."

'Cause, I belong to the Lord and it was from thee that Jesus set me free!"

Today let us proclaim to the Power of Evil that our God, who dwells with us, is more powerful than anything thing that can come at us from the outside.

Today, let us look at the evil temptations of this world, and say,
"Get Thee Behind Me, Satan."

---

[81] For more on the Seven Capital Sins see Bishop Donald Wuerl's article, *"Our Catholic Faith: The Seven Capital Sins,"* Columbia Magazine, August, 1999, The official Magazine of the Knights of Columbus.

YouTube of Faith

By now, most of the world has heard of YouTube. But, for the folks that don't know what it is, YouTube is the latest computer fad that allows almost anyone to upload videos to the internet so that they can be viewed by almost anyone around the world.

If you log on to www.YouTube.com, you can see videos of police chases, old television shows and folks fighting in the streets of America. Some people even upload their personal home videos. That means that you can see videos of Pookie's lil' baby dancing in the streets. You can see pictures of somebody's Uncle Harry falling off of a ladder. You can even see videos of a lady with a belt teaching her teenage son a solid lesson on why you should never talk back to your momma.

By logging on to YouTube, you can see almost anything. Even politicians have come to learn about YouTube. Many of them are uploading their speeches and videos from various public appearances onto the website in hopes of attracting the votes of the younger generation. President Barack Obama has credited YouTube and other video sources like it for helping to promote his agenda to the youth. What the fireside chats on the radio used to be for President Franklin D. Roosevelt, uploads to YouTube have become the venue for the 44th President of the United States.

Now, President Obama and other politicians are not the only folks that are now using YouTube to get their messages out. Even Churches are now using YouTube. If you do a quick search using words like Catholic, Homily, Altar Server, and Catholic Gospel Choir you can find videos of some wonderful Church related stuff. Of course, you also have to weed through a bunch of junk that are just jokes or parodies about our church and our faith.

In fact, I didn't realize my celebrity status until I put my own name in the YouTube search engine and found a video of me saying Mass in Los Angeles, speaking at the National Catholic Youth Conference, and laughing with the youth in the Diocese of Honolulu.[82]

It is amazing how quickly stuff will appear on YouTube. If a politician or athlete or religious leader does anything of note (good or bad), by the time the sun goes down, you can bet that somebody uploaded a video of it on YouTube.

---

[82] In the search engine at www.YouTube.com, type "Father Tony" and prepare yourself to be amazed.

161

When I look at the life of our Church and all of the marvelous events that took place in our history, I was thinking about YouTube. What a blessing it would have been if somebody back then could have shot videos of the big events and then uploaded them to the internet for the world to see. I especially wish that we had videos from the major events in the life of Jesus Christ. Those videos would definitely be the most viewed videos on the world wide web. Unfortunately, there were no video cameras back then. The closest that we can get to being there is through reading and listening to the accounts of the Apostles. Let us thank God for the Gospels, the Acts of the Apostles and the letters that St. Paul and other holy men wrote to their communities.

Scripture is great, but in these modern times, we can all agree that a video would help us even more. If YouTube was up and running back in the time of Jesus, St. Joseph could have uploaded movies from that first Christmas. Mary could have uploaded videos from Jesus' Childhood years, his first Passover Meal, his first day at Hebrew School, and even his first time riding on a donkey. We could also have videos of the stuff that the Apostles experienced. We could download videos of Jesus healing the lame, walking on water and even feeding the multitudes.

A Bible Times version of YouTube definitely would help a lot of us get a better understanding of all that took place back when Jesus walked the Earth. When we read the accounts of the Resurrection appearances, for example, wouldn't it be nice if the Disciples had had a video camera and a computer with them in the Upper Room on that first Easter Night. Although there was no YouTube for us to vividly see everything back then, we are tempted to read the accounts of the Resurrection, as if they were videos from the past, vivid photographic descriptions.

> On the evening of that first day of the week, when the doors were locked, where the disciples were, for fear of the Jews, Jesus came and stood in their midst and said to them, "Peace be with you." When He had said this, He showed them His hands and His side. The disciples rejoiced when they saw the Lord.[83]

What a blessing it would be if we could actually see Jesus coming through that locked door, showing Himself to His friends. We could better share in the rejoicing of the disciples, if we had a video of that blessed moment. Yet, how much greater your experience of faith can be when you don't have a picture or video to prove what you believe in?

---

[83] John 20:19-20

For the disciples, the Resurrection was a vivid experience of faith. Their faith experiences with the Risen Lord was so strong that they dared to do what He did. All of the Resurrection accounts show us people who came to believe very strongly that Jesus was risen from the dead. Once they believed, they were willing to do something about it. They went out and told their friends.

Although they did not have a video to show folks, they still went out and told the world. But, a video of that first appearance would have helped.

We can see, as we read and reflect on those first Resurrection accounts that there were some people in Sacred Scripture that had a hard time believing that Jesus was risen. We can see that the news of the Resurrection that was first brought by the women was dismissed as hysteria. Some of the Apostles thought that the girls were crazy for believing that they had actually seen angels and heard angelic messages of the Lord's rising. Other Scripture Stories tell us of how Jesus reprimanded some of the post-Resurrection witnesses for their lack of faith. Later in John 20, we hear about the greatest time of doubt, as we listen to the story about the Great Apostolic Doubter, *Thomas*. A video would have definitely helped Thomas.

> *Thomas, called Didymus, one of the Twelve, was not with them when Jesus came. So the other disciples said to him, "We have seen the Lord." But he said to them, "Unless I see the mark of the nails in His hands and put my finger into the nail marks and put my hand into His side, I will not believe." Now a week later His disciples were again inside and Thomas was with them.*
>
> *Jesus came, although the doors were locked, and stood in their midst and said, "Peace be with you." Then He said to Thomas, "Put your finger here and see My hands, and bring your hand and put it into My side, and do not be unbelieving, but believe." Thomas answered and said to Him, "My Lord and my God!"*
>
> *Jesus said to him, "Have you come to believe because you have seen Me? Blessed are those who have not seen and have believed."*[84]

In this passage, we can see that although many in that Upper Room probably harbored doubts about all that was being reported, only Thomas had the courage to voices his doubts.

---

[84]John 20:24-29

Thomas basically said, "Unless I see Him and I touch Him, *I'm not going to believe.*"

One week after making such a statement, Thomas did see and touch the Risen Lord. His doubts turned to solid faith. His statements of little faith turned into one of the greatest professions of faith, *"My Lord and My God."*

Through writing the Acts of the Apostles, St. Luke continued writing about the events in the lives of the Apostles after their Resurrection experiences. The Acts of the Apostles speaks of many signs and wonders worked in the Name of Jesus by the Apostles.

> *Many signs and wonders were done among the people at the hands of the apostles. They were all together in Solomon's portico. None of the others dared to join them, but the people esteemed them. Yet more than ever, believers in the Lord, great numbers of men and women, were added to them. Thus they even carried the sick out into the streets and laid them on cots and mats so that when Peter came by, at least his shadow might fall on one or another of them. A large number of people from the towns in the vicinity of Jerusalem also gathered, bringing the sick and those disturbed by unclean spirits, and they were all cured.*[85]

Like Jesus did before them, the Apostles went about doing good deeds in the Name of Jesus: healing the sick, proclaiming the Word and taking care of the poor. Even Peter's shadow had healing properties.

Man, how great it would have been to have a video of St. Peter's shadow passing over somebody being healed.

What we can take from these written accounts is the fact that as the Apostles acted in faith, more and more believers were added to the Lord. In a very real way, the Apostles' faith became contagious. It spread throughout the land.

When you think about it, Old Doubting Thomas shows us what it was that the witnesses to the Resurrection believed. Thomas asked to see the wounds of Jesus. The Risen Lord in whom he would believe was the crucified Jesus, who had suffered and died on a tree.

---

[85] Acts 5:12-16

If that Jesus could show up alive, then God was indeed faithful to the Word who became Flesh, emptying Himself to take on the nature of a slave, becoming obedient even to death. The death of Jesus became for Thomas and the other disciples, what the Gospel of John says it is, a true Passover to the Father.

Jesus, as a human being, risked everything. He gambled that the Father would not let Him down, and He won. Jesus had faith in the Resurrection, long before His Crucifixion!

His Faith called Him to do the Father's Will!
His Faith called Him to shun this World for the Glory that was to come!
His Faith called Him to action!

Well, like Jesus, our Resurrection faith is a faith that calls us to action, too.

When Jesus appeared in the Upper Room to the Disciples, the Bible tells us that He breathed forth the Holy Spirit. It is that Spirit that enables the believer to continue the work of Jesus. In the *Acts of the Apostles*, St. Luke tells us that the apostles dared to imitate the actions of Jesus.

They forgave sins.
They proclaimed the Good News.
They celebrated the Lord's Supper.

Because they believed, they took the risk of acting in the Spirit.

They gambled and won. They understood then, just as we should understand now that wherever He goes, Jesus, the Risen Lord, brings His Spirit of Peace.

The disciples in the Upper Room were far from peace.
They were sad that Jesus had died.
They were frightened that what happened to Him would happen to them.
They were huddled in uncertainty and disappointment.

In coming to them, the Risen Lord dispelled all their pain and fear. And, because of this, "*the disciples rejoiced when they saw of the Risen Lord.*"

The Lord, in the Book of Revelation says, "*Do not be afraid. I am the first and the last, the one who lives. Once I was dead, but now I am alive forever and ever.*"[86]

---

[86]Revelation 1:17-18

People of God, as follower of God, we are called to put our faith in the Risen Lord Jesus. We are called to believe, even though we do not see. We are called to face the sorrows, the disappointments, the pains of life and to keep believing.

We are also called to bring our confidence in the Risen Lord to the world outside of the upper rooms where we are tempted to huddle and hide.

We are invited to bear witness to life when we face death, to bear witness to peace when we see war, and to bear witness to joy when we know sorrow.

If we believe: miracles will happen. If we believe: many will be healed and forgiven, many will be added to the Lord. If we believe: we will never die, but have everlasting life.

You know, I am, so glad that we really don't need YouTube or any other video source to help us believe in the Resurrection of the Lord. All we need is the Sacramental Life of our Church and the power of the Holy Spirit.

For, in the Spirit, with eyes of faith, we can truly see God!

Rich and poor have a common bond: the LORD is the maker of them all.

Proverbs 22:2

SECTION THREE
Lessons from Fr. Tony

Rev. R. Tony Ricard, M.Th., M.Div.
St. Augustine High School
Class of 1982

Standing at the Crossroads:
The Four Moments of the Sun

The Ordinary Passages of Life are amply defined by author Robert Farris Thompson. In his book, *Flash of the Spirit: African and Afro-American Art and Philosophy*, Thompson describes these passages through using "The Four Moments of the Sun" or the Kongo Cosmogram. Thompson writes that all primary elements of life can be compared to the circular movements of the sun. Thus, the circle is one of our most sacred symbols in life.

To the Bakongo People (West Africans), all of human existence is a continuous motion on the Circle of Life. The Rising and Setting of the Sun are used to signify the Birth and Death of human beings (The Rising and Setting of Human Life). The periods in between birth and death are marked by the stages of earthly maturation. Of these earthly maturation periods, the Moment of the Elders receives the highest esteem.[87]

This holistic view of life teaches that the existence of any given community must be seen through the whole. Existence is not found in the particular. The Ancestors, the Elders, the Adult Community, the Child and those Yet-To-Be-Born have special movements in the collective Dance of Mankind.

All persons at The Sacred Transitions of the Sun
must see themselves as distinct representations of the whole.

The First Moment of the Sun contains human life from birth to childhood. The Second Moment moves us from childhood through adolescence. The Third Moment takes us from our youth through our adulthood. The Fourth Moment moves us from adulthood through the period of the Elders.

Our earthly journeys are completed when we move from the Fourth Moment into the Spiritual World, the World of our Ancestors.

By connecting this aspect with our Catholic Faith, we can see that the ideals of the Four Moments of the Sun have consistently been included in our faith traditions and rites.

---

[87]Robert Farris Thompson, *Flash of the Spirit: African and Afro-American Art and Philosophy,* (New York: Vintage Books, 1983), pp. 103-159.

This "African-American Stuff" ain't nothing new to the Catholics. For Catholics, our journey from conception through being Born-Again to reaching the age of reason is achieved in the First Moment of the Sun. The Second Moment takes us from our confirmed full-membership in the community through our ordained or vowed covenants with God and each other. The Third Moment of the Sun moves us from these adult covenants through our roles as Elders, and ordained and lay leaders in the community. Our path as ordained and lay Elders into our time of purification by God occurs in the Fourth Moment. We faithfully believe that our course is completed when we pass on to eternal life with our Creator.

Regardless of our spiritual positions in the Four Moments, we are all worthy of God's Love. *African-American Spirituality consistently stresses that no Moment of the Sun is deemed in and of itself to be better than the whole.*

Our individual dignity is not found in the particular but rather in the communal. We become a truly Catholic Church when everyone in the Four Moments is recognized and made present to the Circle of Christ: The True Circle of Life!

Traditionally, we refer to this common dignity and interconnected Catholic-Circle of Life when we profess our belief in the *Communion of Saints.* We believe that all are connected through the love of Jesus Christ. In Him, the Church is a communion of holy people (*sancti*).

In the *Credo of the People of God: Solemn Profession of Faith,* Pope Paul VI expounds on this by writing,

> "We believe in the communion of all the faithful of Christ, those who are pilgrims on Earth, the dead who are being purified, and the blessed in Heaven, all together forming one Church."[88]

Each person has a specific movement that is needed for the collective Dance of Creation. But, with our movements in this collective dance, there comes responsibility. In particular, those who have entered the Period of the Elders must seize the reigns of the community.

Through their connectedness with the Ancestors, many of whom are rightfully called the "Elders of the Elders", they must lead and guide the people of God. It is their collective charge to shepherd the Sheep of the Creator.

---

[88] *Apostolic Letter of the Supreme Pontiff Paul VI: Credo of the People of God,* paragraph 30

The Bakongo People and most West African communities have always taught that Authentic Elders are fully embodied with *Áshe*.[89] Deep within each of them is the power to make things happen. *Áshe* makes them beacons of "God's enabling light rendered accessible to men and women."[90] One who has fully commanded the powers of *Áshe* is rightfully admitted to the Sacred Council of Elders.[91]

Now, don't think that the concept of *Áshe* is something new or foreign to the Catholic Faith. All I have to do is ask you, "What is Grace?" and I am sure that you will be able to connect *Áshe* with our Faith Traditions.

Áshe is the Wisdom-Filled Grace of God. Thus, those who possess *Áshe* are fully aware of the indwelling of the Holy Spirit which comes through our Baptisms.

Now, the term Elder does not automatically mean that one is chronologically old. Just as the passage of years does not automatically make one an Elder. My Grandmother used to say, "Old age don't make you wise. It only makes you old."

Only the wisdom-filled possession of *Áshe* can allow one into the Moment of the Elders. Some young people have assumed the roles of Elders because of their Divine Gift of Wisdom. The Prophet Jeremiah is a prime example of a chronologically-young Elder. Though he was young, he was given the gifts of Prophetic Wisdom.[92] It was through the grace of God that Jeremiah and all Elders became beacons of the Ancestors to the people in their midst.

Even as we reflect on the Elders, *what must be stressed is that no particular Moment of the Sun is deemed in itself better than the whole.* For, all exist for the sake of the whole. All are responsible for the life of the whole. *"No one has made it, until all have made it."* Thus, we all are called to hold on to each other, making sure that the *"circle will be unbroken."*

---

[89]*Áshe* has also been spelled *axe* in some cultures of African Descendants (especially in Brazil).

[90]Thompson, p. 5.

[91]No one can obtain *Áshe* through their own merits. It is sent through the spiritual world of the ancestors by the Divinity. In possession of *Áshe* one is given the fully-functional gift of wisdom. One, consequently, enters into the Elders' Moment of the Sun.

[92]See, *The Call of Jeremiah* (*Jeremiah* 1:4-11).

As a people, we must proclaim that when any person is missing from the circle, the collective plan for salvation is not being fulfilled.

In Jesus, we are called to invite all peoples to active participation in the dance. Unfortunately, as a Church, we have not consistently sent out this invitation.

Thus, the questions before us this day is, how can we learn to better invite our brothers and sisters to the Banquet Table?

As Church, we are a primary part of the Creator's Dance which is the Circle of Life. We are collectively responsible for assuring our God that the dance will happen according to His Will.

If any Members of the Circle are not present, we are compelled to call them back to the dance. We must be true dancing evangelists. Together, we, the Church will bring the dance to its climax at God's Altar in Heaven. But, for now, we are sending out an invitation to the entire Catholic Community to come to the teaching circle and learn how to dance. That we all might delight in being truly Catholic and truly Free.

> *"And before I'd be a slave, I'd be buried in my grave*
> *And go home to my Lord and be free."*[93]

The glory of young men is their strength,

and the dignity of old men is gray hair.

Proverbs 20:29

---

[93] *African-American Spiritual*

171

My Funeral Plans

Back in April of 1995, just about a month before I was ordained to the priesthood, the Archdiocese sent me a bunch of forms to fill out for my upcoming new job.

There were forms for my health insurance, forms for my dental insurance, forms for my car insurance, forms on what personal property I owned, forms on what type of parish I wanted to be assigned to, forms on what I want to do for vacation, and forms on what I want to do in my future. I even think that there was a form on *how much I liked to fill out forms.*

When you are preparing to be ordained, the Archdiocese wants to gather as much information on you as they can, so that they can better place you in a parish where you can be successful as a minister.

As I filled out all the forms in the package, one of the forms really threw me for a loop. You see, in addition to all the forms that could help the archdiocese plan where they would assign me after I was ordained, there was also a form on which they wanted me to plan my funeral in case I suddenly died.

Talk about an eye opener.

As excited as I was about being ordained, all of a sudden I was being faced with planning my funeral. Wow!

You would think that they were already trying to get rid of me!

Well, as I stared at that form, I can remember thinking about what a funeral for me would entail. I thought about everything, from the music to the readings, and from the Homilist to the pall bearers. If there was going to be a funeral for me, I wanted it to be just right!

It was going to be a simple and quiet event because I'm such a simple and quiet man! OK, just go with the feelings!

Well, it's been a few years since I had to fill out that form. And, I guess that when I take time to update the funeral form, it will probably be a bigger plan than the funeral plan I had back in 1995. You see, that once humble and quiet seminarian has now blossomed into the one that can only be described as *"The Aura that is Tony!"*

Indeed, the plan that I have now for my funeral is a tad bit more extravagant than the one I had back in 1995.

When I go, I want a *throw-down* that is befitting of a Co-heir to the Kingdom. I want a party that folks will remember for decades. I want to go out in style!

First, I want a simple wooden coffin. A nice one can be ordered from the Benedictine Monks over at St. Joseph's Abbey in St. Benedict, Louisiana. Their coffins are beautifully modest. They are old fashioned and look really classy!

For the Funeral Mass, I would like a Jazz Band to play with the Gospel Choir. And, when the Church Celebration is done, I want a Second Line Parade with at least 20 women following the hearse crying profusely because such a good man is gone!

And, let us not forget my outfits. Yep, I said, outfits (with an "s").

Just like the late gospel musician, Raymond Myles had for his funeral, I want to wear at least three different outfits over the span of the three days that it will take to celebrate my Birthday into Heaven.

At the wake or vigil service, I want to be laid out in my Black Cassock, with the little cape flowing and a gold cross blazin'!

At the Morning Visitation, I want to be laid out in my Black Suit with my black Timberland Boots on my feet!

And for the Mass, I have to be laid out in Full Priestly Vestments with a wireless microphone on my head just in case I have something else to say!

When I go, I want folks to be talking for weeks about how good my funeral was and what a *throw-down* we had. Just like our Mardi Gras Masses, I want folks to walk out saying, *"Now, you know that boy just ain't right!"*

Oh, and I think that I am also going to preach my own funeral homily. By the time I go, I'll be able to leave behind a video or a hologram of me preaching from the pulpit.

Heaven forbid I leave it up to someone else to do me justice. Lord knows, can't nobody out preach the *Aura that is Tony*! Plus, can you see the Archbishop's face when he finds out that I am preaching at my own funeral!

People of God, each November, the Roman Catholic Church brings our Liturgical Season to a close. In the final weeks of our liturgical year, our Church calls all of us to reflect on what will happen to all of us at the end of time.

Will we truly be ready when the Savior decides to call us Home?

Are we prepared for the day that they will bury us?

Planning for your funeral is one thing. But, being prepared to die is truly another.

That is why St. Paul, in his First Letter to the Thessalonians, reminds us that we must be ready for our final days, because *"you yourselves know very well that the day of the Lord will come like a thief at night."*[94]

For most of us, we will not know that day nor the hour that the Lord will call us home.[95] We will not have time to plan for our funerals or even more importantly plan for our moment at the Judgment Seat. This means that we have to make sure that we are ready now, just in case today is our last day on Earth.

Like a *thief in the night*, the Angel of Death can creep up on us and usher us through the doorway that connects this world and the world of the Spirits.

Are you ready to stand before the Judgment Seat?
Are you ready to meet God, face to face?
Are you ready to account for what you have done in this world
as you supposedly were getting ready for the *world that is to come*?

Are you ready to answer questions like have you truly come to Know, Love and Serve Jesus as your personal Lord and Savior?
Simply put, are you ready to die?

In Chapter 25 of the Gospel according to our Brother Matthew stresses to us that for some, their moment at the Judgment Seat will usher in a harsh reality. In the Parable of the Talents, Jesus reminds us that everyone has been given certain gifts and opportunities by God.

What you do with all that God has given you will be a deciding factor in whether or not you make it into Heaven. That is why Jesus said to His Apostles,

---

[94] 1 Thessalonians 5:2

[95] See Luke 12:46

"Stay awake, for you know neither the day nor the hour. "It will be as when a man who was going on a journey called in his servants and entrusted his possessions to them. To one he gave five talents; to another, two; to a third, one--to each according to his ability. Then he went away. Immediately the one who received five talents went and traded with them, and made another five. Likewise, the one who received two made another two. But the man who received one went off and dug a hole in the ground and buried his master's money.

After a long time the master of those servants came back and settled accounts with them. The one who had received five talents came forward bringing the additional five. He said, 'Master, you gave me five talents. See, I have made five more.' His master said to him, 'Well done, my good and faithful servant. Since you were faithful in small matters, I will give you great responsibilities. Come, share your master's joy.'

(Then) the one who had received two talents also came forward and said, 'Master, you gave me two talents. See, I have made two more.' His master said to him, 'Well done, my good and faithful servant. Since you were faithful in small matters, I will give you great responsibilities. Come, share your master's joy.'

Then the one who had received the one talent came forward and said, 'Master, I knew you were a demanding person, harvesting where you did not plant and gathering where you did not scatter; so out of fear I went off and buried your talent in the ground. Here it is back.'

His master said to him in reply, 'You wicked, lazy servant! So you knew that I harvest where I did not plant and gather where I did not scatter? Should you not then have put my money in the bank so that I could have got it back with interest on my return? Now then! Take the talent from him and give it to the one with ten. For to everyone who has, more will be given and he will grow rich; but from the one who has not, even what he has will be taken away. And throw this useless servant into the darkness outside, where there will be wailing and grinding of teeth. "[96]

---

[96]Matthew 25:14-30

Some have been blessed with monetary gifts.
How are you using your money for the sake of the Kingdom?

Some have been blessed with physical talents.
Are you using your gift of music, dance or creativity
for the sake of the Kingdom?

Some have been blessed with spiritual talents.
Are you using your gifts to bring others closer to God in prayer?

How are you using the blessing that God has poured down on you?

On the day that you die, will you be prepared to account for how well you used your gifts and talents?

Back in Jesus' day, the word "talents" literally referred to a some of money that was being used. I once read that a talent was equivalent to about fifteen years of wages for an ordinary worker. That's a lot for a Master to hand over to a worker and then just leave.

But, in the parable, Jesus was trying to stress how much trust the Master had in his workers. That's why although he returned unexpectantly, he still expected his workers to have done something productive with what he had given them.

As harsh as it may sound, the one worker who didn't do anything with what the Master had given him, really deserved to be treated they way he was treated. He deserved to be cast out of the Kingdom because he was too lazy to do what God needed him to do.

People of God, all of us are called to look at how God has blessed us in our lives and how we have chosen to use our blessings for the sake of the Kingdom. Because, my brothers and sisters, the day will come when you and I will have to stand before God and account for what we have done with the gifts that God has given us.

For some, it is a scary thing to think about the fact that one day we will die. But, the stark reality is that unless your name is Elijah, and you are expecting a *Fiery Chariot to swing low and carry you home*, you will die some day.[97]

---

[97] See 2 Kings 2:11

But, it is not the death part that you have to worry about. It's standing at the Judgment Seat with which you need to be concerned. So, today, I ask you, "Are you ready to die?"

Some folks think that I am joking about preaching at my own funeral. But, I really am not joking. Ya'll know that I am going to want to have to last word! But, more importantly, I want to make sure that when I die, folks really do remember what was important about my life.

You see, at my funeral, some will remember that I preached all across the nation and in about 20 other countries. Some will remember that I have preached before crowds as large as 20,000 teenagers. Some will remember that I wrote a couple of books and recorded sermons on tapes and CD's. Some will even remember that I was the pastor of not one but two of the greatest parishes in the Archdiocese of New Orleans.[98]

Indeed, they will remember a lot of what I have said and done partially because I am going to leave a list of stuff for them to read off at my funeral. But, for me, I am concerned that most will have never fully understood why I was able to do as much as I did. Some will never get as Kirk Franklin would put it, *"the reason why I sing."*[99]

And that's why I want to preach at my own funeral. Because, as great as it will be for folks to read off all of my accolades, awards and honors, the only thing that will matter in the end is if they knew just two things about me.

In fact, it's the two things that I want inscribed on my grave's headstone:
First: "He loved the Lord and the Lord loved him!"
And, second: "He was his *Momma's Baby*." After that, nothing really matters.

In the celebration of the Eucharist, Jesus continuously preaches to us about all that He wants us to know about Him. In this Blessed Feast, He tells us that He was, is, and will alway be the *"Lamb of God who takes away the Sins of the World."*[100]

---

[98]Our Lady Star of the Sea Church and St. Philip the Apostle Parishes in New Orleans.

[99]*"The Reason Why We Sing"* was a 1993 hit song for Kirk Franklin and The Family.

[100]John 1:29

That is why at His Last Supper, the last time that He got the chance to truly preach to His congregation of disciples before He died, He told them to *"Do this in Memory of Me."*[101]

If folks didn't remember anything about Him, He at least wanted them to remember that He was willing to sacrifice His life for the sake of the world. That is why, in the celebration of the Eucharist, we continuously preach the sermon that Jesus gave on the night before He died.

Today, I pray that God will help you to truly be prepared for the moment that you will stand before the Judgment Seat.

I pray that you will be able to account for all of the gifts and talents the Lord has given you and how you have chosen to use them for the sake of the Kingdom.

And, I pray that following His assessment of your gifts, the Lord will be able to look at you and say,

> *"Well done my good and faithful servant.*
> *Come and inherit the Kingdom that has been prepared for you*
> *since the foundation of the world."*[102]

You know, at my funeral, I really want a major party. I want folks to dress in bright colors and laugh and joke the whole time. From my three outfits to the women following the hearse, when I go out, I want folks to definitely remember that I was here!

But, even if all of that doesn't happen, I just want folks to remember that I did the best that I could do with the few little talents that God has given me.

Once the *Aura that is Tony* leaves this place, Lord knows that there will be a void here on Earth. But, can you imagine how excited the Angels will be when they realize that they'll be a new preacher in town?!

Watch out St. Paul, because a brother is on his way!
And, soon, there will be a pulpit in Heaven with my name on it!

May God help us all be ready for our final days! Amen!

---

[101]Luke 22:19

[102]See Matthew 25:19-34

Book Four

I DON'T MAKE THEM UP!

Reflections, Stories and Jokes from a Faithful Fool

Rev. R. Tony Ricard, M.Th., M.Div.

Published in 2010

Introduction to "I Don't Make Them Up!"

"Consider your own calling, brothers and sisters. Not many of you were wise by human standards, not many were powerful, not many were of noble birth. Rather, God chose the foolish of the world to shame the wise and God chose the weak of the world to shame the strong, and God chose the lowly and despised of the world, those who count for nothing, to reduce to nothing those who are something, so that no human being might boast before God."
(1 Corinthians 26-29)

More times than not, folks who love their God and love their Church have been called "fools" by those who just don't understand. Yet, "Crazy Fools" are definitely those whom we should strive to be in the eyes of the world. For, it is the foolish that God uses to shame the wise.

We are all invited by God to focus on what it means to be a "Fool for the Lord." Through these entertaining Reflections, Stories and Jokes, we can find true joy in the midst of life's great struggles. For spiritual laughter conveys joy to the entire human family, uplifts our souls and energizes our evangelical spirit!

I have been blessed to preach and teach before thousands and thousands of people. In my presentations and homilies, I often use humor to express the love of God, uplift the downtrodden, and celebrate who we are as God's Beloved. Although I can take credit for many of the stories that I've used, I really have to admit that I've "appropriated" most of them from other speakers and presenters. I've especially been known to "borrow" jokes from my ministerial inspirations: Jesse Manibusan, Mike Patin and Paul Florez. Each of them are phenomenal speakers in their own rights.

Once I "digest" a story, I try to retell it in an exciting new way. To make the story more realistic, I usually place myself in it. It is amazing how many folk actually believe that the stories are true.

The Reflections, Stories and Jokes that are included in this book are a collection from many sources. Most of them are jokes that I have heard or have been sent by friends and family. I especially want to thank Carl Kluttz and Norman Howard for the many jokes they have sent to me through the years.

Now you know why at the end of almost all of the jokes that I tell, I say, "I Don't Make Them Up! I Just Repeat Them!"

May this book lift your Spirit so that you too may long to be a Fool for the Lord!

Rev. R. Tony Ricard, M.Th., M.Div.

SECTION ONE
"In the Beginning...."

"God looked at
everything
He had made,
and
He found it
very good."

Genesis 1:31

My Version of the Creation Story
an Introduction

Back in 1990, I got to hear Dr. William Henry Cosby, Jr., the infamous educator, or "Bill Cosby" as we commonly know him, tell a version of the Creation Story that was insightful and yet quite funny.

He has the rare ability to take a familiar story or life experience and share it with his audiences in such a way that only makes them laugh, but has them thinking a bit deeper.

After hearing Bill Cosby's version of the Creation Story, I tried to retell the story in the same manner that he did. Suddenly, I realized that I was no Bill Cosby. No one can really tell a Bill Cosby story quite like he does.

Soon, I realized I had to develop my own version of the Creation Story using my own vision, and combining it with a little flavor of my own.

So, I did.

The most impressionable stories told involve audience participation, I know this first-hand from being a certified elementary school teacher in New Orleans.

So, I incorporated interactive motions from an activity that I learned while directing a youth retreat with the innovative Mike Patin.

He served as the Director of Youth Ministry for the Archdiocese of New Orleans for many years. In a very real way, Mike is responsible for beginning my ministry as a national speaker. He really deserves the credit for presenting "The Aura that is Tony" worldwide.

When I was a seminarian, Mike was the first to recognize my blessings and gifts for Youth Ministry. Not long after I entered the seminary, Mike was beginning to recommend me for speaking engagements and retreats. I was invited to be the keynote speaker for the 1992 Diocesan Youth Conference in the Diocese of Lake Charles, Louisiana. That was my very first time as a keynote speaker.

While directing a retreat with Mike, I watched him engage the youth in an activity that he called, "The Magic Go." This is how it worked. Every time he said the word, "Go," he would direct the kids to complete a series of motions; slaps, claps and even finger snaps.

When I developed my version of the Creation Story, I incorporated Mike's "Magic Go" command with my humorous rendition of the story. But, instead of using the word, "Go," to signal the interactive motions, I switched it to the word, "Boom!"

Every time the youth hear the word, "Boom," in the Creation Story, they are directed to do the following:

1. Slap their legs (once)

2. Clap their hands (once)

3. Snap their fingers (twice)

4. Yell, "Whoop, there it is!"

Adding "Boom!" to the story really brought it to life!

To this day, I thank Bill Cosby and Mike Patin for inspiring me to create one of my most successful stories.

It sure is good!

The Creation Story
Inspired by God - Written by Moses
and Interpreted by Fr. Tony

Once upon a time, or really, "In the Beginning,"[103]
    God was in Heaven and He said to Himself, "Self...."
    (Hey, there wasn't anybody else to talk to!)

"Self, I'm feeling kinda lonely. So, I think that I'll make me something."

On the **First Day,** the Lord said, "Let there be Light!"

Boom!

And the Angels cried out, "Whoop There It Is!"[104]

And there it was. And the Light was everywhere.

And when the Lord looked upon the Light, His Heart was filled with Love.

So, He looked upon the Light and He said,
    "Mmm, Mmm, Mmm, this sure is good!"

Well, that was the First Day.

On the **Second Day**, when the Lord got up, His Heart was filled with Love.
    He loved Him some Light.

But, He realized that there was one small problem. "It don't do anything!"

The Light was like "Hey,.... I'm the Light. That's what I do.... I do Light!"

So, the Lord decided that He would make something that just might do something.

---

[103] Genesis Chapters 1-3

[104] "Whoop There It Is" was the catch phrase made popular in a 1993 Hip- Hop song by Tag Team. The literal translation is "Look, Honey, it's over there!"

So, on the Second Day the Lord created the Sky and the Firmament.

Boom!

And the Angels cried out, "Whoop There It Is!"

And, there they were!

And the Light was doing the Light thing. The Sky was doing the Sky thing and the Firmament was....

(Well, who really knows what the Firmament really was. What ever it was....
    it was the potential from which everything else came into being.)

But, whatever it was....the Lord looked upon the Light, the Sky, and the Firmament and He said, "Mmm, Mmm, Mmm, this sure is good!"

And that was the Second Day.

On the **Third Day**, the Lord got up, and His Heart was filled with Love.
    He loved Him some Light, Sky and Firmament.

But, He realized that there was one small problem. "It don't do anything!"

So, on the Third Day, the Lord decided that He would create something that just might do something.

On the Third Day, the Lord created the Dry Land,
    the Dry Earth and the Sea Vegetation.

Boom!

And the Angels cried out, "Whoop There It Is!"

And, there they were!

So, the Mountain was doing the Mountain thing. The Trees were doing the Trees thing and the Grass was doing the Grass thing.

And, the Lord looked upon the Light, the Sky, the Firmament, the Dry Earth, the Earth and Sea Vegetation and He said, "Mmm, Mmm, Mmm, this sure is good!"

185

And that was the Third Day.

On the **Fourth Day**, the Lord got up and His Heart was filled with Love.
He loved Him some Light, the Sky, the Firmament, the Dry Earth,
the Earth and Sea Vegetation.

But, He realized that there was one small problem.

You see, all this green stuff that He had created didn't know when it was
supposed to grow and not grow.

So, He decided to create a system that would tell the green stuff when to grow.

So, on the Fourth Day the Lord reached up into the Sky and He grabbed that
thing he called the Light.

He made a great big fiery ball, threw it in the air and called it "the Sun."

Then, He took another piece, made another ball and threw it on the dark side of
the Earth and called it "the Moon."

Then, He took a bunch of pieces, chopped them up and threw them in the air.
He called them "the Stars."

Boom!

And the Angels cried out, "Whoop There It Is!"

And, there they were!

And, the Lord looked upon the Light, the Sky, the Firmament, the Dry Earth, the
Earth and Sea Vegetation, the Sun, the Moon and the Stars and He said, "Mmm,
Mmm, Mmm, this sure is good!"

And that was the Fourth Day.

On the **Fifth Day**, when the Lord got up and His Heart was filled with Love.
He loved Him some Light, the Sky, the Firmament, the Dry Earth,
the Earth and Sea Vegetation, the Sun, the Moon and the Stars.

But, He realized that there was one small problem. "It don't do anything!"
(Have you ever tried to play ball with a tree?
After a while, it's going to get boring....for most of us!)

186

So, on the Fifth Day the Lord decided that He would create something that just might do something.

So, on the Fifth Day, the Lord created Birds in the air and Fish in the water.

Boom!

And the Angels, cried out, "Whoop There It Is!"

And, there they were!

The Birds were doing the Birds thing. The Fish were doing the Fishy thing.

And the Lord looked upon the Light, the Sky, the Firmament, the Dry Earth, the Earth and Sea Vegetation, the Sun, the Moon and the Stars, Birds in the air and Fish in the water and He said, "Mmm, Mmm, Mmm, this sure is good!"

Well, that was the Fifth Day.

On the **Sixth Day**, the Lord got up and His Heart was filled with Love.
He loved Him some Light, the Sky, the Firmament, the Dry Earth, the Earth and Sea Vegetation, the Sun, the Moon and the Stars, Birds in the air and Fish in the water.

But, He realized that there was one small problem.

You see, on one-third of this thing that He called the Earth, "There wasn't anything living."

One-third of the Earth is dry land.

So, the Lord decided that He would create something that could live on the dry land.

So, on the Sixth Day, the Lord created Animals upon the earth and Creepy Things that live in Trees!

Boom!

And the Angels cried out, "Whoop There It Is!"

And, there they were!

The Elephant was doing the Elephant thing.
The Monkey was doing the Monkey thing.
The Sheep was doing the Sheep thing.
The Tiger was doing the Tiger thing.

(I'm not going to name them all because there was a lot of them.)

But, the Lord looked upon the Light, the Sky, the Firmament, the Dry Earth,
the Earth and Sea Vegetation, the Sun, the Moon and the Stars, Birds in the air
and Fish in the water, Animals on the Earth and Creepy Things in the Trees and
He said, "I ain't done, yet!"

In looking at all that He had created,
      the Lord realized that as much as He loved the things that He had made,
      the problem was that none of them had the ability to love Him back.

The Lord wanted to create a creature that could freely choose to love Him back.

So, similar to how the African-American Poet,
      James Weldon Johnson described it, the Lord stepped down out of space.

He knelt down beside a river like a Mammy kneeling over a baby
      and He scooped up a hand of clay.

From that clay He created a new being and breathed into him the Breath of Life.

He called him "the Adam!"

Boom!

And the Angels cried out, "Whoop There It Is!"

And, there he was!
      Adam, standing there in all his glory!

Then the Lord looked at Adam and said, "You the Man!"

To which Adam thumped his chest and exclaimed, "I'm the Man!"

The Lord said, "Adam, you have dominion over the whole earth!"

To which Adam thumped his chest and exclaimed, "I've got dominion!"

The Lord said, "Whatever name you give something will be its name!"

Adam thumped his chest, again and said, "I've got names!"

Pointing to a big, fat, gray thing with a long nose,
    the Lord asked Adam, "What's that?"

"That looks like an Elephant to me," Adam replied.

And, the Lord said, "Alright Adam, that's an Elephant."

Looking at another animal with a long neck that was eating leaves
    at the top of a tree, the Lord asked, "Hey Adam, what's that?"

To which Adam replied, "Lord, that looks like a Giraffe to me."

And, the Lord said, "Adam, that's a Giraffe."

Then they saw another big, fat, gray thing with a horn on its nose,
    and the Lord asked, "Hey Adam, what's that?"

"That looks like a Rhinoceros to me," Adam replied.

And, the Lord said, "Adam that's a Rhinoceros!"

Then they saw this thing that looked liked a like a combination between an
Elephant and a Rhino.

And, the Lord said, "Adam, what's that?"

To which Adam replied, "Eleph-phino!" (Get it.... "El - Eph - I - No?")

And so, the Lord said, "Adam man, you just go and have a good time!"

So, Adam set out to enjoy the Earth. He was loving being "the Man."

But, about midway through the afternoon of the Sixth Day,
    Adam realized that there was one BIG problem.

So, Adam headed up to Heaven to have a talk with God.

When he knocked on the Gates of Heaven,
    the Lord answered and asked him, "Adam, is there a problem?"

189

"Oh no, Lord," Adam said,
    "I don't mean to complain because I've got it pretty good."

"But, umm....You see, Lord, every night,
    I see Mr. and Mrs. Elephant go home.
Lord, every night, I see Mr. and Mrs. Giraffe go home.
    Lord, even the Rhinoceros has somebody.
    Umm...., you think you could just....hook a Brother up?"

And the Lord, replied by saying, "Adam....Adam....Adam?

    Are you sure you know what you are asking for?

    Why don't you just go to sleep?"

Well, they say that Adam laid down beside that same river.

In order for the Lord to fashion this new creature out of the very same substance
that He created the first one, the Lord stepped down out of space.

He reached down inside of Adam and pulled out a rib.

From that rib, He fashioned a new being.
    And, He breathed into her the Breath of Life.
    He called her "Eve!"

Boom!

And the Angels cried out, "Whoop There It Is!"

And, there she was standing there in "all her glory."

When Adam woke up and opened his eyes,
    that is when she got her official name.

Because, when he saw her standing there by the river, the first thing he said was
    "Whoa Man!"

    (Get it, Whoa Man....wo----man = Woman!)

Adam looked up to Heaven and he said,
"Lord, You the Man! You the Man!" The Lord smiled down on them and said,
    "Ya'll just head out and have a good time!"

190

As Adam and Eve headed out into the Garden, the Lord looked upon the Light, the Sky, the Firmament, the Dry Earth, the Earth and Sea Vegetation, the Sun, the Moon and the Stars, Birds in the air and Fish in the water, Animals on the Earth, Creepy Things in Trees, Man and Woman, and He said, "Mmm, Mmm, Mmm, this sure is VERY Good!"

Did you know that at the end of the Sixth Day of Creation, the Lord looked upon all that He had created, His Heart was filled with Love.

But, He realized that in creating Eve, He had reached the peak of Creation.
Never again would anything be created greater than Man and Woman.

So, instead of declaring that we were good,
the Lord declared that we were "Very Good."

And, that was the Sixth Day.

On the **Seventh Day**, the Lord got up and His Heart was filled with Love.
He loved Him some Light, the Sky, the Firmament, the Dry Earth, the Earth and Sea Vegetation, the Sun, the Moon and the Stars, Birds in the air and Fish in the water, Animals on the Earth, Creepy Things in Trees, Man and Woman.

On the Seventh Day the Lord realized that Adam and Eve were already teenagers, so He took the Seventh Day off.

He knew that He would never rest again!

On the **Eighth Day**, the Lord went looking for His two kids.
He was yelling, "Adam?....Eve?....Where ya'll at?"

Adam turned to Eve and asked,
"Do you think that He could see us behind this tree?"

To which Eve replied, "Dummy, He MADE the tree!"

So, Adam stepped out from behind the tree and called out,
"Lord, we're right here."

"What are you doing?, the Lord asked.
"We're hiding?" Adam replied.

"And why were you hiding?," the Lord asked.

"Because we were naked.," Adam said.

"Naked? How did you know that you were naked?," the Lord asked.

Adam tried to explain,
"Well, you know Lord, last night, the Woman that you gave me made a wonderful meal. It was so delicious. That girl can really cook!"

The Lord asked Adam, "Where did you get the food for the meal?"

Adam replied, "From the tree in the center of the Garden.
The same tree that you told us not to touch."

And the Lord declared,
"Adam, when I created you, I gave you dominion over the whole Earth.
Everything that I created was made for you to enjoy.
But, the only rule that I gave you to live by was simply this;

you could not touch the Tree in the center of the Garden, that Tree will be forever known as "the Tree of the Knowledge of Good and Evil."

That was it, that was my only rule! But, you had to go and touch my Tree!

Well, guess what? Like all good parents, if you can't live by the rules in My House, then you have to get out!"

And on that day, the Lord put us out of the Garden
and we have been trying to get back in ever since!

Boom!

And the Angels, cried out, "Whoop There It Is!"

SECTION TWO
Biblical Jokes

Jesus opened
their minds
to understand
the Scriptures.

Luke 24:45

Creating Adam's Helpmate

Not long after Adam was created, he was walking around the Garden of Eden and realizing that all of the other creatures had beautiful helpmates and wives.

The Monkeys, the Lions and even the Hippopotamuses
	had beautiful female companions with which they could run and play.

Looking at poor helpless Adam, the Lord knew that it was not good for him to be alone. The poor boy would never be able to figure out the tougher issues of life.

Without the help of a mate,
Adam would never understand things like balancing a household's budget or solving the mystery of who put the toy soldiers in the toilet.

So, God decided that he would strike a deal with Adam
	and finally create for him a friend.

"Adam," the Lord said, "I have come up with a plan that will make you very very happy! I have envisioned for you a companion, a helpmate who will be able to fulfill your every need and desire.

This new creature will be faithful, loving, and obedient to you. She will make you feel wonderful each and every day of your life."

Adam was so stunned by God's vision that he yelled out,
	"Lord, that sounds incredible!"

"Well, it is," replied the Lord. "But it doesn't come for free.
In fact, this is someone so special that it's going to cost you both of your arms.

Lord, Adam," sighed, "I can't live without my arms."

"OK, Adam," the Lord answered, "I can make you someone who won't be as good as my first vision. But, she will indeed be a great helpmate to you. She will be able to solve all of your problems. However, it will cost you both of you legs."

"That's a pretty high price to pay, Lord," said Adam.

" Ummm Lord, how much could I get for a rib?"

Eve's Side of the Story (Rated PG 13)

After three weeks in the Garden of Eden, God came to visit Eve.
"So, how is everything going?" inquired God.

"It is all so beautiful, God," she replied. "The sunrises and sunsets are breathtaking, the smells, the sights, everything is wonderful, but, I have just one problem.

It's these breasts you have given me. The middle one pushes the other two out and I am constantly knocking them with my arms, catching them on branches and snagging them on bushes. They're a real pain."

Eve went on to tell God that since many other parts of her body came in pairs, such as her legs, arms, eyes, and her ears. So, she felt that having only two breasts would help make her body more "symmetrically balanced."

"That's a fair point," replied God, "But it was my first shot at this, you know. I gave the animals six breasts, so I figured that you needed only half of those, but, I see that you are right. I will fix it up right away."

And God reached down, removed the middle breast and tossed it into the bushes.

Three weeks passed and God once again visited Eve in the Garden of Eden.
"Well, Eve, how is my favorite creation?"

"Just fantastic," she replied, "Except for one oversight. You see, all the animals are paired off. The ewe has a ram and the cow has her bull. All the animals have a mate except me. I feel so alone."

God thought for a moment and said, "You know, Eve, you are right. How could I have overlooked this? You do need a mate and I will immediately create a man from a part of you. Let's see, where did I put that useless boob?"

(My best friend, Cathy, thinks that this makes more sense than all that stuff about the rib!)

Dirt

One day,
God was sitting in Heaven having a deep discussion with a noted scientist.

The scientist says to God,
"Lord, we don't need you anymore.
Science has finally figured out a way to create life out of nothing.

In other words, we can now do what you did 'in the beginning'."

"Oh, is that true?
Tell me...."
replies God.

"Well," says the scientist,
"we can take dirt and form it into the likeness of you
and breathe life into it, thus creating man."

"Well, that's interesting." God replies, "Why don't you show Me."

So the scientist bends down to the Earth
and starts to mold the soil.

"Oh no, no, no...."
interrupts God.

(I love this...)

"Get your own dirt!"

SECTION THREE
Prayerful Jokes

If you remain in Me
and My Words
remain in you,
ask for whatever
you want
and
it will be done for you.

John 15:7

Knocking Out Those Hail Mary's

Not too long ago, Our Lady Star of the Sea Church in New Orleans was working hard on renovating and restoring a major light fixture that was the focal point in its 70-feet-high dome. In order to repair the fixture, the restoration company installed scaffolding that took up much of the center of the church. It stretched all the way up to the center of the dome.

Like most Catholic churches, Our Lady Star of the Sea is blessed to have its share of really prayerful folks. At any given Mass, there are at least four or five old ladies who will be working their rosary beads for the entire Mass.

In fact, if you don't have old ladies working those beads,
	your church really ain't Catholic.

Well, one day, as the artist was working on the light fixture, one of the old ladies came into church, knelt down in the front pew and began to recite her rosary.

She was working those beads like a champion,
	knocking out those "Hail Mary's."

As she worked those beads, the artist decided to mess with her.
	In the middle of her "Hail Mary's,"
	he leaned down and yelled to her, "Hello down there!"

Well, when that old lady looked up, she didn't see anybody.

So, she went right back to saying her "Hail Mary's," knocking out those beads.

So, once again, he leaned down from his high perch and yelled down,
	"Hello down there!"

But, when that old lady looked up, she didn't see anybody. So, she went right back to saying her "Hail Mary's," knocking out those beads.

Well, this time, the artist decided that he would really mess with her.
	He leaned down and yelled out, "It's me! Jesus!"

To which the old lady responded,

Hush Up! I'm talking to ya Momma!"

Let Go and Let God

A man was walking in the mountains just enjoying the scenery when he stepped too close to the edge of the mountain and started to fall.

In desperation, he reached out and grabbed a limb of a gnarly old tree hanging onto the side of the cliff.

Full of fear, he assessed his situation.

He was about 100 feet down a shear cliff and about 900 feet from the bottom of the canyon below. If he slipped again, he was definitely going to die.

Filled with fear, he looked up and yelled, "Help me!"

But, there was no answer.

Again and again he cried out for help, but no one answered.

Finally he yelled, "Is anybody up there? "

A deep voice replied, "Yes, I'm up here."

"Who is it?"

"It's the Lord."

"Can you help me?"

"Yes, I can help. Have faith in me."

"Lord, please help me!"

"Let go."

Looking around the man became full of panic. "What?!?!"

"Have faith in me. Let go. I will catch you."

To which the man looked up and yelled out,
      "Uh... Is there anybody else up there?"

St. Jude Candles

Mrs. Jackson was walking down Canal Street in New Orleans
    when she met up with Father Tony.

"Good morning," Father said.
    "Didn't I marry you and you husband about six years ago?"

    "Yes, Father. You certainly did preside at our wedding." she replied.

"Do ya'll have any children, yet?" he asked.

    "No, not yet." she said.

"Well, next week, I am going to be preaching for the St. Jude Novena over
    at Our Lady of Guadalupe Church on North Rampart Street.
If it's alright with you, I'll light a St. Jude Candle for you and your husband."

    "Thank you, Father," she said as they continued on their way.

Quite a few years later, Father Tony ran into Mrs. Jackson again.
    "Well, Mrs. Jackson, how are you doing these days?" he asked.

    "I am doing well." she replied.

Father then asked her, "Do ya'll have any children, now?"

"Oh yes, Father!" she said.
    "Since I last saw you, we've had eleven children:
three sets of twins, and five singles."

"My Lord," Father Tony replied.
    "You guys have been busy! Where is Mr. Jackson?"

She responded,
    "He over by St. Jude, trying to blow out that darn candle!"

SECTION FOUR
Ministry Jokes

There is an appointed time for everything, and a time for every affair under the heavens....

A time to weep, and a time to laugh; a time to mourn, and a time to dance.

Ecclesiastes 3:1.4

It's A Miracle

The other day, Fr. Tony was in the Sacristy preparing for Mass.

As he hurried to get everything ready for the service,
    one of the altar servers rushed in and began to yell.

    "Father, Father, Father!" he said.

"WHAT?" replied the priest.

"Let me tell you what I just saw," he said.

"Well, what did you see?" replied the priest.

"Well, I saw this man coming into church.
    He was walking with crutches.

        He walked up to the Holy Water Font
        and he rubbed some Holy Water on his leg.

        Then, he took his crutch and threw it in the air.

Next, he took some more Holy Water and rubbed it on his other leg.
    And, once again, he threw his other crutch into the air."

"That's a miracle!" exclaimed the priest.

"Where is that man?" he asked.

To which the boy replied,
    "He's flat on his butt, right by the Holy Water!"

The Lie Competition

While walking down the street, one day,
    Father Tony noticed a group of boys who were standing around a dog.

Now, every time he would look in their direction, the boys would start to giggle.

Fearing that they were going to harm the dog, Fr. Tony approached them and said sternly, "Gentlemen, I know that you are not planning to hurt that dog."

One of the boys looked up and replied, "Oh no, Father.
    We're not going to hurt the dog. We love the dog. And, that's why we've decided that whoever could tell the biggest lie could have the dog."

One of the boys raised his hand and said, "My daddy is Michael Jordan.
    He flies home to play basketball with me on every Sunday!"

To which the group replied, "Nah, nah nah!"

Another boy looked up and said, "Well, my daddy is President Barack Obama and I can go anywhere in the country that I want to!"

And, once again, the group replied, "Nah, nah nah!"

A third boy chimed in, "My daddy is Bill Clinton!"
    (All things are possible......)

But, the group still replied, "Nah, nah nah!"

Growing angry at their lies, Father Tony began to scold them for their actions.

"Gentlemen," he said, "Don't you already know that lying is a sin.
    It says it right there in the Bible -
    Thou Shalt Not Bear False Witness Against Thy Neighbor.

    That means that you are not supposed to lie!

    When I was you age, I never told a lie!"

To which one of the boys replied,
    "Give him the dog!"

The Coffin Attack!

The other night, my rottweiler, Pepper Louise, and I were out on an evening stroll. As we walked a block from my rectory, we began to pass the entrance gates to the historic St. Roch Cemetery.

Now, normally, I won't walk past those gates at night. I am easily scared!

But, for some reason, Pepper wanted to head in that direction.

As we passed the gates, we suddenly heard a noise coming from behind the walls of the graveyard. "Thump Thump.............Thump Thump............Thump Thump!"

As the noise got louder, I grew more scared and wondered what could be making the noise. "Thump Thump...............Thump Thump...................Thump Thump!"

However, Pepper was not as curious as I was.

Once she heard the noise, she immediately took off running back to our rectory.

Although she is supposed to be my protection, she wasn't going to be around to see from what I was going to need to be protected!

"Thump Thump.......................Thump Thump.........................Thump Thump!"

Once she took off running, I took off running, too.
"Thump Thump.......................Thump Thump.........................Thump Thump!"

When I look behind us, would you believe that I saw a coffin coming out of the cemetery and heading towards us?

It was standing on it's edge moving in our direction.
"Thump Thump...................Thump Thump................Thump Thump!"

The quicker we ran, the quicker the coffin began to follow us.
"Thump Thump...........Thump Thump............Thump Thump!"

Once we made it to the rectory, we ran inside and locked the doors.
"Thump Thump....Thump Thump....Thump Thump!"

And, the coffin smashed right through the wooden door.

"Thump Thump....Thump Thump!

So, we ran up the stairs.....
    And the coffin followed us.
      "Thump Thump!"

We ran into my bedroom.....
    And the coffin followed us.
      "Thump Thump!"

We ran into the bathroom....
    And the coffin followed us.
      "Thump Thump!"

So, I opened the medicine cabinet,
    hoping to find something to throw at the coffin.

But all I could find was a bottle of Robitussin.
    "Thump Thump!"

So, in horror, I tossed the bottle at the coffin......
    "Thump!"

And, would you believe
    (just hold ya' breath for this one)

The Coffin Stopped

You know why?....
    Because.....Robitussin can always stop a "Coffin Attack!"[105]

---

[105]It's OK to laugh out loud! Don't act like you didn't see that
one coming!

Shall We Gather at the River

As Father John was completing his homily on temperance,
    he concluded by saying,
        "If I had all the beer in the world, I'd take it and throw it into the river."

With even greater enthusiasm, he said,
"And if I had all the wine in the world, I'd take it and throw it into the river."

And then finally, he said,
"And if I had all the whiskey in the world, I'd take it and throw it into the river."

As he sat down, the Choir Director stood very cautiously
    and announced with a smile,
"Today, our closing song will be number #316: 'Shall We Gather at the River.'"

The Army of the Lord

While welcoming visitors to church, Fr. Joseph noticed a unfamiliar young man entering the church. Shaking his hand, Fr. Joseph told him, "Son, you ought to join the Army of the Lord."

To which the young man replied, "I did, Father, but I'm in the Secret Service!"

Illness and Fatigue

While greeting folks after Mass, Father Tony was asked by one of the parishioners, "Why did they move you from your old parish?"

"I was moved because of illness and fatigue," he replied.

"Illness and fatigue?," the parishioner continued.
    "What do you mean you were moved because of illness and fatigue?"

To which Fr. Tony replied, "They were sick of me and I was tired of them!"

SECTION FIVE
Church Folks Jokes

Jesus said to Simon,
"You are Peter,
and upon this rock
I will build
my Church."

Matthew 16:18

The Pope, Billy Graham & Oral Roberts

The other day, the Pope, Billy Graham, and Oral Roberts all died at the same time and went straight to Heaven.

When St. Peter greeted these three holy men at the Pearly Gates, he realized that there was a major problem.

"Oh, this is terrible!" explained St. Peter. "All three of you guys have done some great things in the name of the Lord, and all three of you will be entering into Heaven.

But, we never expected you guys to show up at the same time. I don't know how to tell you this. Your mansions are not ready."

Let me see if I can get someone to put you up for the night."

So, St. Peter picked up the phone and called down to Hell.

When the devil answered the phone, St. Peter said, "Hey Lou, it's me Pete and I need a favor. You see, I have three guys up here who are all getting into heaven but their rooms aren't ready."

"Do you think that they could spend the night with you?"

Realizing that he hadn't done anything for the Lord in a very long time, the Devil agreed to house the three Holy Men. So, the Pope, Billy Graham, and Oral Roberts headed down to Hell.

After about two hours, the phone in Heaven began to ring. When St. Peter answered the phone, he realized that it was the Devil that was calling.

"Hey Pete, it's me, Lou. Man, you've got to come get these boys. They're causing all sorts of problems.

"What type of problems are they causing?" St. Peter asked.

"Well," the Devil replied, "The Pope is down here forgiving everybody, Billy Graham is down here trying to save everybody, and Oral Roberts has raised enough money to buy air conditioning."

Boudreaux and Lent

Each Friday night after work,
Boudreaux would fire up his outdoor grill and cook a venison steak.

But, all of Boudreaux's neighbors were Catholic....
And since it was Lent, they were forbidden from eating meat on Friday.

The delicious aroma from the grilled venison steaks was causing such a problem
for the Catholic faithful that they finally talked to their priest.

The Priest came to visit Boudreaux, and suggested that he become a Catholic.
After several classes and much study, Boudreaux was finally ready to become a
Catholic.

During the Easter Vigil Mass,
the priest poured Holy Water over him and baptized him
"In the Name of the Father, and of the Son and of the Holy Spirit."

Then the priest said to Boudreaux,
"You were born a Baptist, and raised a Baptist, but now you are a Catholic."

Boudreaux's neighbors were greatly relieved.

That is - until the following Lent. On the first Friday of Lent, the wonderful
aroma of grilled venison filled the neighborhood.

The Priest was called immediately by the neighbors.

As he rushed into Boudreaux's yard, clutching a rosary
and prepared to scold him, he stopped and watched in amazement.

There stood Boudreaux, clutching a small bottle of holy water
        which he carefully sprinkled over the grilling meat and chanted:

"You wuz born a deer, you wuz raised a deer, but now you is a catfish."

Jesus in the Bar Room

The other day, Jesus walked into a bar room and began to greet all of the patrons.

As Jesus sat at the end of the bar and talked with all of the patrons,
      a man with a bad leg walked into the bar.

The man looked down to the end of the bar and noticed the Lord sitting there.

So, he called the bartender over and said,
      "Hey Bartender, you can't tell me that
      Jesus the Christ is sitting at the end of this bar."

"Yes, that's Him." the bartender replied.
      "He comes here regularly to meet the people."

"Well dude," the man answered,
      "please do me a favor and send Him a beer from me!"

So, the bartender brought the beer down to Jesus.
      Jesus looked up and gave the man a little wave
      and then returned to talking with the patrons.

As Jesus was talking with the folks,
      a man with a humped back walked into the bar room.

"Bartender," he said, "you can't tell me that lil Jesus, Son of Mary and Joseph,
      is down at the end of this bar."

"Yes, that's Jesus." the bartender replied.
      "He comes here all of the time."

"Dude," the man responded, "send Him some whiskey from me."

So, the bartender brought the whiskey down to Jesus.
      Jesus looked up and gave the man a little wave
      and then returned to talking with the patrons.

As Jesus continued His conversation with the people in the bar room,
      a man with a withered hand walked into the bar.

When he looked down to the end of the bar, he called to the bartender.

"Hey bartender," he said, "is that ol' J.C. down at the end of this bar?"

"Yes, that's Him." the bartender replied.
    "He comes here all of the time.
    He'll go anywhere He needs to so that He can meet the people."

"Well dude," the man said, "send Him some bourbon from me!"

So, the bartender brought the bourbon down to Jesus.
    Once again, Jesus looked up and gave the man a little wave
    and then returned to talking with the patrons.

Well, after having a fun time with the people
    and after drinking all of those drinks, Jesus was feeling really good.

He decided that on his way out of the bar room He would do something special
    for the three men whom did something special for Him.

So, He walked up to the guy with the bad leg and He said,
    "My friend, for your kindness to me, you're healed!"
    And with one touch from Jesus, the man's leg was healed.

Jesus walked up to the man with the humped back and said,
    "My friend, for your kindness to me, you're healed!"
    And with one touch from Jesus, the hump went down
    and the man was healed.

Then Jesus walked up to the man with the withered hand and said,
    "My friend, for your kindness to me...."

But, before Jesus could continue,
    the man immediately stopped Jesus and said,

    "Lord, please don't touch me.... I'm on Disability!"

SECTION SIX
Priests & Nuns Jokes

You are a
Priest forever
according to the
order of Melchizedek.

Hebrews 7:17

Sister Mary Theresa
and O'Malley's Tavern

On a very cold day in Boston, Sister Mary Theresa and a young man found themselves knee-deep in snow while waiting for the city bus.

"Sister," the young man said, "it is way too cold for us to stand out here waiting for a bus. Maybe we should go across the street into O'Malley's Tavern. We could sit near the front window and watch for the bus."

"Well son," Sister said, "if you think that's a good idea."

So, they headed across the street and into the tavern.

"You know," Sister said, "it's probably not a good idea for us to sit in the window. People shouldn't drive by a Nun in a bar room. Maybe we should get one of those booths in the back. Then you could just keep checking for the bus."

"That's cool," said the young man.

"Sister, while I'm in here, I think that I'll have a beer." he said. "Do you want something? Can I get you a some hot tea, or hot chocolate or coffee?"

"Well son," sister said softly, "while we're in here, why don't you get me a double shot of vodka but have them put it in a plastic cup. I don't want people to know what I am drinking."

"Alright Sister, if that's what you want." chuckled the young man.

As the young man walked up to the bar, he said to the bartender, "Please give me one beer and a double shot of vodka but put it in a plastic cup."

To which the bartender replied,
"Don't tell me that Sister is back in here again!"

What Do You Want to Be?

Sister Mary Thomas asked her class what they wanted to be when they grow up.

"I want to be a Doctor." little Michael said.

"I want to be a Nurse," little Malinda said.

"I want to be a Prostitute," little Jane said.

"What?!" sister screamed in shock. "Young lady, I'll see you after class!"

After class had ended, Sister Mary Thomas asked Jane,
"What did you say you wanted to be when you grew up?"

"Sister, I said I want to be a prostitute when I grow up." Jane answered.

After a big sigh of relief, Sister said,
"Oh, I thought you said you wanted to be a Protestant!"

The Catholic Church in Las Vegas

Did you know that are more Churches in Las Vegas than casinos?

During Sunday services at the offertory, some worshipers actually contribute casino chips instead of cash. I would guess that some are sharing their winnings while other are hoping to win.

Since the churches get chips from so many different casinos, the diocese now requires the parishes to send all the chips into the Diocesan Finance Office for sorting.

Once sorted into the respective casino chips, a Benedictine Priest takes the chips to each of the casinos and exchanges them for the cash.

Around the diocese, he is officially known as The Chip Monk.

SECTION SEVEN
Family Jokes

"Sirs, what must I do to be saved?"

And they said, "Believe in the Lord Jesus and you and your household will be saved."

So they spoke the Word of the Lord to him and to everyone in his house....then he and all his family were baptized at once.

Act 16:30-33

Two Little Old Ladies

Two senior ladies met for the first time
      since graduating from high school.

One asked the other,
      "You were always so organized in school,
            did you manage to live a well planned life?"

"Oh yes," replied her friend.

      "That's why I've been married four times!"

"Four times?
      Why four times?" asked her friend.

Well, my first marriage was to a millionaire;
      my second marriage was to an actor;
      my third marriage was to a preacher;
and now I'm married to an undertaker."

Her friend asked,
      "What do those marriages have to do with a well planned life?"

To which she replied,
"One for the money,
         two for the show,
            three to get ready,
              and four to go."

Satan's Sister

Not too long ago, a young priest was standing before his congregation and
    preaching in depth about the degrees of sin in their community.

He preached about fornication.
    He preached about abominations.
        He even preached about confrontations.

He was going on and on and on about the numerous sins that were being
committed by the very same folks who looked so pious on Sunday mornings.

Well, right in the middle of his preaching,
    would you believe that Satan, himself, showed up on the Altar.

Satan looked at the Church and let out a great big roar!
    "AAAHHHHHHHHH!!!" he screamed.
    And half of the church's members ran out of the back door.

""AAAHHHHHHHHH!!!" he screamed, again.
And the other half of the church's members ran out of the back door,
    except for one older man seated in the front row.

So, Satan looked at that man and yelled, ""AAAHHHHHHHHH!!!"
    But, the man just looked at him.

So he yelled again, ""AAAHHHHHHHHH!!!"
    And, the man just looked at him.

So, Satan jumped down off of the Altar ran up the man and yelled a third time,
    ""AAAHHHHHHHHH!!!"
    But, the man just looked at him.

Well, being confused, Satan looked at the man and said,
    "Don't you know who I am? It's me, Lucifer.
    You know, the Lord of Darkness. The Prince of Evil.
    Why aren't you scared of me?

To which the man replied, "Why should I be scared of you?"

    "I've been married to your sister for 27 years."

217

Momma, Please Help Me!!!

Please excuse the rough language in the following story.
I would have deleted them, but the story wouldn't be the same.

After enjoying a wonderful celebration of the Sacrament of Matrimony,
a young couple headed out for their honeymoon.

The Bride truly loved her husband.
She wanted to spend the rest of her life with this wonderful man.

After returning from the honeymoon, the bride immediately called her mother.

"Well," said her mother, "so how was the honeymoon?"

"Oh, Momma," the new bride replied,
"the honeymoon was wonderful! So romantic!"

Suddenly, the bride began to cry.
"But, Momma," she sobbed, "as soon as we returned,
John started using these terrible and disgusting words.
He said words that I have never ever heard!
He was using all kinds of four-lettered words!
Momma, please help me! I have to get out of here!" She cried.

"Jill," responded her mother. "You have to calm down. You are married now
and I can't just come get you because he was using four-lettered words!
Anyway, what could he possibly be saying that would be that bad?

"I just can't tell you!" cried the new bride,
"The words are just too horrible for me to say to my Mother!"

I'm too embarrassed, they're just too awful! COME GET ME, PLEASE!!

'Baby Girl," her mother replied, "Just tell me, I can handle almost anything."
"Tell Momma those horrible four-lettered words that he said to you!"

Sobbing, the bride said, "Oh, Momma, he was using words like;
dust, wash, iron, and cook."

"I'll pick you up in twenty minutes," said the mother.

Fulfilling Their Requests

The other day, three men died
    and found themselves standing before the Judgement Seat.

Before God would allow them to enter Heaven, He gave them each a chance
    to come back to earth as anything they wanted.

The first guy said, "Lord, I want to come back as myself,
    but could you make me 100 times smarter than I am now?

    So God made him 100 times smarter.

The second guy said, "Lord, I want to be better than that guy.
    So, could you make me 1000 times smarter than he is?

    So God made him 1000 times smarter.

The last guy decided that he wanted to be the best.
    So he said, "Lord, could you make me better than both of them?
    Would you make me 1,000,000 times smarter than those two guys?"

So God made him a woman!!!

Love is Eternal

An 85-year-old couple, after being married for almost 60 years, died in a car crash. They had been in good health, mainly due to the wife's interest in health food and exercising.

When they reached the Pearly Gates, St. Peter took them to their mansion. It was beautifully designed with a spacious kitchen, master bath suite and a Jacuzzi.

As they looked around, the old man asked St. Peter how much all this was going to cost. "It's free," St. Peter replied. "This is Heaven."

Next, they went out in the back yard to survey the championship-style golf course that the home bordered. They would have golfing privileges every day. As an added bonus, each week the course changed to a new one representing the greatest golf courses on earth.

The old man asked, "What are the greens fees?"
St. Peter replied, "This is heaven, you play for free."

Next, they went to the club house and saw the lavish buffet lunch with the cuisines of the world laid out.

"How much to eat?" asked the old man.
"Don't you understand yet? This is Heaven. It is free!" St. Peter replied.

"Well, where are the low fat and low cholesterol tables?" the old man asked.

St. Peter lectured, "That's the best part about being in Heaven. Here you can eat as much as you like of whatever you like and you'll never get fat and you'll never get sick either. This is, after all, Heaven."

With that, the old man went into a fit of anger, throwing down his hat and stomping around the room. His wife did her best to calm him down. Once he was calm, she asked him what was wrong.

"This is all your fault," he said.

"If it weren't for all your bran muffins and stupid vitamins, I could have been here ten years ago!"

SECTION EIGHT
Children Jokes

I give you praise,
Father, Lord of Heaven
and Earth,
for although you have
hidden these things
from the wise
and the learned
you have revealed
them to the childlike.

Luke 10:21

Father Tony and the Pre-K Kids

Back in March, Father Tony was walking across the school yard, heading into the building to meet with the principal. As he crossed the yard, the Pre-Kindergarten kids were out on the yard playing kickball.

You should know that whenever Father Tony walked into the school yard, everything seemed to come to a halt. This kids loved him so much that they always stopped what they were doing, waved to him and said "Hello."

Well, as he walked into the yard, the Pre-K kids got really excited. They stopped their game and began to wave and yell.

"Hey Father Tony!" "Hey Father Tony!"

One of the kids knew that she was supposed to say something in front of Tony, but she couldn't remember what to say. So, she yelled out, "Hey Uncle Tony!"

Then, all of the kids ran up to him to give him those "4-year-old, unconditional love hugs!" But as they hugged him, he noticed a little girl who simply stood in the back of the crowd and waved. She quietly said to him, "Hey Father Tony."

Although it was a little confusing to him, Father Tony simply waved back and said, "Hello."

After he completed his meeting with the principal, he headed back through the school yard on way to the rectory. As he stepped into the yard, the entire scene repeated itself.

"Hey Father Tony!" "Hey Father Tony!" "Hey Uncle Tony!"

The kids all ran over, again, and gave him those hugs.

But, the same little girl stood at the back of the crowd and only said, "Hey Father Tony."

Being curious, Father Tony approached the little girl, knelt down and said to her, "Now baby, you are usually one of the first to run up, hug me and say 'Hello'. Why didn't you hug me today?"

"Because I gave you up for Lent!" she said.

The Collar

The other day, Father Mike was walking to the school when a group of young students came running towards him. After stopping to greet each of them, Father Mike asked them if they had any questions for him.

Little Johnny, the youngest one in the group, raised his hand and asked,
"Why do you priests dress so funny?
You look like you have your shirt on backwards."

Father Mike explained to the kids that his Roman Collar was a part of his uniform and that all priests were supposed to wear their uniform when they were doing priestly stuff.

Just like students wear school uniforms, priests wear uniforms that let everyone know that they are priests.

"But, why does it look so funny? And, what's that silly thing on your neck?" Johnny asked.

Becoming a little perturbed by the boy's senseless questioning, tried to flip the script. So, he tarted to ask Johnny some questions.

"How old are you?" the priest asked.

"I'm 5." Johnny said.

"Do you know how to read?" the priest asked.

"Yes, do know how to read!" Johnny snapped back.

The priest took off his collar and handed it to Johnny. On the back of the collar's white tab were raised letters that list the name of the manufacturer.

"Well, Mr. Smarty-Pants," the priest said, "tell me what these letters say."

Looking intently at the letters Johnny said,
"Kills ticks and fleas for up to six months!"

223

To Be Like Jesus

One day, Denzel walked into the family room and asked his Father,
    "Dad, when will I get my own car? I really want a Jeep!"

His Father told him,
    "I don't know when you'll get a Jeep.

    First, your hair is too long.
        Second, your grades are too low.
        And third, you haven't been going to Mass on a regular basis.

    So, until I see some changes in your behavior,
        you can stop hoping to get your own vehicle."

A little perturbed, Denzel decided that he would try to show his Father that he was a changing man. So, he picked-up the Family Bible and headed to his room.

A few hours later, he returned to the Family Room
    to discuss with his Father all that he had read.

"Dad," he said, "I've been reading the Bible and I have decided that
    want to be just like Jesus! I am hoping that if I can be like Jesus,
    you will finally get me my Jeep!"

His Father was elated to hear his son's new revelation.
    And he promised that if his son would be like Jesus,
    he would indeed get a new car.

"Good," Denzel replied, "because I read in the Good Book, that
    Jesus had long hair,
    He hung out with His friends
    and they often had wine to drink!

So, I want to be just like Him!
    If it was good enough for Jesus, then it's good enough for me!"

To which his Father quickly responded,
    "And Jesus also walked everywhere He went!"

    'So Son, you be like Jesus!"

SECTION NINE
Animal Jokes

God made all kinds of
wild animals,
all kinds of cattle,
and all kinds of
creeping things
of the Earth.

God saw
how good it was.

Genesis 1:24-25

Jesus Is Watching You

Late one night, a burglar broke into a house that he thought was empty.

As he tiptoed through the living room, he suddenly froze in his tracks when he heard a loud voice say, "Jesus is watching you!"

As silence returned to the house, the burglar crept forward again.

"Jesus is watching you," the voice boomed, again.

The burglar stopped dead, again.

He was frightened.

Frantically, he looked all around.

In a dark corner, he spotted a bird cage and in the cage was a parrot.

So, he asked the parrot, "Was that you who said Jesus is watching me?"

"Yes,' said the parrot.

The burglar breathed a sigh of relief and asked the parrot, "What's your name?"

"Clarence," said the bird.

"That's a dumb name for a parrot," sneered the burglar.

"What idiot would name a bird, 'Clarence?"

The parrot replied, "The same idiot who named his Rottweiler 'Jesus.'"

Taking Some Penguins to the Zoo

The other day, a man named Kevin was on his job as a city bus driver.

As he drove down the street towards the city's zoo,
    he noticed a large truck that was stranded in the middle of the street.

Being the helpful Christian man that he is,
    Kevin stopped his bus and asked the truck driver if he needed any help.

The truck driver explained that inside his refrigerated truck,
    he had a shipment of penguins that needed to be taken to the zoo.

He asked Kevin if he would be willing to take the penguins to the zoo on the bus.

Initially, the bus driver refused.
    He explained that he knew nothing about transporting penguins.

The truck driver told him that he would give him $100
    if he would be willing to take the penguins to the zoo.

Right away, Kevin agreed to the deal.

So, the truck driver opened back of his truck and together,
    he and Kevin escorted all of the little penguins on to the bus.

Once they were all in their seats and their seatbelts were fastened,
    the bus driver drove towards the zoo.

About two hours later,
    the truck driver saw the bus headed back in the opposite direction.
    It was still loaded with all of the penguins.

After flagging the bus down, he yelled to the bus driver,
"Hey buddy, I thought that I gave you $100 to take these penguins to the zoo."

"You did," Kevin yelled back.
    'We had money left over. So, now we are headed to the movies!"

The Donkey Sale

A priest was trying to sell a donkey. With the economic recession and depression, it is really hard to sell donkeys in this modern age.

After waiting for a day,
> the priest finally found a young man who was willing to buy his donkey.

Once they agreed on the price, the priest said to the young man,
> "Son, before I let you leave with the donkey,
> I have to tell you that donkey had been trained in a very unique way.

> "Instead of using the usual words, like 'getty up' or 'whoa,'
> I used church words to tell the donkey when to go and when to stop.

> So, only way to make the donkey go, is to say, 'HALLELUJAH!.'
> the way to make him stop, is to say, 'AMEN!'"

The young man thought to himself, that's pretty cool.
> It won't be bad to have a religious donkey around the farm.

So, he paid the priest for the donkey
> and immediately got on the animal to try out the preacher's instructions.

"HALLELUJAH!," shouted the man and the donkey started walking.

> "AMEN!,"shouted the man and the donkey stopped.

"HALLELUJAH!," the man shouted again.
> And once again, the donkey started walking.

> "AMEN!,"he shouted and the donkey stopped.

He decided that he would really test out his new religious donkey.

So, he took his donkey to the foot of the mountain,
> climbed on its back and yelled out, "HALLELUJAH!."

The donkey started walking.

Again, he yelled, "HALLELUJAH!"

The donkey started to trott.

"HALLELUJAH!"

The donkey started to run.

Soon, the man realized that he was coming close to the edge of the cliff.

But, the problem was he had forgotten what he was supposed to say to make the donkey stop.

He remembered that it was a church word.

So, he began to yell out anything he could remember.

'Pew!"
"Usher!"
"Candle!"

'Celibacy!" (Everything stops with celibacy!)

As he drew close to the cliff's edge, the guy started to pray.

'Lord, I am your humble servant.
I bought this donkey because I wanted to help the priest.
I can't remember what I'm supposed to say.
But, I know that you know.
I know that you will help me!

In Jesus name, I pray. Amen!"

And, the donkey stopped just at the edge of the cliff!

The young man got so excited that he yelled out, "HALLELUJAH!"

SECTION TEN
Football Jokes

Give thanks to
the LORD
who is good,
whose love
endures forever!

Psalm 107:1

Congratulation to the
New Orleans Saints -
Super Bowl XLIV
Champions
February 7, 2010

A Ticket to the Super Bowl

The other day, a football fan bought a ticket to see the New Orleans Saints play in the Super Bowl. Although he was excited that the Saints were finally playing in the NFL's Championship Game, he was a bit disappointed that his seat was at top of the stadium. It was so high that he could barely see the field.

During the 1st quarter of the game, he noticed a vacant seat down on the third row of the bottom section. It was right in the middle, on the 50-yard line!

So, he watched the seat for that whole quarter. He thought to himself, if no one sits there by the end of this quarter, I am going down to claim that seat.

When the 2nd quarter started, no one had come to claim the seat. So, he walked down from his nose-bleed seat and headed to the bottom section of the stadium. As he got close to the empty seat, he noticed an older gentleman sitting in the seat that was adjacent to the vacant one.

"Excuse me sir," he said to the older man, "is anyone sitting in that seat?"

"No, Son, come on in," the man replied. "Have a seat."

A few minutes later, the Saints fan asked the older gentleman if he knew to whom the seat belonged and why they weren't here at such an important game.

The man explained that he and his wife had been New Orleans Saints Fans since the team came to New Orleans. Each year they promised one another that if the Saints ever made it to the Super Bowl, they would buy tickets for the game.

He went on to explain that a few days ago, his poor wife passed away.

Feeling sorry for the nice man, the young man if he didn't have a child, a friend or even a family member that could have come to the game with him.

The man said, "No Son, they're all at the funeral."

Antagonizing the Nuns

Sister Angela and Sister Greta were at the New Orleans Saints football game and having a great time pulling for their favorite team.

Seated behind them were three young men who decided to mess with the two Nuns. The men were hoping to get the Nuns to move another section so that they could be free to rant and rave or fuss and cuss during the game.

(They could only imagine what would happen to them
if they cussed in front of the Nuns.
They probably had flashbacks to
bars of soap in the principal's office.)

They thought that if they could antagonize the Nuns,
the two Sisters would decide to move.

So, one of the men said loudly to his friends,
"I think I want to move to California.
I heard that there are only 100 Catholics living there...."

The second guy said in reply, "Well, I want to move to Washington.
I believe that there are only 50 Catholics living there...."

The third guy said, "I want to move to Idaho.
I read that there are only 25 Catholics living there...."

One of the nuns turns around and sternly said to the three guys,

"Why don't you go to Hell?
There aren't any Catholics living there."

Safe Haven

There once was a young boy who was taken from his home because he was being physically abused. But, after being in the orphanage for a few weeks, he went to his social worker and told her that he wanted to leave. So, the social worker asked him, "Well, do you want to go back and live with your father, again?"

"No," said, the little boy. "He beats me."

So, the social worker asked, "Do you want to live with your mother?"
    To which the little boy replied, "No, she beats me too."

"Well, then," asked the social worker,
        "If you don't want to live with your father and you don't want to live with your mother, then who do you want to live with?"

And, the little boy answered, "The New Orleans Saints."

"The Saints?" responded the social worker.
        "Why do you want to live with the New Orleans Saints?"

"Because," replied the little boy, "They don't beat anybody."

Three Old Football Fans

Three old football fans were in a church, praying for their teams. The first one asks, "Oh Lord, when will the Dallas Cowboys win another Superbowl?"

God replies, "In the next five years." "But I'll be dead by then," says the man.

The second one asks,
        "Oh Lord, when will the Atlanta Falcons win the Superbowl?"

God answers, "In the next ten years." "But I'll be dead by then," says the man.

The third one asks,
        "Oh Lord, when will the *New Orleans Saints* win the Superbowl?"

And, God answers, "I'll be dead by then!"

233

Book Five

Reflections on Faith, Hope and Forgiveness

Rev. R. Tony Ricard, M.Th., M.Div.

Published in 2011

Introduction to "Keepin' it Real"

Recently, I asked three Seminarians "What does *Keepin' It Real* mean to you?"

"Keepin' It Real means living an authentic life with God at its core.
You recognize those around you as deserving of your love.
You respect them because they are the Children of God.
If one wants to truly keep it real then you will do all you can to know God,
love God, and serve God so that you will be happy with Him in the next world.
Faithfully living out our Christian destiny is *Keepin' It Real*."
- **Daniel H. Green, Seminarian - Archdiocese of New Orleans**

"Keepin' It Real means living in the truth of whom we really are.
This implies that we must get rid of any masks that we may wear to fit in
and be who God created us to be. We are not simply sinners.
We are God's Beloved Children who are called to be Saints!"
- **Josh Johnson, Seminarian - Diocese of Baton Rouge**

"To me *Keepin' It Real* does not simply mean accepting life as it is.
In actuality, it means staying truthful to myself and to my core beliefs.
This truth is rooted in the teaching of our Lord who is my best friend in life.
Keepin' It Real is not always easy
but as it is more important than always being popular."
- **Dennis Caughlin, Seminarian - Archdiocese of New Orleans**

As Seminarians, these three young men are showing the world that they are
Keepin' It Real. They are responding to God's offer of Love and discerning
where God needs them to live out their Call. The only way that they can truly be
authentic Followers of Christ is make sure that they are *Keepin' It Real*.

Just as these three Seminarians have beautifully pointed out, we must stay true to
whom we are in the Eyes of God. The first section centers on being people of
Faith in times of trouble. Although we often feel lost in this world, we know that
God is always by our side. The second section focuses on the gift of Hope which
the Love of the Holy Spirit brings. Even in our darkest hour, we know that the
Lamb of God will lead us to a better day. The third section focuses on our power
of Forgiveness. Although we may never forget hurtful times, we can find
freedom in deciding to forgive.

Through the Love of God, may your life always be one that is *Keepin' It Real*.

Rev. R. Tony Ricard, M.Th., M.Div.

SECTION ONE
Reflections on Faith

Mama Stasia - Fr. Tony's Grandmother

Anestasia Bernadette Carlin Honore'
(Michelle Boutte' - Great-Granddaughter)

**The Faith of Our Ancestors and Elders guides us
on the pathway to Heaven.**

Developing the Faith of a Fool
Truly Keepin' It Real

I was sitting in my office when one of our long-time parishioners came in. As she sat in the chair near my desk, she suddenly burst into tears.

"Miss Lilly, what's wrong?" I asked.

"Well, Father," she sobbed, "I was down at the other church and they refused to bury my Beloved Eddie."

"What do you mean, they refused to bury your Beloved Eddie?" I asked.

"You see, Father," she continued,
    "Eddie and I had been together for almost fifteen years.
    Wherever I'd go, Eddie was by my side.
        If I went to the bank, Eddie was there.
        If I went to the grocery store, Eddie was with me.
        Even when I went to the bathroom,
    Eddie would wait outside of the door until I came out."

    But, for the last few days, whenever I'd put water in his dish,
    he wouldn't drink."

"What do you mean, you'd put water in his dish?" I asked.

"O' Father, Eddie was my dog," she replied.

"I'm sorry, Miss Lilly, but we don't bury dogs." I responded.

Well Father," she began to say, "I was thinking that I would give $10,000 to the priest who would bury my dog."

To which I replied, "Why didn't you tell me that he was a Catholic?"

Why are you so crazy?

That was the question that my former secretary Brenda would always asked me.

Why are you so crazy?

I'm guessing that many folks that have been around me, seen me in action or heard me talk have also asked that very same question.

Why is that boy so crazy?
    Or why is he such a fool?

Well, my goal is to help you and at some level answer that very question.

Through this reflection, I am hoping that you will have a better understanding of what it takes to be a fool.

Not a fool before God, but a Fool for God.

What does it mean to have the Faith of a Fool?

In St. Paul's First Letter to the Corinthians he tells us,

> *"Consider your own calling, brothers and sisters.*
>
> *Not many of you were wise by human standards, not many were powerful, not many were of noble birth.*
>
> *Rather, God chose the foolish of the world to shame the wise, and God chose the weak of the world to shame the strong, and God chose the lowly and despised of the world, those who count for nothing, to reduce to nothing those who are something, so that no human being might boast before God."*[106]

What does it mean to be a Fool?

It means understanding that only what we do for Christ will last.

It means understanding that "If God is for us, who can be against?"

---

[106] 1st Corinthians 1:26-29

It means that "what might seem foolish in the eyes of man may one day be deemed as wise in the eyes of God."

What does it mean to be a Fool for the Lord?

It means that you are willing to commit yourself to the service of God even when others may think that you are crazy!

"God chose the foolish of the world to shame the wise!"

A true fool looks at the world and rejoices because he knows that there's more to life than what this world offers.

So, what does it mean to be a Fool for the Lord?

It means not taking yourself so seriously.

A fool knows that life is meant to be lived. It is meant to be enjoyed. It is meant to bring us happiness. Life is too short for us to be miserable. That means that each day, we need to find something to laugh at, someone to laugh with, and something to help relieve our minds.

We all need to be Fools.

But, we don't need to be foolish fools! Rather, we need to be faithful fools!

A foolish fool doesn't understand what is real.
A foolish fool doesn't understand that life isn't always easy.
A foolish fool doesn't see the reality that lies before him or her.
Because a foolish fool tries to smother the pains of his heart
        behind a facade of joy. But, deep inside, the pain is still there.

Back in 1965, Smokey Robinson said it best in his song The Tracks of my Tears;

"People say I'm the life of the party
        because I tell a joke or two.
Although I might be laughing loud and hearty,
        deep inside I'm blue.
So, take a good look at my face.
        You'll see my smile looks out of place.
If you look closer, it's easy to trace
        the tracks of my tears."

But, if your joy is only momentary; if your joy is only on the outside, then your joy is foolish. And, you are not the kind of fool that St. Paul calls us to be. You are simply a foolish fool rather than a faithful fool.

So, how can one be a Fool without becoming a foolish fool?

Well, one must become a Faithful Fool!
    You need to be a Fool for the Lord.

If God really chooses the Foolish of the world to shame the wise, then to be deemed foolish in the eyes of Man is to truly answer your call from God.

To be a Fool for the Lord, you have to be willing to live by a code of ethics and values that this world will scoff at. You have to be willing to sacrifice for the sake of others. You have to be willing to challenge both the traditional and conventional wisdom of man. You have to be willing to be counter-cultural. When others might want to give up, you have to be willing to stand firm and have faith!

A Faithful Fool relies not on the wisdom of Man but solely on the Wisdom of God.

I know that "Fools rush in where angels fear to tread!"[107] But, sometimes you just have to rush in! I believe that it is better to die the courageous death of a Fool than to live the cowardly life of a King!

When you act counter-cultural, you will be called a fool and will find yourself being ridiculed by man. Yet, sometimes God is calling you to do that very thing. It takes courage to be a fool. It's not easy to always be joyful! But, it sure is worth it.

To be a Faithful Fool, you have to risk failure and loss. Not everything will work out the way that you hoped. But, that's OK.

"It's better to have loved and lost than to have never loved at all."[108] You just have to have the courage of a Faithful and Loving Fool. Taking that risk is way better than selling your soul or not using your common sense just to fit in.

---

[107]"An Essay on Criticism" by Alexander Pope

[108]"In Memoriam: 27" by Alfred Lord Tennyson

So, don't allow the ways of man to get you to go against what your heart is telling you to do. If it doesn't feel right, then it's probably not right.

We all know that No man is always right. Everybody makes mistakes. Everybody is wrong on something. That means that you too must realize that you are not always going to be right, either. That's why we have to rely on the Holy Spirit to give us the wisdom to make the right decisions. We also have to rely on the wisdom of our Ancestors and our Elders. We don't have to cut a new path through the forest of life, we simply need to follow the path that has already been cut for us by those who sacrificed their lives so that we could be here today.

Many of the Saints of God would be considered Fools, today.

Men like St. Dominic and St. Francis were considered fools in their days. They walked away from riches to live a life of poverty and to take care of the needy. Women like St. Katherine Drexel, SBS, and Venerable Henriette DeLille, SSF, were considered fools in their times. They not only walked away from wealth and prestige, they took what money they did have and began ministries that were dedicated to Colored Folks. Now, that was indeed foolish according to the world. Yet, in their foolishness, they became instruments of God's love.[109]

Like them, we must be true to the ideals of faith, hope and love.

As Servant of God, Mother Henriette would say, *"I believe in God. I hope in God. I love. I want to live and die for God."*[110] Anyone who would live by that principle has got to be a Fool.

Being a Fool who wants to live and die for God means that we may be the instruments of God's Love here on Earth! We have to be willing to stand up for the inherit-dignity of all people! We must defend the dignity of the unborn, the poor, the homeless and the hungry. But, we must also defend the inherit-dignity of the rich, the sinful and the criminal.

---

[109]St. Francis of Assisi founded the Order of Friars Minor - The Franciscans. St. Dominic founded the Order of Preachers - The Dominicans. St. Katherine Drexel, SBS, founded the Sisters of the Blessed Sacrament. Venerable Henriette Delille, SSF, founded the Sisters of the Holy Family.

[110]Mother Henriette Delille was born in New Orleans in 1812. This is her only recorded writing. It was written on the inside cover of an 1836 prayer book. www.henriettedelille.com

241

If we believe that everyone is precious in the Eyes of God, we must realize that even those we might despise are still the Children of God. We may not like the things that they do. But, does that make them any less in the Eyes of God than we are?

Their actions may be sinful, but, they still must be seen as God's Children. Maybe by treating them as God's Children we can invite them back into the fold of His family.

It's easy for us to look at the homeless and say that they need our help. It's easy for us to say, "let's defend the unborn" because they cannot defend themselves. It's easy for us to look at the less fortunate and say, "those are the ones who need us" because indeed that is true.

But, a Faithful Fool also knows that they are not the only ones who need us. The rich man and the sinners need God, too.

So, we shouldn't discriminate on whom we should offer God's unconditional love. A Faithful Fool will find a way to love everybody even when you might not like the things they may do.

The Life of a Faithful Fool follows the pathway of Christ.

To help you better understand how to truly be the Fool that God needs you to be, I've come up with a list of four things that I believe must be in the make up of a Fool for the Lord!

A Faithful Fool must be:

1. Loving

2. Caring

3. Giving

4. Forgiving

To be a Loving Fool means that we love with the Heart of Christ. We must love when it is fun and when it hurts. Christ calls us to love everybody, but he doesn't say that I have to like you. You see, *Love* is eternal but *Like* is momentary.

To be a Caring Fool, we have to have a heart that can sympathize and empathize with others. To sympathize is to feel for someone. But, to empathize is to actually share their pain. Our love and concern must be manifested in our action even when our actions may seem foolish in the eyes of man.

I once heard a story about a little boy whose actions showed the world how to care. This four-year old child had a next door neighbor who had recently lost his wife. When the young boy heard the man crying, he walked over to his house climbed onto his lap, and just sat there.

When his mother asked him what he had said to the neighbor, the little boy simply replied, "Nothing, I just helped him cry."

Sometimes, we just need somebody to help us cry. Maybe whatever is wrong can't be fixed, and we just need a good cry!

To be a Giving Fool, we have to be willing to sacrifice the riches of this world for the sake of helping someone out. Francis did it. Dominic did it. Katherine and Henriette did it, too. We don't have to do it on a grand scale. We just have to do what we can. Blessed Teresa of Calcutta once said, "In this life, we cannot do great things. We can only do small things with great love!" Do your small things with great love and you will indeed be on the pathway to becoming a true Fool for the Lord.

To be a Forgiving Fool, you have to be willing to let go of past hurts.

Yeah, it was painful.

Yeah, you have the right to never talk to them, again.

Yeah, it wouldn't be bad if they burned in Hell!

But, you have to let that be up to God.

We have to forgive as Christ has forgiven us!

You see, none of us are perfect. Thus, we can't expect others to be perfect.

We are flawed by the stain of original sin. But, we can overcome that flaw if we are willing to love with the Heart of Christ. We have to be able to forgive. Plus, when we forgive, we actually turn the tables on the very person or persons who have hurt us.

I know that it really messes with folks minds when you walk into a room, greet them with a hug or a kiss even though "they know that you know" what they were saying or doing behind your back!

Don't give them the satisfaction of turning you into a hateful person like them. We don't have time for that foolishness!

To be a true Fool for the Lord, you have to be Loving, Caring, Giving and Forgiving! In that way, God can use you to shame the wise.

Some people don't understand how I deal with all the trials and tribulations of my life and still remain happy. They don't understand that I am a natural fool and I ain't ashamed to proclaim it!

Because, A Natural Fool or a True Fool for the Lord is really touched by God! And, if you really know that the Hands of God are on you, nothing in this world could prevail against you.

At the end of the Beatitudes, presented to us in Gospel of our Brother Matthew, Jesus tells us, not to worry about what others may be saying. As long as we are doing the work of God, just let them call us fools.

In Matthew 5:11-12, we hear,

> *"Blessed are you when they insult you and persecute you and*
> *utter every kind of evil against you (falsely) because of Me.*
> *Rejoice and be Glad, for your reward will be great in heaven.*
> *Thus they persecuted the prophets who were before you."*

In other words, let them call you a Fool! You ain't the First Fool for the Lord and you won't be the last!

The Prophets were considered fools!

The Apostles were called fools.

The Early Church Fathers were fools.

All of the Saints were Fools, too.

So, if we must be considered Fools, at least we know that we're in good company!

Just as *Uncle Sam needs You* to join our nation's army
      and help bring peace and freedom to the World,
The Lord needs YOU to join His Righteous Army
      and become the Fool that God calls you to be.

On this day, may God give you the faith and courage to simply be a Faithful Fool!

May you be willing to put aside childish things and focus on the ways of God and not the ways of men!

May you be a true Fool for the Lord, who understands that only by Loving, Caring, Giving and Forgiving can you truly receive all the blessings that God has promised you!

In Christ, God chooses the foolish of the world to shame the wise. God chooses the weak of the world to shame the strong, and God chooses the lowly and despised of the world, those whom the world thinks are nothing, to reduce to nothing, those who think they are something. So that no one might boast before God.

On this day, may you realize that the only way that you can get into heaven is to be a Fool for the Lord!

Better that they ask, "Why are you so crazy?" and "Who does this fool think he is?" than to be standing before the Judgement Seat and hear the Lord ask, "Who is this fool?"

On a very cold day in Boston, Sister Mary Theresa and a young man found themselves knee-deep in snow while waiting for the city bus.

"Sister," the young man said, "it is way too cold for us to stand out here waiting for a bus. Maybe we should go across the street into O'Malley's Tavern. We could sit near the front window and watch for the bus."

"Well, son," Sister said, "if you think that's a good idea."

So, they headed across the street and into the tavern.

"You know," Sister said, "it's probably not a good idea for us to sit by the window. People shouldn't drive by and see a Nun in a bar. Maybe we should get one of those booths in the back. Then you could just keep checking for the bus."

"That's cool," said the young man.

"Sister, while I'm in here, I think that I'll have a beer," he said. "Do you want something? Can I get you some hot tea, or hot chocolate or coffee?"

"Well, son," Sister said softly, "while we're in here, why don't you get me a double shot of vodka but have them put it in a plastic cup. I don't want people to know what I am drinking."

"All right, Sister, if that's what you want," chuckled the young man.

As the young man walked up to the bar, he said to the bartender, "Please give me one beer and a double shot of vodka but put it in a plastic cup."

To which the bartender replied, "Don't tell me that Sister is back in here, again!"

Today, may you truly be a Fool for the Lord!

Amen!

Momma Stasia
"I Ain't Let Go Yet"

As a child, I was blessed to be raised in a very loving home. My parents worked hard to provide a safe environment for their children where we knew we were loved. Although we may not have had all the luxuries that we would have desired, the one thing that we had plenty of was love.

Although we had no doubt that our Mom and Dad loved us, they were not the greatest source of love in our house. You see, we were blessed to have living with us our maternal grandmother, Anestasia Bernadette Carlin Honore'. And, "Mama Stasia" was indeed a powerful source of pure love. For us, she was the truest example of genuine and unconditional love.

"Mama Stasia" did not have the easiest life in the world but she lived it to the best of her ability. She remained a woman of love even though as a young mother, she had to bury her first born son. He died in a household accident when he was only two years old. She remained a woman of love even though she basically had to raise seven children on her own after a tough divorce from my grandfather. She remained a woman of love even though she often went to bed hungry not knowing from where the family's next meal would come.

Regardless of what life put before her, she remained a woman of love because through it all, she never doubted that God would provide.

Back In 1962, my momma and my sister Deidra left New Orleans to join my father in Munich, West Germany. Back then, my father was serving in the United States Army. Upon their return in March of 1965, they were not only carrying my sister with them. They also were carrying my brother Kevin and the child that would be the crowning point of their creative work (me).

Not many years before my grandmother moved to Heaven, she told me about the very first day that my family arrived back in New Orleans.

On that day, she said, "I saw my skinny daughter get off that bus with her bags and her babies in tow. In her arm, she had this sickly lil' boy. And, when she got off that bus, she put him in my arms, and, 'I ain't let go yet.'"

I am proud to say, that I was that little baby that my momma handed to Mama Stasia. It was my grandmother's loving grip that began on that cold day in 1965 which got me through the tough times of childhood and adolescence.

It was that grip that brought me to church every Sunday. And, it was that grip that helped me to love Jesus so much that I would dedicate my entire life to his service. Indeed, that loving grip helped to change a sickly lil' baby into a devoted man of God.

Back in October of 1988, my grandmother's grip was changed forever. It was in that month that the center of my life suffered a massive stroke.

As they rolled her out of the house, all she could do was hold her eyes open. She could not move any part of her body. As we rushed her to Humana Hospital, All I could think of was how was I going to make it in this world without her.

I prayed to God asking for a miracle. But in my heart, I really wasn't expecting one.

As my family gathered in the waiting room, the doctors worked diligently to try and reveres the damages that the stroke had caused. As we waited, we feared that we would no longer have her with us. As we took turns going back and forth into the emergency room to be with her, we all knew that this could be the day when God would call her home.

Around noon, Fr. Howard Byrd, from St. Augustine High School arrived to celebrate the Sacrament of the Anointing of the Sick. I went back with him and watched as he prayed over her and anointed her with the Oils of the Sick. While he was anointing her, I was still praying for a miracle. I didn't know if a miracle was God's plans, but I surely was hoping to get one if it was.

As we walked out of that emergency room, Fr. Byrd looked at me and said, "You know, she's gonna be all right." Although I appreciated his kind words, I assure you I was not as confident as he was.

For another hour or so, we all continued to take turns going back into the emergency room and keeping vigil. We never wanted her to be back there alone.

As I sat next to her stretcher, I kept assuring her that she was gonna be all right. I could see in her eyes that she was somewhat alert and probably scared. So, I just kept telling her that everybody was praying hard for her.

As I sat back there, afraid of what the future might hold without her, the miracle that "we all had been waiting for" happened. She looked up at me and simply said, "Baby, where's your Momma at?"

I can't tell y'all how much it meant to me to here her speak. Needless to say, I ran out of that room, grabbed my Momma and said, "Your Momma just asked for you."

Right before our eyes, the healing that is promised in the Sacrament of the Anointing of the Sick was taking place. Right before our eyes, we were witnessing "our family's greatest miracle."

While reading the Gospel of our Brother Mark, I can a cross a story that reminded me of that glorious yet scary day at Humana Hospital.

In Mark, we read,

> On leaving the synagogue Jesus entered the house of Simon and Andrew with James and John. Simon's mother-in-law lay sick with a fever. They immediately told him about her.
>
> He approached, grasped her hand, and helped her up. Then the fever left her and she waited on them.[111]

I can't help but think that after grasping her hand, Jesus turn to Peter and said, "You know, she's gonna be all right." She had to be all right, she was holding the hand of the Savior. It can't get any better than that.

How many times in our lives have we found ourselves dealing with illness and longing for the healing touch of God?

How many times have we found ourselves sitting in Hospital waiting rooms and praying for a miracle?

How many times have we hoped that we or someone we love would "just be all right"?

Part of our Journey of Faith is being able to come before our Father and ask for healing miracles.

It's no secret that the world is in need of a healing. The body that we call Earth is racked with the diseases of war and terror. Now, more than ever, we need the Healing Miracle of Peace to come upon the world.

---

[111]Mark 1:29-31

We need God's healing hands to reach down and still the pains and heartaches caused by men and women who control the various nations of this planet. We need God to heal our divisions so that we can indeed receive the Miracles that He is trying to send us.

In our nation, we know that we need a healing. Although the election of President Barack Obama did begin the process of healing many prejudicial wounds. It was also a sign that we are still a hurting nation. The Presidency of Barack Obama has revealed to our nation that the wounds of slavery and segregation have not been completely healed.

The election of 2008 removed the bandages that were applied to our pains by the Civil Rights Movement. But, it has revealed that although we are indeed on the road to recovery, we have not yet been completely healed from the pestering infections of racism and discrimination.

In our families, we know that we need a healing. Many of our families have had to endure the wounds caused by addictions, jealousy and betrayals. The wounds of Alcoholism and drug abuse linger for a long time. They not only hurt the addict, they also injure those around them.

The wounds of jealousy, pride and envy divide families in more ways that we would want to admit. For some, the love of money has replaced their love for the family and their love for God. And, anyone who seems to be doing "a little better than them" becomes the reason why they can't succeed. The wounds of jealousy, pride and envy are tough wounds to heal.

Betrayals by those we love have also ripped open wounds in our hearts. We need God to touch the places where adultery, envy and greed have caused us to turn our backs on those we love.

Our children need a healing.

Our families need a healing.

Our city needs a healing.

Our nation needs a healing.

And, Lord knows our world needs a healing.

If only, we could be like Peter and bring Jesus into our homes so that He could reach out and touch the very place where we are hurting the most.

In the Sacrament of the Anointing of the Sick, we do have a chance to call down the Healing Hands of Christ on individuals we love. In this great Sacrament, we ask God, that if it be His will, the person being anointed receive a healing from whatever is hurting them.

I have seen miracles happen because of this great Sacrament. I have seen folks be healed in mind, body and soul. So, I know that it does work.

But, we also have a chance to bring Jesus into our homes through another Sacrament of Love, the Sacrament of the Eucharist. In the Sacrament that we celebrate here on the Altar of Sacrifice, we are touched by the very same Jesus that walked into the home of Peter and touched the hand of Peter's Mother-in-Law. In the Eucharist, Jesus comes to us and offers the very miracle that we all need. And, He offers it out of pure, unconditional love.

On this day, I challenge you to allow Jesus to enter into your heart and heal whatever it is that may be hurting you, your family and all those you love. Allow the unifying Body of Christ to remove the pains of heartache from you lives and bring about the miracle that you have been longing for. Allow Jesus to be Jesus, today.

"Lord, we are not worthy to receive you, but only say they word and wee shall be healed."

Like my Grandmother, each of us is in need of a specific word of healing. Although we are not suffering from a massive stroke, we are suffering from some form of heartache and pain.

Today, Jesus wants to say the word, so that you can be healed. But, before He can say it, your mind, your ears and you heart have to be opened to receive it.

Today, Jesus is walking into your house and offering you the miracle that you need. But, He can't get in if you never open the door.

Back in 1988, my family was blessed with a true miracle of healing. My Grandmother recovered from her stroke and was with us for another year before she finally moved home to Heaven. Although she's no longer physically with us down here, I know that she's walking the journey of faith with all of her children, and especially me, her baby's baby.

When my Momma and Daddy got off that bus, she said that they put this sickly lil' boy in my arms, and, "I ain't let go yet."

Bless Us O' Lord
Faith in Public

In my first assignment as a priest, at St. Rita's Parish, New Orleans, I met a young man named Steve. For many years, Steve and I traveled across the country speaking at national and diocesan youth conferences. We also presented retreats throughout the south and as far away as South Central Los Angeles. We did a lot together and in the process taught each other some valuable lessons about faith and life.

Some of the lessons that we shared were great and some were small. But, all of the lessons have helped to shape who I am as a priest and who Steve has become as a follower of Christ.

Back when we first started hanging out, Steve taught me something that I have never forgotten. It was a lesson that I love to share with others. In a very real way, its message is important to whom we are as members of the One United Body of Christ.

Back in 1996, during one of the very first times that we shared a meal in a public restaurant, I asked Steve to say, "*Grace.*" He immediately made the Sign of the Cross, and began to pray, "*Bless us O' Lord.......*" When he concluded, he once again made the Sign of the Cross and then we began to eat.

At some point in our meal, we began to talk about how many folks do not say "Grace" before they eat. Even though they may be thankful that God has once again provided a meal, they often forget to say "Thanks to God" for that very meal. Steve pointed out that it's a shame that people don't pray as often as they should, especially at meal time.

While talking about saying "Grace," I commended him on beginning his prayer by making the Sign of the Cross. It was at that point that he shared something profound with me.

He said, "When you are in a restaurant, and you bow your head or hold hands to pray, most of the folks around you will know that you are praying. They will probably assume that you are a Chrsitian and that you are saying 'Grace.' But, when you start by making the Sign of the Cross, not only will they know that you are a Chrsitian, they will also know that you are Catholic. There won't be any doubt as to whom your God is and to what Church you belong. By making the Sign of the Cross in public, people will know that you are committed to Jesus and are a Roman Catholic."

Who would have thought that something so profound could come out the mouth of a 13-year-old boy? This early lesson from Steve illustrates one of the key messages about discipleship and true commitment to the Lord.

True commitment to Jesus Christ means taking a public stance even when others might look at you funny. True commitment to Jesus Christ means taking a public stance even though others might disagree with your faith. True commitment to Jesus Christ means taking a public stance on certain things, even when that public stance might set us apart from other people in our community. True commitment to God means taking risks and accepting challenges. It means making the Sign of the Cross before you say, "*Grace*," when others might not even pray. Even if you might be persecuted for your faith, you still have to stand firm on the Word of God.

The Prophet Jeremiah is a perfect example of one who was persecuted for his commitment to the Lord.

In Book of Jeremiah, we read:

> *"This man ought to be put to death," the princes said to the king; "He demoralizes the soldiers who are left in this city, and all the people, by speaking such things to them; he is not interested in the welfare of our people, but in their ruin."*
> *King Zedekiah answered: "He is in your power"; for the king could do nothing with them. And so they took Jeremiah and threw him into the cistern of Prince Malchiah, which was in the quarters of the guard, letting him down with ropes. There was no water in the cistern, only mud, and Jeremiah sank into the mud.*
>
> *Now Ebed-melech, a Cushite, a courtier in the king's palace, heard that they had put Jeremiah into the cistern. The king happened just then to be at the Gate of Benjamin, and Ebed-melech went there from the palace and said to him, "My lord king, these men have been at fault in all they have done to the prophet Jeremiah, casting him into the cistern. He will die of famine on the spot, for there is no more food in the city."*
>
> *Then the king ordered Ebed-melech the Cushite to take three men along with him, and draw the prophet Jeremiah out of the cistern before he should die.[112]*

---

[112]Jeremiah 38:4-10

Jeremiah was basically condemned to death because he dared to oppose the princes of his region and remain committed to God. Because Jeremiah was willing to preach the *Word of God* in a world that was wreaked with paganism and sin, he was tossed into a well and left to die. Yet God, through the work of Ebed-melech saved him from death. God saved Jeremiah because of his commitment to doing the Will of the Creator.

Many of the early Church Fathers also knew that there will be times when our commitment will cause us to struggle. In the *Letter to the Hebrews*, the author explains that the key to surviving the struggle is found in keeping our eyes fixed on Jesus, who inspires and perfects our faith.

Chapter 12 of the Letter to the Hebrews says,

> *Therefore, since we are surrounded by so great a cloud of witnesses, let us rid ourselves of every burden and sin that clings to us and persevere in running the race that lies before us while keeping our eyes fixed on Jesus, the leader and perfecter of faith.*
>
> *For the sake of the joy that lay before him he endured the cross, despising its shame, and has taken his seat at the right of the throne of God.*[113]

Through constantly keeping Jesus before us, we are given the necessary strength to persevere in running the race which lies ahead: A race that ultimately leads to the Heavenly Kingdom of God.

Sometimes commitment to the service of Christ Jesus may even cause us to oppose our own family.

In the Gospel of our Brother Luke, we hear,

> *"I have come to set the earth on fire, and how I wish it were already blazing!*
>
> *There is a baptism with which I must be baptized, and how great is my anguish until it is accomplished!*
>
> *Do you think that I have come to establish peace on the earth?*

---

[113]Hebrews 12:1-2

No, I tell you, but rather division.

*From now on a household of five will be divided, three against
two and two against three; a father will be divided against his
son and a son against his father, a mother against her daughter
and a daughter against her mother, a mother-in-law against her
daughter-in-law and a daughter-in-law against her mother-in-
law."*[114]

In saying that He has come to *"set a fire on the earth,"* Jesus was describing the
time when the committed followers of Christ will be divided from those who
have been half-hearted disciples.

The fire of Christ will divide the committed mother from the uncommitted father.
It will divide the committed brother from the uncommitted sister. It will divide
the committed child from the uncommitted parents. Those who are committed to
Christ will find themselves on the pathway to Heaven. Others who are less
committed will find themselves on a pathway to Hell.

When Jesus invites us to follow Him, He fully realizes what He is asking of us.
For many of us, it means turning away from the lifestyle that we have grown to
love and accepting new lives in the Lord. In answering the call to be a follower
of Christ, one must be willing to be fully committed to God.

The teachings of Christ cannot be seen as a smorgasbord of morals. Chrsitianity
is not a cafeteria or a buffet! You cannot pick what aspects of the Chrsitian life
you wish to follow. You must be willing to commit yourself to all of God's
commands. A Chrsitian's commitment to Jesus must take priority over
everything else. It cannot be compromised in any way.

In The Gospel of our Brother Matthew, Jesus says to his disciples,

"You are the light of the world,"
*"A city set on a mountain cannot be hidden. Nor do they light a
lamp and then put it under a bushel basket; it is set on a lamp-
stand, where it gives light to all in the house. Just so, your light
must shine before others, that they may see your good deeds and
glorify your heavenly Father."*[115]

---

[114]Luke 12:49-53

[115]Matthew 5:14-16

Like Steve in that restaurant displaying his faith and commitment to God and our Church by the simply making the Sign of the Cross before saying "Grace," we must examine ourselves to make sure that we are fully committed to God.

Where it appears that our commitment to Christ is being compromised, we must change. For, a half-hearted commitment is really no commitment at all.

Through the years, Steve and I have shared hundreds of meals. Still to this day, no matter where we are, Steve says "Grace" beginning with the Sign of the Cross.

Though he has grown out of doing a lot of the things that he used to do as a child, the one thing that he has not grown out of is praying.

In fact, even his prayer at meal time has grown.

You see, because of his days at St. Augustine High School, at the end of saying "Grace" Steve calls on the intercession of St. Joseph and St. Augustine.

So, when he says, "St. Joseph," whoever is at the meals has to respond by saying, "Pray for us."

And when he says, "St. Augustine," you also respond by saying, "Pray for us."

Then you make the Sign of the Cross and can begin eating.

This extended prayer shows that we are not only thankful to God, we are thankful to the Saints for keeping us in their prayers and assisting God's Divine Providence.

So, let us pray,

In the Name of the Father and of the Son and of the Holy Spirit, Amen.

Lord, we come before You, today, asking that You give us the courage to follow You, in not only our private lives but in our public lives, too.

Lord, even though it causes us to be persecuted, as Jeremiah was persecuted, help us to stand firm in our Faith.

Lord, give us the courage to follow you, even though it causes us to struggle, as Sacred Scripture tells us it does.

Lord, give us the courage to follow you, even though, sometimes, it sets us in opposition to our family, as Jesus warns in St. Luke's Gospel.

And finally, Lord, give us the commitment necessary to always be willing to make the *Sign of the Cross* and pray in the crowded restaurants of our lives.

Together we pray,
"Bless us, O' Lord, and these Thy gifts
which we are about to receive from Thy bounty,
through Christ our Lord, Amen.

St. Joseph, "pray for us." St. Augustine, "pray for us."

In the Name of the Father and of the Son and of the Holy Spirit, Amen.

"I believe in God.
I hope in God.
I love.
I want to live and die for God."[116]

Venerable Henriette Delille
(1813 - 1862)
Foundress of the Sisters of the Holy Family

---

[116]Mother Henriette Delille was born in New Orleans in 1812. This is her only recorded writing. It was written on the inside cover of an 1836 prayer book. www.henriettedelille.com

We're Better Than St. Aug
Disciples' Dissension

The City of New Orleans is like no other place on the face of this earth. Having had the chance to travel all across the United States and into several other countries, I have yet to find a place that can really compare to my hometown.

From our fine cuisine of Cajun and Creole foods to our unparalleled styles of Chrsitian celebrations like Mardi Gras and All Saints Day, this place is definitely unique. Folks from around the world travel to New Orleans to experience our unique gifts.

When compared to any place on earth, New Orleans stands out as one of the finest places to live or visit. Whenever I travel to major cities across the United States, I will inevitably run into someone from New Orleans.

Ever since our great Katrina Exodus, our people seem to be everywhere in this country. So, when we get together, we act as if we have known each other all of our lives. Even though we may have not lived in the same neighborhood, if you're from New Orleans, you are part of the family. Being from New Orleans is all the connection you need!

In fact, when I am in other places, folks whom I don't even consider being from New Orleans will claim New Orleans as their home. I'm talking about those foreigners who live in the Greater New Orleans Suburbs. Folks that come from places like places like Slidell, Westwego and Boutte'.

When you are outside of Louisiana and you ask where they are from?, they will automatically say, "New Orleans."

I guess that it's because people in other cities wouldn't be able to find places like LaPlace, Marrero or the great metropolis of Edgard on a map. To halt further questioning they just simply say, "I'm from New Orleans." Even if you live in those places, your family roots are more than likely planted in the Crescent City.

Regardless of where you are in this country, when you meet somebody from this area you automatically become family.[117]

---

[117]And, when you are semi-famous, most of them will claim to actually be your distant cousins.

When I encounter folks from New Orleans, I immediately ask them where they grew up. You and I know that you can tell a lot about a person just by finding out what neighborhood they lived in as children. "Where you come from" does indeed have some bearing on how you see the world. Be it Uptown, Downtown or even the East, "where you come from" helps to shape who you are. It also helps to shape how you see the world.

After finding out where they once lived, we almost immediately go to the question, "What school did you go to?"

Usually if you ask someone what school they attended, they will automatically tell you about their university or college. But, in New Orleans when asked, "what school did you go to?" we don't care if you have a Ph.D. from LSU or you are an M.D. from Tulane University.

In New Orleans, when you ask "What school did you go to?" we don't talk about our advanced degrees, we only talk about our high schools. And, once we get started on our high schools, we are guaranteed to get into the big discussion on whose high school was the greatest!

If you want to see a fight breakout at any New Orleans gathering, just begin to argue on who had the best band or the best football team or the best-looking cheerleaders.

Some of the greatest battles on the Streets of New Orleans during the Mardi Gras Season, is not over who caught the best beads. It's about whose marching band out played the others during the parade.

At Our Lady Star of the Sea Church in New Orleans, the young folks spend an awful lot of energy defending their high schools and talking about who's the greatest. Our parishioners represent our city's greatest schools. We have girls from prestigious Catholic schools like Xavier Prep, St. Mary's Academy, Cabrini, Ursuline, and St. Mary's Dominican High.

We have boys representing Catholic high schools like Brother Martin, Jesuit, Holy Cross, Rummel and Shaw. We have boys and girls from other non-Catholic schools like McDonald #35, John McDonald, Joseph Clark, Lusher, Newman, and Frederick Douglass.

We even have some of the old folks who remember the days of Redeemer-Seton, John F. Kennedy and Francis T. Nicholls High. Although these historic schools are now closed, people in New Orleans still speak about them with love.

And, of course, we have men representing the greatest school of all, St. Augustine High School in downtown New Orleans. Founded in 1951, it is a school that is often imitated but never duplicated. St. Augustine High School is an all-Black, all-male high school that is operated by the Josephite Priests and Brothers. St. Augustine has graduated more Presidential Scholars,[118] more professional musicians, more professional athletes and more Black Catholic Priests than any school in South.

The school's patron is St. Augustine of Hippo. He was a Bishop from North Africa and is considered as one of the greatest theologians of our faith. This Great Doctor of Grace inspires the men of St. Augustine High School to strive toward excellence. *Gratia est Vita* is the school's motto. The school's patron saint reminds us that "Grace is Life!"

Our Lady Star of the Sea is home to every generation of St. Augustine's Purple Knights. I am one of the proudest members of this great fraternity. As a student at St. Augustine High School, I was involved in many activities including the Student Council, the Concert Band and the world renowned "Marching 100." I graduated from St. Augustine High School in 1982 and was blessed to return and teach Theology there from 2002 to 2006.

I am a very proud Purple Knight. I fully believe that my Alma Mater is the greatest school in the city. The quality of all other schools is often determined by comparing them to my Alma Mater. "The Marching 100" band is far superior to all others. That is why you will never hear anyone saying our band is better than Clark or our band is better than Rummel or our band is better than St. Mary's. When arguing that your school has a good band, folks always say, "Our band is better than St. Aug's Marching 100."[119]

If you want to be the best, you have to somehow claim that you are better than the best! But, we all know who the best is! Go Big Purple!

While reading through the Gospel Reading of our Brother Mark, I came across a passage that reminded me of New Orleans and all the folks who argue over whom the best is.

---

[118] A Presidential Scholar is selected by the U.S. President as one of the top 140 students in the nation.

[119] For more information on the best high school in the nation, St. Augustine High School, visit www.PurpleKnights.com

260

In the Gospel of Mark, we read,

> *Jesus and his disciples came to Capernaum and, once inside the house, He began to ask them, "What were you arguing about on the way?"*
>
> *But they remained silent. They had been discussing among themselves on the way who was the greatest.*
>
> *Then He sat down, called the Twelve, and said to them, "If anyone wishes to be first, he shall be the last of all and the servant of all."*
>
> *Taking a child he placed it in their midst, and putting His arms around it He said to them, "Whoever receives one child such as this in My name, receives Me; and whoever receives Me, receives not Me but the One who sent Me."*[120]

In this passage, as the disciples walked with Jesus through the regions of Galilee, they discussed with one another whom they thought was the best disciple of the Lord. Rather than arguing whether Jerusalem High School or Bethlehem Prep had the greatest band or the best shepherd team, they were arguing as to which one of them was the greatest of all of Jesus' disciples.

Now, how the disciples were arguing, we could only guess. Maybe they were discussing who among them seem to have the deepest faith. Or which one of them was doing the most to help Jesus with His day-to-day needs. Or which one of them was having the most success with their own preaching ministry.

The disciples were trying to determine who was the best in the Band of Men that walked, talked and ministered with Jesus on a regular basis. They wanted to know who was the greatest of all.

When Jesus heard his disciples discussing who was the greatest, He reminded them that what they may consider as great may not be the criteria that God would use to determine greatness. Where they may have been concerned with greatness in the eyes of man, Jesus was focused on what it means to be great in the Eyes of God.

---

[120]Mark 9:33-37

You see, right before their deep discussion on greatness, Jesus had just finished telling them that His path to greatness was not the path that the Jewish people had been expecting.

In Mark 9:31-32, Jesus says,

> *"The Son of Man is to be handed over to men and they will kill Him, and three days after His death He will rise."*

Rather than being raised to greatness through a triumphant battle or by an Angelic Army, He was going to reach His destined glory through the passion and death of crucifixion and His ultimate Resurrection from the dead. He would become great on earth because He was going to lay down His life for the sake of the world.

Once His Path down the Way of the Cross was over, greatness would no longer be measured by whom you are. It would then be measured by one's willingness to give to those in need. It will be measured by one's willingness to sacrifice his or her own joys for the sake of others.

Basically, Jesus was telling his disciples and telling us that if you really want to be great in the Eyes of God you have to be willing to be least in the eyes of man; you have to be willing to serve.

I assure you that being considered great on earth will not automatically get you counted amongst the great people in Heaven. In fact, if your only goal is to be great here on earth you will probably not be great in Heaven. You may not even make it into Heaven.

That is why Jesus placed a child in the middle of his disciples and explained that if you really want to be blessed by God, make sure that you are treating people like God would treat them.

Jesus told them,

> *"Whoever receives one child such as this in My name, receives Me; and whoever receives Me, receives not Me but the One who sent Me."*

In other words, greatness in the Eyes of God will be determined by how often you have worked to take care of the children, the poor and the needy in our midst. This means that to be great in Heaven you have to be a true servant of the Lord on earth.

A lot of times, we spend our energy arguing over what is greater in this world. We compare our schools. We compare our families. We compare our parents. We even compare our children. We spend a great deal of energy trying to show how what we have or who we are is somehow greater than what another person has or is.

Part of what we must realize is that through the Blood of the Lamb and the Feast of the Eucharist, we are all great in the Eyes of God. By the sacrifice of Christ Jesus, we have become the Sons and Daughters of our Heavenly Father. There's nothing on earth that could be greater than being one of God's Children.

You know, down in New Orleans we are passionate about a lot of things. When we "get to fussin'" about the things we love, folks had better watch out.

From the NFL New Orleans Saints to the NBA New Orleans Hornets, to our old neighborhoods and our cherished high schools, we will have heated discussions about who was the greatest.

Today, we ought to realize that every neighborhood has its degree of greatness, every high school has something that made it great.

Just in case there is any doubt about which high school has the greatest marching band, all I can say is if your band has marched and played for Blessed John Paul II, eight U.S. Presidents, the Rose Bowl Parade, Macy's Thanksgiving Day Parade, Monday Night Football, The Sugar Bowl, NFL Super Bowls, led Mardi Gras Parades, and was featured in major motion pictures, then we can argue who's the greatest.

But until then, we'll just let the legacy of our legendary Band Director, Mr. Edwin Harrell Hampton, speak for itself.[121]

Today, may you be blessed so that like the St. Augustine "Marching 100" you too can truly be the Best!

Amen!

---

[121] Mr Hamp - Edwin Harrell Hampton was the Band Master of St. Augustine High School for more than 50 years. He moved to Heaven in July of 2009. The Purple Knights of St. Augustine High School will never forget the lessons of love and dedication that Mr. Hamp taught us.

How Will They Remember Me
When I Die?

On June 25, 2009 the world was rocked by the news of the death of the one and only Michael Joseph Jackson.

Michael Jackson - world renowned entertainer
    -multi-millionaire and a devoted father.

Michael Jackson - the King of Pop
    or as Quincy Jones put it simply the Greatest Entertainer whoever lived.

Michael Joseph Jackson - definitely, a man who is "gone too soon."[122]

After his death, there were daily news reports regarding his life, his family or even the circumstances surrounding his death. The world heard an awful lot about how Michael Jackson lived, and who he truly loved.

Although he's physically gone, there is no doubt that Michael Jackson will be remembered for many years to come!

He will be remembered for his musical gifts and talents. He will be remembered for his generosity to hundreds of charities around the world. He will be remembered for his ability to capture people's hearts and sing directly to their souls. Indeed, he will be remembered.

It is amazing how the life and death of one man from the small town of Gary, Indiana has touched and affected the lives of millions. "It don't matter if you're Black or White," Michael's work at some level has been a part of everyone's life.

In the wake of all that has been on reported about Michael, I began to wonder, what will folks say about me when the "Aura that is Tony" passes on to the next world.

How will they remember me when I die?

---

[122]The song "Gone Too Soon" was written by Michael Jackson. It was dedicated to the memory of Jackson's friend Ryan White. Ryan was a teenager from Kokomo, Indiana, who came to national attention, after being expelled from his school for having HIV/AIDS.

Whenever someone famous or active in the City of New Orleans dies, they usually merit a few reports on television and in the Times-Picayune newspaper. So, I imagine that when I finally move to Heaven, they'll be reports and articles about me. Even the Pope may come to New Olreans to be at my funeral!

Which leads me to wonder, *How will they remember me when I die?*

Will they recall the work I have done with terminally ill children?

Will they recall the time I have spent teaching in the public schools?

Will they recall the phenomenal homilies I gave and how I inspired the masses with my great wisdom and eloquence?

Will they remember just how humble I truly was?

"How will they remember me when I die?"

Quite often in his preaching, the Prophet Jeremiah criticized men who apparently never stopped to ask, how they would be remembered when they died? In Jeremiah's time, the political and religious leaders of Judah were known for being selfish, for being men who looked after their own needs and seriously neglecting the flock entrusted to them by God. When these leaders died, the only thing the people could remember was how much they did to better their own life.

In the 23rd Chapter of Jeremiah, we hear,

> *"Woe to the shepherds who mislead and scatter the flock of my pasture, says the Lord. Therefore, thus says the LORD, the God of Israel, against the shepherds who shepherd my people: You have scattered my sheep and driven them away. You have not cared for them, but I will take care to punish your evil deeds."*
>
> *"I myself will gather the remnant of my flock from all the lands to which I have driven them and bring them back to their meadow; there they shall increase and multiply. "I will appoint shepherds for them who will shepherd them so that they need no longer fear and tremble; and none shall be missing, says the Lord"*[123]

---

[123] Jeremiah 23:1-4

Apparently, they failed to be generous. They failed to live according to God's Will. They failed to be good leaders. The only thing that people remembered about them was that they only cared for themselves.

They should have stopped at some point in their lives and asked, *"How will they remember us when we die?"*

Had they stopped to ask that question, maybe they would have changed their ways and been better leaders of the people. They would have definitely been more devoted Servants of God!

The lives of the leaders of Jeremiah's time should let all leaders know that they need to periodically stop and ask themselves "How will folks remember me when I'm gone?"

Regardless if they are a religious leader, a political leader or the leader of a family, they ought to be conscious of the legacy that they will leave behind. By doing this, it will help them keep their priorities straight and in-line with the Will of God.

I fully believe that this introspection, these moments of looking inside of one's own heart, is how Jesus was able to keep His priorities straight!

With all that was within Him, Jesus could have taken for granted His role in this world and the role that was given to Him by His Father in Heaven. But, rather than taking it for granted, He constantly asked His disciples if the folks really understood whom He was and what He had come to do.

While He was with us here on earth, Jesus wondered how people would remember Him. Time and time again, He asked the disciples, *"Who do people say that I am?"*[124]

Like most people, Jesus cared about what folks thought of Him and His work. But, rather than leaving it up to others to come up with good memories of Him, He gave them images remember him by.

In the Gospel of our Brother Mark, Jesus gives us an image of how He would like to be remembered.

---

[124]Matthew 16:13-15

In the 6th Chapter of Mark, we read:

> *The apostles gathered together with Jesus and reported all they had done and taught.*
>
> *He said to them, "Come away by yourselves to a deserted place and rest a while." People were coming and going in great numbers, and they had no opportunity even to eat. So they went off in the boat by themselves to a deserted place.*
>
> *"People saw them leaving and many came to know about it. They hastened there on foot from all the towns and arrived at the place before them. When He disembarked and saw the vast crowd,*
>
> *His Heart was moved with pity for them, for they were like sheep without a shepherd; and He began to teach them many things"*[125]

In this passage, St. Mark gives us an image of Jesus as a generous shepherd, taking the Apostles away for needed rest and yet ready to teach the people Himself. In seeing Jesus as the Good and Generous Shepherd, we spiritually remember Him as a good man with a good heart.

In the image of the Shepherd, Jesus gives us an example of not only how we should remember the time He spent with us on earth, but also how we are called to live our own lives and hopefully be remembered by those who know us. Because we have been baptized and share Jesus' life as Priest, Prophet and King, we too, are called to be good and generous shepherds. Like Jesus and the Apostles, each and every baptized Chrsitian is called to be a spiritual shepherd to the people of our world.

Spiritual shepherds lead wisely, fulfilling the hope expressed by Jeremiah.

> *"Behold, the days are coming, says the Lord, when I will raise up a righteous shoot to David; As king he shall reign and govern wisely, he shall do what is just and right in the land."*[126]

---

[125] Mark 6:30-34

[126] Jeremiah 23:6

Spiritual shepherds lead through honest prayer and their service of others. They pray regularly and consistently. For in prayer, God helps them to bring up whatever it is that may be interfering with their relationship with God and their love for others.

Honest prayer always leads us outside of ourselves, it puts us in communion with many other people seeking an assurance that God is good and that God has time for our individual concerns.

Jesus not only calls us to be shepherds who live sincere lives of prayer. He also calls us to be spiritual shepherds who lead through examples, who lead by serving others.

As Baptized Chrsitians, we can provide the kind of shepherding that someone needs. This can be done by showing how to forgive by actually forgiving or showing how to respect each person by paying attention even if only for a short time to what matters.We can make a difference in the lives of others. That is how we will be remembered when we die.

In a 1985 interview that I did with Bishop Harold Robert Perry, SVD, the first Black Bishop in modern times and my childhood Pastor, I asked him "How did he want to be remembered?"[127]

He simply said, "When through one man, a little more love, a little more goodness, a little more light and a little more truth comes into the world, then the man's life has meaning."

In the life of Bishop Harold Perry, a courageously humble Servant of God, he has given true examples of how to live as a spiritual shepherd. True spiritual shepherds are rarely in the spotlight, but somehow their presence or absence is always noticed or felt.

Most people don't have the public lives as Pope, Archbishop or even Bishop Perry. Lord knows that no one will ever be as famous as Michael Jackson. However, that should not stop us from trying hard to be the spiritual shepherds that all of us have been called to be.

---

[127]Bishop Harold R. Perry, SVD, was ordained to the priesthood on January 6, 1944. He became the first African-American Bishop in the 20th Century when he was ordained as an Auxiliary Bishop of New Orleans on January 6, 1966.

Now, It is true that one day I might become the Cardinal or Archbishop of New Orleans. But, if I don't become a Cardinal or Archbishop, I can be content with just being a good and generous shepherd right here.

You see, we don't have to be famous or occupy a prestigious office to truly have a positive impact on the lives of others. We can make a difference right here and right now!

Just think about it, for most of us the people who have had the most positive impact in our lives probably were not on the front page of newspapers or on the covers of entertainment magazines. Yet, their impact was no less important on our lives.

Just remember, something you do today for someone else could have a lasting impact on their life. Even small things can affect the rest of a person's life, and they will remember you forever.

Each day, we should take time to remember Jesus, the Good and Generous Shepherd. In doing so, He joins us on our journey to the Kingdom of Heaven.

When we remember our Spiritual Ancestors, those Spiritual Shepherds who have affected our lives, they too are made present to us through the love they shared with us.

Sometimes I wonder if, when all is said and done, when our lives have reach their ends, will we be recalled in the midst of an assembly?

Will family members speak our names with sincere reverence?

Will they tell the story of our prayers, our service and our lives?

How will we be remembered by those whose lives we've touched?

In one of his greatest messages to the world, Michael Jackson told us that everybody ought to spend a little time talking to "The Man in the Mirror." You should take a little time to access who you are and how you are living out the Call that God has given you.

Are you truly the man or woman that God needs you to be?

How are your words and deeds impacting those around you?

Now is the time to really assess our personal response to Jesus' call to us to be Good and Generous Spiritual Shepherds.

In the words of the King of Pop, "I'm starting with the Man in the Mirror. I'm asking him to change his ways. And, no message could have been any clearer. If you wanna make the world a better place take a look at yourself, and make a change!"[128]

You know, listening to the King of Pop can help you to get ready to meet the King of Kings!

If you really want to meet Jesus, the only way you can truly be ready is by starting with the Man or Woman in the Mirror!

In Christ Jesus, you have the chance to take a look at yourself and be prepared to make a change!

How will they remember you when you die?

Amen!

Sirach 44

Now will I praise those godly men, our ancestors, each in his own time:
The abounding glory of the Most High's portion, his own part, since the days
of old. Subduers of the land in kingly fashion, men of renown for their might,
Or counselors in their prudence, or seers of all things in prophecy;
Resolute princes of the folk, and governors with their staves; Authors skilled in
composition, and forgers of epigrams with their spikes;
Composers of melodious psalms, or discoursers on lyric themes;

Stalwart men, solidly established and at peace in their own estates--
All these were glorious in their time, each illustrious in his day.
Some of them have left behind a name and men recount their praiseworthy deeds;
But of others there is no memory, for when they ceased, they ceased.[129]

---

[128]The song "Man in the Mirror" was recorded in 1988 as a part of Michael Jackson's "Bad" album.

[129]Sirach 44:1-9

SECTION TWO
Reflections on Hope

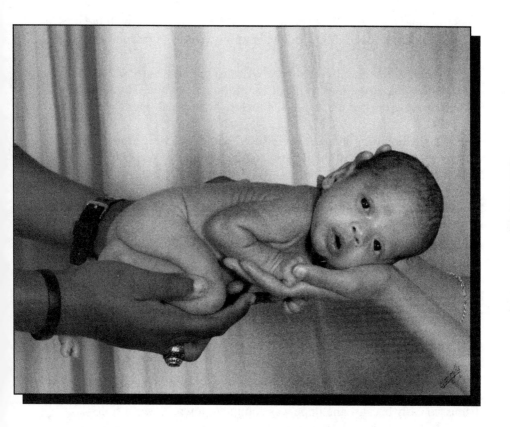

Justin James Smith, Jr. - Born September 3, 2010

Babies exercise a very import ministries in our churches.

They are Ministers of Hope!

They are the new cells in the Body of Christ!

Behold the Lamb of God
Who Takes away the Sins of the World

On a very warm morning in September of 1987, I had the joy of accompanying a group of young people from Our Lady of Lourdes Parish on a very special trip to the Louisiana Superdome. On that morning, we were all excited because we were going to see and possibly greet one of the most popular men in the entire world.

On September 12, 1987, the City of New Orleans was graced with the presence of Cardinal Karol Joseph Wojtyla, better know to us as Pope John Paul II.[130]

On the days that the Pope visited New Orleans, our entire city was abuzz. We had been preparing for this papal visit for quite a while. The Louisiana Superdome was decked out in gold and white, with papal flags flying all around.

Notre Dame Seminary and the Archbishop's residence were immaculately cleaned, in anticipation of the Pope spending a couple of nights in the Archbishop's home.

Even the street in front of the Archbishop's residence was spruced up with new palm trees and freshly painted light posts that were decked out in banners of gold and white. Excitement was truly in the air.

At the time of the visit, I was teaching third grade at Lafayette Elementary School, a school that is located directly across the street from the Seminary and Archbishop's house.

On the Friday that the Pope was to arrive at the seminary, our school was closed early and the Secret Service took over our building, positioning lookouts and rifle marksmen on the roof of the school to protect the Pope from any possible assassination attempts. We were the only public school in New Orleans that was dismissed early because the Pope was coming to town.

Out on the Lakefront, near Southern University of New Orleans and the University of New Orleans, a large stage was erected for the Papal Mass that would be attended by more 400,000 devoted Chrsitians. That stage was probably the most high tech Altar ever built.

---

[130]On May 1, 2011, Pope Benedict XVI is scheduled to celebrate the beatification of Pope John Paul II. Soon, Pope John Paul II will be formally known as Blessed John Paul II.

Along with the enormous lighting and sound equipment, it also included an Altar table that was actually a secret elevator. In the event of an assassination attempt, the Pope was instructed to drop down under the Altar and the Altar would immediately descend into the platform which was a protective building. That building was stronger that most bomb shelters.

Indeed, the city was ready for the arrival of this holy man. I can remember going into the Superdome with the youth from Our Lady of Lourdes Parish. Everyone was excited about seeing the Holy Father. We had talked about it for weeks. They even had their own nickname for the Holy Father. In the weeks building up to his visit, the youth referred to Pope John Paul II as "J.P. Deuce."

Inside the Dome, we were seated in the upper level. From that vantage point, we could see everything that was happening on the main floor. That was pretty cool. When the time came for the Pope to arrive, a wave of electricity seemed to flow throughout the crowd. The person whom we had been longing to see was finally about to enter the Dome. Finally, we were going to be in the presence of one of the holiest men on earth. We were about to see the Pope.

Without being prompted, the entire Dome all turned towards the Poydras Street Entrance of the Superdome as we anticipated the Holy Father's entrance. I can't tell you how proud I was to see coming through the tunnel, marching with great procession and style, the St. Augustine Marching 100. There they were, my Alma Mater, entering a stadium that was packed with thousands of faith-filled youth.

And, right behind the greatest band in the land, riding in a glass-encased float was the man for whom we had all been waiting. Right behind my high school's band was the Pope, himself!

When the Pope mobile entered the Dome, the crowd got so excited that you would have thought that we were at a rock concert. That group of almost 70,000 youth were cheering the arrival of the Pope like folks back then cheered the arrival of Michael Jackson or the Beatles.

There he was, John Paul II, himself. The most powerful religious leader in the world: the Pope, our Pope, the Vicar of Christ.

Needless to say, I have never forgotten that day. I have never forgotten what it felt like to be in our Superdome, watching our St. Augustine High School's "Marching 100," and seeing our Pope. It truly was one of the best days of my life.

For several years, the city of New Orleans anticipated the arrival of the Holy Father. His actual visit was the culmination of many years of waiting. But, our time of waiting can't really compare to the time of waiting that was endured by the folks in the City of David. You see, for quite a long time, the children of Abraham had been anticipating the arrival of a Holy Man in the City of David.

Like the preparations that were being made for the arrival of Karol Joseph Wojtyla in New Orleans, people had been spiritually preparing for the arrival of a very Holy Man in Jerusalem and throughout the regions of Galilee. People had been preparing for centuries for the arrival of the Son of God: the One who would save the world.

Almost from the days of Abraham, folks had been anticipating the arrival of the Savior. Moses talked about it. David sang about it and Solomon preached about it. For centuries, folks waited for God to send His Son.

Much of the Prophet Isaiah's writings focus on the Israelites' time of anticipation. We read one of his greatest passages when we gathered to celebrate the Solemnity of the Nativity of our Lord.

In our first reading from Midnight Mass on Christmas Morning, we read,

> *The people who walked in darkness have seen a great light; upon those who dwelt in the land of gloom a light has shone. You have brought them abundant joy and great rejoicing, as they rejoice before you as at the harvest, as people make merry when dividing spoils. For the yoke that burdened them, the pole on their shoulder, and the rod of their taskmaster you have smashed, as on the day of Midian. For every boot that tramped in battle, every cloak rolled in blood, will be burned as fuel for flames.*
>
> *For a child is born to us, a son is given us; upon his shoulder dominion rests. They name him Wonder-Counselor, God-Hero, Father-Forever, Prince of Peace. His dominion is vast and forever peaceful, from David's throne, and over his kingdom, which he confirms and sustains by judgment and justice, both now and forever.*
>
> *The zeal of the LORD of hosts will do this!*[131]

---

[131] Isaiah 9:1-6

Isaiah knew that his people were anxiously awaiting the arrival of the Messiah. He wanted to make sure that everyone understood that the One who was coming would bear a new light to the world. With that new light, God would send justice and peace to the world. God's justice would bring a right judgement against those who lived according to the ways of the world and not according to the ways and laws of God.

Isaiah also promised freedom to the Children of God. The freedom he promised was freedom not from earthly bondage but rather a freedom from the ravages and control of sin. He promised freedom from that which would lead us to the eternal darkness of hell. He reminds us that the Messiah would be a light to the nations: A light that would bring salvation to all.

Part of Isaiah's challenge to us is to examine how we live in the Light that has come into the world. That is why in the Letter from St. Paul to the Corinthians, St. Paul reminds us that we are all called by God to be bearers of the light. We are called to be holy men and women of faith. Paul tells us that we have been made holy by the presence of the long awaited Messiah.

In the introduction to his letter to the Corinthians, Paul writes,

> Paul, called to be an apostle of Christ Jesus by the will of God, and Sosthenes our brother, to the church of God that is in Corinth, to you who have been sanctified in Christ Jesus, called to be holy, with all those everywhere who call upon the name of our Lord Jesus Christ, their Lord and ours.
>
> Grace to you and peace from God our Father and the Lord Jesus Christ. I give thanks to my God always on your account for the grace of God bestowed on you in Christ Jesus, that in him you were enriched in every way, with all discourse and all knowledge, as the testimony to Christ was confirmed among you, so that you are not lacking in any spiritual gift as you wait for the revelation of our Lord Jesus Christ.
>
> He will keep you firm to the end, irreproachable on the day of our Lord Jesus (Christ). God is faithful, and by him you were called to fellowship with his Son, Jesus Christ our Lord.[132]

---

[132] 1st Corinthians 1:1-9

St. Paul remains us that we can indeed remain holy because God has already given us the necessary gifts of holiness. We have been sanctified in Christ Jesus! Thus, we already possess all that we need to remain faithful to our calling. We also have been made ready for the day when Christ will return to usher in the Final Days.

Through his letter to the Corinthians, St. Paul lets us know that Jesus is the man for whom our Hebrew Ancestors had been waiting. His arrival marked the end of an ancient Advent. But, by ascending into Heaven, Jesus also began a new period of waiting. However, this time of waiting will end when Christ returns to present us to His Heavenly Father.

In this letter, St. Paul offers us an Isaiah- like challenge. He calls us to be excited while waiting for the Lord. But, he also reminds us that as we wait, we must strive to be as holy as possible. Like the excited youth that were waiting for Pope John Paul II to enter into the Superdome, we have to share a hope-filled anticipation for the Second Coming of the Lord.

Right before Jesus made His public appearance as an adult, there was a great deal of hope-filled anticipation. People would travel from miles around to the region of Galilee in hopes of seeing the Messiah. Although Jesus had not yet made a public appearance, many believed that the Messiah had indeed arrived. Some even thought that John the Baptist could have been the one for whom they had been longing.

In the Gospel of John, we read,

> When the Jews from Jerusalem sent priests and Levites (to John) to ask him, "Who are you?" he admitted and did not deny it, but admitted, "I am not the Messiah."
>
> So they asked him, "What are you then? Are you Elijah?" And he said, "I am not." "Are you the Prophet?" He answered, "No." So they said to him, "Who are you, so we can give an answer to those who sent us? What do you have to say for yourself?"
>
> He said: "I am 'the voice of one crying out in the desert, "Make straight the way of the Lord,"'as Isaiah the prophet said."[133]

---

[133] John 1:19-23

The Israelites had been waiting for the Messiah for thousands of years. So, it is not hard to understand how they could have thought that John was the Messiah. But, can you imagine what it had to have been like on the morning that the Messiah was finally revealed to them?

I can only imagine the excitement that flowed through the crowd as John told them about the One, who would be coming who would be baptize them with more than river water.

In Luke, St. John the Baptist says,

> *"I am baptizing you with water, but one mightier than I is coming. I am not worthy to loosen the thongs of his sandals. He will baptize you with the Holy Spirit and fire."*[134]

For centuries, the prophets pointed to the Savior's arrival. For years, John the Baptist got folks pumped-up in anticipation of the Messiah. It had to be exciting an exciting time. It had to be like the Superdome was on the morning of September 12, 1987 as we waited for Blessed John Paul II to arrive.

The Gospel of John describes the moment of the Savior's arrival like this.

> *(When John) saw Jesus coming toward him and said, "Behold, the Lamb of God, who takes away the sin of the world.*
>
> *He is the one of whom I said, 'A man is coming after me who ranks ahead of me because he existed before me.' I did not know him, but the reason why I came baptizing with water was that he might be made known to Israel."*[135]

Like the entrance of the St. Augustine High School's "Marching 100" did for the Pope in the Superdome, God used John the Baptist to formally introduce Jesus to the world.

t t the River Jordan that God formally presented to the world, though John, the One for whom the prophets and preachers had been waiting. It was at that moment that God revealed to the world, His only begotten Son, Jesus.

---

[134] Luke 3:16

[135] John 1:29-31

At the moment of Jesus' baptism by John, God, the Father, made it perfectly clear that Jesus indeed was the Messiah. Through voice from Heaven, God the Father to Jesus *"You are my beloved Son; with you I am well pleased."*[136]

If you think that the crowd was excited when John pointed Jesus out to them, imagine how exited they had to be when they saw the Heavens open and the Spirit of God descend on Jesus like a dove that they heard the voice of God proclaim that the wait was over. Now, they could finally behold the Lamb of God!

I would give anything to be able to go back in time to be a part of that moment on the banks of the river. What a glorious day it would be, to be able to sit in the presence of John the Baptist and be a part of the moment when Jesus the Son of the Living God was formally revealed to the world.

But, unfortunately, as humans, we are tied to time and space, and will never be able to transcend that dimension. But, if we could, I surely would.

Yet, when you think about it, we are given the opportunity to feel the same level of excitement that the folks of Galilee felt. We are given the opportunity to feel the same level of excitement that they felt on the day that Jesus, the Son of God, was brought into their midst.

But, do we fully understand the opportunity that we have?

Are we fully aware of what God will do for those who love Him?

I don't think that we are.

Every time we gather as the Children of God to celebrate the Eucharist, we are given the chance to feel the same excitement that the folks who sat along the Jordan River once felt.

Every time we gather as a faith community, we have to opportunity to welcome Jesus the Son of God in our midst.

Every time we celebrate Mass, we are privilege to be in the presence not of the Vicar of Christ, but of the Christ, Himself. Through the Eucharist, Jesus, the Beloved Son of God, joins us.

---

[136]Luke 3:22

278

But, far too many of us never fully understand what is happening. Far too many of us have been caught up by the traps of this world and never get a chance to fully see the Lamb of God.

Far too many of us enter this place preoccupied by life's troubles, fully consumed by life's burdens, that they never get a chance to see the one who was sent to free them from that very darkness.

Far too many of us never get a chance to *Behold the Lamb of God who takes away the sins of the world*, because they have chosen to live in the blinding world of sin rather than allowing Son of God to finally bring them to the level of peace that all of the Prophets promised us.

Through the celebration of the Eucharist, we as Roman Catholics believe that the Body and Blood of Jesus is made present to us through concept of transubstantiation.

Transubstantiation means that the bread and wine that are offered on the Altar, through the miraculous prayers of Christ and His Church, are changed into the Body and Blood of the Lord. Though the physical structures of the bread and wine remain the same, the internal substance (the essence of what it really is) changes forever. The essence of the gifts we present to the Altar, become for us the Body and the Blood of Jesus.

Just, as the physical body, the cells that made up the body of Baby Jesus was able to house the essence of the Lamb of God, the physical structures of the bread and the wine are able to house the essence of Christ.

The Eucharist that we receive at Communion time is indeed the Savior of the World. It is not a facsimile. We are not pretending. It is Jesus, the Lamb of God who takes away the sins of the world.

Can we fully understand this theological principle? I would say, "No."
Is it truly miraculous? I would say, "Yes!"
Do I believe in miracles? I would say, "Without a doubt!"
And, I pray that you do, too.

will never forget that blessed September morning when God allowed me to sit in that Superdome and experience the electricity that filled that place when Pope John Paul, II, visited New Orleans. It was and still is one of the true highlights in my personal faith journey. But, the excitement of the arrival of the Pope cannot even come close to the excitement that the folks of Galilee felt when they finally got a chance to see and experience the presence of Jesus.

The excitement of being in the presence of the Pope cannot even come close to what we ought to feel when we realize that every time we celebrate Mass, Jesus the Son of God, is in our midst.

In the Eucharist, the one about whom Moses talked; the one about whom David sang and the one about whom Solomon preached joins us to offer in a timeless manner His Body and Blood for the salvation of the world.

During the consecration of the Eucharist, I am privileged to join the Holy Father and all the priests of the world, standing *in persona Christi*[137] and offering my body for the sake of the world.

But, even more, I am privileged to stand *in persona Johannes Baptista*[138] and present to you God's Beloved Son, in whom He is well pleased.

Today, may God allow you to open your eyes of faith so that you might see the one whom the prophets anticipated and for whom the people longed.

May you open your ears of love so that you might hear the Word of God that is made incarnate in our midst.

May you open your hearts of joy so you might feel the excitement of the ages, and realize *just how privileged we are* to be in the presence of our Savior.

Today, *Behold the Lamb of God Who Takes away the Sins of the World.*

And, once you have held Him in your hearts, don't allow the Devil, the master of the world of sin, to take the Lamb away from you.

In the name of all that is holy, I beg you to make yourself ready to behold the Lamb!

---

[137] "In the person of Christ"

[138] "In the person of John the Baptist"

Airport Security and Anxiety

Over the past 20 plus years, I have been blessed with the chance to travel all around the world. From preaching along the Sea of Galilee to walking through the Canadian Rockies, I've been to a lot of places and met thousands of God's beloved children.

One of my most favorite places to visit and preach is on the Islands of Paradise, the great State of Hawaii. I have had a chance to visit Honolulu on five different occasions. It really is tough to be me!

Not too long ago, I had the chance to direct a Vocations Retreat for the Diocese of Honolulu. It was held at St. Stephen Diocesan Center which is on the Island of Oahu. More than 30 young men and women gathered at this retreat center that overlooked the ocean. We had a great time as we reflected on the beauty of nature and our common call to be disciples of the Lord.

On this particular trip to Hawaii, I brought my usual "oversees" traveling companion, my momma. She and I have traveled to more than nine countries together. We always have a great time on our journeys. But, this trip was a bit different. This time, we also brought my dad.

Traveling with my parents was truly an enriching experience. We really enjoyed the beauty of Hawaii and the love of the Hawaiian people.

In this day and age, anywhere traveling has become a bit more difficult than it used to be. Ever since September 11, 2001, just getting through security has been a true experience. Because of the terrorist attacks on New York, Washington, D.C., and Pennsylvania, airport security has been extremely tight. From dealing with the extra security guards to passing through those "invasive" metal detectors, just getting to the plane is a journey of faith.

The new metal detectors are so powerful that they can detect a crumpled-up, foil-wrapper from a piece of gum that you had in your pocket. I know this because it happened to me!

The security folks are doing a pretty good job making sure that travelers are safe. So, unlike many I usually don't complain when you have to go through all of the security stuff. I know that the reason for the heightened security is not to harass the passengers, but to make travel safer for all of us. The security checks help to keep out dangerous weapons and dangerous people. They also keep out all those evil folks who try to smuggle in illegal wads of chewing gum!

The airport security team is there to guard over our sense of peace. They are there to help alleviate our anxieties and concerns. They are there to help God keep us calm.

In St. Paul's Letter to the Philippians, we are told,

> *Have no anxiety at all, but in everything, by prayer and petition,*
> *with thanksgiving, make your requests known to God.*
> *Then the peace of God that surpasses all understanding will*
> *guard your hearts and minds in Christ Jesus.*[139]

In this, St. Paul tells us that God and not just the airport security folks will bring security to our minds and hearts. God's peace will stand guard so that no destructive thoughts, no emotions or unnecessary anxiety will disturb our inner peace.

Not only will God's peace stand guard against threats from outside of us; God's peace will also guard and fill our inner thoughts as well. In this letter, St Paul gives several keys to achieving God's inner peace. He says that we should

> *Rejoice in the Lord always. I shall say it again: rejoice!*
> *Your kindness should be known to all. The Lord is near.*[140]

We should all rejoice because the Lord is on His way back to claim us! We may not be able to rejoice in all of life's circumstances. But, we can rejoice in the Lord because He is always near to help us. He is near to strengthen us, to guard our hearts and to give us His peace.

With rejoicing, we are also told to be kind. That means we shouldn't be self-centered. We must be focused on the needs of others. It's by focusing on the needs of others that we are able to take our minds off our own troubles and put them in perspective. That can help us become less anxious about our own problems.

We should bear in mind that unnecessary anxiety robs us of our inner peace. St. Paul tells us to "Have no anxiety at all." We need to stop worrying about everything and ask God for a true sense of peace and serenity.

---

[139]Philippians 4:6-7

[140]Philippians 4:4-5

We all know that serenity comes when you can
"accept the things you cannot change;
have the courage to change the things you can;
and (have) the wisdom to know the difference."[141]

God doesn't want us to worry about stuff. That is why there are 365 times in the Bible in which God tells us not to worry, not to be anxious or not to be fearful about things that may come our way.

Now, don't get me wrong, anxiety is a natural emotion that can be good or bad. I know from experience that a little anxiety before a performance or a speaking engagement is good. It can get the adrenalin flowing and heighten your senses to the needs of the community. However, too much anxiety can get out of our control and begin to paralyze you to the point in which you can't do anything.

That is why we must be willing to surrender to God all those problems that are not ours or problems that are beyond our control. That is why we need "the wisdom to know the difference."

We must also begin to work harder at thinking positive about life. People often ask me, "Why do you always see to be so happy?" It is because I usually am happy.)

I have come to understand that negative thinking can rob you of your inner peace. When negative thoughts come along, we need to flood them out with positive thinking. We need to overload our minds by thinking about good things!

St. Paul understood that a flood of good thoughts can truly crowd out the bad images that might enter our minds. That is why in his letter to the Philippians, he lists many positive thoughts that we can use to replace anxious or negative thoughts.

In his letter, Paul tell us to think about

Whatever is true, whatever is honorable,
whatever is just, whatever is pure,
whatever is lovely, whatever is gracious,
if there is any excellence
and if there is anything worthy of praise,

---

[141]The Serenity Prayer was written by Reinhold Neibuhr (1934)

283

think about these things.
Keep on doing what you have learned and received and heard
and seen in me.

Then the God of peace will be with you.[142]

Thinking about *"whatever is true"* means that we ought to avoid spreading rumors about folks. We ought to stop gossiping and talking behind other people's backs. Instead, we should spend our energy focusing on the Truth that is God. We should spend our energy reading Sacred Scripture or filling our mind with other inspirational stuff like Gospel Music and evangelical preaching.

Thinking about *"whatever is honorable"* means that we should respect others and the roles they play in our lives.

Thinking about *"whatever is just"* means that we need to crowd out the temptation to cheat or be greedy. We need to focus on "doing the right thing" and making decisions that are honest and trustworthy.

Thinking about *"whatever is pure"* means that we have to be on guard not to allow the ways of the Devil to invade our minds. Purity of mind and heart is not easy in this day and age. Our purity is constantly being challenged by the media of today. We have to have the wisdom of being able to decipher what is right and wrong in the things we see on TV, on the Internet, and in the movies.

Thinking about *"whatever is lovely"* means that rather than focusing on the negative things in life, we should focus on the magnitude of God's love for us, focus on the grandeur of nature, the softness of a baby's face or the magic of music.

Thinking about *"whatever is gracious"* means that first we ought to realize that it is only through the Grace of God that we are who we are. Filled with His grace, we must then, extend the gift of God's grace and mercy to others. Remember, only those who show mercy will be shown mercy.

The last thing that Paul says, for us to think about is that which is *"praiseworthy."* This means that we should compliment each other for the good that we do. Focus on the good qualities of your family members and your friends, and then let them know the gifts you see in them. We work harder to achieve greatness when others tell us that they see a mark of greatness in us.

---

[142]Philippians 4:8-9

Finally, Paul tells us to *"keep on doing what you have learned."* That means in order for all these good thoughts and feelings to be effective in our lives, they have to be followed up with good actions and signs of love. It takes time for our negative feelings and deep-rooted worries to change. But, eventually, we know that if we flood them out with good stuff, we can change how we see things and how we live our lives.

I fully believe that if we put into practice all the virtues that St. Paul listed in his *Letter to the Philippians, "the God of peace will be with us."* Not just guarding our hearts and minds, but truly with us, one with us, living within us. The eternal, omnipotent, invincible, and triune God will be with and within each of us.

> *Then the peace of God that surpasses all*
> *understanding will guard your hearts and minds*
> *in Christ Jesus.*[143]

Traveling to Hawaii with my parents was an awesome experience. While they spent time on an all-expense-paid vacation, I spent time preaching the Word of God. As we headed back home, all three of us packed our bags with all sorts of souvenirs. We also packed our hearts with many wonderful memories of our time in paradise.

Going through security at the Honolulu Airport wasn't all that bad, either. Although my folks seemed to flow through the security check without any problems, I ended up having to be patted down by a security person.

I have to confess to you that I actually enjoyed the pat down. You see, the Hawaiian security person that patted me down wasn't your usual "security man." She was a very cute, Hawaiian girl. And, if you have to get patted down by a cute Hawaiian girl, then, "You gotta do what cha gotta do!"

Aloha!

Amen!

---

[143]Philippians 4:7

Silence Is Golden
Cancer Awareness

Back in the old days, I often heard people say, "Silence is golden."

At times, that indeed is true. In a movie theater, silence is golden. In a room with a sleeping baby, silence is golden. Even while watching certain parts of a heated football game, silence is golden. But, there are times in our lives when we go from the point where silence is considered to be golden to where our silence can truly become deadly.

Far too often, there are times in our lives when we have chosen to remain silent when we should have been speaking up. We should have been speaking out. We should have been taking action. But, we chose to be silent rather than speaking out and risking the serenity that our silence once brought up. In the society in which we now live, we must realize now more than ever that we cannot remain silent when our silence can become deadly.

Back when I was growing up, there once was a time when what we are doing today would have been considered a taboo. Today, as we openly address the realms of cancer, especially cancer in the African-American community, we are breaking the silence of many ages.

We are breaking the silence that has indeed become deadly.

I can remember back in the 1970's, when a family member was diagnosed with cancer it was often kept as a secret amongst the relatives and friends. Although hundreds of thousands were dying from cancer each year, it seemed like no one wanted to openly discuss what was happening in our society.

Back when I was a child, my family would often travel to Plaquemine, Louisiana to visit my great-grandmother and all of our "country" relatives who lived "down da bayou."

One of my most favorite places to visit was the home of my Uncle Winton and Aunt Inez. Their house was always filled with love and laughter. Part of it was because they had six children living in a six room house. But the greater part was because they just loved being together and sharing the love of their family with others. When we went to their house, even if we were sleeping on a pallet on the floor under the kitchen table, we knew that we were at home.

My Uncle Winton worked for the Dow Chemical Plant. He loved his job almost as much as he loved his family. And, oh how proud we were of him. A hard-working man, who was doing all he could do to take care of his family and also spending much of his life helping to take care of his aging mother and other families, too. In my eyes, my uncle Winton was the epitome of life and love.

Uncle Winton seemed to be able to handle anything that came his way. From the trials and tribulations of being a good father to the struggles of keeping a house over his family's head when Black folks in the country were still struggling for Civil Rights, my Uncle Winton seemed to be a man who could handle anything.

But, the day came when Uncle Winton was faced with something that he could not defeat. The day came when Uncle Winton's once strong body became painfully frail. The day came when his home that was once filled with laughter and joy suddenly seemed dark and lonely.

The day came when the sounds of life in that little Plaquemine, Louisiana home were silenced. And because no one truly understood what was happening, no one wanted to talk about it. They especially would not say much to the children.

As I look back at those days, I realize now more than even that silence is not always golden. My Uncle Winton died from cancer in a time when no one would openly talk about it. They would whisper that he had "it"or they might say he had the "C." No one could fix their mouth to openly say he had cancer and that the cancer was taking his life. Everybody just stayed silent in a time when silence was neither golden nor glittery. Silence became deadly because no one, back when I was a child, would talk about the "C."

Today, we cannot remain silent in the face of cancer. We cannot remain silent and allow cancer to continue to plague our world. We cannot remain silent, if we are going to be able to help our God and our doctors to truly be able to do the work of healing and eradicate the deadly diseases that fall under the banner of cancer from our society. When it comes down to defeating these deadly diseases, silence cannot help. It can only hurt.

In their closing reports for 2008, the American Cancer Society reported that the African-American community has the highest death rate and shortest survival of any other racial or ethnic group in the United States for most forms of cancer.

Although the causes are complex, when combining economics and access to adequate health care, it is clear that part of the struggle come from the silence that can prevent early detection and know where to go to seek proper treatment.

In 2003, the death rate for all cancers combined continues to be 35% higher in Black men and 18% higher in Black women. Combined with the other diseases that plague our society such as heart disease, AIDS and Hepatitis, the life expectancy is lower for African Americans than for non-African Americans. Although the average White man is expected to live to see his 75th birthday, the average Black man is only expected to live to see his 69th birthday.

It is time for us to stop being silent. We cannot keep sitting back and watching our brothers and sisters die from many diseases that can be defeated. We have to begin to speak up, to shout it out, and to say to the Devil, "It's time for this to stop!" We have to break the silence if we are going to defeat these diseases.

Two of the leading cancers in our community are breast cancer and prostate cancer. In this year alone, it is estimated that more than 19,000 new cases of breast cancer will be found in African-American women: making breast cancer the most common cancer among Black women.

Although it is the most common form of cancer with our women, it's rates are stabilizing among women who are 50 and older and actually decreasing among women under 50. Part of these changes are coming because of the successor of self exams and mammography. Although having an annual mammography is not the most pleasant thing for a woman to do, it can save you life. Not knowing is the most deadly thing that can happen to you. Early detection is the key to winning this battle.

Among our men, prostate cancer accounts for 37% of all cancers diagnosed in our community. More than 30,000 new cases were expected to be discovered in 2009. Like women and breast cancer, we men don't really want to discuss prostate cancer. And, we definitely don't want to discuss how difficult it is to go through a prostate check. All I will say is it involves a rubber glove and going where no man has gone before. So, rather than getting regular checks, we would much rather remain silent and live in the unknown.

But, my brothers, we too, cannot stay quiet when it comes to fighting prostate cancer. We cannot keep thinking that "it won't happen to me." We cannot hide from what has become second only to lung cancer in our community. We cannot remain silent because that kind of silence is never golden.

We do not die from cancer as some form of remediation for our sins. We do not die from cancer because we somehow deserve it. We are dying at alarming rates because we just don't want to talk about it. We don't want to face the reality that it is real. It is in our midst.

Well, it is time for the silence to be broken. It is time for us to cry out to the Lord to save us.

In the Gospel of Mark, there is a story of a blind man who knew that breaking his silence was the only way he could possibly be healed.

In the 10th Chapter of Mark's Gospel, we hear,

> *As Jesus was leaving Jericho with His disciples and a sizable crowd, Bartimaeus, a blind man, the son of Timaeus, sat by the roadside begging.*
>
> *On hearing that it was Jesus of Nazareth, He began to cry out and say, "Jesus, Son of David, have pity on me."*
>
> *And many rebuked him, telling him to be silent. But hhe kept calling out all the more, "Son of David, have pity on me."*
>
> *Jesus stopped and said, "Call him." So they called the blind man, saying to him, "Take courage; get up, He is calling you."*
>
> *He threw aside his cloak, sprang up, and came to Jesus.*
>
> *Jesus said to him in reply, "What do you want Me to do for you?" The blind man replied to Him, "Master, I want to see."*
>
> *Jesus told him, "Go your way; your faith has saved you." Immediately he received his sight and followed Him on the way.*[144]

In this story, we see how a blind man named Bartimaeus cried out to Jesus as the Lord passed along the road. Although Bartimaeus could not see Jesus with his eyes, he could feel the presence of the Lord in his midst. And, so, humbling himself before the Lord, he cried out, "Jesus, Son of David, have pity on me!"

"Have pity on me!"

With faith in his heart, and the courage of his ancestors, he cried out and Jesus heard his pleas. When Jesus asked him what did he really want, the blind man simply said, "I want to see."

---

[144]Mark 10:46-52

He didn't give Jesus a long explanation on what seeing would truly mean to him.

He didn't explain to the Lord how long he had been blind or how much heartache he had endured.

He simply said, "I want to see." And, it was in his simple but faith-filled request that the Lord healed him. Without asking how did you get it or why do you have it, Jesus simply said, "Go your way, you faith has saved you!" And with that, the blind man's sight was restored.

Today, we as a community must cry out like a blind man on the side of the road. We must cry out as we feel the presence of Christ in our midst. We must cry out while others would have us sit on the side of the road and continue to beg for pity or simply just fade away.

We cannot remain silent if we are going to eradicate these deadly diseases from our society. We cannot remain silent. We must encourage our men, women and children to take advantage of the medical procedures that God has allow doctors and researchers to discover.

By being proactive in our battle with cancer, we can indeed prevent or detect early some of the deadliest cancers in our community.

We must encourage doctors and health care providers to do all that they can to make sure that adequate health care facilities are provided in our community. Everyone must have the same access to all of the newly developed, life-saving procedures.

We also must contact our elected officials and tell them that we want affordable health care for everyone. We cannot remain silent. We must speak out if we are going to save our community.

Like Bartimaeus, we have to cry out to the Lord of Life, Jesus Son of David, have pity on us. And just like with Bartimaeus, we don't have to go into lengthy discussions on how we got it or how bad it is. We only have to say, "Today, Lord, we want to be cancer free."

Today, we must break the silence that once filled our hearts. We must break the silence that once darkened my Uncle Winton's country home. We must break the silence that has been killing our men, women and children for far too long. We must be resolved to end the one thing that has been the greatest plague in our community.

It's not the cancer that has been our great killer. It is not talking about it, not taking actions that can bring about early detection, and not facing it head on. We have to be just as brave just as Bartimaeus was when he approached Jesus to be healed.

It's not cancer that kills us. It's the silence.

And, proof that silence is not always golden.

Today, we say to our Lord,
   "Jesus Son of David, have pity on us for being silent."

Today, we, as a people, want to be cancer free.

Amen!

We Stand Firm on God's Promises

Yet it was our infirmities that he bore,
our sufferings that he endured,
While we thought of him as stricken,
as one smitten by God and afflicted.

But he was pierced for our offenses,
crushed for our sins,

SECTION THREE
Reflections on Forgiveness

Forgive Us Our Trespasses

As We Forgive Those Who Trespass Against us

True Forgiveness is Never Easy

Late one afternoon, Father Joe went up to Father Frank and said,
"I am SICK and TIRED of always having to be the priests.
I wish that we could have just one night where we could just go out and let loose. We could go to the casino, go to the bar and just have a good time. I just want one night when we could just 'party like it's 1999.'"

Father Frank was shocked. "Are you nuts?" he shouted.

"This is a small town and everyone knows us. If we go to any of the local clubs, we're all but guaranteed to run into someone we know."

Fr. Joe said, "That's all right, Frank, because I've got a plan.

We could drive over to our neighboring state and go to their casinos. Over there, we could play the slot machines, play blackjack and poker and even drink if we want to drink. Nobody knows us over there."

"Well Joe," said Fr. Frank, "if you think that it will work, let's give it a try."

So, later that night Fr. Joe and Fr. Frank headed across the state border.

They had a good time going from casino to casino.
They played cards and drank beers seemingly forgetting that they were both priests.

After dragging themselves back into the Rectory at about 5 o'clock the morning, Fr. Fred began to feel really bad.

"Joe, man, we should have never done that" said Fr. Frank.
"As priests, we should never be hanging out in casinos, gambling and drinking. It's just not right! Even if the people never find out what we've done, God will always know."

"I understand how you feel," said Fr. Joe, "and I've got a plan.

"Tomorrow morning, we'll get up and go into the church.
You can hear my confession and I can hear your confession.
That way, we can make this right with God."

"That's a great idea" said Fr. Frank.

Early the next morning, Fr. Frank put on his vestments and headed into the confessional. Not long after, Fr. Joe came in, knelt down and said,
"Bless me, Father, for I have sinned. Last night, my priest friend and I went over to the casinos. We gambled, got drunk and dragged ourselves into the rectory at about 5 o'clock in the morning. I really do feel bad. I hope that God and you will forgive me."

Fr. Frank answered, "The Lord is patient and forgiving, and so shall I be. For you penance, why don't you say 5 Hail Mary's, 5 Our Father's and donate 10 dollars to the poor and you will be absolved of your sin."

"Thank you," said Fr. Joe.

After a short while, they switch sides and Fr. Frank began his confession.
"Bless me, Father, for I have sinned." he said.
"Last night, my priest friend and I went over to the casinos. We gambled, got drunk and dragged ourselves into the rectory at about 5 o'clock in the morning. I also do feel bad. I hope that God and you will forgive me."

After a short pause, Fr. Joe shouted, "I don't believe this!

How DARE you call yourself a priest!

If you even want to be forgiven, you will do 500 "Our Father's", 500 "Hail Mary's", you will donate all your money for the next month to the church, and go around the church 500 times on your knees praying for the Lord's forgiveness. Then come back and we'll discuss absolution, but I'm not promising you anything!"

"WHAT??!!" Father Frank was shocked. "What's wrong with you Joe?"

"Hey," Fr. Joe replied,
"What I do with my free time is one thing, but I take my job seriously!"

Lord, Lord, Lord, forgiveness is big business!

From the dawn of time, God has called us to focus on the Gift of Forgiveness. Unlike Frank and Joe's arranged forgiveness, God wants us to truly focus on real forgiveness. The kind of forgiveness that comes when it is least expected. The kind of forgiveness that comes from our hearts.

Much of the Hebrew Scriptures[145] were written to somehow unite us with the love of God and the love of our neighbor. Each of the books of the Old Testament was written in anticipation of the arrival of the greatest source of forgiveness: Jesus the Christ.

In the Book of Sirach[146], for example, we are told that forgiveness is not an easy task.

Sirach says,

> *Wrath and anger are hateful things, yet the sinner hugs them tight.*

> *The vengeful will suffer the Lord's vengeance, for He remembers their sins in detail.*

> *Forgive your neighbor's injustice; then when you pray, your own sins will be forgiven.*

> *Should a man nourish anger against his fellows and expect healing from the Lord?*

> *Should a man refuse mercy to his fellows, yet seek pardon for his own sins?*

> *If he who is but flesh cherishes wrath, who will forgive his sins?*

> *Remember your last days, set enmity aside; remember death and decay, and cease from sin! Think of the commandments, hate not your neighbor; of the Most High's covenant, and overlook faults.*[147]

---

[145]The Old Testament

[146]Another name for the Book of Sirach is The Book of Ecclesiasticus

[147]Sirach 27:30-28:7

Our human inclination is to be a people who hold grudges and seek vengeance when we are wronged. But, the author of this book reminds us that if we do not forgive as we should, one day it will all come back on us.

That is why the author says, *"The vengeful will suffer the Lord's vengeance, for He remembers their sin in detail."*

That is why we are told to *"remember your last days (and) set aside enmity."* In other words, remember that one day you will have to stand before God and account for the bitterness that you have carried in your hearts.

Don't go to your grave carrying a grudge on your heart because a heavy heart will make it hard for you to climb the stairway to Heaven!

That is why the call to forgive others is primarily a call to conversion of the heart.

Believe it or not, one of the highest forms of conversion is found in being able to forgive someone who has deeply hurt you. In order to forgive, you have to swallow your pride and allow God to deal with the situation at hand and with any judgement that might need to be rendered.

In the 103ʳᵈ Psalm, we are also told that one day we will have to account for our sins and our bitterness. But, we can take comfort in knowing that unlike human beings, God is a loving and forgiving God. Thus, we should rejoice and praise God in all we say and all we do.

Psalm 103 tells us,

> *Bless the LORD, my soul; all my being, bless his holy name!*
> *Bless the LORD, my soul; do not forget all the gifts of God,*
> *Who pardons all your sins, heals all your ills,*
> *Delivers your life from the pit, surrounds you with love and*
> *compassion, Fills your days with good things; your youth is*
> *renewed like the eagle's. The LORD does righteous deeds, brings*
> *justice to all the oppressed. His ways were revealed to Moses,*
> *mighty deeds to the people of Israel. Merciful and gracious is the*
> *LORD, slow to anger, abounding in kindness. God does not*
> *always rebuke, nurses no lasting anger, Has not dealt with us as*
> *our sins merit, nor requited us as our deeds deserve.*[148]

---

[148]Psalm 103:1-10

Unlike human beings, God does not hold grudges against those who have repented of their sinfulness. In fact, the psalmist tells us that when it comes to the sins that we have confessed, *"As far as the east is from the west, so far have our sins been removed from us."*[149]

The Psalmist also tells us that *"As a father has compassion on his children, so the Lord has compassion on the faithful. For He knows how we are formed, remembers that we are dust."*[150] Ultimately, God knows that we are limited beings. Having made us from dust, He knows that we are not perfect and will always be in need of His unconditional love.

St. Paul fully understood what his ancestors spoke about in the Hebrew Scriptures. In reflecting on his own limited nature, he tells all of us that we need to be ever grateful for God's unchanging hand and unending love. As God's children on earth, we are destined to be with the Lord in Heaven. The only thing that we need to do is remain faithful to our calling from God.

In *St. Paul's Letter to the Romans*, we are reminded that our lives do not belong to us. For, through the ultimate sacrifice of forgiveness, Jesus Christ purchased us and our salvation. As the disciples of Christ, we have become the children of God. That means that we belong to the Lord. In this letter, St. Paul writes,

> *None of us lives for oneself, and no one dies for oneself. For if we live, we live for the Lord, and if we die, we die for the Lord; so then, whether we live or die, we are the Lord's.*[151]

This means that we must be Christ to one another. We must treat others as Christ treats us. This is why we must be willing to forgive one another.

Those, who hold grudges and backbiting vengefulness, are not living as folks who belong to the Lord. They are living as if they belong to some other power. If you are refusing to forgive, you are really living according to the power of Satan and not the power of God. Rather than holding on to grudges, you ought to be saying, "Get thee behind me," to the grudges that might be weighing heavy on their hearts.

---

[149]Psalm 103:12

[150]Psalm 103:13-14

[151]Romans 14:7-8

The Life, Death and Resurrection of Jesus Christ assure us that we can find salvation when we find God in our brothers and sisters. We must always keep in mind that we are fashioning our eternal future by the way we treat others.

In the Gospel of our Brother Matthew, St. Peter approached Jesus and asked,

> *"Lord, if my brother sins against me, how often must I forgive him? As many as seven times?"*
>
> *Jesus answered, "I say to you, not seven times but seventy-seven times."*[152]

In saying that we should forgive someone *"not seven times but seventy-seven times"*, Jesus was basically addressing the limitless nature of real forgiveness. Real forgiveness must be based in unconditional love. That means that our love must not have prerequisites or requirements.

Jesus wasn't implying that after seventy-seven times of forgiving someone, you could give up on them. What He was implying was that forgiveness should not be held to a specific amount of times. True forgiveness cannot be measured in quantity. It can only be measured in quality. Real forgiveness, heartfelt forgiveness has no limit.

We should also remember that in reciting the *Lord's Prayer,* we pray that God will *"Forgive us our trespasses as we forgive those who trespass against us."*[153] So, if we do not forgive those who have hurt us, how can we possibly expect God to forgive us when we hurt Him with our sins?

You know, it really is easy to answer the question, "How often must I forgive someone who has sinned against me?" All you have to do is ask yourself, "How often do I expect God to forgive me when I sin against Him?"

When you put it in that perspective, then countlessly forgiving someone is not as hard as you may think. To constantly hold grudges, to constantly seek vengeance, to constantly refuse to forgive anyone who has hurt you makes a mockery of the forgiveness we celebrate through the Death and Resurrection of Jesus Christ. Holding on to grudges says that you do not fully understand what we do when we gather for prayer or to celebrate the Eucharist.

---

[152]Matthew 18:21-22

[153]Matthew 6:12

As Roman Catholics, we believe that the Eucharist is the ultimate reminder of God's gift of reconciliation. On the Altar of Sacrifice, we recall the Life, Death and Resurrection of One who was sent to redeem the world, to reconcile us with the Father.

Now, if Jesus could give us His Body and Blood, in order that our sins might be fully forgiven by our God, surely there is nothing that you cannot sacrifice for Him. Even if it means you have to give up that hurtful thing that you have carried in your heart for years.

On this day, let us call to mind anything that might be separating us from one of God's children.

Let us think about the folks who have hurt us and we have refused to forgive them.

Let us take whatever it is that might be weighing heavy on our hearts and on this day, give it over to the Savior.

Whoever it is, whatever it was, whatever it might be, take it, this day, and lay it at the foot of the cross. For then and only then, will you truly be able to understand the forgiveness that God has given you.

Forgive us our trespasses as we forgive those who trespass against us.

Forgive us our debts as we forgive our debtors.

"Lord, if my brother or sister sins against me, how often must I forgive, . . . seven times?

"Not seven times, but seventy-seven times."

Amen!

Forgiving the Unforgettable

How do I forgive you?

How do I forgive you when I know that you hurt me on purpose?

How do I continue to look you in the eye when I know that you haven't stopped trying to hurt me?

How do I live with the knowledge that although I never intentionally tried to hurt you, you did everything in your power to hurt, defame and destroy my life?

How do I forgive you when I know you hurt me on purpose?

One of the harshest realities of life is the fact that we hurt one another and we often do it on purpose.

We do it with our words. We do it with our deeds. We do it with our bad intentions and our pretentious desires.

We hurt one another. And, we often do it on purpose.

In facing this harsh reality, we are also faced with an even tougher position: How do I forgive you when I know you hurt me on purpose?

I once heard that "to err is human and to forgive divine."[154] I wonder if that means that I don't have to forgive people since I'm not divine but forgiveness is.

If forgiveness is divine, maybe only God has to forgive people for their sins.

But, "to err is human." So, even if I don't have to forgive, I have to at least realize that I am human and I will err. I will do something that is wrong and I will do it on purpose.

So, what's so divine about forgiveness? What makes the act of forgiving so holy?

First, we must realize that true forgiveness comes directly from God. Time and time again, our Heavenly Father has had to *"forgive us our trespasses."*[155]

---

[154]"An Essay on Criticism" by Alexander Pope

[155]Matthew 6:12

Quite often, God has had to touch our very souls and wipe away our sins. When we sinned against God and His Church, He forgave us. When we broke one of His Commandments, He forgave us. When we hurt Him by hurting one of His earthly sons or daughters, He forgave us.

God has forgiven us far more times than we have ever deserved. That is why "to err is human" - that is part of the reality of our lives - "but to forgive is divine" - that is part of the reality of our God.

But, we must be keenly aware that in forgiving us of our trespasses, God turns to us and calls us to then *"forgive those who trespass against us."*

Forgive those who trespass against us - knowingly or unknowingly. Forgive those who hurt us - on purpose or unintentionally. *"Forgive those who trespass against us."* In doing this, we do for others what God has repeatedly done for us. But, we should also be aware that the act of forgiveness is not an act of just giving to others. It is also an act of freeing one's self.

I once read:

> The act of "forgiveness is the miracle of a new beginning. It is to start where we are, not where we wish we were, or the other person was.
>
> It is to hold out a hand; to want to renew a friendship; to want a new relationship with husband, father, (son,) daughter, friend, or indeed (my) enemy.
>
> It may not take away the hurt. It does not deny the past injury. It does not ignore the possibility and need for repentance and a change in the relationship.
>
> It means being willing to take the initiative in dealing with any barriers that I may be raising towards a restored relationship.
>
> It means that I am willing to have a relationship with the other party that is based on Christian love and not on what has happened in the past, if the response of the other person makes that possible." [156]

---

[156] http://www.christianity.co.nz/forgive3.htm

In other words, I must strive to forgive those who have hurt me - not just for their sake - but really for my own sake. In offering forgiveness to another person, I really am offering freedom to myself. Letting go of the hatred in my heart makes room in my heart for the blessings of God!

Another reality of forgiveness is the fact that no one can make me forgive a person who has hurt me. Forgiveness is part of the internal forum. It is part of the mind, heart and spirit. Thus, I must choose to forgive someone. It can't be forced.

I remember back in the old days, when I was in elementary school. Whenever we had a fight on the school yard, the teachers would make you stand up in front of the person you were fighting and say, "I'm sorry." And after, the other person said, "I'm sorry," too, you then shook hands as a sign of forgiveness.

But, more times than not, as you were looking each other in the eyes, you were not offering forgiveness, you were probably saying, "Three O'clock at the Oak Tree - Let's finish this!" Even though it looked like forgiveness was being offered, reconciliation was not actually taking place.

Today, God calls us to be men and women of true forgiveness - not just because it will be an act of letting go and letting God be the judge but because it is an act of freeing oneself. *"To err is human but to forgive divine."* To err is to bind up yourself and others - to forgive is to set yourself and others free.

Through the Grace of God, may you finally be able to let go of the past hurts of your life. May God give you the strength to loosen the bounds of your heart and allow self-healing to begin. May you see the err of your unforgiving ways, and work now to be the loving person that God has called you to be.

In the name of Jesus, our Suffering Servant, May God forgive you as you forgive those who trespass against you.

How do I forgive you when I know you hurt me on purpose?

The only way that I can do it is by looking to the cross and realizing that Christ forgave me, even though He knew that I put Him there on purpose.

Now is the time for forgive.

Lord, *"forgive us our trespasses as we forgive those who trespass against us."*

Amen!

MANTENIENDOLO REAL

Reflexiones Sobre la Fe, la Esperanza y el Perdón

Rev. R. Tony Ricard, M.Th., M.Div.

Publicado en 2011

303

Introducción - *Manteniendolo Real*

Mis querido hermanos y hermanas:

La parte más emocionante de la escritura *Manteniendolo Real* era mi deseo de tener lo tradujo al Español. A pesar de que no era capaz de tener datos a continuación, todo traducido, espero que disfruten de mis esfuerzos iniciales. Quiero agradecer a la señora Bélgica Coignet para la traducción de estas reflexiones. Usted me está ayudando a expandir mi ministerio.

Sé que habrá algunos errores gramaticales en las traducciones. Por lo tanto, pido disculpas por ellos. Hay algunas tildes que faltan y las palabras mal escritas. Sólo recuerde que estoy tratando muy duro para llegar a su comunidad. Tengo muchas ganas de presentar más de mi trabajo a la comunidad Latina.

Los centros de la sección primera en ser personas de Fe en tiempos de problemas. Hay tiempos que se sienten perdidos en este mundo, sabemos que Dios está siempre a nuestro lado. La segunda sección se centra en el don de la Esperanza que el Amor del Espíritu Santo trae. Incluso en nuestra hora más oscura, sabemos que el Cordero de Dios nos llevará a un mejor día. La tercera sección se centra en nuestro poder del Perdón. A pesar de que nunca se puede olvidar veces hirientes, podemos encontrar la libertad en la decisión de perdonar.

A través del Amor de Dios,
que tu vida siempre que se lo *Manteniendolo Real.*

Rev. R. Tony Ricard, M.Th., M. Div.

Desarrollando La Fe De Un Tonto

Estaba sentado en mi oficina, cuando uno de nuestros parroquianos Viejo llego. Ella se sento en la silla cerca de mi escritorio, de repente se pone a llorar.

"Senora Lilian que le pasa? Yo le pregunte.

"Bueno Padre,"Ella sollozaba, "estuve abajo en la otra iglesia y ellos se negaron a enterrar a mi Amado Eddie."

"Usted quiere decir que no quisieron enterarle a su Amado Eddie?" Pregunte.

"Usted ve Padre" Ella continuo, "Eddie y yo hemos estado juntos por quince anos; adonde yo iva el estuvo a mi lado. Si iva al bano, Eddie estuvo alli. Si iva al Mercado, Eddie iva conmigo, aun cuando yo iva al bano, Eddie me esperaba atras de la puerta.

Pero en los ultimos dias, cada vez que le ponia agua en su plato, el se negaba a beber."

"Que usted quiere decir que cuando le puso agua en un plato?" Yo pregunte.

"O Padre, Eddie fue mi perro," Ella contesto.

"Lo siento, Senora Lilian, pero nosotros no enterramos perro." Le conteste.

"Bueno Padre," Ella comenzo a decir, "pensaba darle diez mil dolares al sacerdote que entierre a mi querido perro."

Yo le respondi, "porque no me dijo que el era Catolico."

Porque usted es tan Loco?

Esa era la pregunta que mi secretaria anterior Brenda siempre me preguntaba.

Me imagino que mucha gente que han estado alrededor mio, me han visto en accion o me han escuchado seguro se hacen la misma pregunta.

Porque ese chico tan loco?
    O Porque tan tonto?

Bueno, mi objetivo es de ayudarles de alguna forma contestar esa misma pregunta. A traves de este libro, yo espero que tendran una mejor comprension lo que toma para ser un tonto.

No un tonto ante Dios, pero un tonto para Dios.

Que esto significa de tener la fe de un tonto?

En la primera carta de San Pablo del Corintios nos dice;

Pues mirad, hermanos, vuestra vocación, que no sois muchos sabios según la carne, ni muchos poderosos, ni muchos nobles;

sino que lo necio del mundo escogió Dios, para avergonzar a los sabios; y lo débil del mundo escogió Dios, para avergonzar a lo fuerte; y lo vil del mundo y lo menospreciado escogió Dios, y lo que no es, para deshacer lo que es, a fin de que nadie se jacte en su presencia. [157]

Que significa ser un tonto?

Significa que has entendido que solo lo que hacemos para Dios es lo unico que dura.

Entendiendo que si Dios es para nosotros, quien puede estar en contra?

Significa que lo que se vea como una tonteria ante los ojos del hombre, puede que un dia se vea como una sabiduria ante los ojos de Dios.

Que significa ser un tonto para el Senor?

Significa que tu estas de acuerdo a ser el sirviente de Dios, incluso cuando otros creen que tu estas loco.

"Dios escoge a los tontos para avergonzar a los sabios."

Entonces, cual es el significado de ser el tonto para tu senor?

Significa que no tomes las cosas demasiado en serio.

---

1 Corintios 1:26-29

Un tonto sabe que la vida se debe vivir, tienes que gozarla.Tienes que atraer la felicidad. La vida es muy corta para que nosotras seamos miserables. Eso significa que cada dia, necesitamos encontrar algo en la vida para reirnos, y algo para que nuestra mente descanse.

Todos no necesitamos ser payasos. Pero necesitamos ser fieles tontos!

Mas bien ser los mas tonto fieles.
Un insensato no comprende lo que es verdadero.
Un tonto insensate no comprende que la vida no es siempre facil, ve la realidad que esta enfrente de el o antes ella.

Porque un tonto insensato trata de sofocar los Dolores del Corazon detras de una fachada de alegria.

Pero si su alegria es solo momentanea,si su alegria es solo por fuera, entonces su alegria es insensata.
Pablo nos llama a ser. Eres simplemente un tonto insensato antes que un tonto fiel.

Entonces como puede uno ser un tonto sin llegar a ser un tonto insensate?

Asi que uno tiene que ser un tonto fiel.
Debe ser un tonto fiel para el senor.

Si Dios escoge realmente el insensato del mundo para avergonzar al sabio, entonces ser creido insensato en los ojos del hombre es de contestar sinceramente la llamada de Dios.

Para ser un tonto para el senor usted tiene que estar dispuesto a vivir por el codigo de la moralidad y volores que este mundo escarnecera. Tienes que estar dispuesto a sacrificarse por otros. Tiene que estar dispuesto a desafiar tanto al tradicional como al convencional sabiduria del hombre. Tiene que estar dispuestos a ser contra cultural. Cuando otros quizas quieren abandonarle tiene que mantenerse firme y tener fe.

Un tonto fiel confia no en la sabiduria del hombre pero unicamente en la sabiduria de Dios.

Se que los tonto corren donde los angeles temen pisar. Pero a veces usted debe apurarse y entrar corriendo.

Yo creo que es mejor tener una muerte valiente de un tonto que vivir la vida que vive un rey cobarde.

Cuando actua contra-cultural sera llamado un tonto y encontrara que usted mismo sera ridiculizado ante el hombre; pero a veces Dios te llama a ser eso mismo. Hay que tener valor para ser un tonto. No es facile estar siempre feliz! Pero vale la pena.

Para ser un tonto fiel, tienes que arriesgar el fracaso y la perdida. No todo sale de la manera que tu esperaba, pero eso esta bien.

Es preferible haber amado y haber perdido, que nunca haber amado. Solo tienes que tener valor y ser fiel y un adorado insensato. Tomando ese riesgo es mejor que vendiendo tu alma o no utilizando tu sentado comun para que les gustes.

Nunca dejes que la manera del hombre te hagan cambiar los que tu Corazon te esta diciendo que hagas. Si no se siente bien probablemente no es bueno. Bueno yo se que no todo hombre es correcto, todos hacemos errores.

Todos nos hemos equivocado en algo, eso solo significa que tu has realizado que no siempre vas a estar en lo correcto. Es pore so que tenemos que contar con el espiritu santo, para darnos la sabiduria para hacer la decision correcta. Tambien tenemos que contar con la sabiduaria de nuestros antepasados y los ancianos. No tenemos que cortar un camino Nuevo a traves de la foresta de la vida, simplemente tenemos que seguir el camino que esta ahi cortadas por aquellos que sacrificaron sus vidas para que nosotros estuvieramos hoy aqui.

Muchos de los santos de Dios son considerados tontos hoy. Hombres como San Dominique y San Francisco eran considerados tonto en sus tiempos. Ellos dejaron sus riquezas para vivir la vida de los pobres y ayudar a los necesitados. Mujeres como Santa Katherine Drexel y la Madre Henrietta De Lille fueron considerados tontas en sus tiempos. Ellas no solamente dejaron sus riquezas y el prestigio, ellas tomaron el dinero que tenian y empezaron unos ministerios que dedicaron para ayudar a la gente de color.Eso de acuerdo con el mundo fue una tonteria. Pero en sus tonterias se convirtieron en instrumentos para el amor de Dios.

Como ellas, debemos ser ideales de la fe, la esperanza y el amor.

Como sirvientes de Dios ,la Madre Henrietta dijo que *'Creo en Dios, mi esperanza esta en Dios, adoro a Dios y yo quiero vivir y morir por Dios."* Cualquiera que viviera por ese principio tiene que ser un tonto.

Ser un tonto que quiere vivir y morirse por medios de Dios, que podemos ser los instrumentos de Dios aqui en la tierra! Tenemos que estar dispuesto a defender nuestra herencia y dignidad de todas las personas, debemos defender la dignidad del que no ha nacido,el pobre y la gente sin hogar,y el hambriento. Pero tambien debemos defender la heredada dignidad del rico,el pecador y el criminal

Si nosotros creemos que todos somos precioso ante los ojos de Dios, nosotros debemos entender que aunque despreciamos algunos, ellos tambien son hijos de Dios. Quizas no nos guste lo que ellos hagan, pero ante los ojos de Dios eso no los hace menos que nosotros.

Mas sus acciones pueden ser pecadoras pero,ellos todavia deben ser vistos como ninos de Dios. Quizas tratandolos como ninos de Dios, podemos invitarlos para que apoyen el doble de su familia.

Es facil para nosotros ver la gente sin hogar y decir que necesitan nuestra ayuda. Es facil para nosotros decir "defendamos al nino que no ha nacido" porque ellos nose pueden defender asi mismo. Es facil para nosotros mirar al desafortunado y decir "Esos son los que no necesitan" porque verdaderamente es la verdad.

Pero, un tonto fiel tambien sabe que ellos no son los unicos que nos necesitan,el hombre que es rico y los pecadores necesitan a Dios tambien.

Entonces nosotros no debemos descriminar a quien le debemos ofrecer amor sin condicion de Dios. El tonto fiel encontrara una manera para adorer a todos aun cuando usted no le guste lo que ellos ofrecen. La vida de un tonto fiel sigue la senda de cristo.

Para ayudarte a comprender sinceramente lo que el tonto fiel que Dios necesita que seas, hize una lista de cuatro cosas que creo deba estar en el que quiere ser un tanto fiel de Dios.

★   Amor
★   Cuidarlo
★   Dar
★   Perdonar

Para ser un tonto amoroso significa que adoramos con el Corazon de Cristo. Tambien debemos adorer cual es divertido y cuando duele.Cristo nos llama a adorer a todos, pero el no dice que tengo que quererle. Ve el amore s eterno, pero el querer es momentaneo.

Para ser un tonto amoroso, tenemos que tener un Corazon que compadezca y se comprometa con ellos. Para compadecerte tienes que sentir el dolor por alguien pero comprometete. !tu necesitas vivir su dolor! Nuestros amor y preocupacion tiene que ser manifestada por nuestros acciones, incluso cuando eso parezcan tonto ante los ojos del hombre.

Una vez oi una historia sobre un ninito que le enseno al mundo lo que es amor. Este ninito de 4 anos tenia un vecino que habia perdido su esposa recientemente. Cuando el ninito oyo al hombre llorando, el fue a su casa y se le sento en sus piernas, y se quedo ahi sin decir nada.

Cuando su madre le pregunto que el le habia dicho al vecino, el nino constesto simplemente, "Nada, solo lo ayude a llorar."

Aveces necesitamos a alguien que nos ayude a llorar, quizas lo que el tenia no habia arreglo y todo lo que necesitaba era llorar!

Para ser un tonto generoso, tenemos que estar listos para sacrificar todas las riquezas de este mundopor la unica razon de ayudar a alguien. Franis lo hizo. Dominiq lo hizo. Katherine y Henrietta lo hicieron tambien. No tenosmos qu ehacerlo en una gran escala, solo tenemos qu ehacer lo que podemos. Beato Teresa de Calcutta una vez dijo, "En esta vida, no podemos hacer obras grandes. Solo podemos hacer pequenas obras pero con una amor grande." Has obras pequenas con mucho amor y tu verdaderamente estarias en el caino de ser un tonto verdaderamente para tu Dios.

Para ser un tonto que perdona, tienes que aprender a olvidar las cosas que te hirieron.

Si, fue doloroso.
Si, tienes el derecho de nunca hablarle.
Si, no seria malo si se quemaran en el infierno!
Pero tienes que dejarle a Dios que desida.

Tenesmos que perdonar como cristo nos perdono!

Ya ves, ninguno de nosotros sommos perfecto. Por eso no podemos esperar que los otros sean perfectos.

Nosotros estamos imperfectos por el pecado original. Pero, podemos supera ese imperfect si desidieramos amar con el Corazon de Cristo. Tenemos que aprender a perdonar. Ademas cuando perdonamos, viramos la mesa contra la persona o personas que nos hirio.

Yo se que le molesta a esa persona cuando tu la vez y la saludas o le das un abrazo o un beso "aunque ellos saben que tu sabes" lo que ellos hagan dicho o han hecho a tus espaldas!

No le des la satisfaccion de convertirte en una persona mala como ellos. No tenemos tiempo para sus payasadas!

Para ser un tonto de Dios, tienes que ser amoroso, generoso, cuidadoso y perdonar. Y de esa manera Dios te usa para avergonzar al sabio.

En Mateo 5:11-12,

"Bienaventurados sois cuando por mi causa os vituperen y os persigan, y digan toda clase de mal contra vosotros, mintiendo. Gozaos y alegraos, porque vuestro galardón es grande en los cielos; porque asi persiguieron a los profetas que fueron antes de vosotros."

En otras palabras, dejar que se llama a un tonto! Tu no eres el primer tonto de Dios y no eres el ultimo.

Los profetas eran considerados tontos.
Los profetas les llamaron tontos.
La primera iglesia de padres era tonta.
Todos los santos eran tontos tambien.

Si nos consideramos tontos, almenos sabemos que estamos en buena compania!

Asi como el tio Sam nos necesita para la armada y ayudar a traer la paz y la libertad al mundo, Dios te necesita en su armada y que te conviertas en el tonto que Dios quiere que seas.

En este dia que Dios teda la fe y la fuerza para ser un fiel tonto.

Que tu puedas podenar a un lado las cosas de nino y ponte tu la fuerza de Dios y no lo que el hombre quiere Espero que seas un tonto para el Senor, que entiendas que solo los que aman, los que cuidan y los que perdonan pueden verdaderamente resivir la bendicion que el senor te prometio.

En Cristo, Senor escojemos las tonterias del mundo para avergonzar al sabio. Dios escoje al mas debil del mundo para avergonzar al fuerte y Dios escoje al humilde y al despreciado del mundo, a eso los que el mundo piensa que son nada, esos que piensas que valen algo. Para que nadie pueda alabarse ante Dios.

311

En este dia , espero que sepas que la unica manera que puedes entrar en el cielo es ser el tonto del Senor.

Mejor eso ellos preguntan "porque eres tan loco" o "quien se cree ese tonto" que estar enfrete de el para que me juzgue y oigo a Dios preguntarme, "quien es este tonto?"

Un dia muy frio en Boston, la hermana Maria Teresa y un hombre joven se encontraban hasta las rodillas en la nieve mientras que esperarban el bus.

"Hermana," dijo el muchacho, "hace demasiado frio para estar parado aqui esperando el bus. Usted no cree que deberiamos cruzar la calle y entrar a la taberna O'Malley`s. Nos podemos sentar cerca de la ventana para ver cuando el bus llegue."

"Bueno hijo," dijo la hermana, "si usted piensa que es una buena idea."

Asi fueron hacia la taberna.

"Tu sabes" dijo la hermana, "no creo que es Buena idea de sentarnos cerca de la ventana. La gente van a ver una monja sentada en una cantina. Deberiamos sentarnos en la parte de atras, y tu pudes vigilar para ver si viene el bus."

"Eso esta bien,"dijo el muchacho.

"Hermana ya, que estoy aqui, creo que me voy a tomar una cerveza," dijo el. "Usted quiere algo? Le puedo traer un te caliente, o un chocolate o café?"

"Bueno hijo", dijo la hermana, "mientras estamos aquí, porque no me traes un trago doble de vodka pero dile que le pongan en un vaso de plastico. No quiero que la gente sepa lo que estoy bebiendo.

"No hay problema hermana, si eso es lo que usted quiere," medio sonrio el muchacho.

Cuando el muchacho fue y le dijo al mesero que le diera una cerveza y un trago doble de vodka pero que lo pusiera en un vaso de plastico.

A eso el mesero le contesto, "no me digas que esa hermana esta aqui de Nuevo!"

Que hoy tu seas verdaderamente un tonto por tu senor.

Amen!

Dr. Tony Ricard M.D.

Cuando era nino yo sone con lleguar hacer medico. Yo queria ser conocido Dr. Tony Ricard un pediatra renonbrado mundialmente. A los 12 anos yo habia decidido a que iba a asistir a la Universidad de Tulane Médica de la Escuela.

Despues de graduarme de la facultadad de medicina yo estaria muy ocupado con todas las peticiones para mi servicio, pero aceptaria una oferta de un despensario pedratrico muy grande para convertirme en el medico principal.Despues de haber trabajado ahi como 10 anos, me convirtiria en el jefe principal del hospital del nino aqui en Nueva Orleans.

Ese fue mi sueno de ninez, ser el Dr. Tony Ricard. M.D., en la vercion de Nueva Orleans del Dr. Marcus Welby, M.D. Pero yo no tenia la menor idea que desde nino, Dios tenia diferentes suenos para mi. No paso mucho tiempo cuando Dios entro en mis suenos y me pidio que en vez de ser Doctor el queria que yo fuera un sacerdote catolico romano.

En el Evangelio de Mateo, nosotros oimos la historia de cuatro hombres que probablemente crecieron sonando con ser pescadore.

Cuando andaba en el mar de Galielea, el vio a dos hermanos, Simon que es llamado Pedro y su Hermano Andres. Lanzando una red en el mar, eran pescadores.

Dijo a ellos, si me sigues yo los hare Pescadores de hombres. Inmediatamente dejaron sus redes y lo siguieron.

Andando Jesús junto al mar de Galilea, vio a dos hermanos, Simón, llamado Pedro, y Andrés su hermano, que echaban la red en el mar; porque eran pescadores. Y les dijo: Venid en pos de mí, y os haré pescadores de hombres. Ellos entonces, dejando al instante las redes, le siguieron.

Pasando de allí, vio a otros dos hermanos, Jacobo hijo de Zebedeo, y Juan su hermano, en la barca con Zebedeo su padre, que remendaban sus redes; y los llamó. Y ellos, dejando al instante la barca y a su padre, le siguieron.

Y recorrió Jesús toda Galilea, enseñando en las sinagogas de ellos, y predicando el evangelio del reino, y sanando toda enfermedad y toda dolencia en el pueblo.[158]

---

[158]Mateo 4:18-23

Pedro, Andrés , Jacobo y Juan, eran todos de una familia de pescadores y probablemente seguian los pasos de sus padres. Yo apostaria que eran muy Buenos en sus negocios y proporcionaban unos ingresos solidos para sus familias vendiendo los pescados que atrapaban.

Los cuatro crecieron alrededor del mar de Galilea. Cada dia cuando eran jovenes, ellos probablemente veian a los pescadores recojiendo sus redes llenas de pescado. Ellos seguramente jugaron por el mar con sus barquitos de juguetes y buscaban con sus redes pequenas, sonando con el dia que dirijirian los barcos grandes y traer sus cargas de pescados.

Bueno ese dia llego. Ellos se convirtieron en Pescadores. Pero con ese dia, vino un llamamiento que cambio sus vidas.

Un dia glorioso cuando trabajaban con redes y barcos, Jesus anduvo por las costas y empezo a decirles que dejaran sus barcos y que se convirtieran en sus dicipulos.

El les dijo, *"siganme y los convertire en Pescadores de hombres."*[159]

El no pedia que vinieran a una misa especial del domingo. El les pedia que abandonaran sus suenos de ninez y sus sustentos actuales para llegara hacer sus apostoles y para ayudarles en su ministerio. San Mateo nos dicen que abandones inmediatamente nuestros redes y nos convirtieramos en sus seguidores.

Te puedes imaginara estar en tu trabajo, sentado en tu escritorio y mirar hacia arriba y ver a Jesus llamandote?

Sabiendo lo que sabemos hoy, seria definitivamente una decision facil para nosotros, levantarse y llegar hacer sus seguidores. Pero para los primeros apostoles tuvo que haber sido una decision dura. Sabian muy poco de este hombre de Nazaret. Habían oído probablemente algunas historias acerca de lo que predicaba y puede haber visto a Juan cuando se lo bautizó en el río de Jordania, pero eso fue todo.

Fue duro decidir abandoner un trabajo seguro para seguir a un hombre, que en sus propias palabras no tenia ningun lugar *donde descanzar sus cabezas.*[160]

---

[159]Mateo 7:19

[160]Lucas 9:58

314

Alli tenia que haber algo hacerca de ese hombre que hizo que ellos abandonaran sus redes para segurilo. De una manera muy honesta estos cuatro Pescadores tuvieron que haber sentado la presencia del Senor.

Aunque ellos no se percataron que Jesus, el hijo de Maria y Jose, el carpintero fuera realmente el hijo de Dios. Ellos si sintieron la presencia de Dios. Y fue esta presencia que ellos desearon.

En Jesus ellos sintieron la luz que Isaias proclamaba. En Jesus ellos ya no anduvieron a oscuras.[161] Porque esa era sinceramente una gran luz. Una luz que cambio los corazones y les dio una luz de suenos.

Les tomo poco tiempo para que Pedro, Andrés, Jacobo y Juan realizaron que tan brillante la luz de Cristo era. Una vez que se dieron cuenta dedicaron sus vidas a server y abandonaron sus vidas terrenal se convirtieron el en los defensores de El.

Mis hermanos y hermanas,
Igual que esos Pescadores, cada uno de nosotros es llamado por Jesus para que te conviertas en su seguidor. Cada uno de nosotros nos llamara para que seamos sus dicipulos, ser uno de aquellos que usa sus talentos y regales para expresar las buenas noticias.

Pero estariamos preparados para hacer lo que Pedro, Andrés, Jacobo y Juan hicieron y abandonar nuestras redes para inmediatamente seguirlo?

Es que estamos de acuerdo para haceruno de sus seguidores sin importarnos las consecuancias que pasen?

Es que estas listo para entregarte a Jesucritos?

La diferencia entre los cuatro Pescadores, Jesus no te esta pidiendo que abandones tu trabajo, o que te conviertas en predicadores iterantes. Pero, lo que el te pide es que apesar de todo seas su seguidor.

Esto significa que si eres abogado seas el abogado de Cristo.

Si eres maestro ensena la palabra de Cristo.

Si eres ama de cas haslo para Cristo.

---

[161]Isaias 9:1

No importa cuan sea tu papel en la vida, no importa lo que hagas, solo hazlo en el nombre de Cristo.

En cualquier aspect de tu vid debes ser autenticamente Cristiano, Catolico y hosnesto con tus valores y ensenanzas que han sido trasmitidos con los apostoles desde los dias de los apostoles. Tu no puedes ser cristiano honesto y hacer cosas que estan encontra de las creencias Cristianas. Como Ccristianos nos conocen por las buenas obras que hacemos.

Cuardate; *ellos sabran que somos Cristianos por nuestros amor.*[162]

Este joven que sonaba con algun dia ser doctor, escucho la llamado de Jesus y se convirtio en sacerdote; un llamado de un sueno que se convirtio en realidad. Y verdaderamente creo que muchas de las personas que lean este libro tendran un llamado como el mio.

Pero otros su llamado a server a Cristo y a su iglesia de una manera diferente. Muchos son llamados por Dios para que sean ministros de la iglesia y par aparticipar en la misa del domingo, como ministro eucaristico, lectores, mienbros del coro, servidores y servidores del altar. Otros nos prueban que son seguidores autenticos de cristo cuando se convierten en maestros de religion, maestros de la doctrina, gremio de senoras, club de hombres y grupo de jovenes. Hay muchas maneras para seguir a Cristo y debe estar listo para server a nuestros hermanos y hermanas.

Tenemos que decidir que si escuchamos el llamado de Cristo, no solo si le vamos a contestar y a seguirle.

Resemos juntos para que Dios nos ayude a entender nuestros papel en el mundo alrededor y nuestra comunidad Cristiana.

Recemos con este entendiemiento que si el nos llama tendremos el valor de contestarle.

Finalmente recemos juntos porque asi quizas continuemos la Buena obra que empezo con el carpintero y los cuatro Pescadores.

El les dijo, "siganme y los convertire en Pescadores de hombres."
Ellos inmediatamente abandonaron sus redes y se convirtieron en sus seguidores.

---

[162]Juan 13:35 - "En esto conocerán todos que sois mis discípulos, si tuviereis amor los unos con los otros."

Mamá Stasia - "Nunca Me Solto"

Cuando era nino, yo fui vendecido por haber crecido en un hogar lleno de amor. Mis padres trabajaron duro para proporcionarnos un ambiente seguro en donde nosotros teniamos mucha felicidad. Aunque nosotros no teniamos todos los lujos que abriamos deseado; lo que si tuvimos fue mucho amor.

Aunque estuvimos seguro que nuestra mama y nuestro papa nos adoraban, ellos no fueron la fuente mas grande del amor en nuestro hogar. Ve fuimos bendecidos para tener viviendo con nosotros nuestra abuela maternal Anestacia Bernadette Carlin Honore'. Y la "Mamá Stasia" fue verdaderamente una fuente ponderosa de puro amor. Para nosotros, ella fue el ejemplo mas verdadero y un amor sin condiciones.

La "Mamá Stasia" no tuvo la vida mas facil del mundo pero la vivio a lo mejor de su capacidad. Ella fue una mujer con mucho amor aunque como una madre joven,ella tuviera que enterrar a su primer hijo. El murio en un accidente de casa cuando solo tenia dos anos de edad. Se quedo una mujer que tenia mucho amor, aunque tuviera basicamente que criar siete ninos sola despues de un divorcio duro. Se quedo una mujer con mucho amor aunque a menudo se acostara con hambre y no sabiendo de donde iva a venir la proxima familia para su familia.

A pesar de lo que la vida puso ante ella, ella se quedo una mujer con mucho amor porque a travez de todo, ella nunca dudo que Dios proporcionaba.

En 1962, mi mama y mi hermana Deidra dejaron Nueva Orleans para unirse a padre en Munich, Alemania occidental. Donde mi padre servia en el ejercito de los Estados Unidos. A su regreso en marzo de 1965 ellos no solo llevaban a mi hermana con ellos y a mi hermano Kevin y al nino que seria el punto que alerdiaba que su trabajo habia creado (YO).

Unos anos antes de que mi abuela se mudara al cielo ella me conto hacerca del primer dia que mi familia regresaban a Nueva Orleans.

Ese dia, ella dijo, "vi a mi hija flaca, se bajo del bus con sus bolsas y sus bebes en remolque. En sus brazos ella tenia s este pequeno enfermo nino. Y cuando se bajo del bus ella lo puso en sus brazos y nunca me solto."

Estoy orgulloso de decir que fui ese bebe pequeno que mi mama entrego a la "Mamá Stasia" . Fue su puno amoroso que empezo en ese dia frio de 1965 que me guio y ayudo a travez de los tiempos dificiles de la nines y juventud.

Fue ese puno que me trajo a la iglesia todos los domingo y fue ese puno que me ayudo a adorer a Jesus tanto que dedicaria mi vida a sus servicios.

Verdaderamente ese puno adorado ayudo a cambiar un bebe enfermamente pequeno en un hombre dedicado a Dios.

Fue en Octubre de 1988, que el puno de mi abuela fue cambiado para siempre. Fue en ese mes que el centro de mi vida sufrio un derrame cerebral.

Cuando se la llebaban de la casa, solo lo que podian hacer era tener sus ojos abiertos. Ella no podia mover ninguna parate de su cuerpo. Cuando apurabamos a llebarla al Hospital de Humana, lo unico que podia pensar era como iva a sobrevivir en este mundo sin ella.
Yo le pedia a Dios por un milagro. Pero mi cirazon no esperaba uno.

Cuando la familia llegaba a la sala de espera, los medicos trataban fuerte para tratar de inverter los danos que el derrrame habia causado. Mietras esperabamos, temiamos que nosotros no la hibamos a tener con nosotros mas. Nos turnábamos para ir a la sala de emergencia para estar con ella, todos sabiamos que este Podria ser el dia cuando Dios la llama a su casa.

Alrededor del medio dia, el padre Howard Byrd del colegio secundario San Agustin habia llegado a darle los aceites de los enfermos, volvi con el como oro sosbre ella y le ponia loas aceites del enfermo.

Mientras que él era su unción, yo todavía estaba orando por un milagro. Yo no se si un milagro estaba en los planes del Senor, pero yo esperaba sin duda que yo resibier a uno.

Cuando salimos de la sala de emergencia el padre Byrd me miro y dijo, "sabes, ella va a estar bien." Aunque yo aprecie sus palabras amorosas, yo les aseguro que yo no Estaba tan seguro como el.

Como una hora y algo, todos continuamos Tomando turnos en la sala de urgencias y mantener una vigilancia. Nosotros nunca deseabamos que ella estuviera aya sola.

Cuando me sente junto a su camilla, yo le aseguraba que iva a estar bien. Podria ver en sus ojos que estabas un poco alerta y probablemente con miedo. Asi que yole dije que todos estaban resando por ella.

Cuando estaba sentado ahi atemorizado de lo que el future traeria si ella no Estaba aqui, el milagro que "todos habiamos estado esperando sucedio." Ella me miro y dijo simplemente, "Mi Nino donde esta tu mama?"

Yo no le puedo decir cuanto significa a mi oirla hablar. No es necesario decir nada, yo Sali del cuatro corriendo hacia mi mama y dije, "Su Mama la llama."

Y ahi frente a mis ojos, la cura que es prometida en el sacramento del aceite enfermo sucedio. Ahi enfrente de mi ojos nosotros presenciabamos nuestro milagro ms grande de la familia.

Al leer el evangelio de nuestro hermano Marco yo encontre una historia que me recordo de que aquel diatan espantosoy glosrioso en el Hospital Humana.

En Marcos, nosotros leemos

Al salir de la sinagoga, vinieron a casa de Simón y Andrés, con Jacobo y Juan. Y la suegra de Simón estaba acostada con fiebre; y en seguida le hablaron de ella.

Entonces él se acercó, y la tomó de la mano y la levantó; e inmediatamente le dejó la fiebre, y ella les servía.[163]

Yo me pongo a pensar que despues de agarrar su mano, Jesus miro a pedro y le dijo, "sabes ella va a estar bien." Tuvo que estar bien ella sostenia la mano del senor; que seria mejor que eso.

Cuantas veces en nuestras vidas nos encontramos con una enfermedad y anehelo y el toque de la mano de Dios?

Cuantas veces nos hemos encontrado en una sala de espera de un hospital y orando por un milagro?

Cuantas veces nosotros hemos esperado que nosotros o alguien que amamos iva a estar bien?

Parte de nuestras jornada de fe es venir a nuestro padre y pedir un milagro curativo.

---

[163]Marco 1:29-31

No es secreto que el mundo necesita ser curado con los aceites. El mundo que llamamos la tierra es atormentada con las enfermedades de la Guerra y temor. Ahora mas que nunca, necesitamos el milagro curative de la paz, para que cure el mundo.

Necesitaos la mano curative de Dios para que alcance todas la penas y dolores causados por los hombres y Mujeres que controlan las varias naciones de este planeta. Nosotros necesitamos a Dios para curar nuestras divisions para que podaos resivir los Milagros que el trata de enviarnos.

En nuestra nacion, nostros sabemos que necesitamos una cura. Aunque la eleccion del presidente Barack Obama empeso el proceso de curacion de las heridas perjudiciales. Se fue tambien una senal que todavia estamos con mucho dolor. La presidencia de Barack Obama a revelado en nuestra nacion que las heridas de esclavitud y segregacion no ha sido curadas completamente.

La eleccion del 2008 quito los vendajes que fueron aplicados a nuestras heridas causdas por el movimiento civil del derecho humano. Pero, ha revelado que aunque estemos verdaderamente en el camino de la recuperacion, nosotros todavia no hemos sido curados ocmpletamente de las infecciones que molestan del racismo y la descriminacion.

En nuestras familias nosostros sabemos que necesitamos que alguien nos cure. Muchas de nuestras familias han tenido que aguantar las causas de heridas por acciones, heridas de cellos y traiciones. Las heridas del Alcoholism y el abuso de drogas por mucho tiempo. Ellos no solo duelen los adictos tambien hieren los que alrededor de ellos.

Las heridas delos celos, el orgullo y la envidia puso una linea divisor entre las familias en maneras que queriamos admitir. Para algunos el amor por el dinero ha reemplazado su amor por la familia y su amor por Dios. Y cualquiera que parece estar haciendo un poco mejor que llos no llega hacer la razon porque eloos no tienen exito. Las heridas del celo, envidia y orgullo son duras de curar.

Las traiciones por esos que nosotros adoramos tambien han descarrado nuestras heridas y corazones. Nosotros necesitamos a Dios para tocar los lugares donde el adulterio, la enviadia y la abaricia ha causado que dieramos la espalda a esos que adoramos.

Nuestros ninos neocccsitan la cura.

Nuestras familias necesitan la cura.

Nuestra ciudad necesita la cura.

Y Dios sabe que el mundo necesita la cura.

Si solamente podriamos estar como Pedro y traer a Jesus a nuestros hogares para qu epueda alcanzar fuera y adentro en el lugar donde nos duele mas.
En el Ssacramento de Ungir del Enfermo, tenemos una aportunidad de llamar las manos sagradas de cristo en individuos que nosotros amamos. En este gran sacramento, nosotros preguntamos a Dios que si es su voluntad la persona que resive la cura a lo que ellos les duele.

He visto milagros que suceden a causa de este gran sacramento. Yo he visto las gentes que son curadas en la mente, el cuepo y el alma, asi se que trabaja.

Pero nosotros tambien tenemos unas oportunidad de traer a Jesus a nuestros hogares a travez del sacramento del amor, el Sacramento de Eucaristia. En el sacramento que celebramos aqui en el altar de sacrificios, nosotros somos tocados por el misimo jesus que anduvo en el lugar de pedro y toco la mano de la suegra de pedro.

En la Eucaristia, Jesus viene a nosotros y ofrece el milagro que todos nosotros necesitamos. Y, El le ofrece fuera de puro amor incondicional.

En este dia, yo los desafio a permitir a Jesus entrar en sus corazones y curar lo que les esta doliendo, su familia y todo eso que usted ama.

Permita que el cuerpo que unifica de Cristo para quitar los dolores de pena de su vida y produce el milagro que usted ha estado desean siempre.

Permita que Jesus sea Jesus hoy.

"Senor, nosotros dignos de resivirte, solo di la palabra y nosotros seremos curados."

Como mi abuela, cada uno de nosotros necesita una palabra especifica de curacion, aunque nosotros no sufrimos de golpes masivos, nosotros sufrimos de alguna pena y dolor.

Hoy, Jesus quiere decir la palabra para que pueda ser curado, pero antes de que lo pueda decir, su mente, los oidos y su corazon tiene que estar abbierto para resivirlo.

Hoy, Jesus anda en su casa y le frece el milagro que usted necesita. Pero, el no puede entrar si usted nunca abre la puerta.

En 1988 mi familia fue bendecido con un milagro verdadero cuando el curo. A mi abuela se recupero de su derrame cerebral y estuvo con nosotros por un ano mas antes de que ella se mudara al cielo. Aunque ella no esta fisicamente con nosotros aqui se que anda en el viaje de la fe con todos sus ninos y especialmente yo el bebe de sus bebes.

Cuando mi mama y mi papa se bajaron de aquel bus, ella dijo, "Ella lo puso en sus brazos y nunca me solto."

Bueno, yo le puedo contar que con todo y que su puno se mudo al cielo yo todavia en mis momentos mas duros los siento. El puno de Cristo es similar, el puno del amor es eterno. Y por eso, yo estoy contento que mi santa en el cielo todavia aguanta. Entonces la "Mamá Stasia" patrona de mi familia por favor no nos sueltes!

"El Senor, yo no soy digno de resivirte pero solo dime la palabra, y yo sere curado."

Hoy, que tu recibas el apoyo del Senor porque el no te suelta todavia!

Amén!

Mama Stasia - Abuela de Padre Tony

Anestasia Bernadette Carlin Honoré

La Fe de nuestros Antepasados nos guía en el camino al Cielo.

Porque Los Sacerdotes
Se Visten Tan Gracioso

Un dia del otono pasado, Yo caminaba hacia la escuela cuando un grupo de estudiantes corrian hacia mi. Depues de parar para saludar a cada uno de ellos, yo les pregunte si tenian alguna pregunta para mi.

El pequeno Juancito, el mas joven del grupo, levanto la mano y pregunto, "Porque los sacerdotes se visten tan raro? Pareciera que se pusieron la camisa al reves." Bueno yo les explique, que mi cuello Romano era parte de mi uniforme t todos los sacerdotes estaban supuesto a usarlo cuando estan haciendo cosas saerdotal. Igual como los estudiantes usan uniformes escolares, sacerdotes usan uniformes porque asi la gente sabe lo que somos.

"Pero porque es tan gracioso? Y que es esa cosa tonta en tu cuello?" Juancito pregunto.

Me puso un poco inqieto por las preguntas insensatas del nino, yo le cambie el tema. Asi que yo les hice
unas preguntas.

"Que edad tienes?" Pregunte.
    "Yo tengo cinco anos," contesto.

"Sabes leer?" Pregunte.
    "Si yo se como leer!" Juancito contesto.

Asi, que me quite el cuello y se lo ofreci a Juancit. Adentro del collas habian unas letras que era de la fabrica.

Bueno sabelotodo, dije yo, dime que dicen esas letras.

Miro atentamente a las letras y Juancito dijo,
    "Mata garrapatas y pulgas por seis meses!"

Y como mi mama decia, ya termine con el.

Mateo 11:25

En aquel tiempo, respondiendo Jesús, dijo: "Te alabo, Padre, Señor del cielo y de la tierra, porque escondiste estas cosas de los sabios y de los entendidos, y las revelaste a los niños."

¡Cuantas veces me he encontrado con ninos que parecen ser muy sabios para su eded! Ahora yo no estoy hablando de ninos que creen que son adulto! Eseo es algo otor. Yo estoy hablando de ninos que son inteligentes de verdad. Tan sabios,que tu te preguntas que si han estado aqui anteriormente.

Yo pienso que parte se su sabiduria viene, porque pueden ver la vida sin habiendo experimentado algunas de las desilociones y las luchas que vienen cuando uno crece. Ellos no han tenido que luchar por los problemas que cada dia nos trae y los doleres cabeza y del corazon que solo pasan a los adultos. O tratando de mantener a una familia en este mundo materialista y aveces despiadado.No, ellos no pueden ver la vida por lo que es verdaderamente: Un Regalo de Dios que lo debes vivir completamente.

Si solamente nosotros los adultos podriamos aprender de la sabiduriade nuestros pequenos. Pero, *"Aunque Dios haya ocultado estas cosas del sabio y el aprendio que los ha revelado a los pequenos."*

Aunque todas las Escrituras,la Sabiduria del Amor de Dios es evidente (se vemos y escuchamos las Escrituras con la perspectiva del nino). En el Libro de el Profeta Zacarias, por ejemplo, dos dicen que no importa lo que pase en la vida, tenemos que alegrarnos.

En el Capitulo 9 de Zacarias, oimos,

Alegrense con ganas, O hijas de Zion, pega el grito de alegria,O hijas de Jerusalen! Veale, tu Rey vendra a ustedes, un justo salvador es el, cabalgando en un asno y, en un potro,el potro de un asno.Desterrara el carruaje de Efrain, y el caballo de Jerusalen; El arco del guerrero sera desaparecera, y el proclamara la paz en las naciones. Su domino sera de mar a mar y del Rio a los ines de la tierra.

Estosignifica que debemos de alegrarnos ansiosamente porque muy, muy pronto,nuestro Rey vendra a rescatarnos de todos los tributo y tribulaciones de esta vida. Y,cuando venga, todos recibiran sus justas recompensas. Aquellos que han estado fieles a Dios se uniran a El y su Reino y su dominio sobre la tierra.

Aquellos que no han sido fieles se encontraran desterrados del Nuevo Jerusalen,que es el Reino Del Cielo. Como en la sabiduria de un nino,es verdaderamente simple y es el porque en cual debes alegrarte.

En la Carta de San Pablo a los Romanos, nuestro hermano Pablo nos recuerda que como los ninos, nosotros vivimos segun la Voluntad de Dios.

En esta carta, Pablo dice,

Así que, los que están en la carne no pueden agradar á Dios. Mas vosotros no estáis en la carne, sino en el espíritu, si es que el Espíritu de Dios mora en vosotros. Y si alguno no tiene el Espíritu de Cristo, el tal no es de él. Empero si Cristo está en vosotros, el cuerpo á la verdad está muerto á causa del pecado; mas el espíritu vive á causa de la justicia. Y si el Espíritu de aquel que levantó de los muertos á Jesús mora en vosotros, el que levantó á Cristo Jesús de los muertos, vivificará también vuestros cuerpos mortales por su Espíritu que mora en vosotros.[164]

Esto significa que debemos vivir de acuerdo al Espiritu que vive dentro de nosotros. Si vivimos de acuerdo a lo carnal y dejamos los deseos de este mundo que controle nuestras vidas,nunca podremos disfrutar de la vida como Dios espero que sus Hijos la difrutaran.,

Vivir de acuerdo a la carne significa estar enredados en las trampas de este mundo.Si las trampas de este mundo te causan que te quemes en el infierno.

Un buen ejemplo de vivir segun de acuerdo a la carne, estara haciendo la adquisicion de bienes materiales mas importante que servir a Dios.Otro ejemplo seria de dejar que tus deseos sexuales y fisicos sean tan importante que amar a Dios de verdad.Y preocuparte por tus vecinos.Tambien dejando que tus deseos se conviertan en tu trabajo principal,que sea mas importante que visitar a tu familia y este ejemplo de vivr segun la carne.Vivir segun los medios carnal que los valores de este mundo comienzan a desbancar los valores que Dios y su familia le han ensenado a usted.

San Pablo nos asegura que si vivis segun la carne usted se morira.Y esa muerte no sera solo fisica,pero,la vida como tu la sabias tambien morira.

En Mateo 6:24, Jesus dijo,
Ninguno puede servir á dos señores; porque ó aborrecerá al uno y amará al otro, ó se llegará al uno y menospreciará al otro: no podéis servir á Dios y á Mammón."

Sensillamente puesto,o el Dios de Abrham,Isaac,Jacobo seran su Dios o las maneras de este mundoseran su Dios.

---

[164]Romanos 8:8-11

326

En el evangelio de nuestro Hermano Mateo, Jesus nos dice que nuestras vidas como adultos deben ser tan simple como nuestras vidas cuando eramos ninos. En el Capitulo 11 de Mateo, Jeus dijo,

"En aquel tiempo, respondiendo Jesús, dijo: Te alabo, Padre, Señor del cielo y de la tierra, porque escondiste estas cosas de los sabios y de los entendidos, y las revelaste a los niños.

Sí, Padre, porque así te agradó. Todas las cosas me fueron entregadas por mi Padre; y nadie conoce al Hijo, sino el Padre, ni al Padre conoce alguno, sino el Hijo, y aquel a quien el Hijo lo quiera revelar.

Venid a mí todos los que estáis trabajados y cargados, y yo os haré descansar. Llevad mi yugo sobre vosotros, y aprended de mí, que soy manso y humilde de corazón; y hallaréis descanso para vuestras almas; porque mi yugo es fácil, y ligera mi carga."[165]

Cuando pequenos, Dios nos revela que El continuamente a revelado a sus hijos a travez de las generaciones. Una revelacion infantil sencilla de este pasaje del Evangelio dice que la unica manera que nosotros podemos venir a conocer a Dios que es el Padre a travez de Jesus, su Hijo. Asi como un nino viene a saber de Dios por las palabras amorosas y actos humanitarios de sus padres,nosotros venimos a conocer a Dios el Padre por las palabras amorosas, y los actos del Espiritu lleno de Jesus, nuestro Salvador.

Otra revelacion infantil que viene de este pasaje que nosotros como adultos encontramos descanso de verdad solamente cuando vamos a Dios y se lo pedimos.Al final del dia, un nino sabe que el lugar seguro y comodo en la tierra es en los brazoz amorosos de su Madre o su Padre.En la noche, un nino se duerme en los brazos de sus padres, simple porque en los brazos de sus padres el se siente que nada en este mundo lo puede erir.En los brazos de Dios, encontramos la misma paz que un nino encuentra en los brazos de sus padres.Envuelto en los brazos de Dios,nosotros podemos encontrar sinceramente descanso.

---

[165]Mateo 11:25-30

La tercera revelacion infantil viene del pasaje que esta presente en Jesus y el nos dice, *"Llevad mi yugo sobre vosotros, y aprended de mí, que soy manso y humilde de corazón; y hallaréis descanso para vuestras almas; porque mi yugo es fácil, y ligera mi carga."* Al escuchar estor con los oidos de adultos, y interpretan este pasaje con la sabduria adulta, sabemos que esa parte del mensaje es la prueba que Dios nunca nos dara, mas de lo que podemos aguantar. Por, "Su Yugo es facil, y su luz de carga."

Pero, si usted escucha la revelacion con la sabiduria infantil, usted recibira otro mensaje. Por, el entendimiento simple del nino, tu vienes a realizar que Jesus dijo, *"Llevad mi yugo sobre vosotros."* El no dijo, toma Mis arreos sobre usted o sea enjazado con mis cargas. Esa es la clave a que debemos dar atencion.

Por, un arreo es lo que pones en un caballo o mula para que ese animal pueda alr un arado o un vagon.Pero, el sabe que la Yugo no es un arreo.

La Yugo es un aparato que se le pone en la nuca de los animales, casi como un arreo doble que asi pueden alar algo,bien pesado como un arador o un vagon. En otras palbras con una revelacion del nivel de un nino cuando Jesus dijo,"Toma mi Yugo sobre usted y aprende de ell. El decia, Mi Yugo, juntos nosotros podemostirar todas las cargas que la vida coloca en sus hobros. Pero, con Mi yugo, sera enjazado en un lado y yo sere enjaezeado con usted en el otro lado.Asi, juntos,nada en este mundo,ninguna lucha de la vida adulta, ninguna carga carnal, ningunos problemas en su trabajos jamas le pondrian desgastar.

Para la ayuda de Jesus, lo ayuda a tirar lo que el Padre permita llegar a tus hombros,usted no solo lo hara, pero, como un nino,al final del dia,encontrara descanso:un descanso pacifica en los brazos protectores de Dios,el Padre.

Aveces cuando la vida llega a ser tan pesada que nosotros no podemas resover que hacer, debiamos girar y mirar a los problemas de la vida atravez de los ojos de un nino. Pues Jesus dijo, *"Te alabo, Padre, Señor del cielo y de la tierra, porque escondiste estas cosas de los sabios y de los entendidos, y las revelaste a los niños."*

Si solamente,cuando nos convertimos en adultos,nosotros pudieramos ver atravez de los ojos del nino.Entonces,nosotros vivieramos no de verdad como Diosintento que vivieramos.

Un Sabado en la manan, una madre hacia crepe para sus dos hijos,Kevin y Tony, cuando de repente los dos se pusieron a discutir sobre quien tomaria el primer crepe.

Viendo la moral del dilema, la madre decidio usar la situacion
para ensenarles un leccion valiosa.

Ella, miro a sus hijos y dijo.:
"Si Jesus tuviera sentado aqui, ahora mismo,
que ustedes piensan que el diria a su hermano?"

En otras palabras, cuando viene a coger el primer crepe: Que Jesus haria?"

El hermano mayor miro hacia arriba y repondio, diciendo, "
Mama, Jesus probablemente diria, permito que mi hermano tenga el
primer crepe.Y, yo esperare."

"Excelente repuesta," contesto la madre."Y acuerdense que nosotros somos llamados a ser como Jesus."

Y el hermano menor miro a su hermano mayor y dijo,
"Esta manan tu seras Jesus."

"Te alabo, Padre, Señor del cielo y de la tierra, porque escondiste estas cosas de los sabios y de los entendidos, y las revelaste a los niños."

Aunque hara todo El lo hace para proteger a Sus Hijos, aunque signifique que El tiene que dar hasta la ultima gota de su sangre para salvarnos a nosotros. Dios no pararia a nada para salvar la vidas de Sus Hijos.

Amen!

El Hombre Topita de Sotuta

En Agosto de 1990, fue bendecido cuando entre el Seminario de Nuestra de Dama. Esta bella escuela en Nueva Orleans, es conocida en a travez de toda la Nacion, por el buen trabajo que hacen entrenando jovenes que se convierten en Sacerdotes Catolico Romano. Obispos y Director de Voracion de muchas ciudades americanas y algunas naciones de Africa han enviado coherentemente a sus seminaristas a nuestro seminario de la Dama, para que ellos quizas se beneficien de la excelente instruccion que ofrece.

Al estudiar en el seminario, futuros sacerdotes toman cursos academico en diferente areas espirituales. Una de las mejores areas de estudios es en el programa de Teologia Pastoral.En esta area, seminaristas aprenden sobre ministerios a travez de clases de trabajo y a travez de tareas pastoral en varias partes de la comunidad.

Mientras que estaba en Nuestra Dama, Yo complete tareas de verano como seminaristas en la iglesia Santa Monica, como asistente del Director dela Universidad Xavier para los estudios de Negros Catolicos,y como un capellan en el Hospital de Ninos, y como un Diocino-Interno en la Parroquia de Santa Francia De Cabrini. Tambien fui voluntario por un ano,trabajando como maestro de lenguage norteamericanos por senas en la Escuela Elemental de Lafayette.

Un punto culminante de mis experiencias pastorales fue un viaje de mision que mi clase de seminario tomo en Yucatan. En la pequena aldea mejicana de Sosuta,nosotros trabajamos para ayudar a mejorar las condiciones de vida del pobre en esa region.

Ese viaje sera grabado en mi memoria para siempre. En esa aldea pequena yo encontre a personas cuyos hogares eran chozas de una habitacion, hechas de palos, tejados de barro y paja cuya riqueza fue medida por los pocos animales que poseian, cuyos ninos fueron negado el derecho de una escuela de bajo nivel y cuya practica de Religion es controlada por el gobierno. Todavia.en rsas mismas personas yo vi un amor por Dios muy inmenso y la lealtad a la Iglesia Catolica que fue un dia indudable.

Cada dia, mis hermanos seminaristas y yo fuimos a varias partes de Sotuta, y las aldeas vecinas a ayudar en la reparacion de los tejados de paja de easa casas. Cada equipo de seminaristas subia encima de los hogares de palos y barro, quitabamos el techo viejo y poniamos nuevos materiales.

El material del tejado,que nosotros utilizamos son llamados "Lamina". Son nada mas que hojas de carton y alquitran.Estas hojas son colocadas en los tejados de paja y asegurados a las vigas de las cabanas utilizando una barra de herremientas. La barra es hecha de tapas de botella de sodas y alambre.

En mi equipo yo era el hombre de Topitas. Permaneci abajo y hacia topitas. Permaneci abajo y hacia topitas y entretenia a los ninos del vecindario mientras que mis companeros se subian a los techos. Yo queria ser el hombre Topita porque asi no tenia que ensuciarme. Mientras mis hermanos hicieron todo el trabajo sucio yo me sentaba con los ninos a hacer topitas y entretenerlos con ruidos de animales y diciendoles chistes en espanol.

(Lo graciosob era el hecho que mi espanol fue tan limitado que muy raramente comprendia los chistes que me contaban. Por supuesto los ninos sabian que mi espanol era limitado eso hizo los chistes aun mas graciosos. Ellos no podian entenderme y yo no le compredia!)

Yo honestamente le puedo decir que durante el tiempo que yo estuve con la gente de los Maya de Yucatan, Dios me envio muchos regalos. Ellos fueron uno de mis momentos mas felices del seminario y que yo experimente alla.Estoy muy agradecio por el amor que Dios me mostro y a mis hermanos seminaristas a travez de los corazones de los Mayas.

Uno de los regalos mas grandes que recibi, fue la oportunidad de encontrar a personas que no tenian nada en que confiar solo su Fe en Dios y el amor por uno y el otro. Mientras tratabamos de recuperarnos de la devastacion del Huracan Katrina, yo pense acerca de las personas de Sotuta, Mejico. Asi como ellos sabian depender de Dios para todas sus necesidades, nosotros tambien debemos fiarnos de que Dios proporcionara a todo lo que necesitamos

La Escritura Sagrada a menudo afirma nuestra fe totalmente por las personas Mayas,y por los ninos de Dios aqui en America y en muchas otras regiones.En el Libro de Exodo,por ejemplo,nos dan ejemplos de muchos hombres y a las mujeres que dependieron sinceramente de Dios para proporcionar todo lo que necesitan.

En el capitulo 17 de Exodos,nos ensenan el nivel de confianza en Dios que tiene Moses, Aaron y Hur. Ellos sabian que Dios estaba de su lado y que nada prevalecera contra ellos.

En Exodus leemos,

Entonces vino Amalec y peleó contra Israel en Refidim.

Y dijo Moisés a Josué: Escógenos varones, y sal a pelear contra Amalec; mañana yo estaré sobre la cumbre del collado, y la vara de Dios en mi mano.

E hizo Josué como le dijo Moisés, peleando contra Amalec; y Moisés y Aarón y Hur subieron a la cumbre del collado.

Y sucedía que cuando alzaba Moisés su mano, Israel prevalecía; mas cuando él bajaba su mano, prevalecía Amalec.

Y las manos de Moisés se cansaban; por lo que tomaron una piedra, y la pusieron debajo de él, y se sentó sobre ella; y Aarón y Hur sostenían sus manos, el uno de un lado y el otro de otro; así hubo en sus manos firmeza hasta que se puso el sol.

Y Josué deshizo a Amalec y a su pueblo a filo de espada.[166]

Levantando el personal de Dios y la mano durante la batalla,Moises sirvio como un recordatorio constante a sus tropas que Dios estuvo con ellos. Asi podrian luchar bien sin el temor de perder.

Yo creo que la fuente que dio a los israelitas la energia para triunfar sobre sus enemigos es la misma fuente que conduce a personas en muchos paises de mision para defender el Mundo de Dios que otorgo a nosotros a travez de Jesucrito. Tenemos que estar dispuestos a defender el Mundo De Dios a donde vallamos. Es por eso en su Segunda Carta a Timothy, San Pablo escribe,

Pero persiste tú en lo que has aprendido y te persuadiste, sabiendo de quién has aprendido; y que desde la niñez has sabido las Sagradas Escrituras, las cuales te pueden hacer sabio para la salvación por la fe que es en Cristo Jesús.

Toda la Escritura es inspirada por Dios, y útil para enseñar, para redarg:uir, para corregir, para instruir en justicia, a fin de que el hombre de Dios sea perfecto, enteramente preparado para toda buena obra.

Te encarezco delante de Dios y del Señor Jesucristo, que juzgará a los vivos y a los muertos en su manifestación y en su reino, que prediques la palabra; que instes a tiempo y fuera de tiempo; redarguye, reprende, exhorta con toda paciencia y doctrina.[167]

---

[166]Exodus 17:8-13

[167]2 Timoteo 3:14-4:2

San Pablo desafío Timothy y sus seguidores a que prediquen la palabra contra la oposicion que ellos quizas encuentren.en la misma manera, estas palabras las mandas a los hombres y mujeres que han dedicado sus vidas para servir genter en tierras extranas.

En el evangelio de nuestro Hermano Luke, Jesus Jesus nos dice pararabola que nos da a nosotros un gra ejemplo de como ser persistente nos ayuda a nuestro beneficio.

En el Capitulo 18 de Luke, Jesus dice,

Había en una ciudad un juez, que ni temía a Dios, ni respetaba a hombre.

Había también en aquella ciudad una viuda, la cual venía a él, diciendo: Hazme justicia de mi adversario.

Y él no quiso por algún tiempo; pero después de esto dijo dentro de sí: Aunque ni temo a Dios, ni tengo respeto a hombre, sin embargo, porque esta viuda me es molesta, le haré justicia, no sea que viniendo de continuo, me agote la paciencia.

Y dijo el Señor: Oíd lo que dijo el juez injusto.

¿Y acaso Dios no hará justicia a sus escogidos, que claman a él día y noche? ¿Se tardará en responderles?

Os digo que pronto les hará justicia. Pero cuando venga el Hijo del Hombre, ¿hallará fe en la tierra?[168]

En esta parabola acerca de un juez injusto y una viuda persistente, el punto importante de esta parabolano es que Dios es injusto como el juez,pero que nosotros debemos ser tan persistente en nuestras oraciones como la viudad estuvo en sus peticiones.

Jesus nos llama a ser persistente cuando le pedimos a Dios lo que necesitamos. El nos dice que llamemos a Dios dia y noche. A diferencia del juez, Dios nos da lo que necesitamos sinceramente en un justo y rapido asunto. Es por eso que debemos tener fe que Dios te contestara tus oraciones de acuerdo a su voluntad.

---

[168]Luke 18:2-8

Yo creo firmemente que esta es la base de fe de lso Catolicos y Cristianos que viven y trabajan en America, the Yucatan y otras mision del area. Cada uno es llamado a ser persistente en nuestras oraciones pero no solo a nuestras necesidades, pero tambien orar por nuestros hermanos y hermanas a travez de mundo.Cuando unimos los corazones con la fe, y llenar los corazones de todos los Cristianos persistentes damos un paso mas cerca de nuestra ultima union con nuestro Dios.

Mis experiencias en el Yucatan me ayudo a realizar que la gente pobre o aquellos de tierras lejanas no son menos digno en los ojos de Dios que cualquier Cristiano en la tierra. El alma de un nino golpeado por la pobreza tiene tanto valiosa para Dios como alma de un sacerdote en nuestra Iglesia.

El alma de una madre golpeada por la pobreza es tan valiosa para Dios el alma de la Madre Bendita Theresa De Calcutta.

El alma de un padre golpeado por la pobreza es tan valioso a Dios como el alma de Beato Juan Pablo II.

No ser humano es intrinsecamente mas alto en los ojos de Dios que cualquier otro ser humano.A nosotros se nos dan las mismas oportunidades para escoger "amar a Dios y nuestros vecinos" como nuestro primer objetivo.Asi, aquellos que pueden ayudar a otros como es nuestro deber que Dios nos enseno.

Aquellos que constantemente se niegan a querer y ayudar a sus hermanos y hermanas que han sido tocado por la pobreza tienen que culparse asi mismo cuando caminan hacia el sendero eterno de la condenacion.

Nuestra fe en Dios tiene que ser una fe de accion. Si fe no es evidente en lo que hacemos, entonces debemos preguntar, es que es verdadera fe en Dios, que siempre ha sido un Dios de accion?

Las gentes que cnoci en Yucatan eran verdadera gente de accion. Sus oraciones, liturgias y celebraciones de la Eucaristia fue siempre lleno del espirito y honestamente elogiaban a Dios. Con nuestra asistencia devota, su compromiso persistente a la celebracion del altar de Dios y la persistencia de la gente en otras areas de la mision puede ser reforzada.

A travez de nuestra ayuda persistente y oraciones, ellos podran continuar su servicio a Dios como creyentes que se reunen a sus Altar. Podemas ayudarlos a esparcir la Buenas Noticias de Jesucristo a aquellos que no hallan tenido el privilegio de oir y recibir Su Palabra.

Rezemos que Dios oira nuestras oraciones persistente mientras que predicamos las Buenas Noticias y llamar a otros para que reciban nuestra felicidad.

Jesus pregunto a sus dicipulos, "Cuando el hijo del hombre venga, encontrara alguna fe en el mundo?"

A travez de los efuerzos en nuestro pais y de aquellos en paises de mision, yo tengo seguro que Jesus encontrara gente de fe en cualquier parte de la tierra. Y con oraciones que sean persistente quizas las gentes alla en Soluta,Mejico, volveran a ver aquel Hombre Topita.

Amen!

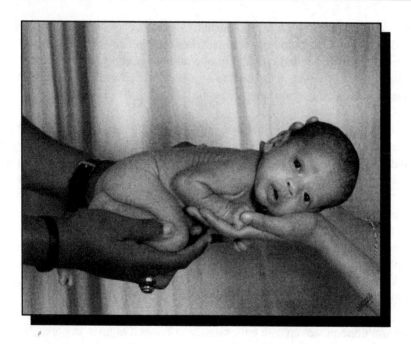

Justin James Smith, Jr. - Nacido Septiembre 3, 2010
Los bebés son Ministros de la Esperanza!

Son las nuevas células en el Cuerpo de Cristo!

Nosotros Somos Mejores Que
San Agustin

La Ciudad De Nueva Orleans es un lugar como ninguno en el mundo. He tenido la oportunidad de viajar alrededor de los Estados Unidos y en varios paises, todavia no he encontrado una ciudad que se compare con la mia. Desde nuestra cocinasy nuestras comidas criollas, hasta nuestro estilo de Cristianos que no es paralelo a la Celebracion como el Carnaval y el Dia De Los Muertos, este lugar es definitivamente unico.las gentes de otros paises viajan a Nueva Orleans para experimentar nuestros regalos unicos.

Cuando comparamos con otros lugares en la tierra, Nueva Orleans sale como uno de los mejores lugares para vivir y visitar. Siempre que viajo a otras ciudades en los Estados Unidos,siempre me encuentro con alguien de Nueva Orleans.

Despues de nuestro Gran Desastre Katrina, nuestras gente para esta ren otras partes del pais. Asi cuando nos reunimos, nos compartimos como si nos hubiesemos conocido toda la vida. Aunque no hemos vivido en el mismo vecindario, si eres de Nueva Orleans tu eres parte de la familia. Ser de Nueva Orleans es toda la conexcion que necesitas.

Es un hecho, que cuando estoy en otros lugares, las gente que no consideramos que son de Nueva Orleans, hasta ellos llaman a Nueva Orleans su casa. Yo estoy hablando de los extranjeros que viven en los suburbios de Nuestra Gran Nueva Orleans. Gentes que vienen de lugares como Slidell,Westwego and Boutte.

Cuando te encuentras fuera de Louisina y le preguntas de donde eres? Ellos automaticamente dicen, "ueva Orleans." Me imagino que eso es porque en otras ciudades no encontraria como La Place, Marrero, la gran metropolis de Edgar en un mapa. Para cortar las preguntas, simplemente dicen que "Yo soy de Nueva Orleans." Aunque usted viva en esos lugares, las raices de tu familia seguramente estan enterradas en Ciudada Medialuna.

No importa donde estes en este pais, cuando conoces a alguien del area automaticamente nos convertimos familias. (Y cuando seas semi-famoso, la mayoria diran que tu eres un primo lejano.)

Cuando encuentro personas de Nueva Orleans, yo inmediatamente les pregunto en donde ellos crecieron. Usted y yo sabemos que podemos saber mucho de una persona por el vecindario donde vivio "De donde eres" quizas tenga mucho que decir de como tu miras al mundo. Ya sea en centro o afuera hasta el Oeste, "En donde vivistes" ayuda a moldar lo que tu eres hoy.

Despues que sepas donde ellos vivieron, nosotros inmediatamente nos dirigimos a esta pregunta, "A que escuela fuistes."

Usualmente cuando le preguntas a alguien a que escuela fueron, automaticamente te diran, la universidad o colegio. Pero en Nueva Orleans cuando preguntamos, "A que escuela fuiste"? No nos importa que tengas un titulo como PH.D de LSU o tienes un M.D de Tulane.

En Nueva Orleans cuando tu preguntas "A que escuela fuistes?" Nosotros no hablamos de titulos avanzados, Nosotros hablamos de la Escuela Secundaria. Y en el momento que comenzamos a hablar de la escuela secundaria, pueden estar seguro que tendremos unas discusiones serias de que escuela es mejor.

Si usted quiere ver una pelea en cualquiera reunion en Nueva Orleans, solo empiece a discutir quien tiene la mejor banda o el mejor equipo de football o las mejores animadoras. Una de las batallas mas grandes en las calles de Nueva Orleans durante el tiempo de Carnaval, no es quien recogio los mejores collares. Es sobre que banda toco mejor nque las otras ndurante el desfile.

Nuestra Senora La Estrella Del Mar, los jovenes gastan mucha energia defendiendo sus escuelas y diciendo quien es el mejor. Nuestras parroquias representa nuestras mejores escuela.Nosotros tenemos muchachas que vienen de las mejores escuelas Catolicas como; Preparatoria de Xavier, Academia de Santa Maria, Cabrini, Ursuline y Dominican

Tenemos muchachos que representan escuelas como Brother Martin, Jesuit, Holly Cross, Rummel y Shaw. Tenemos jovenes de otras escuelas como McDonald 35, John McDonald, Joseph Clark, Lusher, Newman, Frederick Douglas. Hasta tenemos algunas gente que se acuerdan de aquellos dias de Redeemer-Seton, John F. Kennedy o Francis T. Nichols. Aunque estas escuelas historicas estan cerradas, la gente en New Orleans todavia hablan de ellas con carino.

Y por supuesto tenemos a hombres representando una de nuestra escuela maravillosa, la Escuela Secundaria De San Agustin en Nueva Oreleans. Fundada en 1951, es una escuela que muchos la emitan pero nadie la a duplicado. Es una escuela solo para masculinos de raza negra, que es dirigida por Sacerdote Josephite. La escuela que ha graduado a Presidentes Escolares,[169] musicos profesionales, y Sacerdotes Negros mas que cualquier otra escuela en el sur.

---

[169]Un Erudito presidencial es selecionado por el presidente como una de las mejores 120 estudiantes de la Nacion.

San Agustin de Hippo era Obispo de Africa del Norte y es consideramo uno de los mejores Teologos de nuestra fe.Este Gran Doctor de la Gracia inspira a los hombres de la escuela de San Agustin para esforsarse hacia la excelencia. *Gracia es Vida* es el lema escolar. El patrono escolar nos recuerda esa Gracia Es La Vida!

Nuestra Senora La Estrella Del Mar es la casa de toda generacion de los caballeros purpura de San Agustin. Yo soy el mas orgulloso de todos los miembros de esta fraternidad. Como estudiante de San Agustin yo participe en el Concilio de estudiantes, la banda de concierto y a la reconocida mundial la banda de la *"Marching 100."* Yo me gradue en 1982 de la escuela secundaria de San Agustin y fui bendecido con la oportunidad de volver y ensenar Teologia del 2002 al 2006.

Yo soy un Caballero Purpura muy orgulloso. Creo completamente que mi Alma Matta es la escuela mas grande en la ciudad. La calidad de las otras escuelas puede ser determinada comparandolas con mi Alma Matta! La banda de la *"Marching100"* es mucho mas superior que las otras. Es por eso que nunca oiras a nadie diciendo que nuestra banda es mejor que la de Clark o que nuestra banda es mejor que la de Rummel o que nuestra banda es mejor que Santa Maria. Cuando discutimos que sus escuelas tienen una buena banda, siempre decimos "Nuestra Banda es mejor que la de San Agustin *"Marching 100."*

Si quieres ser el mejor, de algun modo reclama que tu eres el mejor de los mejores. Pero nosotros sabemos quien es el mejor! Vamos con Los Purpuras!

Mientras que leia el Evangelio de nuestro Hermano Mark, encontre un pasaje que me recordo de Nueva Orleans y todas las gentes que discuten sobre quien es el mejor.

En el Evangelio de Mark, leemos,

Y llegó a Capernaum; y cuando estuvo en casa, les preguntó: ¿Qué disputabais entre vosotros en el camino?

Mas ellos callaron; porque en el camino habían disputado entre sí, quién había de ser el mayor.

Entonces él se sentó y llamó a los doce, y les dijo: Si alguno quiere ser el primero, será el postrero de todos, y el servidor de todos.

338

Y tomó a un niño, y lo puso en medio de ellos; y tomándole en sus brazos, les dijo: El que reciba en mi nombre a un niño como este, me recibe a mí; y el que a mí me recibe, no me recibe a mí sino al que me envió."[170]

En este pasaje, como los dicipulos anduvieron con Jesus a travez de las regiones de Galileo, ellos discutieron entre ellos quien era el mejor dicipulos del Senor. En vez de discutir de que La escuela secundaria de Jerusalen o que la escuela de Belen tenia la mejor banda o los mejores pastores,ellos estaban discutiendo sobre quien era el mejor disipulo de Jesus.

Ahora, como los dicipulos estaban discutiendo,solo podemos imaginar. Quizas ellos estaban discutiendo quien entre ellos tenia la Fe mas profunda.O cual de ellos estaba dando mas ayuda a Jesus con sus quehaceres de cada dia. O cual de ellos tenia mas exito con su propio predicar en el ministerio.

Los dicipulos estaban tratando de decifrar quien era el mejor de la Banda de Hombres que hablaba,caminaba, y predicaba porsu ministerios todos los dias. Ellos querian saber quie era el mas grande de todos.

Cuando Jesus escucho a sus disipulos discutiendo quien era el mejor, El les recordo que lo que ellos consideran grande puede que no sea por la criteria de Dios que usamos para determinar una grandeza. Donde ellos estaban preocupado por la grandeza en el ojo del hombre,Jesus estaba enfocado en lo que significa ser grande ante los ojos de Dios.

Usted ve,antes de tener esa profunda discusion sobre la grandeza, Jesus habia terminado de decirles que su sendero hacia la grandeza no era el sendero que los Judios estaban esperando.

In Marco 9:31-32, Jesus dijo,

"El Hijo del Hombre será entregado en manos de hombres, y le matarán; pero después de muerto, resucitará al tercer día."

Antes de ser levantado a la depresion de la grandeza de una batalla triunfanta o por un ejercito Angelico, El alcanzaria su gloria de su destino por la pasion y la muerte de su crusifixion y El viva a dar su vida por el mundo.

---

[170]Marco 9:33-37

En su sendero hacia la Via De La Cruz se termino; su grandeza no se iva a medir por quien tu eres.se mediria por el deseo de que tu obsequias a los necesitados. Sera medido por aquel que consientemente se sacrifica sus alegrias por otros.

Basicamente, Jesus le decian a sus dicipulos y a nosotros nos decia que si tu realmente quieres ser grandioso en los Ojos De Dios, tu tienes que estar listo antes los ojos del hombre,tu tienes que estar listo a servir.

Te aseguro que estar considerado Grandioso en la tierra no quiere decir que vas a ser contado como igual que los grandes hombres del Cielo. De hecho, si su unico objetivo es de ser grandioso en este mundo, usted probablemente no sera grandioso en el Cielo Quizas ni siquiera llegues al Cielo.

Es por eso que Jesus,puso un nino en el centro de sus dicipulos y explico que si tu realmente quieres ser bendito por Dios, ten por seguro que estas tratando a las personas como Dios lo haria.

Jesus les dijo,

"El que reciba en mi nombre a un niño como este, me recibe a mí; y el que a mí me recibe, no me recibe a mí sino al que me envió."

En otra grandeza de las palabras en los Ojos De Dios, sera determinado por, con que frecuencia usted a trabajado para cuidar los ninos, el pobre y al necesitado entre nosotros. Esto significa que para ser grande en Heaven tu tienes que ser un verdadero sirviente del Senor aqui en la tierra.

Muchas veces perdemos energia discutiendo de que es lo mas grande en este mundo. Comparamos nuestras escuelas, nuestras familias,nuetros parientes, y hasta nuestros hijos. Nos las pasamos perdiendo el tiempo tratando de ensenar lo que tenemos y quien es el que tiene mas que otra persona tiene o es.

En parte lo que tenemos que realizar es que atravez de la Sangre de la Oveja y el Banquete de la Eucarista que todos somos gran en los Ojos de Dios. Por el Sacrificio de JesuCristo, nos convertimos en los hijos y hijas de nuestro Padre Celestial. No hay nada en la tierra que puede ser mas grande que ser unos de los Hijos Del senor.

Sabes alla en Nueva Orleans somos pasionados aproximadamente por muchas cosas. Cuando empezamos a discutir acerca de las que nosotros adoramos, las gentes deben tener cuidado.

Desde la NFL Los Santos de Nueva Orleans, hasta el NBA Las Avispas De Nueva Orleans, a nuestros vecindario viejos y nuestras escuelas que queremos y tenemos discusiones caliente acerca dequien fue el mas grande.

Pero hoy debemos realizar que cada vecindario tiene un grado de grandeza, y toda escuela secundaria tiene algo que los hace grandioso.

En caso tal que haiga alguna duda que cual escuela secundaria tiene la mejor banda marchante de musica, te puedo decir que si tu banda a tocado para el Beato Papa Juan Pablo II, ocho presidentes de los Estados Unidos, El desfile de las Rosas, el desfile de Macy's del Dia de Gracia, Football de los Lunes, el Sugar Bowl, NFL Super Bowls, dirigio los desfiles del Martes de Carnaval, y fueron presentados en mayores peliculas y despues de eso podemos hablar de quien es el mejor.

Pero hasta entonces permiteremos que la legacia del legendario director de la banda Edwin Harrell Hampton habla por si mismo.[171]

Que hoy sea bendecido como la Marchante de 100 de San Agustin, para que verdaderamente seas el mejor.[172]

Amen!

---

[171] Senor Hamp - Edwin Harrell Hampton fue el maestro de banda de San Agustín por más de 50 años. El se mudo al cielo en Julio nde 2009. Los Caballeros Purpuras de la escuela secundaria de San Agustin nunca se olvidara de las lecciones de amor y dedicacion que el Senor Hamp nos enseno.

[172] Para mas informacion de la mejor Escuela Secundaria de la Nacion, San Agustin, visite www.PurpleKnights.com

Mis Hermanos y Hermanas en Cristo,

Gracias por leer estas reflexiones.

Espero que les gustaba.

Por favor, perdona los errores.

Que Dios te bendiga
y te guarde fuerte!

La Paz,

Padre Tony

Book Six

The Eagle Story

Rev. R. Tony Ricard, M.Th., M.Div.
Illustrated by Anthony A. Jones

Published in 2012

"My Momma was a Chicken.
My Daddy was a Chicken.
I live on a Chicken Farm.
I do Chicken things and I eat Chicken food.

I'm telling you. I'm a Chicken!"

Introduction to The Eagle Story

When I entered the Seminary back in 1990, I began working towards a Master of Divinity Degree at Notre Dame Seminary in New Orleans. At the same time, I enrolled at Xavier University of Louisiana to begin working on a Master of Theology Degreethrough the Institute for Black Catholic Studies. Although I earned a great deal at Notre Dame, much of what I do now as a speaker and teacher comes from my years at Xavier University.

My style of preaching, my flare for dramatics, my good looks (wait, that came from my Momma), and even my story-telling are all gifts and talents that I was able to refine while studying at Xavier University. The Institute for Black Catholic Studies was truly a focal point of my training and formation for the priesthood.

During a course on Catechesis in the African-American Community, I came across a wonderful story about overcoming the tough odds of life, The Eagle Story. It is a story that I heard as a child. So, I was delighted to hear it again. This inspirational story was handed down by enslaved Africans and has been told nationwide and in several other countries. As best as I can tell, my version of the Eagle Story can be traced back to a folktale from the West African country of Ghana.

The Eagle Story helps us realize that we are the Children of God. As such, we are destined to leave this Chicken Farm that we call Earth and soar like Eagles in the Kingdom of Heaven. Our task is to stand firm in faith and believe in our minds and our hearts that we are not Chickens. We are God's Eagles.

"He gives power to the faint, abundant strength to the weak.
Though young men faint and grow weary, and youths stagger and fall,
They that hope in the LORD will renew their strength,
they will soar on eagles' wings;
They will run and not grow weary, walk and not grow faint."

Isaiah 40:29-31

"We Are Eagles! We're not Chickens!"
- Turk, the Eaglet

The Eagle Story

Once there was a Chicken Farmer, and on his farm he had some Chickens.

One day the Chicken Farmer was talking to his friend and he said, "My friend,
I've got this problem. You see, my Chicken Farm ain't doing too well."

His friend replied, "I'll tell you what you ought to do. You see, just the other day,
I was up in the mountain and I spied this great big Eagle.

If you could somehow catch that Eagle, bring her down and put her in a cage,
people would pay you money to see that Eagle.
You could call it the Eagle Zoo."

"That's a great idea," the Farmer said, "That's just what I will do."

So early the next morning, he got up and he tucked his eagle-catching net under
his arm and headed up the mountain.

But as he climbed up that mountain, the Eagle heard him coming.
So, she sat up in her nest.

When the Farmer got really close, the Eagle took off flying in the air.

Well, he took his net and threw it on the Eagle trapping her wings.

She immediately plummeted to the ground and died.

(Because she busted her head on a rock.)

Seeing the dead Eagle, the Farmer panicked and ran down the mountain
to see his friend.

"I killed the Eagle, Man! I killed the Eagle!" he shouted.

"Did you check the nest?" his friend asked.

"Well, Maybe there was something in the nest that you could sell."

So, early the next morning the Farmer climbed back up the mountain.

When he got really close to the nest, he reached up and put his hand inside it.
    And, there he found two Eagle eggs.

He grabbed those two eggs and he hurried down the mountain.

    Getting back to his Chicken coop, he rushed inside.

There he looked for the biggest and fattest hen he could find.

He lifted her up, put those eggs down under her and then looked at her and said,
    "Girl, do your thing."

Well, she took her big fat Chicken tail and sat on those eggs.
    And she sat and she sat and she sat.

Before you knew it, one of those eggs began to hatch. Out popped the prettiest,
little brown Eaglet that you could ever want to see.
    (Eaglet is what they call baby Eagles.)

At feeding time, when they would throw the corn to the left and he'd run to the
left to get some corn. And when they would throw the corn to the right, he'd run
to the right to get the corn.

He was just as happy as ever being a Chicken.

Soon, the other egg began hatch and out popped another little Eaglet.

Well, when they would throw the corn to the left and he'd go get the corn.

And when they would throw the corn to the right, he'd walk over
    and get some more stupid corn.

But, after a while he was getting tired of all this Chicken....mess.

Soon, he began spending most of his days lying out in the field
    looking up at the clouds.

One day, while he was staring at the clouds,
    he spied this great big brown dot in the sky.

That dot was going 'round and around and around.
    He began to realize that this dot was a bird.
    A great big bird.

347

When he looked up, that bird flew down and landed right beside him.

So, he looked up at that bird and that bird looked down at him.
He looked up and the bird, and the bird looked down at him.

He looked up at the bird and he said, "Hey, who are you?"
And the bird replied, "I am an Eagle. And, just who are you?"

"Well," the Eaglet said, "They call me Turk, and I am a Chicken."

"Turk" the big Eagle said,
"You're not a Chicken. You're an Eagle!"

Turk looked up at him and said, "Let me tell you one thing:

My Momma was a Chicken.
My Daddy was a Chicken.
I live on a Chicken Farm.
I do Chicken things and I eat Chicken food.

I'm telling you.
I'm a Chicken!"

"Let me tell YOU something," said the Eagle.

"Your Momma was an Eagle, the Queen of all the birds.
When your Momma took off to fly all of the other birds would stop to
watch her soar.

And, your Daddy, boy....,
your Daddy was an Eagle, the King of all the birds.

Your Daddy ran all of the Birds' Meetings.
When your Daddy spoke, everybody listened.

I'm telling you, Boy....you're an Eagle."

Turk looked up at him and said, "Let me tell you one thing:

My Momma was a Chicken.
My Daddy was a Chicken.
I live on a Chicken Farm.
I do Chicken things and I eat Chicken food.

I'm telling you.
        I'm a Chicken!"

"Well," that Eagle thought to himself,
        "Tell you what I'm gonna do. I'll take him to the top of the tree."

So he put his big brown wing around Turk and flew up him to the top of the tree.

From the top of the trees, he looked at Turk and he said, "Jump!"

Turk looked up and him and said, "You must be crazy!
        I have told you before, I am a Chicken.
        Now I might make it from the coop to the fence, but that's about it."

The Eagle looked at Turk and said,
        "I've told you before, you are an Eagle. So, Jump!"

And Turk said, "Let me tell you one thing:

My Momma was a Chicken.
My Daddy was a Chicken.
I live on a Chicken Farm.
I do Chicken things and I eat Chicken food.

I'm telling you.
        I'm a Chicken!"

The Eagle once again, thought to himself,
        "Tell, you what I'm gonna do. I'll give him a little push."

So, he snuck up behind Turk and BAM!....
        kicked him right in the tail!

There Turk went, falling towards the ground.

Now when Turk got close to the ground,
    he had two things between which he could decided.

He could spread out his little brown wings and try,
    or he could bust his head on a rock!

Well, as you guessed, Turk, spread out his wings and voooom!
    He took off flying in the air.
Flippin' and a floppin,' and a floppin'
    and a flippin', because that's what Eagles do.

He flew back to the top of the tree and said,
    "I've got to go tell my brother. I've got to go tell my brother!"
So, Turk flew down onto the Chicken Farm landing right next to his brother.

Turk excitedly said to him, "We're Eagles, Man, we're Eagles!"

His brother looked at Turk and thought to himself, "Turk is going crazy!
    I wonder what he has been out there doing?"

Turk said hurriedly,
    "This great big Eagle came down and he said that Momma was a Queen.
    Daddy was a King. Momma flew, Daddy talked.
    We're Eagles, Man, we're Eagles!"

His brother looked at him and said,
    "Now Turk, I have told you before:

Our Momma was a Chicken.
Our Daddy was a Chicken.
We live on a Chicken Farm.
We do Chicken things and we eat Chicken food.

I'm telling you, Turk,
    we'z Chickens!"

Turk thought to himself,
    "Tell you what I am gonna do. I'll take him to the top of the tree."

So, Turk put his little brown arm around his brother and flew up him to the top of the tree. And when they reached the top of the trees, he looked at his brother and said, "Jump!"

His brother looked back at him and said,
    "Turk, if you don't get me down off this tree, I'm going to kill you!"

"We're Eagles Man, Jump!" hollered Turk. "Jump!"

And his brother replied, "I have told you before:

Our Momma was a Chicken.
Our Daddy was a Chicken.
We live on a Chicken Farm.
We do Chicken things and we eat Chicken food.

I'm telling you, Turk,
    we'z Chickens!"

So, Turk thought to himself,
    "Tell you what I'm gonna do. I'll give him a little push."

So he snuck up behind his brother and BAM!....
    Kicked him right in the tail
sending his brother soaring towards the ground.

Well, as he got closer and closer to the ground,
    he had two things between which he could decide.

He could spread out his little brown wings and try
    or he could bust his head on a rock!

And as you guessed, when he got close to the ground, BAM!

He died.

And that's how the story ends.

(What do you think, every story has a happy ending?)

You see, the problem was, in the mind of Turk's brother, he was still a Chicken.

And, no matter what people said, and no matter what people did,
    until he believed in his heart that he was an Eagle, he'd always be a Chicken.

351

El Cuento de el Aguila

Habia una vez un granjero, y en su granja tenia un gallinero.

Una dia el granjero estaba platicando con un amiga y le dijo, "Amigo tengo un problema, mi gallinero no va bien".

El amigo le contesto, "Yo se que debes de hacer. El otro dia andaba en la montaña y vi una águila muy grande. Si de alguna manera pudieras atrapar a el águila y ponerla en una jaula, la gente te pagaria dinero para verla. Podrias llamarle el Zoologico del Águila."

"Es una buena idea," dijo el granjero, "Es lo que voy hacer."

El dia siguente, el granjero se levanto y tomo su red para captar águilas y se dirigió hacia la montaña.

Cuando iba subiendo la montaña, el águila lo oyó venir y se sento en su nido. Cuando el granjero se acercó, el águila se hecho a volar. Pronto tomo su red y se la tiro a el águila atrapandola por las alas.

Inmediatamente el águila se desplomo al suelo y se murió.

Viendo lo que le paso al el águila, el granjero entro en pánico y corrió por la montaña a buscar a su amigo.

"¡Maté a el águila, maté a el águila!" gritó el granjero.

"¿Revisaste el nido? Quizas hay algo en el nido que puedas vender," le contesto el amigo.

Al dia siguiente el granjero subio la montaña por segunda vez. Se acerco al nido y encontro dos huevos de águila. Agarro los huevos y corrió por la montaña.

Llegando a su gallinero se apuró y buscó la gallina mas grade y gorda, la levanto y colocó los huevos de águila debajo de la gallina. La voltió a ver y le dijo, "¡as lo tuyo chica!".

La gallina se sento sobre los huevos de águila y esperó, esperó, y esperó.

Despues de un corto tiempo una de las águilitas empezo a nacer. Nació el águilita mas bonito que se hubiera visto.

A la hora de comer aventaban el maiz a la izquierda y el águilita corría a la izquierda para comer maiz.

Aventaban el maiz a la derecha y el águilita corría a la derecha a comer maiz.

El águilita era muy feliz siendo un pollito.

Un dia la otra águilita nació. Y tambien aventaban el maiz a la izquierda y el águilita corría a la izquierda a comer maiz. Aventaban el maiz a la derecha y el águilita corría a la derecha a comer maiz.

Pero después de un tiempo el águilita empezo a cansarse de todo el "pollijeo". Él empezo a pasar sus dias acostado en el pasto viendo hacia el cielo.

Un dia mientras miraba el cielo, vio un punto café. El punto café estaba dando vueltas y vueltas y mas vueltas. El águilita empezo a reconocer que el punto café era un pajaro. Un pajaro muy grande.

Voltió hacia arriba y el pajaro voló hacia el águilita y atterizo enseguida de él. Voltió a ver a ese pajaro, y el pajaro lo miraba a él.

Miró al pajaro y le pregunto, "¿Y tu, quien eres?", el pajaro le contesto, "Soy un águila, y tu, quien eres?"

"Me llamo Turk y soy un pollo," le contesto.

"Turk" dijo el águila grande, "¡tu no eres un pollo, eres una águila!"

Turk miró a el águila grande y le dijo, "Dejame decirte una cosa, mi mamá era una gallina, mi papá era un gallo, vivo en un gallinero, hago las cosas como los pollos y como comida de pollo. ¡Te digo que soy un pollo!"

"Pues dejame decirte halgo a tí," dijo el águila grande, "tu mamá era una águila, la reina de todos los pajaros. Cuando tu mamá volaba todos los pajaros se detenian no mas para verla. Y tu papá, bueno, tu papá era un águila, era el rey de todos los pajaros. Tu papá organizaba todas las juntas de los pajaros, y cuando tu papá hablaba todos ponian mucha atencíon. Hazme caso cuando te digo que tu eres una águila."

Turk voltió a ver a el águila grande y le dijo,
"Dejame decirte una cosa,
mi mamá era una gallina,
mi papá era un gallo,
vivo en un gallinero,
hago las cosas como los pollos y como comida de pollo.
¡Te digo que soy un pollo!"

Bueno, penso el águila grande y dijo, "Voy hacer una cosa, te voy a llevar a lo
mas alto de un árbol."

El águila grande abrazo a Turk y voló a lo mas alto del árbol. De los mas alto del
árbol el águila
grande voltió a ver a Turk y le dijo, "¡Brinca!"

Turk lo miró y le contesto, "¡Has de estar loco! Ya te dije que soy un pollo.
Quizas puedo volar del gallinero al cerco, pero nada mas."

El águila grande miró a Turk y le dijo, "¡ya te dije que eres un águila, ha si es que
brinca!"

Turk le contesto, "Dejame decirte una cosa,
mi mamá era una gallina,
mi papá era un gallo,
vivo en un gallinero,
hago las cosas como los pollos y como comida de pollo.
¡Te digo que soy un pollo!"

El águila grande se puso a pensar y le dijo, "¿Sabes que voy hacer?... te voy a dar
un empujoncito."

Se colocó detras de Turk y "¡SAS! Lo empujo.

Turk empezo a caer. Cuando Turk se acercaba mas a suelo, tuvo dos opcíones,
podia estirar sus alitas y tratar de volar ó se podria romper la cabeza en una
piedra.

Bueno, tu lo adivinaste, Turk estiró sus alitas y "VOOOOM" empezo a volar.
Empezo a dar vueltas, y vueltas y mas vueltas por que eso es lo que hacen las
águilas.

Voló hacia lo mas alto de un árbol y penso, "tengo que decirle a mí hermano."
Turk voló hacia el gallinero y aterrizo enseguida de su hermano.

Turk exclamó, "¡Somos águilas, hermano, somos águilas!"

El hermano miró a Turk y penso, "¡Turk se esta volviendo loco! Quien sabe que anda haciendo."

Turk le explicó a su hermano, "una águila grande me dijo que mamá era una reina y papá era un rey. Mamá volaba y papá hablaba. ¡Somos águilas hermano, somos águilas!"

El hermano miró a Turk y le contesto, "mira Turk ya te he dicho mamá era una gallina, papá era un gallo, vivimos en un gallinero, hacemos las cosas como los pollos y comemos comida de pollo. ¡Te digo que somos pollos!"

Turk se puso a pensar y le contesto, "voy hacer una cosa, te voy a llevar a los mas alto de un árbol." Turk abrazo a su hermano y voló hacia lo mas alto de un árbol. Al llegar miró a su hermano y le dijo "¡Brinca!"

Su hermano lo miró y le dijo, "¡Turk si no me bajas de aqui te voy a matar!" "¡Somos águilas tonto, brinca!" le grito Turk. "¡Brinca!"

Su hermano le contesto, "Turk ya te he dicho mamá era una gallina, papá era un gallo, vivimos en un gallinero, hacemos las cosas como los pollos y comemos comida de pollo. ¡Te digo que somos pollos!"

Turk se puso a pensar y le dijo a su hermano, "Ya se que tengo que hacer, te voy a dar un empujoncito."

Se colocó detras de su hermano y "¡PAZ!" lo empujo, mandando a su hermano hacia el suelo.

Cuando su hermano se acerco al suelo tuvo dos opciónes podria estirar sus alitas y tratar de volar ó se podria romper la cabeza en una piedra.

Bueno tu lo adivinaste, se acerco al suelo y "¡SAS!" se murio.

A si termina esta historia, ¿que pensabas, que todas las historias tienen un final feliz?

Pues como vez el problema del hermano de Turk era que en su mente el era un pollo. Y no importaba lo que le dijieran ó lo que hicieran todos, mientras que él no sintiera en su corazon que en verdad era una águila, siempre seguiria siendo un pollo.

355

Book Seven

Diary of
An Unapologetic
Roman Catholic Priest

Rev. R. Tony Ricard, M.Th., M.Div.

Published in 2013

Dear Readers and Fans of Fr. Tony,

While searching for a definition of "truth," I came across
an old song by Johnny Cash that speaks directly to the concept
of Truth. It was a song that I had never before heard.
Needless to say, I loved it.

Not many folks know that I am a big fan of Country Music.
My best friend Cathy Allain knows it because for the past
25 years, we have ridden together to Louisiana Lions Camp
in Anacoco, Louisiana. That is where we host Camp Pelican and
Camp Challenge, our two camps for kids with disabilities. It is
all but inevitable that at some point during our 5 hours drive,
I will tune the radio to a Country Music Station and sing along
with whatever song that is playing. (She has already earned
100 days out of Purgatory for having had to endure my singing!
That is, of course, if Purgatory still exists.)

Cathy knows that I especially love the songs of old. I grew up
listening to Crystal Gayle, Dolly Parton and Loretta Lynn.
I love me some Conway Twitty, Randy Travis and Kenny Rogers.
I even love Garthe Brooks and Kenny Chesney - even though
they are relatively new when compared to Johnny Cash and
Charlie Pride. What I love about old country songs is the fact
that more often than not, they answer questions about "Truth."

There is something about country music singers that allow them
to speak to the truth. They speak about true in love. They
speak about true in heartaches. They speak about the true ups
and downs of life. They simply speak about the truth.

In 1970, Johnny Cash record a little know song called,
"What Is Truth?"

In his song he wrote,

> The old man turned off the radio
> > Said, "Where did all of the old songs go
> > Kids sure play funny music these days
> > They play it in the strangest ways"

> Said, "it looks to me like they've all gone wild
> > It was peaceful back when I was a child"

> Well, man, could it be that the girls and boys
> > Are trying to be heard above your noise?
> And the lonely voice of youth cries "What is truth?"

In this **Diary**, I hope to answer the question, **"What is Truth?"**

Through sharing this series of letters from my personal diary, I present to you many of the truths of the Holy Roman Catholic Church, the struggles of our society, the traps of sin and the ways of the world. In these 52 simple letters, I speak the truth as I know it. I also invite you to write your own letters of truth.

Some of my letters deal with tough issues like Racism, Abortion and Homosexuality.

Others deal with the controversial debates such as the Catholic Church's approach to the Presidency of Barack Obama.

Still others teach the truth as it was taught to me by my Momma, my Daddy and my Elders.

All of them speak the truth as I know it and as the Roman Catholic Church has taught it.

You know, there are times when a true preacher or a **Preacher of the Truth** must speak a word that might ruffle a few feathers or wrinkle a few cassocks. It is in those times that he or she will face opposition from both inside and outside of the Church walls. Although the opposition might "get ugly," a Preacher of the Truth must still "tell it like it is!" He must do it in a pastoral but **unapologetic** manner.

As a **Preacher of the Truth**, I should not be expected to apologize for speaking the **Truth of God**. For as Aunt Ester on Sanford and Son would say, "The Truth shall set you free!"

Of course, she was only quoting Jesus who said, "If you remain in my word, you will truly be my disciples, and you will know the truth, and the truth will set you free." (John 8:32)

Although some folks will take issue with some of the letters, they too will have to face the Truth and realize that everything that I have written is in accordance with the Truth as it is presented to us by the Holy Spirit, the Magisterium and our Early Church Fathers.

People of God, this the Truth as I know it!

"And the Truth Will Set You Free."

Sincerely,

Fr. R. Tony Ricard

Rev. R. Tony Ricard, M.Th., M.Div.,
An Unapologetic Roman Catholic Priest
and a Preacher of the Truth

Dear God the Father, Creator of All That Is,

I want to thank you for all that You have done for me.
I am so blessed to be who I am. That is why I hope that You know
that I don't take "being me" for granted. Yet, sometimes,
I do wonder, "Why did You make me?"

This question is not a new question at all. Back in the old days when
dinosaurs roamed the earth, the nuns used to ask this question to the
children. It was the lead question in the old Baltimore Catechism.
Back then, every good Catholic child knew that the answer was simply,
"God Made me to Know Him, to Love Him and to Serve Him in this
world and to be happy with Him in the next."

So, I know that you made me to know, love and serve you. But, I guess
that I am wondering just how I am supposed to do that in this modern
world. Is it really possible to truly know you, honestly love You and
fully serve You with all of the many distractions of today? I guess
that I need to really spend time thinking about how I can fulfill the
purpose of why You actually made me.

I know that I have been made to know You to the best of my ability.
That is why I have been working so hard to read Your words of love in
Sacred Scripture. There is no better way to come to know You than
through Your own words.

It is in reading Your words that I realize just how much you love me.
In fact, not only do You love me, You love everybody. I guess that all
You really want from us is for us to love You back. Loving You is really
easy when I realize just how much You love me!

Now, as to loving You with my whole heart, my whole mind and my
whole soul, that's not as easy as it sounds. So, when I mess up and let
something else get into my heart or mind, would You please keep
protecting my soul until I realize what I am doing?

Knowing You and loving You as much as I do does make serving You really easy. There is no one on this earth that has been better to me than You. Even my Momma can't claim to love me more than You do. So, dedicating my life to You has just been a natural thing for me to do. Although I have been called to be dedicated to You as a Roman Catholic Priest, I know that You have called others to serve You in many different ways.

Some have been called to be priests, deacons, religious women (sisters or nuns) and men (brothers). Others have been called to be parents and grandparents. Still, others have been called to the single life. No matter what our call may be, as long as we are knowing, loving and serving You to the best of our abilities, I am confident that we will make it into Heaven.

So, Father God, I may still often ask, "Why did You make me?" However, I know that whatever the reason, it was out of pure love. For that love, I want to say, "Thank You!"

Thank You for making such a beautiful world for us. I really do like this place. Thank You for writing the Bible. I know that it was written on our hearts. Thank You for sending Jesus. I know that it wasn't easy to sacrifice Your Only Begotten Son for the sake of others. Thank You for being You. I don't even know how people could put a false god before you.

And, Lord, Thank You for making me . . . well, me! It definitely was Your way of showing the world just how good of a creator You are!

I'm glad that You are my God!

Sincerely,

Fr. Tony

Tony, Your Gracious Creation

Dear Jesus, God the Son, Savior of the World,

Sometimes I wonder why do You love me so? I know that more often than not, I fall short of Your grace. Yet, somehow, You keep loving me. It is as if You know me better than I know myself.

When I look back at all You have done for me, I am struck with awe. You are really an awesome Savior. I realize that nothing I have done has ever made me deserving of all Your love. Nothing I could ever do would be enough to repay You for Your sacrifices for me. So, I guess that all I can really do is work to show You how much I appreciate You and Your love.

During the Christmas season, we stop to remember that You came to us in the form of a baby. Why did You come as a baby? Was it because You wanted to truly be united with mankind?

I know that by coming as a baby and growing up to be a strong young man, You experienced all the joys and pains of our lives. You knew what it was like to scrape Your knees as You learned how to walk. You knew what it was like to bring anxiety to Your mother's heart when You remained behind in the temple after the Passover feast was completed. You knew what it was like to grieve the death of someone You loved when You had to bury Saint Joseph, Your foster-father. You knew what it was like to be betrayed by Your family and friends as You hung upon a cross.

So, I guess that You came to us as a baby because You wanted to really be united with us in all the things that we experience in our lives.

But, I wonder, Lord, why did You have to die on the cross? Didn't You have the power to come down from that tree and usher in the New Kingdom without having to die?

362

I guess that by dying on the cross, You showed the world that You would stop at nothing to save us. Your pain on that cross opened for us the gates of Heaven.

You know, I can't wait to get up there to see You. I can only imagine just how beautiful the "place that You have prepared for me" will be. But until I get there, can I please ask You for a few favors.

Would You please watch over my family and friends? I love them so much and want to see all of them live a good life.

Would You please watch over our Church? It's hard to be a Christian in this sometimes not-so-Christian world. So, we need all the help that we can get.

And, would You please watch over our babies? They are our most precious gifts from You. So, please make sure that we don't do anything to mess-up their journey towards You.

Lord Jesus, may my life and my love be acceptable in Your sight. May I never forget just how much You love me and all the people of the world.

Sincerely,

Fr. Tony

One of Your Coheirs to the Kingdom

Dear Holy Spirit, Source of Grace,

As a child, I had no idea just how important you are in my life.
I used to think that you were just the source of God's Grace.
I didn't realize that You are indeed our God.

I remember praying, "Come, Holy Ghost, fill the hearts of
Thy faithful, and enkindle in them the Fire of Thy Love.
Send forth Thy Spirit, and they shall be created;
And Thou shalt renew the face of the earth."

But, I didn't really know what all of those words meant.
I had no idea just how powerful You are.

Holy Spirit, most children don't realize that it is through You that
we receive all that grace we need to be successful in this world.
Some children think that it is because of their parents that they live
in good houses, attend nice schools or even have enough food to eat.
Little do they know that nothing is possible without Your grace.

As an adult, I have come to realize that You are the loving Spirit of
God. You are the Source of God's love. You are God indeed.

Although You are often overshadowed by the Father and the Son, You
are equal in majesty and consubstantial with the Father and the Son.

So, today, I come to You and ask that You send forth Your love and
renew the face of the earth.

I don't need to tell You that the earth is hurting and needs Your help.
This place is filled with sin. There seems to be more people hating
each other rather than folks who love each other.
Somehow, they have become disconnected from You.

So, if it be Your Will, please come down and help us.

You have the power to put an end to the endless hatred that plagues our world. Through Your love, we can put an end to the physical, mental and spiritual wars that we are fighting today.

We need You now more than ever!

You are the only One who can unite us.

St. Paul tells us, "For in one Spirit we were all baptized into one body, whether Jews or Greeks, slaves or free persons, and we were all given to drink of one Spirit." (1 Corinthians 12:12)

Lord, please make us drink of that one Spirit, again. Regardless of whom we are, where we may live or even whom we might choose to love, only You, the Holy Spirit, can find a way to unite us.

In the song, "Veni Creator, Spiritus" we sang,
"O comforter, to Thee we cry,
O heavenly gift of God Most High,
O fount of life and fire of love,
and sweet anointing from above."

Holy Spirit, the world is desperate for that
"sweet anointing from above"!

So, please send it as fast as you can!

Sincerely,

Fr. Tony

Your Faithful Servant

Dear, Blessed Virgin Mary, Jesus' Momma,

Were you scared when the angel Gabriel appeared to you?
I know that I would've been scared.
It's not that often that angels appear in people's homes.
What did the angel look like? Did he have wings?
Was he wearing a dazzling white robe? Did he have on shoes?

I guess that I will have to wait until I get to Heaven to get some of the answers to my questions.

Well anyway, I wanted to write to you to first thank you for saying "Yes" to the Archangel Gabriel when he announced to you that God had chosen you to be the bearer of Jesus into this world. I know that you had to be a little scared when you realized that the Holy Spirit was going to visit you and that you would "conceive in your womb and bear a son." (Luke 1:31)

When you said,
"May it be done to me according to your word" (Luke 1:38), you risked everything. You risked facing the shame of the community if they did not believe you. You risked the disappointment of your parents, Saint Joachim and Saint Anne. And you definitely risked losing your betrothed, Saint Joseph. He above all knew that the child was not his son. You were willing to "put it on the line" for God. And because of that, you have been crowned as the Queen of Heaven.

Thank you for your willingness to be the Mother of God. I know that it was through you that Jesus learned how to be a Man of God. You taught Him to have a heart of compassion. You showed Him how to feel the hearts of God's people. Your life defined for Him the essence of faithful dedication. You were not only the instrument through which God the Father brought His Only Begotten Son into this world. You were the instrument though which God taught His Son how to love.

Sometimes, I wish that other mothers would realize that they have the same role to play in the lives of their children. Mommas are not only called to be care givers and providers. They are also called to be the first teachers of the ways of Christ. It is difficult for a child to fully understand unconditional love if they never experience that kind of love from their mother.

I fully believe that it was you love that gave Jesus the strength to finish the work of His Father in Heaven. I can only imagine the power your eyes conveyed to Him as He carried His cross on the road to Calvary. I know that just the strength from His Momma's eye helped Him to get up each time He fell and do what God needed Him to do. You were His rock when He most needed you.

While hanging on the cross, your Son offered to us the greatest gift that His Father had given Him. It was from the cross that He gave you to us to be our Mother. I know that Jesus told us, "No one has greater love than this, to lay down one's life for one's friends." (John 15:13) Ultimately, His death on the cross was the greatest act of love that He could give us. But, I believe that His giving us His Mother was His second greatest act of love.

Please continue to pray for all of your children on earth. Ask the Father to help us deepen our relationship with your Son. It is only through the salvation offered by your Baby Boy that the world can be saved. Lord knows that we need your Baby now more than ever.

Thank you for being our Mother.

Sincerely,

Your Son

Dear Saint Augustine of Hippo, Great Doctor of Grace,

Back in 1978, I walked through the doors of St. Augustine High School to begin my journey as a Purple Knight. As a thirteen-year-old kid, I didn't know much about you. However, I did know that I was entering a school that was known for its championship athletic teams, its world-renowned band and its ground-breaking role in the Civil Rights battles in the South. Although I didn't know much about you, my new school's patron, I did know that I was becoming a part of an academic icon.

St. Augustine High School was founded in 1951 by the Society of Saint Joseph of the Sacred Heart - The Josephites. Back then, Xavier University Preparatory School was the only Catholic High school that an African-American young man could attend. Although Xavier Prep was doing a great job in educating young men and women of color, the Archdiocese of New Orleans realized that there was a great need for additional opportunities for young Black men to receive a solid Catholic education. That is why Archbishop Joseph Francis Rummel entrusted the care of this new high school to the Josephites.

As a freshman at St. Aug, I quickly learned that you were, and still are, one of the greatest men in the history of Christianity. The Josephite Fathers and Brothers taught us that you were from North Africa and are formally known as the "Great Doctor of Grace." You were given this title back in 1298 when you were selected as one of the first four Doctors of the Church. You were honored with this title because your writings have been recognized as some of the greatest works of faith. Folks all around the world have been inspired by your works.

Although many have been touched by your eloquence and grace, I was inspired more by your life than by your books and writings.

You see, I learned that although you are a saint now, you definitely weren't a saint when you were in your youth. You spent a lot of years searching for the pathway to peace. In The Confessions of St. Augustine, you wrote, "You have made us for Yourself, O Lord, and our heart is restless until it rests in You." Through these words you described your earnest desire to better know, love and serve the Lord.

As a young man, you continuously searched with a Restless Heart for the meaning of life. You searched in the secular world: living a less-than-Christian lifestyle. You searched is the philosophical world: studying various forms of philosophy and heresies. You even search in the world of sin: living with a woman without the benefit of marriage and fathering an illegitimate son named Adeodatus. Indeed, you searched with a Restless Heart.

But, through the prayers of your mother, St. Monica, and the Bishop of Milan, St. Ambrose, you began to search for true rest in the comfort of God's Love. Your Restless Heart was filled with a true desire for the knowledge and love of the truth. And since Jesus is the way the truth and the life, you realized that you could only find "The Truth" when you finally "found Jesus."

St. Augustine, all of us have a built in desire to find the "True Truth." That is why some many seem lost in this world. They are still searching for a pathway of freedom, a pathway of Truth.

May your love for Jesus and your constant prayers help to guide them to the altar of Christ. It is only there that they will find the peace that cans settle a Restless Heart.

Sincerely,

Fr. Tony

A St. Augustine Purple Knight

Dear Virgin of Guadalupe, Patroness of the Americas,

For more than 480 years, the people of our world have marveled in your beauty. When you appeared to Saint Juan Diego Cuauhtlatoatzin, you forever changed the face of our devotions to you as the Mother of Jesus.

In 1531, you first appeared on Tepeyac Hill outside Mexico City to declare to the world that you were our most Blessed Mother and the protectress of all mankind. In your apparition, Saint Juan Diego said that you were as beautiful as an Aztec Princess. As proof of your appearance, you instructed Saint Juan Diego to gather roses in his tilma (cloak) and to present them to the bishop. When Saint Juan Diego unfolded his tilma before Bishop Juan de Zumárraga, they realized that your beautiful image had been miraculously imprinted on Saint Juan Diego's garment.

The beauty of this image conveys that you are truly the Mother of our Universal Church. By coming to us through the beauty of the Aztec people, you have declared that no one is unworthy of God's love and protection.

In 1999, the world rejoiced as Pope John Paul II proclaimed you to be the Patroness of the Americas, Empress of Latin America, and Protectress of the Unborn. We are forever grateful for your love and watchful care.

Back in 2002, Pope John Paul II celebrated the canonization of Juan Diego Cuauhtlatoatzin. The Holy Father praised Saint Juan Diego for his simple faith and his humility before God.

In his homily, Blessed John Paul II quoted Saint Juan Diego who said to you: "I am a nobody, I am a small rope, a tiny ladder, the tail end, a leaf."

Like Saint Juan Diego, many of your children often feel as if they are nobody or as insignificant as a leaf. Yet through your love, you have helped us to understand that even the tiniest leaves are very important to God.

Regardless of whom you are, where you live, or the abilities that you may or may not have, everyone has been made in the image and likeness of God. All of us have been offered a seat at the Banquet Feast in Heaven.

Today, I ask that you unite your love with the hearts of our Abuelas and Abuelitas as they continue to pray for their children and their children's children.

Through your intercession, may we be ever conscious of your loving protection and your willingness to step down from Heaven and make holy the soils of the Americas.

May your image continue to bring blessings upon the people of Mexico and the entire world.

May we never forget the beautiful Virgin of Guadalupe.

Sincerely,

Fr. Tony

You Devoted Son

Dulce Madre, no te alejes, tu vista de mi no apartes.
Ven conmigo a todas partes y nunca solo me dejes.
Ya que me proteges tanto como verdadera Madre,
Haz que me bendiga el Padre, el Hijo y el Espíritu Santo.

Amén.

Dear Rev. Dr. Martin Luther King, Jr.,

It has been more than 40 years since you stood on the steps of the Lincoln Memorial and proclaimed to the world, "I have a dream." Back then, you dreamed of the day when your "four little children" would one day "live in a nation where they will not be judged by the color of their skin but by the content of their character." Well, Dr. King, I am happy to say that day has arrived.

Although we still live in a nation where some folks are still filled with the misconceptions of racial superiority, the overwhelming majority of our nation's citizens have come to understand that we have all been created equal in the eyes of God. We no longer live in a land where only a few are allowed to exercise the civic duties of voting or the greater comforts of life are reserved for just a select few. We now live in a nation where it is frowned upon when someone faces discrimination based on race, creed or color.

Dr. King, we have come a long way. However, we still have not reached the mountain top of which you so eloquently spoke. We are still climbing up the rough side of the mountain. But like you, I too dream of the day when we will get there.

Unfortunately, We still are dealing with racism in America.

It was never more evident than during the presidential elections of 2008 and 2012. With the presidential candidacy of Barack Hussein Obama, much of the racial hatred of the days before I was born began to surface again. Racism has once again become a festering sore on the protective skin of the American body. Although the sore is much smaller than in the past, we have to admit that it still exits and that we still need healing. We cannot just cover it up with political correctness. We must reach deep into the wound and anoint it with the Balm of Gilead. But before we can begin to heal the wound, we have to first admit that the wound still exists.

Racism and prejudice can exist whenever human beings are involved. If we are not judging folks by the color of their skin, we are finding other ways to prejudge them. We discriminate against folks because of their race, their countries of origin, their faith tradition and even their sexual orientation. We will discriminate over their gender or how much money they have. It's amazing how often we will find a reason to prejudge another Child of God.

Dr. King, in the shadows of Abraham Lincoln, you said, "I have a dream that one day every valley shall be exalted, every hill and mountain shall be made low, the rough places will be made plain, and the crooked places will be made straight, and the glory of the Lord shall be revealed, and all flesh shall see it together."

Like you, I also have that same dream.

I dream of the day when we will not have to apologize for having dreams that stretch the collective mind of our nation and calls us to love one another as Christ loves us.

I dream of a day when the pains of racism will be forever erased by the love of God and the power of the Holy Spirit.

I dream of a day when your dream will be fulfilled and our children will be free to dream even bigger dreams than ours.

Dr. King, may God help us to fully make your dream a reality and the dreams of Christ our focus.

Thank you for having the courage to preach, to teach and to dream!

Sincerely,

R. Tony

Your Brother Dreamer

Dear Bishop Harold Robert Perry, My Pastor,

You were born in Lake Charles, Louisiana, to Frank and Josephine Perry on October 9, 1916. Your father worked in the rice mills while your mother toiled as a domestic cook. They worked together to provide a loving Catholic home for you and your five siblings. Although the broader community looked upon you and your siblings as inferior because you were of African descent, your parents never allowed you to use your race as a reason "not to strive" for greatness.

Back in the 1920's and 1930's, much of our nation was divided along color lines. In the hearts and minds of many, people of color were considered less significant than folks from the dominant cultures. Some even believed that African-Americans were created by God for the sole purpose of serving others.

Even the Holy Roman Catholic Church was segregated by race. They used to force African-Americans to either sit in the back pews of the church or to attend churches that only ministered to people of color. It is hard for me to imagine the many hardships that you had to face simply because you were "colored."

At the age of thirteen, you decided to answer God's Call and pursue a vocation to the priesthood. After entering the Society of the Divine Word, your love for God blossomed and your zeal for the church brought many to the faith.

Following your ordination to the priesthood on January 6, 1944, you serve as pastor of a few parishes. In 1964, you the Provincial Superior of the Southern Province of the Divine Word Society in the United States. That same year, you also became the first African American clergyman to deliver the opening prayer in United States Congress.

On September 29, 1965, Pope Paul VI appointed you as the Auxiliary Bishop of New Orleans. Your episcopal ordination on January 6, 1966, made you the first African-American Bishop in modern times. Your ordination forever changed the face of the Catholic hierarchy in the United States.

In 1975, you were appointed as the Pastor of my childhood parish - Our Lady of Lourdes in New Orleans.

I was so excited to meet "the bishop." Little did I know the impact that your life and ministry would have on my life. You were my model of faith and courage.

Bishop, you are my model of a true priest. Much of what I do is a reflection of you. I strive to be the kind of priest that would make you proud.

Although we had many conversations in my early years, our most memorable exchange took place on Sunday, December 1, 1985. It was then that I formally interviewed you about your life and your ministry. By that time, you were suffering from the beginning stages of Alzheimer's Disease. I prayed that you would be in a "remembering mood" when I called you. I thank God that you were.

Through that interview, I realized the courage it took for you to accept your appointment as the First Black Bishop in the 20th Century. You knew that you were going to be used by God to open the doors of the episcopacy to other men of color.

As the only Black Bishop, you faced a lot of racial hatred in your early years. But, you handled it with the love of Christ. In discussing the racism that you faced, you said, "If I would have reacted with anger and spoke without holiness, it would have taken many years for another Black to become bishop. I was the trailblazer, sent as a trial."

Bishop, God truly used you to cut a pathway of justice through the tangled webs of inequality and the fight for Civil Rights.

In summoning up your life, you said,

"When through one man, a little more love, a little more goodness, a little more light and a little more truth comes into the world, then the man's life has meaning."

Back in January of 1991, the Archdiocese of New Orleans gathered to celebrate the 25th Anniversary of your ordination as a bishop. It was at that celebration that I spoke with you for the last time.

By then, you mind was trapped by Alzheimer's and I wondered if you would recognize me. When I approached you, I simply said, "Bishop, my name is Tony and you were my Pastor for almost 10 years."
I went on to tell you that I was a new seminarian and that you were one of the reasons why I decided to enter the seminary. You smiled and simply said, "And so, you remember me."

From that final encounter, I walked away realizing just how important it was to you that folk never forget the life and ministry that you were blessed to live. Today, I am a part of your legacy and I promise you that as long as I live, you will never be forgotten.

May your soul and all the souls of the faithful departed rest in peace.

Sincerely,

Fr. Tony

Your Altar Server

Dear Archbishop Gregory M. Aymond, Archbishop of New Orleans

From 1986 to 2000, you were blessed to serve as the Rector and President of Notre Dame Seminary in New Orleans. In your ministry of priestly formation, you helped to guide hundreds of young men through the waters of discernment to restful shores of the Altar of Christ. Through your guidance, hundreds of priests and deacons confirmed that they were being called by God and joyfully received the Sacrament of Holy Orders.

I began my seminary journey during the summer of 1990. I know that you were blessed to serve as my rector. Any rector would be honored to have the future "Fr. Tony" in their seminary. I am sure that I brought a lot of joy and excitement to your life. I am also sure that there were times when you were ready to strangle me over something I said or did. Yet in our good times and bad, I never questioned your love and concern for my spiritual life and my discernment of the Call.

After my ordination in 1995, you continued to support me and the various ministries that I was doing. Although you no longer were responsible for my work, you still took pride in the fact that this phenomenal young priest" trained under your tutelage.

In 1997, we all rejoiced as God called you to serve as a bishop in our Church. Your ordination as an Auxiliary Bishop for the Archdiocese of New Orleans was an exciting time for all of the young men who studied under your guidance. You served us well until you were appointed as the Coadjutor Bishop of Austin and later became the Ordinary of their Diocese in 2000. Although we were sad to see you leave our Archdiocese, we were confident that God was calling you to do great things for our brothers and sisters in Texas.

Nine year after you left us, you were asked by Pope Benedict XVI to return to the Archdiocese of New Orleans and be installed as the 14th Archbishop of New Orleans.

I don't think that you can fully understand just how excited I was to know that you were returning. At the welcome gathering that was held for you by the priests, I remember telling you exactly how I felt.

Your return to New Orleans was like the return of a favorite uncle who had gone off to war. While you were gone, we missed you and thought about you often. When you came back, the family celebrated that you had made it home safely.

In a very real way, you are a member of my family. I see you as both my brother in Christ and my father in priestly ministries. As my Archbishop, you are responsible for all that I do as a priest. You have also been given charge by God to watch over my mental, physical and spiritual well-being. It can't be easy having to be responsible for me!

In our first private meeting upon your return, I talked to you about all that I endured following Hurricane Katrina. Almost everyone that I knew lost their homes and were displaced by the storm. Many of my friends had not yet returned to New Orleans and some were never coming back.

I talked to you about how hard I had to fight to keep Our Lady Star of the Sea Parish from closing. I explained that Star of the Sea was not in the Archdiocesan Plans and that Archbishop Alfred Hughes had graciously allowed us to remain open. Of course, we had to do it without the benefit of help from the Archdiocesan flood insurance or from the money that was collected in other dioceses. We were left to fend for ourselves.

It wasn't an easy thing to do. We had to raise the funds that would be needed to repair our buildings, re-institute all of our ministries and meet the pastoral needs of our parishioners. On many days, I felt as if I was a priest without the benefit of support from the priestly fraternity. I felt all alone.

Luckily, Bishop Shelton Fabre was appointed as an Auxiliary Bishop of New Orleans in 2006. Through his help and support, some of the stress from "trying to survive" was relieved. Although the battle was not over, I no longer felt isolated from my archdiocese.

I am sure that you don't even realize how God used you to minister to me in that private meeting. You opened the meeting with a prayer and then began to thank me for all that I had done to keep the parish from closing. That was the very first time that anyone from the archdiocese stopped to recognize what we had accomplished.

Archbishop, I didn't fight to keep Our Lady Star of the Sea open because I wanted personal recognition. I fought to keep it open because I fully believe that it was in God's plans that the doors wouldn't be closed. But, I do have to admit that every now and then even a popular priest likes to hear words of appreciation. It also felt good to know that my former rector and new spiritual father approved of the priest that I have become.

Archbishop, I pray that you and your brother Bishops never forget the role you have in the lives of your priests. You are very important to our personal and ministerial lives. You are the shepherds called to not only care for the sheep in the pews. You also are called to also care for the ordained sheep at the Altar.

May God bless you in your ministry as our Father and Shepherd.

Sincerely,

Fr. Tony

One of Your Ordained Sheep

Dear Momma
Dear Iva O'Rita Honore' Ricard, My Momma,

June 19, 1964, had to have been the happiest day of your life. It was on that day that God blessed you with the gift of me! Although you already had my sister and my brother, I know that you only had them to fill in the time until I would come along. That's why I'm your youngest child. After having me, you knew that you and my daddy had reached the peak of your creative powers. You could have never created another child that would be as good as "the baby."

For all of my life, I have worked hard to make you and daddy proud. I know that you both have sacrificed a lot for the sake of your family. I could never repay you for all that you have done for me. I guess that the only repayment is to just be the best man that I could be.

I will never forget the day that I announced to you and daddy that I was entering the seminary. It was on March 18, 1990, when I returned home from the Handicapped Encounter Christ retreat. I walked into the den, turned off the television and told you both of my big decision. After hearing my announcement, you started screaming and my daddy started crying. I remember thinking to myself, "Well, I hope that they are happy!" You said to me, "I always knew that you were going to be a priest." When I asked why you hadn't told me this, you simply said, "I knew that it had to be on your and God's time."

Five years later, you and daddy walked me into St. Francis Cabrini Church in New Orleans to celebrate the Sacrament of Holy Orders. Following my priestly ordination, we went together into the rectory of the church to meet with Archbishop Francis Schulte and to receive the letter for my first assignment.

As we waited for the Archbishop, our Auxiliary Bishop, Most Rev. Nicholas D'Antonio, O.F.M., came over to congratulate both you and daddy. "You know," he said, "When you have a child ordained or enter religious life, it's an automatic ticket to Heaven for the parents."

Daddy got excited because he knew that he definitely needed help with getting his Heavenly ticket. After talking about your ticket to Heaven, Bishop Nick then turned to you and asked you a question that left you stunned. He simply asked, "Aren't you glad that you didn't abort him?"

Later you told me that you really didn't know how to answer that question. If you said "yes" then it meant that you thought about aborting me. If you said "no" then it meant that you wanted to abort me. All you could say to him was "Bishop, I am glad that I have my baby." Momma, I want to thank you for not aborting me.

You were only 19 years old when I was conceived. At that time you were living in Munich, Germany with my daddy. As he went about his duties in the United States Army, you were at home caring for Deidra who was only two years old and for Kevin who had just celebrated his first birthday. In addition to your two babies, you also were dealing with an alcoholic husband who would rather get drunk than help you with the children. According to the ways of the world, you had more than enough reasons to justify "getting rid" of me. The last thing that you needed was another baby.

I hope that you realize now that if you had chosen to abort me, the world would've never been blessed with the "Great Aura that is Tony!" If you had aborted me, I wouldn't have been able to become the priest that I am and affect as many lives as I have been blessed to touch. Momma, I am who I am today because you chose to let me live!

I pray that God will continue to bless you for being my Momma. May you always know how much I love you and cherish the fact that God has given me the best Momma in the world. Thanks for letting me live!

Sincerely,

Your Baby

Dear Rodney Joseph Ricard, My Daddy,

It is no secret that for much of my childhood years, you were losing your battle with alcoholism. Almost everywhere you went and everything you did involved drinking. You drank when you were gathered with the family and when you were alone. You drank when you were happy and you drank when you were sad. No matter what you did, you made sure that alcohol was there.

There were times in my life when I wished that you would stop drinking and just be the daddy that Deidra, Kevin and I always dreamed of having. We wanted a daddy like we watch on the Brady Bunch or Good Times. We would have even been happy with Herman Munster as long as our daddy didn't always seem drunk. We simply wanted to have you without the bottle.

Although you were never physically abusive, we were often hurt by your words and your lack of words. Some times, you would tell us some really hurtful things that left us in tears. As hurtful as those words would be, I think that it was really the lack of words that hurt most. You see, there were always a few things that we longed to hear. We waited to hear you say. "I love you" or "I'm proud of you."
We just wanted to know that we mattered.

In 1979, you finally decided to become the daddy that we wanted. It was on November 18, 1979, that you took your last drink! For the past 30 plus years, you have been working hard to be a father in whom all three of your children could be proud. Well, I hope that you know just how proud we are of you! You "put that bottle down" because you loved us and didn't want to lose your family. You showed the world that we meant more to you than a bottle of vodka or a can of beer.

I cannot count the number of times that you have apologized to our family for your years of drinking. There is no doubt that you know how much hurt your drinking brought to our lives. Well, I hope that you realize now just how much joy we have in telling the world that our daddy is a recovering alcoholic. Although you will always be an alcoholic, it's the recovering part that makes the difference.

For years, I was ashamed to tell folks that I grew up in an alcoholic's home. I feared that folks would look down on me and think that I wasn't worthy of being around them. But now, I realize that it is nothing to hide. I also realize that I am not the only person to have lived with an alcoholic. There are many folks who are just like us.

In sharing your story with the world, I am praying that young folks who are dealing with alcoholic parents or those dealing with alcoholic spouses will know that they still can achieve greatness. They need to know that I didn't come from a perfect home. I wasn't raised on Leave It to Beaver. I came from the real world and lived in a home that dealt with real problems. Although I wish that things were different in the past, I know that I am the man that I am today because of the roads that God allowed me to walk. We all become who we are because of both the good times and the bad times of our lives.

Daddy, you have shown the world that a man can conquer the greatest demons in his life. Your victory over alcoholism has taught your children that with God, there is nothing that we cannot do. Also, you should know that it's time for you to stop apologizing. We have already forgiven you. Just keep doing what you are doing because we finally have that daddy that we wanted. We finally have a daddy who we know loves us and is very proud of us. We just hope that you know we love you and are very proud of you, too!

May God continue to bless you, our Daddy, in your recovery!

Sincerely,

Your Pride and Joy

Dear Mr. and Mrs. Tom Benson, Owners of the New Orleans Saints and the New Orleans Hornets[173],

For as long as I can remember, the phrase "Who Dat?" has been a part of my vocabulary. I can remember hearing my grandmother answering the front door of our uptown house by yelling "Who Dat?" I can also remember being in high school and cheering "Who Dat?" on St. Augustine High School's "Marching 100" Band's bus. The rhythmic shouts of "Who Dat?" have been around for quite a while and have had many powerful meanings.

When we chant "Who Dat?" at the beginning of every New Orleans Saints home game, you can feel the foundation of the Louisiana Superdome vibrating under our feet. If the Dome didn't have a roof, I think that folks as far away as Baton Rouge and Thibodaux would be able to hear us cheering. Following our 2010 victory over the Indianapolis Colts in Super Bowl XLIV, it seemed that the whole world was singing "Who Dat?" with the Who Dat Nation.

"Who Dat?" means so much to the people of New Orleans. It not only connects us as fans of our beloved Saints. It also connects us as Hurricane Survivors and folks who have shown the world that we will never give up. Although most folks think of "Who Dat?" being only about football, we all know that it's about a people who will never quit.

Since Hurricane Katrina, "Who Dat?" has also taken on even deeper meanings. You see, "Who Dat?" also talks about the folks in our community who have stepped up to make sure that the whole community would be all right. From the many church folks and volunteer groups who came down to the region to help our city recover to the major corporations that have given major contributions to help offset what the government was not doing, "Who Dat?" is about them, too.

---

[173]The New Orleans Hornets' became the Pelicans in 2013.

However when I think about who sits in the heart of the Who Dat Nation and has helped keep that heart beating, I need look no further than you, Tom and Gayle Benson. In a very real way, both of you have helped to keep the pulse of the city pumping at a steady beat. Together, you are the heart of the Who Dat Nation.

Mr. Benson, God has blessed you with great success in the business world. The greater blessing is how you have used what God has allowed you to accomplish to help keep the heart of New Orleans beating. It seems that every time our city has needed someone to step up and help save an important piece of our heart, you have come to our rescue. You are a true blessing to our community.

Mrs. Benson, if Mr. Tom controls the beat of the city, you definitely have to be the one who controls the flow of our "Who Dat?" blood. Like Mr. Tom, you are a phenomenal gift to your hometown and to the world. The love that you have for the people of our community is evident every time you stop to talk to anyone. You treat everyone as if they are royalty. It's no wonder that Mr. Benson fell in love with you. The entire city has fallen in love with you, too.

Neither of you has forgotten that once you were just little kids walking the streets of New Orleans. You have shown the world that God will continue to bless those who "have" as long as they never forget that once "they had not."

May God continue to shower you and your family with His Grace asa you share your blessings with the world.

When it comes to loving God and our city, if the question is "Who Dat?" then the only real answer has got to be "You Dat!!!"

Sincerely,

R. Tony
The Holy Who Dat

Dear President Barack Hussein Obama, 44th President of the United States of America

On November 4, 2008, you rocked the nation with your election as the 44th President of the United States of America. It was on that day that you became the first African-American to be elected to our nation's highest office. For the first time in the modern era, a Black man was chosen to be the leader of the free world. Although many rejoiced on the day of your election, many others shivered with fear and began to spew the words of hatred that had not been publicly spewed since the days of racial segregation.

As you moved into the White House, walked behind the desk in the Oval Office and sat in the President's chair, the ugliness of racism boiled all around you.

Many openly discredited you based on the color of your skin. They did not want to accept that you were the President simply because you are Black.

Other cloaked their racism in the noble banners that they claimed were in defense of our citizenship. They called themselves the "birth'ers" and tried to prove that you were not a citizen of the United States and that your birth records from Hawaii were not valid. There were even a few folks who claimed that you were born in Kenya and were in fact a citizen of that wonderful African nation. It was amazing how folks tried to cloak their racism by focusing their attention on absurd theories and principals. Even after you had served for four years as our nation's President and sought reelection to this noble office, they still were trying to prove that you were not a true American.

President Obama, secular folks weren't the only ones cloaking their racism in noble causes as they sought to discredit you. There were some church folks who also did not like you because you are Black.

Rather than focusing on your race, they began to focus on your position in our battle against legalized abortion. Many came out hard against you not because of the abortion issue but because of the color of your skin. They simply used your "Pro Choice" stance as a way of saying that you were not worthy to be the President.

As a Roman Catholic Priest, let me be perfectly clear in writing that I do not and cannot agree with your stance on abortion. I fully believe that it is against God's will to kill anyone. Thus, abortion is murder and must be stopped.

With that being said, I also cannot agree with those who somehow expect African-American Catholics to not be proud of your presidential election. We are a people who after 246 Years of slavery, 100 years of Jim Crow laws and 44 years of prejudice and discrimination were finally able to witness someone who looks like us take up residence in the White House.

As an African-American man, I couldn't help but be proud. You are proof to our sons and daughters that they can reach the highest peaks in our nation. With your election, they now can truly believe that we are living in the land of the free and the home of the brave.

Mr. President, I can assure you that simply by writing this letter, some will begin to dislike me and even hate me because I have chosen to speak the truth. It is my prayer that they will first reflect on their own feelings and ask themselves what is at the root of their disapproval.

I am a Roman Catholic Priest and am called to take stances that are counter cultural and are at times not very popular. Just as with the prophets of old, I cannot be afraid to confront the ills of society for fear that other might not like me. I must be willing to speak up even when I know that some will attack me for simply "telling it like it is." It is my calling from God and my obligation as a priest.

To those who might disagree with what I have written to you, I say that is their right. We live in a free country and are members of a God- fearing Church. Everyone is free to believe whatever they choose to believe. But, before they write to me, before they send me literature on abortion or before they write to the Archbishop of New Orleans to complain about what I have said, I ask that they first go before the Altar of God and make sure that root of their disagreement is not planted in the soils of racism or being feed by the fertilizers of hatred.

I am proud to be an American but I am even more proud to be an Unapologetic Roman Catholic Priest.

Sincerely,

Fr. Tony

A Proud Catholic American

God Bless America
by Irving Berlin

"While the storm clouds gather far across the sea,
Let us swear allegiance to a land that's free,
Let us all be grateful for a land so fair,
As we raise our voices in a solemn prayer."

God Bless America,
Land that I love.
Stand beside her, and guide her
Thru the night with a light from above.

From the mountains, to the prairies,
To the oceans, white with foam
God bless America,
My home sweet home.

Dear Parents of Young Children and Old Ones, Too

On March 17, one of God's greatest gifts to the world was born. Although on March 17, 1963, my brother Kevin was born, I am really taking about the birth of Miss Chortni Henderson. She was born on March 17, 2010. She is my New Best Friend and is also the daughter of Mr. Chris Quest, II. Chortni has become the light of my life. I don't know if there are any places that I have visited since 2010 that have not heard about my little buddy. She definitely has walked through the front door of my rectory and walked out with my heart.

Chortni is in her third year of life and is living it to the full. Each day, she is growing and developing and learning new things. It is amazing how much a baby or a toddler learns before they enter Kindergarten. This is why parents have to be extremely conscious of what they are teaching their children in those early years.

Sometimes I wonder why some folks are allowed to have children. Almost all of the problems that we have in our society can be traced back to a person's childhood. Far too often, our problem adults are the result of being raised in homes when the parents were not conscious of their charge from God to be good models. Although some bad adults go astray on their own, many of them never learned the lessons of right from wrong. They never were taught how to "act" in public and how to "treat" other folks. Many of the hateful attitudes and prejudicial opinions that adults may possess can be traced back to their childhood years. No child is born a racist. No child is born a sexist. No child is born a homophobe. At some point in their lives, someone has to teach them how to hate.

Parents, you must realize that your children are gifts to you from God. On the day that you stand before the judgment seat, you are going to have to account for how well you developed the gifts that God sent you. You must guard against teaching your children anything that is against the love of God.

389

In the Gospel of our Brother Mark we hear, "And people were bringing children to Him that He might touch them, but the disciples rebuked them. When Jesus saw this, He became indignant and said to them, 'Let the children come to Me; do not prevent them, for the kingdom of God belongs to such as these. Amen, I say to you, whoever does not accept the kingdom of God like a child will not enter it.' Then He embraced them and blessed them, placing His hands on them." (Mark 10:13-16)

I hope that you noticed that Jesus became indignant when the disciples were preventing the children from getting close to Him. Christ will very be indignant with you too if you do anything that will cause your child to go astray. It is tough for Jesus to embrace a child whom a parent hinders from getting to the Lord.

In the celebration of Baptism, in the blessing that is given to father of the child we pray, "God is the giver of all life, human and divine. May He bless the father of this child. He and his wife will be the first teachers of their child in the ways of faith. May they be also the best of teachers, bearing witness to the faith by what they say and do, in Christ Jesus our Lord." In this, we remind the father and the mother that their child will be watching and listening to everything they say and do. You have to make sure that you keep yourself in check.

Being a parent is not a right. It is a privilege. My prayer is that you will always realize the blessing that you have as parents in this world. May God give you the strength to deal with the "Terrible Two's" and the "Terrible Teens." May you reach a happy old age in company of your children and your children's children. May you be the best Christian Parents that you can possibly be!

Sincerely,

Fr. Tony

A Parent Watchdog for God

Dear African-American Males, My Younger Brothers,

Since its founding, the American society has been rocked by a great fear. This fear is embodied in a horrendous monster which threatens the existence of the before mentioned society. What makes this fear deadly is society's inability to name and claim the fear. This enormous fear has essentially stopped all progression toward freedom. In fact, some may argue that America has reversed its course and is sliding backwards: falling into the errors of its past sins. For most Americans, the monster has become the prime target for hatred and denigration. In the minds of many and in the hearts of some, the removal of this monster would solve America's problems.

The fear is manifested through the ideology of racism. Racism is an internal cause which denies the rights and dignity of an individual solely on the basis of racial or cultural differences. As a result of this abhorrent fear, a monster has become evident in the mind-set of the American society. This monster, which instills fright in almost everyone, is you, the African-American Male.

To speak of you, we have to speak of the horrors in the American Society. Who else has had his dignity and human qualities stripped from his very being? Who else has witnessed his personhood being denied by the laws of a nation? The African-American Male, enduring centuries of pain, has become the monster which scares America.

I once heard that to write is to give voice to inner thoughts. To not write is to silence the thoughts; rendering them unworthy of existence. That is why I am writing to you, today. When your society devalues your images, it also sterilizes your potential to be all that you can be. It cuts off your roots, hindering your growth. St. Paul, in his letter to the Romans (11:16), writes, "If the root is holy, then the branches are also holy." Without your roots, you cannot survive. You cannot achieve holiness.

If "Black is not Beautiful, then you are not beautiful." If beauty lies in what you cannot achieve because of pigmentation, then you can never be wholly beautiful or beautifully holy.

In redefining beauty, the wider society has successfully recast you into a discouraging plight of double-consciousness. As William Edward Burghardt DuBois would say, the African-American Male must forever view himself through the "eyes of others...One forever feels his twoness, - an American, a Negro; two souls, two thoughts, two unreconciled strivings; two warring ideals in one dark body, whose dogged strength alone keeps it from being torn asunder." (This was taken from his book, The Souls of Black Folks)

My brothers, you are not monsters. You are precious gifts from God. This is why you must move beyond your monstrous definition. You cannot just keep existing without understanding that God made each of you with a purpose. The Roman Catholic Church supports the recognition and validation of whom you are. Its position stands firm through its many documents on Social Justice. This great Church asserts, through interpreting revelation, that all of God's creations are beautiful: these creations include the African-American Male.

Today, I pray that you will begin to see yourselves in the same light that God sees you. You are His beloved sons. You are Jesus' coheirs to the Kingdom of Heaven. You are destined for greatness. You can achieve that greatness by first showing the world that you are not a monster! You are our brothers and we must love you as such!

May God's Fatherly Grace lead you to see who you really are.

Sincerely,

Fr. Tony

Your Big Brother

PS: Pull up your pants! Old people don't want to see your underwear!

Dear African-American Young Women, My Sisters,

I wonder if you know just who you are. You are the princesses and queens of our society. You are the manifestation of God's beauty and the peak of Creation. When God made you, I know that He exclaimed, "Mmm, Mmm, Mmm.... This sure is very good!"

Knowing that you are the expression of God's love, I am struggling with understanding why you don't expect others to treat you as such. Time and time again, you allow society and especially young Black men to disrespect you. You allow them to treat as less than you are.

I have grown weary with how often I hear young men refer to you as B*%$# and Wh*%#. You are not female dogs and you are definitely not prostitutes. You are our beautiful sisters. You should demand that you be addressed as such. Of course, you have to stop referring to each other in such a manner. You need to stop giving boys permission to call you anything but a Child of God.

I also can't understand why you would pay to attend a hardcore Rap concert or purchase hardcore Rap music. Why do you pay to have someone degrade you? You will pay $50 for a concert ticket and then sit for hours listening to young men disrespect who you really are. You are not just an object to be possessed and used for sexual gratification. You are young ladies and you deserve to be treated in a respectful manner.

My sisters, you are descendants from a long line of powerful women. You are the daughters of the Queen of Sheba and the Blessed Mother, the daughters of Saints Perpetua and Felicity, the daughters of Saints Crispina the Bold and Josephine Bakhita. You are the daughters of many great and holy women whom have walked this land before you.

You are also the representatives of our ancestral history. You are the descendants of Harriet Tubman, Sojourner Truth and Mary McLeod Bethune. You are the legacy of Phyllis Wheatley and Rosa Parks. You are the reasons why they endured slavery, lived through segregation and fought for Civil Rights. You are the answers to their prayers.

It is time for you to say to the world, "Enough is enough!" I assure you that young men will not call you "out of your name" if you make it know that it is unacceptable. You have to hold yourself in high esteem if you expect others to do so. You are God's beloved daughters. So, make sure that everyone treats in a manner that you deserve. Don't settle for less!

Also, remember that your bodies are precious gifts. Your precious gifts of sexuality and virginity are gifts that God has given you to share with your husband. Don't allow anyone to unwrap your gifts until they have made a lifelong commitment to you on the Altar of God!

Sometimes, boys will try to coerce you into having sex by saying, "If you love me, you would let me." Well, you need to respond with "If you really love you, you wouldn't ask me!" Sex before marriage is a mortal sin. If you really love someone, you wouldn't want to risk them burning in Hell for committing a grave matter in the eyes of God.

My sisters, you are much more than this world wants you to believe. You are not objects to be used, abused and treated like refuse. You are our princesses and queens! So, claim your crowns and make sure that no one is allowed to tarnish them or knock off your jewels!

May God bless you in great abundance.

Sincerely,

Fr. Tony

Your Big Brother

Dear Members of the Gay Community, Our Family,

A great deal of energy has been spent trying to figure out if folks are born gay or is it something that develops because of their environment. Who really knows how one's sexual orientation is determined? Although many scientists have their own theories, no one has been able to present a definitive answer. After all of the data has been analyzed, we still don't know.

Sometimes I wonder if the battle over nurture vs nature is just a smoke screen that is constantly being thrown up so we don't have to deal with the real issue. To me, the real issue is, does God love heterosexual people more than He loves those who are homosexuals?

Well, I am writing you to let you know that God loves you just as much as He loves anybody else. We are all made in the image and likeness of God. The time and energy that God puts into creating heterosexuals are the same amount of time that He put into creating you. We are all precious in His sight.

The Catechism of the Holy Roman Catholic Church is really clear when it speaks about homosexuality and homosexual acts. In the Catechism, we read: Homosexual acts are "contrary to the natural law. They close the sexual act to the gift of life. Under no circumstances can they be approved." (Catechism pp 2357)

That means that we are called to love you as God loves us. Although we cannot approve of any act that goes against natural law, we can and must love you for whom you are. The Catechism goes on to say, you "must be accepted with respect, compassion, and sensitivity. Every sign of unjust discrimination in their regard should be avoided." (Catechism pp 2358)

In this, we are being reminded that discrimination based on anything is just wrong. No one has the right to treat you as less than human simply because your orientation is not like their own.

Finally, the Catechism says, "Homosexual persons are called to chastity. By the virtues of self-mastery that teach them inner freedom, at times by the support of disinterested friendship, by prayer and sacramental grace, they can and should gradually and resolutely approach Christian perfection." (Catechism 2359)

The reason why the Church calls homosexuals to Chastity is because we believe that sexual intercourse is designed by God for two purposes. First, it is for the union of the couple. The second purpose is for the procreation of life. Sexual intercourse was designed by God for loving couples to make babies. Whenever either of the two purposes is missing, we are called to remain in the state of Chastity. It does not matter what your orientation may be. If you are not open to the permanent union of the couple or to the creation of a child, you are called to Chastity. Premarital sex, adultery, and the use of contraception by a married couple all fall under this same understanding. In each situation, one of the purposes of sexual intercourse is missing. In each situation, it is considered a sin.

We could argue for years about our Church's teachings on Homosexuality. Everybody has their own opinion on many of our Church's teachings. One thing that is perfectly clear is that God has never and will never hate anybody. We are called to love you just as we are called to love anybody else. No one is excluded from God's love.

You are children of God. You are our brothers and sisters. Whenever you are missing from us, the Body of Christ is incomplete. I pray that God will continue to shower you with His love and protect you from the hatred of those who think that they can speak for God.

I look forward to seeing you at the Banquet Feast in Heaven!

Sincerely,

Fr. Tony

Your Loving Brother in Christ

Dear Brothers at Elayn Hunt Correctional Center,

I will never pretend that I can understand the mind of a convicted felon. What makes a man hurt another person? What drives a man to take another person's property? What makes a man believe that it's all right to take the life of another individual?

The last time I checked, the Ten Commandments were still the Laws of God even if then have not been fully observed in the laws of man.

You know better than most that human beings are capable of hurting other in ways that most folks could never conceive. You also know the consequences of your actions when you choose to hurt someone, take their property or destroy their lives.

From your side of prison, I would bet that you could teach the world hundreds of lessons on what we should or should not be doing. I also think that you could teach the world some valuable lessons about the unconditional nature of God's love.

On a couple of occasions, I have been blessed to visit with you guys to celebrate the Eucharist and to speak at your Vocational Graduation Ceremony. I was also blessed to join you for your Black History Program. Each time that I have visited you, I have walked away with a better appreciation of God's love and a deeper love for each of you.

When I am with you, I do not see criminals. I see the Children of God!

Deep down inside each of you is that blessed Spirit that God shared with you on the days of your Baptisms. Part of my gifts is the ability to see what God sees in everyone. So, I didn't drive over to Saint Gabriel, Louisiana, to come and see criminals. I drove over to come and see my brothers in Christ. I drove over to come and see the face of God.

In the Gospel of Matthew, Jesus speaks of the Judgment that will come upon the nations. In Matthew 25:34-40, we hear "The righteous will answer him and say, 'Lord, when did we see you hungry and feed you, or thirsty and give you drink? When did we see you a stranger and welcome you, or naked and clothe you? When did we see you ill or in prison, and visit you?' And the king will say to them in reply, 'Amen, I say to you, whatever you did for one of these least brothers of mine, you did for me.'"

My brothers, when I come to see you,
    I am actually coming to visit my Lord.

In 1816, St. Eugene DeMazenod, O.M.I., founded the Oblates of Mary Immaculate with the specific intent of serving the poor. One of his primary missions was also to serve those who were in prison. Even before starting his community, he was being touched by those who were incarcerated. In 1807, he wrote to his father expressing how meeting with the prisons taught him the importance of showing mercy to others. "It is the task of justice, with both equity and severity, to establish guilt...." he said. "Our duty is to ease their sufferings by every means in our power."

St. Eugene understood that everyone who commits a crime must face the appropriate punishment for that specific crime. He also understood that prisoners were still the Children of God and needed the Grace of God just as much (if not more) than the folks who were walking the streets.

I have been extremely blessed to visit with each of you. I love celebrating Mass and spending time just talking with you. I also loved having the honor of hearing your confessions through the Sacrament of Penance. The depth and sincerity of your confessions were far greater than most that I have heard. You understand the need for God's forgiveness and unconditional love better than most of the folks who are walking the streets.

You also help me to own up to my sinfulness. None of us are perfect. Each of us has things that we need to bring to the Foot of the Cross. Jesus would not have had to die if He was only coming to save the righteous. He came specifically for sinners like you and me.

I guess that all those who stand in judgment of you had better pick up their Bibles and turn to Matthew 7:1-2. The old translations would say, "Judge not least you too shall be judged." The newer translations say, "Stop judging, that you may not be judged. For as you judge, so will you be judged, and the measure with which you measure will be measured out to you."

I am going to keep "measuring" you with love and compassion because I will surely need Jesus to measure me in the same way when I reach the judgment seat.

May God keep you close to His Heart as you turn away from sin and promise to be faith to the Gospels of the Lord.

Sincerely,

Fr. Tony

Your Brother, a Sinner

Dear Students of St. Augustine High School,

In 1978, I walked through the doors of St. Augustine High School in New Orleans to begin my journey as a new Purple Knight.
St. Augustine High School is an all-male institution that primarily serves young men from the African-American community. At the request of the Archbishop of New Orleans, it was founded in 1951 by the Society of Saint Joseph of the Sacred Heart - The Josephites.

As a Ninth Grader, I really didn't know what being a "Purple Knight" would mean to me. I was only 13 years old and was barely 5 feet tall. I was so small that I wore a size $3\frac{1}{2}$ adult shoe. Needless to say, I really was a small fish entering into a big pond.

I can remember walking down the halls to my freshman classes and marveling at all of the big dudes that were the juniors and seniors. They were the future State Championship Football players from the class of 1979 and 1980. They were the drum majors of the world-famous "Marching 100". They were the Presidential Scholars and the National Achievement Scholars. I had a lot of major icons in the school to emulate. That is why I often wondered if I would ever be as good as they were.

Many of them went on to become professionals in sports, music and science. A few of them are now back at St. Aug as teachers and administrators who are handing on the legacy that was given to us.

Since graduating from St. Augustine High School in 1982, I have been blessed to have a few successes of my own. I am a former public school teacher and I have a couple of master degrees in Theology and Divinity. I have preached all around the world and have also written a few highly successful books. I have been truly blessed to be who I am.

I think that the foundation of my success, all started at St. Augustine High School. It was at St. Aug that I developed from being a somewhat shy little kid to a man who can stand on a stage and preach to a crowd of more than 23,000 teenagers. You see, St. Aug taught me to identify my gifts from God and to be confident that God would be with me wherever I would go.

I credit my being in the "Marching 100" band with my ability to preach in front of thousands. Although some find it hard to believe, I really was a pretty shy kid when I entered high school. I can remember that for my fourth grade play, I only wanted to be the tree. It was because the tree person only had to stand in the background and hold up a cardboard tree.

However, as a member of the Marching 100, I found myself in one of the greatest bands in our nation. In that band, I stood on the floor of the Louisiana Superdome and listened to crowds of more than 68,000 folks give our band standing ovations. I marched down the streets of New Orleans and watched as thousands of Mardi Gras Revelers danced to the beat of our drums. I was small part of a major piece of New Orleans' history and I like it a lot!

I was able to overcome my shyness because in my mind the massive crowds were looking at the entire band and not just at me. However, by my senior year, I wasn't that shy kid anymore. In fact, I was so cocky that I started to think that the crowds were coming just to see me. The other guys in the band were just there to be my backup musicians.

Being in our band helped me to realize that I had many gifts that I could share with the world. I was destined for greatness and it all began in the Marching 100.

I know now more than ever before that I am only a small piece in the legacy of our historic institution. I have returned to our school to serve as the Special Assistant to the President and as the Campus Minister because I want to help you fully understand the legacy that you have joined.

As the children of God and my brother Purple Knights, you are destined for greatness. You are marked by God to achieve more than you can even imagine at your young ages. Each of you has been given special gifts by God. You will know where your future successes lie once you figure out where God needs you to begin using those gifts.

My young brothers, I pray that you will never forget that we are interconnected by our faith, our school experiences and our school pride. Like our faith community, we are not only connected with those currently in our school, we are also connected with the thousands of men who have graduated from St. Augustine High School. We are forever connected because in us, the Legacy Lives!

May God bless you and continue to bless St. Augustine High School - Home of the Purple Knights!

Sincerely,

Fr. Tony

Class of 1982

Dear Me,

Man, life has surely taken me to places that I never thought I would go. I have been blessed to preach in hundreds of places to thousands of people. I've given presentations in the shadows of the Canadian Rocky Mountains and along the sands of Waikiki. I've preached to youth in Ontario and celebrated Mass with my Momma along the Sea of Galilee. Indeed, I have literally been around the world proclaiming the Good News of Jesus Christ.

When I look back at my life, I realize that I've had the chance to do a lot in a relatively short period of time. For that, I am eternally grateful to God.

Although it has been a fun journey, it has not always been easy.

It is not easy to be the popular guy. So many folks seem to misunderstand what I am about and misinterpret what I truly believe. If only they would take the time to really get to know the real "Fr. Tony," maybe their opinions of me would change.

So then, who am I?

What do I really believe?

Well legally, I am Rodney Anthony Joseph Ricard but most folks know me as "Fr. Tony." I am the son of Rodney and Rita Ricard and the brother of Kevin and Deidra. I am blessed to be the uncle of Corey, Andy, Shanna, Albert and Kristen. I am definitely their best uncle.

As a child, I was blessed to live in a "shotgun" double house in uptown New Orleans. On one side, I lived with my parents, my siblings and my maternal grandmother - Mrs. Anestasia Carlin Honore'. On the other side, was my Nanny's family. She lived there with my uncle Cyril A. Coulon, Sr., and my cousins - Cyril, Jr., Debbie and Darryl.

403

I am the Godson of Mrs. Felicie "Nanny" Honore' Coulon and the late Mr. Karl Ricard. Although my Uncle Karl was my Godfather on the baptismal records, my real "Godfather" was my late Uncle Cyril. He and my Nanny were definitely instrumental in my becoming the man that I am today. They have been some of my greatest supporters.

I am also blessed to be the mentor and surrogate father of Dernattel (Sr.), Steve, Daniel, Chris, Shannon, Denzel and Tevin. I am also "Paw Paw Tony" to Jada, Lil Dee and Chortni.[174]

I also have a grand baby that now lives in Heaven. Her name is Carly Madine Ackers. She is the daughter of Marilyn Madine - my grown child - form Our Lady Star of the Sea Parish.

My best friends are Cathy Allain and Glenn Chenier. I have been knowing them for decades. They probably know me better than I know myself.

I am also close friends with Diane Dooley and Cindy Capen. Both have been instrumental in my life and ministry as a priest.

As a child, was I a pretty shy kid. I was always afraid of large crowds. At Mardi Gras parades and at family gatherings, I used to hang onto my Momma's leg because I was so afraid of other people. I never could imagine that I would be doing what I am doing today

Even now, I still get really nervous in front of large congregations or packed arenas. My butterflies have butterflies!

---

[174]**2016 Update:** Since "Diary of an Unapologetic Roman Catholic Priest" has been published, I have been blessed to add a new grandson (Landon Quest) and a new surrogate son (Brandon Grace) to our family.

I was also scared of the dark when I was younger. As a result, I slept in my grandmother's bed until I was in the 8th Grade.

Back then, I never liked watching horror movies and hated going into Haunted Houses. Although I am an adult and a priest, I am still a little scared of the dark, today. I still hate horror movies and will only go into a Haunted House if it was designed by Walt Disney.

Although I really enjoy doing what God is allowing me to do, it is not as easy as some may think. I really have to work hard at being me.

I love reading Sacred Scripture and preaching about the Gospel of Jesus Christ. There is nothing that can compare to knowing that you are helping draw people closer in their relationships with God.

I have never taken for granted the blessings that I have in being a Roman Catholic Priest. Each day, I try to thank God for allowing me to serve Him and His people. I know that it is truly by the Grace of God that I get to do what I do.

I know that I don't bring a lot of gifts to the table. That is why I am constantly amazed at what God can do with just my "Two fish and five loaves."

I am not as confident as I may come across to others.

My confidence has grown through the years. Although I still sometimes doubt myself, I have learned to place my weaknesses on the shoulders of Christ. I know that God is using me to speak to tens of thousands each year. I pray that I will always preach what God needs me to preach.

There are times when I feel taken for granted or even used by others. Sometimes folks think that because "I am usually happy" that I don't have "feelings." But, I do.

Like everybody else, I want to know that folks really do appreciate the sacrifices that I make to keep everybody else happy.

It is not easy to be the popular guy. I can't go to a grocery store or department store without meeting folks who know me. I always laugh when folks begin to take an inventory of what's in my shopping cart. They always want to know what I am purchasing.

Sometimes, it would be nice to just be able to "shop," but I know that it is the price of fame. It is part of the journey that God needs me to be traveling. (That is why I sometimes go shopping when most folks are at work or asleep!)

Since being ordained, I have worked hard to win the approval of others. I especially have longed for the approval of other priests. Although some have commended me on my ministry, I have never really felt the "fraternal love" for which I have longed.

Part of the problem is that I am keeping myself too busy with my various ministries. I don't take time to stay connected with my brother priests. I am always busy writing sermons, preparing for speaking engagement or writing new books. I do have close priest friends like Fr. James Derran Combs, OFM, and Fr. Joseph Brown, SJ. Unfortunately, I don't stay in contact with them like I should. I need to make better efforts at staying connected with my brothers in the clergy.

Part of why I don't have a lot of priest friends is because I also have felt the unjust disdain and "judgmental" feelings of other priests. I feel as if many look at me as some sort of "side show" act. I am only here for "entertainment purposes only."

They believe that I only do what I do so that I can be the "popular priest." In a very real way, I have had to deal with the envy and overbearing jealousy of the very guys whose approval I sought.

If they only would take the time to get to know the real me, maybe they wouldn't judge me so harshly.

Once while doing a revival in Chicago, I heard a young Rapper speak about the life and ministry of Fr. Augustus Tolton. When Fr. Tolton was ordain in 1886, he became the first "recognizably Black" priest in the United States.

Fr. Tolton dealt with a lot of hated and jealousy from other priests. Some hatred him because of his race. Others hatred him because of his success in connecting with his parishioners. His popularity also fueled the clerical envy. They did not like the fact that he was not only popular with the "colored" parishioners. He was also popular with the "white" parishioners, too.

In his rap about the life of Fr. Tolton, this young artist presented a line that has reverberated in my heart since I first heard in back in 2006. In speaking about Fr. Tolton, this rapper said, "No good priest will be without his Pharisees!"

Although that young guy was talking about Fr. Augustus Tolton, he was speaking straight to my heart. It was then that I realized that I needed to keep doing what I do in the manner that I do it.

If my "Pharisee" needed to continue judging me, that will be between them and God. I just needed to stay true to myself and to my Call from God.

I realize now that the negative comments and snide remarks that I have gotten from some priests really do not represent the feelings of the entire priesthood. In my most recent years of ministry, I have begun to feel the fraternal love that I once thought would forever elude me. I am especially grateful for the paternal and fraternal love that I feel from Archbishop Gregory Aymond. He really is my spiritual father and my presbyteral brother.

Although I will probably still have to deal with a few "Pharisees," I am confident that their numbers are dropping. Hopefully, after 18 years of being a priest, they have finally figured out who I am and what I am about.

I am just a simple "colored boy" from Uptown New Orleans who has been blessed by God to "get the Call."

By now, I have preached or taught about almost every part of the Bible. I know for certain that I have preached about every part of the Gospel. God has blessed me with many opportunities to break open His Word and to bring our Savior's journey to life.

Although I enjoy all of the passages from the Gospel, there is one passage that has been ringing loudly in my ears. It is the passage that recounts Jesus' encounter with Pontius Pilate on the steps of the praetorium.

As the crowds called for Jesus to be crucified, Pilate, the Roman Governor, asks Jesus, "Are you a king?"

Jesus's answer stuns Pilate. I would bet that Pilate expected Jesus to deny His Kingship in order to save His life. But instead of denying that He was a King, Jesus simple says,

> "You say I am a king. For this I was born and for this I came into the world, to testify to the truth. Everyone who belongs to the truth listens to my voice."

> Feeling the shocked, Pilate said to Him,
> "What is truth?"

> (John 18:37-38)

Most of our lives are built on trying to discover the Truth.

Well, here are my truths. Here is the truth that is Fr. Tony:

I am a Child of God. I am not better than anybody else. However, in the eyes of God, there is no one better than me.

I am a disciple of my Lord and Savior - Jesus Christ. I fully believe that Jesus is the only direct pathway to the Kingdom of Heaven.

I am a sinner in constant need of the Savior's help. There are times when I do things that I know are wrong and I do them on purpose. That is why most of my "Don't Be Stupid" talk is directed at me.

Like all good preachers, I usually preach to myself and hope that it can help somebody else.

With that being said, I am realize that I not responsible for anybody's salvation except my own. My vocation is to introduce folks to Jesus who is "the way, the truth and the life." It is up to them as to whether or not they accept the Truth that is Jesus.

I am my Momma's Baby and my Daddy's Pride and Joy. As long as they are happy with me, I can face almost anything in this world.

I am not the conceited and self-centered person that some think that I am. In fact, I am just the opposite. I worry a lot about "meeting the needs" of God's people. I also have a deep-rooted and genuine fear of not having enough to say when I am in the pulpit or on a stage. I still get very nervous when I have to speak or preach in front of a crowd.

I am a priest of the Archdiocese of New Orleans and I am very excited to be the Special Assistant to the President and Campus Minister at St. Augustine High School. I know that I am exactly where God needs me to be.

I have been blessed to have written six best-selling books. Hopefully, with this book, that number will increase to seven best-selling books. Although folks think that I must have a lot of money in the bank, all of the proceeds from the books and products have gone directly back into my ministries.

For six years following Hurricane Katrina, I spent a lot of money supporting and helping to save Our Lady star of the Sea Parish in New Orleans. I also have contributed to youth ministry programs and paid for kids to attend national conferences. In addition to that, I have helped to keep at least 20 kids in Catholic schools and helped to pay the college tuition of a few. Although my book sales have been great, I don't have a hidden pot of gold.

Finally, I really do love being me. I feel honored to represent God to so many people. I pray that God is pleased with whom I am and what I do. Although I am not perfect, I think that I am becoming the best "Fr. Tony" that I can be. I am also glad that God isn't finished with me, yet.

When I die, I hope that I am remembered as a dedicated Child of God and my Momma's Baby. Everything else is just lagniappe. It's just a little extra from God as a pure gift to the world.

I also pray that God will bless you and all you love!

Thank you for loving and supporting this humble servant of God!

Sincerely,

Fr. R. Tony Ricard

Rev. R. Tony Ricard, M.Th., M.Div.,
An Unapologetic Roman Catholic Priest
and a Preacher of the Truth

Book Eight

A New Purple Heart
Reflections and Poems by
Young Purple Knights

Rev. R. Tony Ricard, M. Th., M. Div.
Mr. Chad Smith and the Younger Students of
St. Augustine High School

Published in 2014

Introduction to *A New Purple Heart*

"You Have Made Us for Yourself, O Lord, and Our Heart Is Restless until it Rests in You."

These are the words that our school's patron, St. Augustine of Hippo, used to describe his earnest desire to better know, love and serve the Lord.

As a young man, St. Augustine continuously searched with a Restless Heart for the meaning of life. He searched in the secular world: living a less-than-Christian lifestyle. He searched is the philosophical world: studying various forms of philosophy and heresies. He even search in the world of sin: living with a woman without the benefit of marriage and fathering an illegitimate son named Adeodatus. Indeed, he searched with a **Restless Heart**.

But, through the prayers of his Mother, St. Monica, and the Bishop of Milan, St. Ambrose, St. Augustine began to search for true rest in the comfort of God's Love.

St. Augustine's **Restless Heart** was filled with a true desire for the knowledge and love of the truth. And since Jesus is the way the truth and the life, St. Augustine could only find "The Truth" when he finally "found Jesus."

All of us have a built in desire to find the "True Truth."

Created by Lyndon Barrois '82

This collection of Reflections and Poems, offer you an insight into the **Purple Hearts** of the 6th and 7th Grade Students from St. Augustine High School. As you look into the **Restless and Purple Hearts** of these young **Purple Knights**, may the Holy Spirit come upon you and bring you a true sense of hope for our future.

This is **A New Purple Heart** - Reflections and Poems by Young Purple Knights.

Rev. R. Tony Ricard, M.Th., M.Div., St. Augustine High School '8
Mr. Chad Smith, St. Augustine High School '9

Section One

✠✠✠✠✠✠✠✠✠✠✠✠✠✠✠✠✠

The Heart of
the Purple Knight

The Code of the Purple Knight

The **PURPLE KNIGHT** is a man of **CHRISTIAN VIRTUE** and a man of **HONOR.**

The **PURPLE KNIGHT** is **LOYAL** to his God, to his family, to his friends, to his country, and to his school, and will never knowingly disgrace them.

The **PURPLE KNIGHT** is a man of **CHARACTER** who values **COURAGE** and **HONESTY.** He embraces manly virtue, and with St. Paul has put aside all childish ways.

The **PURPLE KNIGHT** is always a **GENTLEMAN**; He is Considerate of others, sympathetic, cheerful and kind. He manifest his Christian joy his readiness to come to the aid of those in need.

The **PURPLE KNIGHT respects his God** by keeping the Commandments and frequently celebrating the Church's Sacraments.

The **PURPLE KNIGHT respects his teachers** for he understands that through their instruction and discipline they serve as guides on his way to productive life.

The **PURPLE KNIGHT** is **CHIVALROUS** by first of all having a devotion to Mary, the mother of Jesus, and flowing from that devotion a respect for all women, young and old.

The **PURPLE KNIGHT** shows **respect for his school** by striving to make it the best that it can be, by care he shows for its physical structure and equipment, and by the spirit and enthusiasm he exhibits for its activities.

The **PURPLE KNIGHT** is **DEVOTED** to his studies because he understands that education is the key to a successful and productive life.

The **PURPLE KNIGHT** realizes that **through his baptism** he has put on **Jesus Christ** and that his life-long vocation is to make that identity come into sharper focus by **devoting himself to the services of God and others.**

Section Two

✠✠✠✠✠✠✠✠✠✠✠✠✠✠✠✠✠✠✠

The Purple Heart of Father Tony

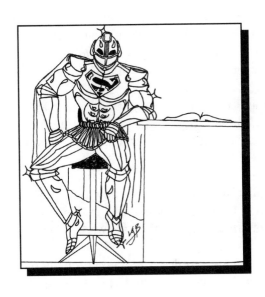

Thank You, Lord, for His Restless Heart!
by Rev. R. Tony Ricard and Chris A. Quest, II

Father God,
If You don't mind, we'd like to take a minute out of Your time to thank You for the gift of a man who gave almost all of his time to our glorious school.

You See, Lord, we have been really thinking about the Blessing that came upon St. Augustine back when the school, itself, was just in its infancy.

As the Members of the Josephite Community were laying the foundation for what would become one of the greatest institutions of Secondary Learning, a young, energetic man was invited by the Josephites to lay the foundation of what has become the crowning Jewel of our School.

That young energetic man was
Mr. Edwin Harrell Hampton.
(Lord, we called him, Mr. Hamp.)

Thank You, Lord, for the multitude of gifts that You developed in Mr. Hamp. His musical abilities and his creative genius are "often imitated but never duplicated." **You see, they'll never be another one like him.**

Through Your Grace, he has been recognized by men and women around our country for his gifts to the world of Music. He truly was (and still is) a blessing, and for that we thank You.

But, Lord, we wonder how many people know that the greatest gift that Mr. Hamp brought to the school had nothing to do with his musical talents or his ability to design mind-boggling field shows.

You see, Lord, the greatest gift that Mr. Hamp brought to the school was the gift of his heart. **Thank You, Lord, for His Restless and Purple Heart!**

Lord, in Mr. Hamp, we came to know a man of true love.

His dedication and commitment to our School Family was unquestionable.

And, his love for *his boys* is eternal. Anyone who has came into contact with his **Restless Heart** will testify to the love they felt flowing from this blessed man.

His genuine love for the *Men of St. Augustine* is evident by the many men who continually streamed back to the school and to the games hoping to get a chance to speak to him and thank him for the impact he has made on their lives.
Thank You, Lord, for that impact.

Lord,
Mr. Hamp was the **Elder Statesman** of **St. Augustine High School.** Though his role at our school shifted because of his age, his vocation never really changed.

When you saw him, you saw **St. Aug.**
When you saw him, you saw the **Marching 100.**
When you saw him, you saw the **Love** that laid the foundation upon which many great lives have been launched.

You see, Lord, even to this day as he rest with you in **Heaven,**
Mr. Hamp is still the **embodiment** of true "Knight Pride" and a pure "Purple Heart."

He Is the Restless Purple Heart of this Great Body of Purple Knights.
He Continues to Maintain the Beats That Keeps Us Marching on the Zion.

So, Lord, if You don't mind, We'd like to take a minute out of Your time to thank You. Thank You for creating one of the greatest blessing our school will ever see. **Thank You, Lord, for Mr. Hamp.**

And, when You get a chance, send Your blessing upon Him so that he can continue to be our Ancestor in Faith and our truest example of a **Restless** and **Purple Heart.**

Rev. R. Tony Ricard '82
Proud Alumnus of the Marching 100

Chris A. Quest '06
Proud Drum Major of the Marching 100

417

Skies Full of Promise
by St. Augustine of Hippo

God of Life,
    there are days when the burdens we carry chafe our shoulders
    and wear us down; when the road seems dreary and endless,
    the skies gray and threatening;
when our lives have no music in them and our hearts are lonely,
    and our souls have lost their courage.

Flood the path with light, we beseech you;
    turn our eyes to where the skies are full of promise.

Eyes Full of Promise
by Rev. R. Tony Ricard

Lord, I made the mistake one day of looking into the Eyes of a Child.
    In those eyes, I saw the hope for our future.
    In those eyes, I saw the dreams of our past.

In those eyes, I saw the very reason why Your Child, Jesus,
    came to save the world.

Lord, when I am growing weary
    from the sometimes over whelming task of teaching your children,
    help me to once again look into their eyes.

Help me to see what I saw long ago.
    Help Me to See Eyes Full of Promise.

(Thank You, Lord, for letting me look into The Eyes of Your Child.)

418

In His Image
by Rev. R. Tony Ricard

My image of God
    is easy to see.
He's Young, Gifted and Black.
    Yeah, He's just like me.

On that day
    when we first met,
I hoped it wouldn't be
    something I'd regret.

He was sittin' on the corner
    right near my place.
He wasn't saying anything
    But, I surely could read His
face.

For some reason
    He wanted to be my friend.
His eyes were saying open you heart
    so my love could get in.

Now the tears were
    tricklin' down His face
Cause' He was filling me
    with His holy Grace.

There ain't much
    that me and him won't do.
You see I love Him, now,
    and He loves me, too.

Now me and God
    we have lots of fun.

We shoot ball with the fellas.
    You should see Him run.

But you know what's best
    about my God?
It's that fact that he loves me
    even when it's hard.

He's my friend when I'm BAD.
    Yeah, BAD meaning good.
But he's also my friend
    when I don't do what I
should.

I guess He knows me
    better than most.
And, it's of this knowing
    that I can boast.

My image of God
    is easy to see.
He's Young, Gifted and Black.
    Yeah, He's just like me.[175]

---

[175]Fr. R. Tony Ricard created this piece while studying at Notre Dame Seminary, back in 1992.

Shoes
by Rev. R. Tony Ricard

While waiting outside of Church one day,
I over heard a mother of the Church turn to a boy and say,
   "Boy, you better get back home
   and do something 'bout your hair.
   'Cause looking like that, they ain't goin' let you in there."

Seizing the opportunity, she looked him up and down
   And started to tell him how to dress,
   When visiting this side of town.

"You gotta straighten-up your back,
   but bend your knees when you pray
   'cause that's the only way you can hear
   what God got to say."

"And while I'm telling you all the stuff
   that you've gotta do,
   you betta practice holding your Bible like this
   and your Holy Rosary, too."

"Now once you get all cleaned up,
   and you done practice all you can,
   come on back to our Church,
   so you can be a real prayin' man."

After hearing that Church mother talk,
   And taking in all her stuff,
   The boy raise his hand to God and said,
   "Lord, Enough is Enough."

He prayed, " Heavenly Father, I done all I can do.
   I go to Church most every Sunday,
   And I try to say what's true.
   But, the folks in the Church, they seem to be
   So worried about my looks,
   They done forgot about the love they read
   In their own Holy Books."

"They're so worried about my outsides,
       my hair, my clothes, my skin,
       that they'll never ever get to see the Spirit I hold within."

"So, Father, I give them to You,
       to do with what You please,
       and maybe while they're in there,
       praying on bended knees,
       they'll think about Your words,
       and their souls will begin to see,

"Most people pay You lip service,
       when their hearts are far from thee."

And when he finished praying, that lady looked all about,
       And she saw that boy's momma coming,
       So this Church mother began to shout,

"Girl, come get your boy, wash his hair,
       and clean him up, just right.
       Then maybe he can come to our Church
       for the service Saturday Night."

"But, till he's looking better,
       he better not come here again,
       'Cause, this is the house of the Lord,
       and not everyone's gettin' in."

The Mamma looked at that Church mother,
       As she blocked the Church's doorway,
       And with a soft voice and tear-filled eyes,
       That Mamma began to pray,

           "I've got shoes, You've got shoes,
           All of God Children got shoes to wear.
       When I get to heaven I'm goin' to put on my shoes.
           Goin' to walk all over God's Heaven.
               Heaven, Heaven,
       Everybody talking 'bout Heaven ain't goin' there.
               Heaven, Heaven
           Goin' to walk all over God's Heaven."

She looked down at her son and said, "Jesus, let's go home."

421

Section Three

✳✳✳✳✳✳✳✳✳✳✳✳✳✳✳✳✳✳✳✳✳✳✳

The Purple Hearts of
Grade Six

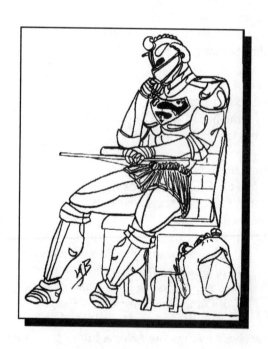

Brothers
by Kendal Rowan   6th Grade

I am my brother's keeper,
Both in two ways,
My biological brother and my St. Augustine brothers;
All of my brothers help me if I need help.

　　　Some are older, others are younger,
　　　some are thin, and some are tall,
　　　Some are serious, and some are playful,
　　　All help each other in one way or another.

We travel in packs,
We take charge of each other.

If one gets in trouble,
We all get in trouble; then we help each other out.

My biological brother always helps me,
Because he is strict,
That shows he cares about me.

　　　He says he is my keeper and I respect that.

He does just as my St. Augustine brothers
　　　and he always will;
We are all **BROTHERS** in one way or another.

I Am My Brother's Keeper!

My Spotlight
by Semaj Davis   6th Grade

In elementary school, Dwayne came to my talent show to support me as my group performed. My part of the performance was to rap and the entire group danced.

It was me and three of my guy friends, and we were making some magic on stage.

My brother sat on the back row, so that he would not be seen and create a big seen or steal my spotlight.

After the entire talent show was over, I went back to the hotel with my brother and his entourage.

We ordered room service, talked and watch the Miami Heat game on the television.

It was one of the times
that I felt really close to my brother.[176]

---

[176]Semaj's big Brother is Dwayne Carter. Dwayne is the Grammy Award winner who's better known to the world as the rapper, Lil Wayne.

Go to School!
by Derek Dunbar   6th Grade

Go to school, that's what my mother says
Go to school and be on time

Don't listen to what a man without an education says because
      he is not exercising his mind

Get up early and be prepared

Eat a good breakfast and have your supplies

No need to play around, it's just not that time

Right now! Its time for me to go hard.

      Right now! Its time for me to turn it up.

This is my moment to shine.

It's time for me to "Go to School!"

Thank The Lord
by Kris Augustine   6th Grade

Every day I wake up and thank the Lord
    for giving me another day to live.

I'm also grateful that I have someone to say good morning
to. Those people would be my parents and beautiful sisters.

hey encouraged me to come to St. Augustine High School,
and make a better person out of myself. If I didn't have
this family, there would be no telling where I would be.

That's why I am blessed to have a "glorifying God" family
and a warm – hearted family to go home to.

I go home to them every day after a hard learning session.

My Favorite

by Kris Augustine   6th Grade

My favorite color is Green.

My favorite seafood is Oysters.

My favorite food is Gumbo.

My favorite sport is Football.

My favorite family member is my Dad.

My Life

by Future Lee   6th Grade

Dark and mysterious

Crazy and delirious

Ups and downs

Smiles and frowns

Happiness and excitement

Hearts lightened

Music's my passion

I just love rapping

Intelligence, I already have

God leads the way so I can make a better path

Instead He saves me from His wrath

I make mistakes - I'm a human being

You treat me like I'm other things

That's not fair

But no one cares

But that is why we are all brothers

we're supposed to respect and love each other.

The Master Plan for Me
by Denero Dunbar   6th Grade

And we know that all things work
Together for the good
of them who love the Lord….

No matter what happens in
My life it will all work for
My good, even if friends
Leave me, they should have it.

Even if in class I fail a test,
I'll tell myself I did my best and
ask God to bless the rest, because
he has the master plan for me.

Even if goals sometime seem
Hard to reach, one day I
Will succeed, I will achieve
I will be the best Denero I can be.

Section Four

✳✳✳✳✳✳✳✳✳✳✳✳✳✳✳✳✳

The Purple Hearts of Grade Seven

Freedom
by Curtis Bibbins Jr.   7th Grade

Freedom to give, freedom to live, freedom to question why.

Freedom to walk, freedom to talk, freedom to live or die.

Freedom to sing, freedom to swing, freedom to walk on by.

Freedom to speak, freedom to seek, freedom to laugh or cry.

Freedom to work, freedom to shirk, freedom to spend or buy.

Freedom to please, freedom to tease.

Freedom to smile or to sigh.

Freedom to see, freedom to aspire high, freedom to touch.

Freedom to clutch, freedom to grant or deny,

Freedom that's mine.

Freedom divine,

Freedom no money can buy.

Life
by Broderick Martin   7th Grade

Living life is a foreign and humorous action that everyone experiences. As a young man, I can see how my life and other people's lives never stay the same because the world revolves around change.

Change is part of our day and our daily lives.

Sadly, there are two parts of living, life and death.

Life is like a game and if you play it well then you will continue to go on to the next level. However, if you do not play correctly and do not oblige by the rules, then you will continue to stay on the same level and continue to fail.

An example is of my twenty-one year old cousin who passed away last week. He played the game the best he could, but could not continue to play by the rules.

My mother said that she believes his next level was premature and thinks that he should have had more life to live.

I think life is worth living, no matter what level you are on.

Everyone should be able to experience the foreign and humorous things that life has to offer.

In God's Name
by Will Spears   7th Grade

Who ever thought who I would be today,
a 7th grader balling like a king.

Just a young boy trying to follow my dreams.

Who would have ever thought it would be me.
It's no front, I'm not trying to stunt.

God blessed me with this amazing talent,
without him I would not be who I am today.

So when you hear my name;
Just know I do what I do in God's name.

You Think You Know Me
by Tyler Wilson   7th Grade

I am black, young, and proud; however,
    you think you know me.

You look at my apparel to discriminate against me,
    but you still think you know me.

I eat and drink like you but you still choose to hate me.

You look at my home
        and think you know all of the things I go through,
        but instead of trying to help me, you criticize me.

We were all born equal,
    but you think you are better than me.

You characterize me
    by the color of my skin, clothes, home, and lifestyle.

However, at the end of the day you still don't know me.

Warning to the World
by Marc A. Barnes   7th Grade

Dear World,

I am writing this to warn you that I'm coming.
I'm coming and I'm not stopping. I won't stop until I'm at the top
and everyone knows my name.

I just thought it would be best to let you know that the first person to
run the universe will be me.

Do not worry though; I will be a just ruler.
I will listen as well as talk and I will try to correct all wrongs.

I just thought it was best to warn the world that I will win almost all
the time and on that rare times when I lose, I will lose like a winner,
proud with my head held high, knowing I will win next time.

World, I know you are trying to figure out how to prepare for me.

All you have to do is wait, you don't have to create the doors for
opportunities, I'll make them and you don't even have to tell people
about me, I'll make sure they know. So I just thought it was only fair
that I warn you that I will own you one day.

Yours truly,
Marc A. Barnes,
Future Ruler of the World

Book Nine

The Gumbo Pot
Stirring Up Some Faith

Rev. R. Tony Ricard, M.Th., M.Div.
A Priest of the Archdiocese of New Orleans

Published in 2015

Introduction to *The Gumbo Pot*

There is nothing like my Nanny's Gumbo!

For as long as I can remember, my Nanny always made the best Gumbo in the world. Gumbo is a dish that was created back in the days of slavery when people of African Descent could only gather a few food scraps from the master's table. By using leftover scraps, Women of Color were able to create dishes that could feed the multitudes. Gumbo is a mixture of a little this and a little that. It looks a little like soup, but it tastes a hundred times better. The name "Gumbo" was derived from the African-Congo word for okra. The West-African and Bantu people called okra *"ki ngombo"* or *"quingombo"*.

In my Nanny's Gumbo Pot, you might find shrimp, crabs, smoked sausage, chicken, gizzards and whatever else she could find to nourish the family. With the addition of some okra, *file'* and her special seasoning, her Gumbo Pot became the magnet that drew our entire family together.

The steaming bouquet that emerged from her Gumbo Pot was as sweet as the fragrance of frankincense at Christmas Eve's Midnight Mass. Like Jesus on a mountain top, my Nanny could work miracles with that pot.

I have had Gumbos in many places but none has ever been able to come even close to what flowed out of my Nanny's Gumbo Pot - although some Gumbos have been pretty good. They have never been able to reach the delicious status of what my Nanny was able to do at her stove. Her Gumbo was simply the best. When I think about the ingredients that my Nanny added to her Gumbo Pot, I realize just why her Gumbo was so good. You see, my Nanny added more than shrimp or crabs to her pot. She added more than sausage, chicken or even okra. The best thing that my Nanny threw into her Gumbo Pot was her love.

Her Gumbo drew people to her kitchen because it was filled with unquenchable faith and awe-inspiring love. In addition to her endless love, she added an awful lot of forgiveness. As she stirred her Gumbo Pot, she would think about her family and everyone else who would be drawn by its Creole aroma. While humming "Amazing Grace" or "Blessed Assurance", she would fill her Gumbo Pot with more than the stuff that would nourish our bodies. She would also be adding stuff to nourish our souls.

The Catholic Church's Cardinal Virtues (or ingredients) are Faith, Hope and Love. My Nanny's Cardinal Ingredients were Faith, Forgiveness and Love!

Although my Nanny's Gumbo Pot was used to nourished my soul. It is not the only pot in which I found both physical and spiritual foods. I have been blessed to have been nourished by the pots of a few other phenomenal ladies of Faith. The pots that were stirred by the Blessed Mother, my Maternal Grandmother, my Mexicana Mother and my West Coast Rock, all worked to fill my spiritual belly with more than just a spoon full of yummy-ness.

The Faith Pot of Mary, the Mother of Jesus, has nourished me with perfect love. Her example of discipleship has continuously nourished me in times of troubles.

The Red Beans Pot of Mrs. Anestasia Bernadette Carlin Honore', Momma Stasia, my maternal grandmother, filled my childhood with hours of prayer and an endless flow of encouragement.

The Mole Pot of Mrs. Angelita Ybarra Florez, my Mexicana Momma, helped me to see the connectedness of all cultures and peoples.

The Chicken Dumplings Pot of Mrs. Constance May Osmond Wichman, Cindy's Momma and part of my Redland's Rock, helped to lay a foundation of love that has nourished me through many trials and tribulations.

It is always amazing to see how women of faith can take a few scraps and fill a pot with enough goodness to nourish the world.

This book is a tribute to my Nanny's Gumbo Pot and her endless love. It is filled with stories and reflections on Faith, Forgiveness and Love. I pray that it will nourish your spirits so that one day folks will remember your works as much as I remember the miracles that arose from my Nanny's Gumbo Pot!

"It's time for us to get to cooking!"

In Christ, I remain,

Rev. R. Tony Ricard, M.Th., M.Div.
A Priest of the Archdiocese and
My Nanny's Favorite Godson!

438

Ain't Nothing Too Good for My Momma!

Over the span of the last twenty years, I have had the pleasure of enjoying many new things as a Roman Catholic Priest. I have celebrated the Sacraments, preached to throngs of youths across the nation and traveled around the world, *"proclaiming that the Reign of God is at hand."* Indeed, I have been thoroughly enjoying my life as an ordained minister of the Archdiocese of New Orleans.

Not long after I was ordained, I had the chance to travel to the Holy Land. This is one of the greatest gifts that I have received because I decided to say "yes" to God and dedicate my life completely to Him as a member of the clergy.

Back in 1996, Deacon Jerry Martinez and I led a group of eleven Believers through the sacred regions of Jordan, Israel and Egypt.

We visited the Church of the Nativity in Bethlehem where we saw the birthplace of our Lord. We visited the Church of the Holy Sepulcher in Jerusalem and were able to touch our hands to the top of Mount Calvary. We visited the Great Pyramids in Egypt and The Ancient City of Petra in Jordan. The entire trip was an unforgettable experience.

Looking back on that trip, I know that I have been blessed with many great opportunities. But, the greatest part of the trip was not visiting any of the ancient sites or sacred places. It was not standing inside of the pyramids or even praying inside of the Tomb where the Earthly Body of Christ once laid. The greatest part of the trip was the gift I was able to bestow on the person in my life who means the most to me.

A few months before the trip, I called my Mother and the conversation went something like this:

"Hey Ma, go stand by your calendar on the kitchen wall." (So, she did.)

"Now, tell me whatcha doing around November 5th?" ("Nothing, Baby.")

"Well, that's Good," I said.

439

"Do you think that Daddy could do without you for a couple of weeks, cause I want to take you with me to the Holy Land, free of charge?"

(After a brief moment of silence) My momma said, "Baby, you know you have been fulfilling my dreams for most of your life. But, *this is more than I could have ever dreamed of.*"

It was at that moment that I told her and have no shame announcing to the world, **"Ain't nothing too good for my momma."**

People of God, I fully believe that if Jesus were in my shoes, and had the chance to give his Momma a special gift, like a trip to the Holy Land, he would have done the same thing.

Time and time again, Jesus has said to His Followers, "Ain't nothing too good for my momma."

In fact, His very last Human Act was to make sure that somebody would be there to take care of His Momma. While He hung on a cross, He looked to the Disciple John and told this Beloved Disciple, "Take Care of My Momma." It was at that moment that Jesus gave the world one of the most precious gift that the Creator had given to Him: Mary, His Momma.

Jesus indeed loves His mother as much as I love my mother. In fact (*though I don't know how it could be possible*), Jesus loves His mother even more than I could ever love my mother.

No one would argue against the point that Mary was one of the most influential persons in Jesus' Life.

★   She committed herself to the Will of God by saying "yes" to His angelic messenger. It was through Mary that Jesus entered this world.

★   She gave birth to Him in the Little Town of Bethlehem.

★   She changed His diapers during the flight to Egypt.

★   She raised Him in the town of Nazareth.

★   She urged Him to perform His first miracle at the wedding feast in Cana.

★ She listened to Him preach throughout the Holy Land.

★ She stood by Him when his friends abandoned and betrayed Him.

★ She gave Him the strength to get up from the ground when He fell while carrying His cross.

★ She stood on Mount Calvary at the foot of His cross and watch her baby die.

★ She held His dead body close to her pierced heart when it was taken down from the tree.

★ She helped to lay him in the Tomb.

★ She wept as He lay dead in a hollowed grave.

She rejoiced on the day of the Resurrection.

★ She dined with Him at His Post-Resurrection appearances.

★ She was filled with the Holy Spirit on the Day of Pentecost.

★ She lived a long life continuously proclaiming to God, *"How Great thou Art."*

Indeed Mary the Mother of Jesus, Mary the Mother of God, Mary the Protectress of the Poor, Mary the Immaculate Conception, Mary the Blessed Mother, ever Virgin, Mary the Queen of Heaven and Earth, was and is a primary person through whom we have come to know and believe in Jesus, the Son of God.

Through Mary's "yes" to God, He blessed humanity through the Incarnation of His Only Begotten Son.

Through Mary's "yes" to God, our human bodies were lifted to a new and holy state.

Through Mary's "yes" to God, the human body became the Living Temple of the Holy Spirit and a "sacrament to all of Creation."

441

Mary's "yes" to God, elevated humanity above all creatures because it was through this one human being that we have come to share in His Divinity, Who humbled Himself to share in our humanity.

When the Angel Gabriel came to Mary and announced that she would be the instrument through which God would be united with all of mankind, you could bet that it wasn't easy for her to say "yes." In fact, who could have blamed her if she would have said "no?" Just think about all saying, "Yes to God," would do to her life.

She was a teenaged girl who was suddenly being told that she could possibly be an unwed mother. She was already engaged to marry a good Man and could possibly lose him because of this pregnancy. So, you could bet that St. Ann and St Joachim, Mary's Mom and Pop, would not have been happy if Mary had somehow messed up her engagement to Joseph.

Just think about it: St. Joseph was a good catch. He was the kind of man that most girls look for. He was definitely no *fix-her-upper*. He already owned a nice home, with a two-donkey garage. He owned his own business, *Joe's Carpentry Shop*. He was respected in the community. And no matter what happened, he never said a word. Mary had a lot to lose if Joseph would not believe her.

Yet, even with all she could lose, Mary said yes to God.

It is no wonder that the Roman Catholic Church has proclaimed Mary, the Mother of God, as the First of all the Saints, Queen of Heaven and Earth. She was the very First Disciple of the Jesus. She was the first to talk to Him. She was the first to touch Him and to be touched by Him. She was the first to dedicate her life in service to Him. Yes, Mary is Number One among all the Saints and Jesus would have it no other way.

In 1950, Pope Pius XII declared to the Christian World that when Mary's earthly life ended, her Baby Boy honored her with a gift that was more than she could have ever dreamed of. Rather than taking His Momma on a trip to the Holy Land, to the land promised long ago to Abraham, Isaac and Moses, Jesus saw fit to take her the Holiest of Lands, to the Promised Land that is the Eternal Kingdom of God.

Jesus loved His Mother so much that He refused to allow her body to know earthly decay. He assumed her, body and soul, into Heaven. This was the greatest gift that He could possibly give her.

442

Through the earthly life and ongoing works of the Blessed Mother, we are given an example of perfect commitment to God.

Never has Mary ever ask that she be given the Glory. In everything she says and in everything she does, she consistently points to her Child as the only road to salvation.

She is not the Savior of the World. She is not the Fourth Person of the Holy Trinity. She is not God. Mary is simply a Proud Momma who wants everyone to know and love her baby boy.

As followers of Jesus and the modern day children of our Blessed Mother, our present task is to shape our lives into the Christian patterns set by Mary and the many great saints who have come before us.

Each day, we are called to say "Yes" to God. Just as Mary said, "Yes" and allowed the Holy Spirit to use her as the means of bringing the Son of God into the world, we must respond positively to God's call and bring His Son into the world in which we live.

Through the Eucharist, the Church, and the prayers of the Blessed Mother and all of the Saints of God, may we have the strength and courage to answer God's Call and be true Ambassadors of Christ.

You know, traveling to the Holy Land with my Momma is indeed one of the greatest highlight of my life as a priest. I pray that God will give me other opportunities to bestow gifts upon *this lady who means so much to me.*

Today, we join with Jesus, who crowned Mary, His Momma, the Immaculate Conception, as the Queen of Heaven.

Let us unite our hearts and our minds as we proclaim,

"Ain't nothing too good for our momma."

God's Still In Heaven

Back on August 29, 2005, my life changed when the costliest storm in American history struck the Gulf South. At last count, Hurricane Katrina caused more than 108 Billion dollars in damages and lead to the death of 1,836 people.

My family and I evacuated the city on the day before the storm hit. We were extremely blessed to have gotten out of town before 80% of New Orleans filled with flood waters. We were blessed to find safety at the Louisiana Lions Camp in Anacoco, Louisiana. To this day, I thank Ray Cecil and the Lions Camp staff for helping to provide a refuge for my family.

In the wake of Hurricane Katrina, I remember sitting in my little office at camp and wondering "What are we gonna do now?"

By the time the news reported the massive flooding throughout the city, we had already figured that it wasn't going to be an easy journey. Although we knew that God was with us, we still wondered about our future. What do you do when you've lost everything in a moment, in a blink of an eye?

Like most folks, I evacuated with only three days of clothing and enough cash in my pocket to feed my folks for those three days. Once those resources ran out, I really didn't know what I was going to do next to make sure that all of my people were all right.

The one thing that I did know was that God was still God and that we had to trust that He would indeed provide all we would need. We had to rely on God because everything that we could rely on was already under water.

As the flood waters ripped through our neighborhoods, the only thing we could do was turn to our God. Luckily, we could turn to Sacred Scripture to find out that we were not the first people to go through tough times. That is why we knew that we could survive the aftermath of that great storm. Our spiritual ancestors survived their disaster. So, surely, we would survive, too.

In the Book of the Prophet Isaiah, for example, we listen to the journey of our ancestors who often believed that God had abandoned them. As a people, they had endure slavery in Egypt, exile by the Babylonians and ineffective leadership. Many began to wonder if somehow God had left them. Had the Lord forsaken them?

In Isaiah 49:14-15, God proclaims through the prophet,

> Zion said, "The LORD has forsaken me; my LORD has forgotten me."

> Can a mother forget her infant, be without tenderness for the child of her womb?
> Even should she forget, I will never forget you.

In other words, no matter what hardships come your way, you should trust that God is still with you and will indeed help to see you through. God will never forget you.

Like Isaiah, St. Paul also calls us to stand firm as disciples of the Lord, no matter what might come our way. Quite often in Sacred Scripture, St. Paul was dealing with all kinds of divisions in the Christian community. He especially had to address troubling times in the town of Corinth. Some believed that only in their allegiance to certain individuals could they be truly blessed by God.

Some were followers of Paul. Some were followers of a guy named Apollos. Others followed a preacher named Cephas. Although all of them were followers of Christ, they often argued over whose followers or whose church was the greatest in the eyes of God.

In his First Letter to the Corinthians, Paul was telling them that it did not matter to which church they belonged. The only thing that mattered was that they were true follower of Christ. The blessings of God were abundant enough to take care of all of God's Children. No one particular group would have a monopoly on the blessings of God. God's greatest concerns are the things in our hearts and not the groups we belong to or the things around us.

That is why Paul tells us that God "will manifest the motives of our hearts, and then everyone will receive praise from God."[177]

In the aftermath of Katrina, we had to trust in our hearts that God would indeed bless us and provide even our most basic needs.
Paul was able to rely on the words of Jesus to realize that God would provide for His children. Jesus had already shown His love for those whom God had given Him. Thus, Paul knew that God's providence was real.

---

[177] 1 Corinthians 4:5

In Matthew 6:25-34, Jesus says,

> "I tell you, do not worry about your life, what you will eat or drink, or about your body, what you will wear. Is not life more than food and the body more than clothing?
>
> Look at the birds in the sky; they do not sow or reap, they gather nothing into barns, yet your heavenly Father feeds them. Are not you more important than they?
>
> Can any of you by worrying add a single moment to your life-span? Why are you anxious about clothes?
>
> Learn from the way the wild flowers grow. They do not work or spin. But I tell you that not even Solomon in all his splendor was clothed like one of them. If God so clothes the grass of the field, which grows today and is thrown into the oven tomorrow, will he not much more provide for you, O you of little faith?
>
> So do not worry and say, 'What are we to eat?' or 'What are we to drink?' or 'What are we to wear?' All these things the pagans seek.
>
> Your heavenly Father knows that you need them all.
>
> But seek first the kingdom of God and his righteousness, and all these things will be given you besides. Do not worry about tomorrow; tomorrow will take care of itself. Sufficient for a day is its own evil."

As we watched Katrina's waters take over our homes and businesses, it wasn't the easiest thing for us to do. We couldn't help but worry about what we would eat or where would we find clothes for those who did not pack enough stuff.

In September of 2005, the people of New Orleans were all worried about what our immediate and long-term future would hold. But in this Gospel Passage, Jesus also asked us, " Is not life more than food and the body more than clothing?"
In other words, although we may have lost everything but the clothes on our backs, the fact that we were all still alive was reason enough to rejoice and trust in God. Although many had lost their lives in the storm, we were still here; we were still alive. And, ultimately, our lives were far more important than any of the stuff that we may have lost in the storm.

446

Just as God takes care of the birds in the sky, the wild flowers and even the grass in the fields, our heavenly Father will take care of us, too. Like the sparrow, we need only trust that God would provide.

That is why Jesus tells us to not "worry and say, 'What are we to eat?' or 'What are we to drink?' or 'What are we to wear?'... Your heavenly Father knows that you need them all."

Christ promises us that God will take care of His beloved children. When in need, we only have to turn to Him and allow God to take care of it. But before we can turn to Him, we have to make sure that our hearts are right and that we are placing nothing above our love for God.

That is why Jesus says, "Seek first the kingdom of God and his righteousness, and all these things will be given you besides." In other words, if you place God first in all things, God will never forsake you or leave you orphaned.

With God on our side, we shouldn't worry about tomorrow because Jesus tells us "tomorrow will take care of itself."

When I think back to our first days after Katrina, I can remember wondering from where would our next meal come.

Where would we find clothes?

Where would we find long-term shelter and the money that was going to be needed to keep us going since almost everyone's jobs were under water, too?

How were we going to make it through the darkest times of our lives?

But, in the matter of days, the phones at Lions Camp began to ring with offers of help and support. Red Cross and Food Stamps helped to take care of our need for food and clothing. And, FEMA began to help with our needs for immediate shelter and long term housing. Friends and family from all around the country began to do what they could to help us survive. Even strangers began to pitch in, too.

Before we knew it, we began to see the light and realize that somehow we were going to make it through the storm.

Only a few days after the storm, my momma said, "As long as there's a God in Heaven, I know that we're gonna be all right." Those words kept me from losing my mind and giving up.

As long as there's a God in Heaven, I know that we're gonna be all right. Though a mother could forsake her child, our God in Heaven will never forsake us.

We are His beloved children.

We are His disciples.

We are His precious Sparrows.

We are indeed precious in the eyes of God.

God knew that there would be times in our lives when we would feel lost and forgotten. There will be times when we would wonder if we mattered at all. So, He left us this Eternal Feast to remind us just how important we are to Him.

In the Eucharist, Jesus Christ shows us that we are indeed the beloved of God by continuously sacrificing His life for the sake of the world. At the Eucharistic Table, Christ Jesus gives us *all that we need* to make it through the tough days of life and to somehow rejoice even in our darkest hours.

The Eucharist feeds our souls and clothes our Spirits in robes of majesty.

That is why we don't have to worry about tomorrow because on this Altar we cannot only see our future. We can also taste what awaits all who seek first the Kingdom of God.

On this day, may you allow God to take care of all your worries and fears. Allow God to handle all the stress you have and know that He will never forsake or forget you.

On this day, may you realize that if God can get us through the worst storm of our lives, none of our little storms will be too much for Him to bear.

For as my Momma said, "as long as there's a God in heaven, I know we're gonna be all right."

Saying Grace

On May 27, 1995, I was blessed to be ordained to the Roman Catholic Priesthood. In my first assignment as a priest, at St. Rita's Parish, uptown, I met a young man named Steve who became my surrogate son.

Together, Steve and I traveled the country speaking at National and Diocesan Conferences and giving retreats for youth. Together, we did a lot and in the process taught each other some valuable lessons. Some of the lessons have been great and some of the lessons have been small. But, all of the things that we taught each other have been valuable to some degree.

Back when we first started hanging out, Steve taught me something that I have never forgotten. And, even to this day, I love to share this lesson with others. Because, in a very real way, it is import to *who we are* as members of this Church.

Back in 1996, on one of the first times that we sat down to eat in a public restaurant, I asked Steve to say *"Grace."* It has always been the tradition with my boys and myself that the youngest person at the table was responsible for leading us in "Grace."

So, Steve immediately made the Sign of the Cross, and began to pray, *"Bless us O' Lord..."*

When he concluded, he once again made the Sign of the Cross and then we began to eat.

At some point in our meal, we began to talk about how many folks do not say, 'Grace", before they eat. Even though they may be thankful that God has once again provided a meal for them to eat, they often forget to say, "Thanks to God" for that meal. Steve pointed out that it is a shame that people don't pray as often as they should (especially at meal time).

While talking about saying "Grace," I commended him on beginning his prayer by making the Sign of the Cross. And, it was at that point that he shared something profound with me.

He said, "When you are in a restaurant, and you bow your head or hold hands to pray, most of the folks around you will know that you are praying. They will probably assume that you are a Christian and that you are saying 'Grace.' But, when you start by making the Sign of the Cross, not only will they know that you are a Christian, they will also know that you are Catholic. There won't be any doubt as to who your God is and to what Church you belong. By making the Sign of the Cross in public, people will know that you are committed to Jesus and the Catholic Church."

Who would have though that something so profound could come out of the mouth of a 13-year-old? This early lesson from Steve illustrates what true commitment to God is really all about.

True commitment to Jesus Christ means taking a public stance even when others might look at you funny.

True commitment to Jesus Christ means taking a public stance even though others might disagree with your faith.

True commitment to Jesus Christ means taking a public stance on certain things, even when that *Public Stance* might set us apart from other people in our community.

True commitment to God means taking risks and accepting challenges. It means making the Sign of the Cross before you say "*Grace*" when others might not even pray.

Sometimes, true commitment to Jesus will cause us to be persecuted. But it is that very commitment that we help us withstand the persecution and emerge victorious.

A great example of this commitment can be found in the Book of the Prophet Jeremiah. It is quite clear that Jeremiah was persecuted in his times. Through the words of the prophet, we learn that Jeremiah was basically condemned to death because he dared speak up for God and oppose the princes of his region. Because Jeremiah was willing to preach the Word of God in a world that was wreaked with paganism and sin, he was tossed into a well and left to die.

Jeremiah 38:4-6, 8-10 says,

> In those days, the princes said to the king: "Jeremiah ought to be put to death; he is demoralizing the soldiers who are left in this city, and all the people, by speaking such things to them; he is not interested in the welfare of our people, but in their ruin."
>
> King Zedekiah answered: "He is in your power"; for the king could do nothing with them.

And so they took Jeremiah and threw him into the cistern of Prince Malchiah, which was in the quarters of the guard, letting him down with ropes. There was no water in the cistern, only mud, and Jeremiah sank into the mud.

Ebed-melech, a court official, went there from the palace and said to him: "My lord king, these men have been at fault in all they have done to the prophet Jeremiah, casting him into the cistern. He will die of famine on the spot, for there is no more food in the city."

Then the king ordered Ebed-melech the Cushite to take three men along with him, and draw the prophet Jeremiah out of the cistern before he should die.

In this passage, we see that God saved Jeremiah because of his commitment to doing the Will of the Creator. Like Jeremiah, we too have to stand strong. Sometimes our commitment will cause us to struggle. It may even cause us to question our commitment to God and God's commitment to us.

In his Letter to the Hebrews, St. Paul tells us that the key to surviving the struggle is found in keeping our eyes fixed on Jesus, who inspires and perfects our faith. Through constantly keeping Jesus before us, we are given the necessary strength to persevere in running the race that lies ahead: A race that ultimately leads to the Heavenly Kingdom of God.

In Hebrews 12:1-4, Paul says,

Since we are surrounded by so great a cloud of witnesses, let us rid ourselves of every burden and sin that clings to us and persevere in running the race that lies before us while keeping our eyes fixed on Jesus, the leader and perfecter of faith.

For the sake of the joy that lay before him, he endured the cross, despising its shame, and has taken his seat at the right of the throne of God.

Consider how he endured such opposition from sinners, in order that you may not grow weary and lose heart. In your struggle against sin you have not yet resisted to the point of shedding blood.

Men like Jeremiah are not the only ones that inspire us. Our ultimate inspiration comes from the commitment that Jesus had to His Father in heaven. He endured the cross before he received the glory of the Resurrection.

Looking at Jesus' journey on Earth, we can take courage as we walk our pathway to the Kingdom of God. As He endured the Cross, so can we endure our suffering.

One thing that is very clear in Sacred Scripture is that true commitment to the service of Christ Jesus is not easy. There will be times when folks will reject you because of your love for God. You may actually face times when your family will oppose you because of your love for God.

In Luke 12:49-53, Jesus says to His Disciples,

> "I have come to set the Earth on fire, and how I wish it were already blazing!
>
> There is a baptism with which I must be baptized, and how great is my anguish until it is accomplished!
>
> Do you think that I have come to establish peace on the Earth?
>
> No, I tell you, but rather division.
>
> From now on a household of five will be divided, three against two and two against three; a father will be divided against his son and a son against his father, a mother against her daughter and a daughter against her mother, a mother-in-law against her daughter-in-law and a daughter-in-law against her mother-in-law."

The fire of Christ will divide the committed followers of Christ from those who have been half-heartedly committed to Christ. It will divide the committed mother from the uncommitted father. It will divide the committed brother from the uncommitted sister. It will divide the committed child from the uncommitted parents.

Those who are committed to Christ will find themselves on the path way to heaven. Others who are less committed will find themselves on a path way to hell. When Jesus invites us to follow Him, He fully realizes *what* he is asking of us.

For many of us, it means turning away from the lifestyle that we have grown to love and accepting new lives in the Lord. In answering the call to be a follower of Christ, one must be willing to be fully committed to God.

The teachings of Christ cannot be seen as a smorgasbord of morals. Christianity is not Picadilly! You cannot pick what aspects of the Christian life you wish to follow. You must be willing to commit yourself to all of God's commands.

A Christian's commitment to Jesus must take priority over everything else. The Christian's commitment to light and truth cannot be compromised in any way.

In Matthew 5:14-16, Jesus says to his disciples,

> "You are the light of the world. A city set on a mountain cannot be hidden. Nor do they light a lamp and then put it under a bushel basket; it is set on a lamp stand, where it gives light to all in the house.
>
> Just so, your light must shine before others, that they may see your good deeds and glorify your heavenly Father."

Like Steve in that Restaurant displaying his Faith and Commitment to God and our Church by the simple act of making the Sign of the Cross before he says, "Grace," we must examine our lives to see if the way we live out our faith shows that we are fully committed to God.

Where it appears that our commitment to Christ is being compromised, we must change. For, a half-hearted commitment is really no commitment at all.

Through the years, Steve and I shared hundreds of meals. And, no matter where we were, Steve said, "Grace," beginning with the Sign of the Cross. Though he has grown out of doing a lot of the things that he used to do as a child, the one thing that he has not grown out of is praying. In fact, even his prayer at meal time has grown.

You see, now, because of his days at St. Augustine High School, at the end of saying "Grace," Steve often calls on the intercession of *St. Joseph* and *St. Augustine*. So, when he says, "St. Joseph," whoever is at the meals has to respond by saying, "Pray for us." And when he says, "St. Augustine," you also respond by saying, "Pray for us." Then, you make the Sign of the Cross and can begin eating.

In a very real way, this extended prayer shows that we are not only thankful to God and committed to Him in faith, we are also thankful to the Saints of God for keeping us in their prayers and assisting God in His ministry and Divine Providence.

Like Steve, I, too, think that it is good for us to say "Grace." But, I'd add that we should not only say, "Grace" before meals. We should actually say, "Grace" before everything we do. Giving thanks to God will indeed flood our lives with even more reasons to say, "Grace."

When the praises go up, the blessings come down!

And so let us pray, In the Name of the Father
    and of the Son and of the Holy Spirit, Amen.

Lord, we come before You, today,
    asking that You give us the courage to follow You,
    In not only our private lives but in our public lives, too.

Lord, even though it causes us to be persecuted, as Jeremiah was persecuted,
    help us to stand firm in our Faith.

Lord, give us the courage to follow you,
    even though it causes us to struggle, as Paul tells us it does.

Lord, give us the courage to follow you, even though, sometimes,
    it sets us in opposition to our family, as Jesus warns in the gospels.

And finally, Lord, give us the commitment necessary to always be willing to make the *Sign of the Cross* and pray in the crowded restaurants of our lives.

As we approach our journey of life may we always pray,

    "Bless us, O' Lord, and these Thy Gifts which we are about to
    receive from Thy Bounty, through Christ our Lord, Amen.

St. Joseph, "pray for us." St. Augustine, "pray for us."

In the Name of the Father and of the Son and of the Holy Spirit, Amen.

454

Tell It Like It Is

Back when I was in the seminary, we were required to take a few classes on preaching. Now, I can honestly tell you, that the way I preach today and the way they taught us to preach are not really the same.

You see, in the seminary, they told us that when you preach, you should never use the word, "I." You should limit the use of personal experiences as examples. You should speak about yourself only in the third person. And never, just never, address any individual group or section of society by itself because you may somehow offend them by addressing them specifically.

Another thing that they taught was when you have to speak about a tough issues, make sure that you use a calming image to soften the blow!

"We must be cautious," they told us, "not to offend any particular person or group. Just, challenge them, in general."

As y'all could guess, back when I was sitting in those homiletic classes, I can honestly say that I was thinking to myself, "Whatever happened to Priests who just tell it like it is?"

Sometimes folks need to just hear the truth even when it might hurt. Because, the truth is the truth. And, as Aunt Ester taught us, "The Truth will set you free." Sometimes, it is good for folks to hear the plain truth. They need to have the Word of God broken down into plain English so that there is no room left for misinterpretations.

Sometimes, folks just need to hear a priest, quote Aaron Neville and just *"Tell It like It Is!"*

Well, I have decided to do just that. Right now, I am gonna just *"Tell It Like It Is!"*

Please know that I do not intend to hurt anyone's feelings or to alienate anyone from the Church or it's members. But for whatever reason, I feel the need to just speak the truth!

The basic truths of our lives are quite simple. God is God. And, He is Good.

None of us here is God - and that's the Truth!

Anything that turns a person away from God is called SIN. And, Sin is bad.
God is Good - Sin is Bad!

God is the source of love. Because, God is Love. The Devil is the source hatred
and that makes him the Lord of Sin.

A Sin is a Sin. No matter how big or how small. It, in some way, shape or form,
hurts your relationship with God and with His people.

That's why we should be going to confession - To be reconciled with God and
his people. I'll touch on that later.

The basic definition of sin is quite simple:

1. It's a grave matter. That means that it's serious!

2. You have full knowledge of what you are doing.
That means you know that it's wrong.

3. You are doing it of your own free will.
That means that "ain't nobody" making you do it.

It's time to get rid of the confusion about sin!

In the year 2015, I fully believe that the waters that once separated the banks of
the Promise Land, the land where God exists, and the banks of Slavery, the Land
of Satin, Himself, have somehow been muddied by our personal sins. The
problem is, folks sometimes have no idea that through their sins, they are casting
mud into the River of Life. So, in order to help everybody out, here is a basic list
of some of the mud that God sees as Sin.

- Greed is a Sin. Living "for the love of Money" is a Sin!
- Stealing is a Sin. If it does not belong to you, you should not take it!
- Not giving to God what belongs to God is a sin.
- Breaking things that do not belong to you is a sin. That's the same as stealing.
- Gossiping is a sin. Talking behind people's Back is a Sin!
- Lying is a Sin That's like stealing the truth!
- False Pride is a Sin.
- Uncontrolled Anger is a Sin.
- Using the Name of God in Vain is a Sin.

- Lust is a sin.
- Pornography is a sin.
- Adultery is a Sin.
- Pre-Marital Sex is a Sin.
- Living together, Cohabitation, or as the old folks would say, "shacking-up" is still a Sin.
- Using Illegal Drugs is a Sin!
- That includes Smoking Weed!
- Abusing Alcohol is a Sin!
- Abusing your child, be it physical, mental or emotional is a sin.
- Abusing your Spouse, be it physical, mental or emotional is a sin.
- Child neglect is a sin.
- Being a Dead-beat Dad or Mom, not caring for the children you create is a sin.
- Abusing or neglecting a senior citizen is a sin.
- Cursing at your parents is a sin.
- Disrespecting your elders is a sin.
- Not attending Church on Sunday or a Holy Day of Obligation is a still a Sin.
- Making anything or anyone more important than serving God and your Church is a sin.

Put plainly, Stuff that was a sin in the past is still a sin today!

God has not changed. His ways are always constant!

Thus, if it was wrong when you were growing up, it still is wrong today!

Plainly put, a sin is a sin is a sin. And, we all by now know exactly what a sin is. No matter how much you try to dress it up or to explain it, anything that turns a person away from the Love of God and away from showing that love for one another is called SIN. And, Sinning is unacceptable.

For, to knowingly do anything that goes against the Will of God will hurt your relationship with the Lord. And, that is unacceptable!

As a priest, as a minister, as a clergyman, sometimes, *"I've gotta just tell it like it is!"*

When we look throughout Sacred Scripture, we can see places where Jesus got in trouble because he dared to tell it like it is.

In Gospel of John, for example, the Jews were murmuring because Jesus Christ dared to challenge their beliefs and share the truth with them.

In John 6:41-51, we read,

> The Jews murmured about Jesus because he said, "I am the bread that came down from heaven," and they said, "Is this not Jesus, the son of Joseph? Do we not know his father and mother? Then how can he say, 'I have come down from heaven?'"
>
> Jesus answered and said to them, "Stop murmuring among yourselves.
> No one can come to me unless the Father who sent me draw him, and I will raise him on the last day.
>
> It is written in the prophets: They shall all be taught by God. Everyone who listens to my Father and learns from him comes to me. Not that anyone has seen the Father except the one who is from God; he has seen the Father.
>
> Amen, amen, I say to you, whoever believes has eternal life. I am the bread of life.
>
> Your ancestors ate the manna in the desert, but they died; this is the bread that comes down from heaven so that one may eat it and not die.
>
> I am the living bread that came down from heaven; whoever eats this bread will live forever; and the bread that I will give is my flesh for the life of the world."

You see, Jesus was this young, cute and popular preacher that was attracting hundreds of followers. He was packing churches across the region with His dynamic style of preaching and His knack for speaking directly into folks hearts. (Hmmm...)

The problem was, whenever He hit on a topic that ruffled their feathers, they began to discredit Him and ask themselves *"Just who does he think he is?"*

That's kind of what happens to priests, today. The moment you speak about something that might ruffle folks' feathers, instead of reflecting on themselves, they try to find something wrong with the Priest! That's why many ministers hesitate to tell it like it is.

But, in this episode from the Gospel of our Brother John, Jesus did not hesitate. This challenge to the Jews comes right after Jesus had fed the five thousand men (not counting the women and children) on the mountain. He told them that they could eat like this forever if they only accepted the fact that He was sent by God the Father to deliver them from Sin.

However, this did not sit well with them. So, they began to murmur and bicker. But, when you think about it, Jesus was just "telling it like it is."

If you want to get to heaven, if you want to dine at the Banquet Table in the Kingdom, you need to make sure that you accept Jesus as you personal Lord and Savior and live your life according to the Master's Plan. It is that simple. This means that we can't play with the Lord.

You can't get to heaven by being a Christian on Sunday Morning and then acting like a demon on the rest of the days. God has no room in the Kingdom for hypocrites. You have to be a Christian All of the time. As a minister, I have to be willing to tell folks when they are doing something that is not only detrimental to their life on Earth, but is also detrimental to their life in the Kingdom of Heaven.

People of God,

It is time for us to wake-up from our sleep and truly follow Jesus, the Bread of Life. It is time for us to live our lives as if today will be our last day on Earth.

It is time for us to take a good look at our own life and eliminate anything that might be calling us away from the love of God.

Part of the truth, as I understand it, is the fact that John 3:16-18 tells us,

> God so loved the world that he gave his only Son, so that everyone who believes in him may not perish but may have eternal life. Indeed, God did not send the Son into the world to condemn the world, but in order that the world might be saved through him. (Therefore,) Those who believe in him are not condemned.

This means that every person, male or female, young or old, black or white, straight or gay, educated or illiterate, able-bodied or physically-challenged, visually-impaired or with good sight, every person on the face of God's Green Earth has the chance to live eternally with God in the Kingdom of Heaven.

That is why Jesus came and built this Church. That is why we are here. Jesus the Christ, calls us to recognize our broken-ness, to repent for our sins and to be reconciled with God and the Church.

You know, I find it amazing how so many folks can sings God songs of praise and never admit that they are sinners. When I think about how few people come to confession on Saturdays or call to set up an appointment for confessions, I wonder if we have truly come to understand "why" Jesus set up this Church. It was so that we could be cleansed of our sins and be nourished by His body and blood. But, most folks just don't understand.

In the Eucharist, we have the real presence of the Lord. In the Sacrament of Penance, we have the real forgiveness of the Lord. It's time for folks to not only be nourished at the Table of the Eucharist. They need to also be cleansed at the Seat of Reconciliation.

Today, may you have the courage to bring it before God. And may other priests have the courage to just speak the truth.

And, may my teachers at the seminary forgive me this day for just "telling it like it is!"

Amen and Amen!

Tooka and Chris' Seafood Platter

Back on May 27, 1995, I walked into St. Francis Cabrini Church to celebrate my ordination to the Priesthood. On that date, I knelt before Archbishop Francis Bible Schulte and promised to dedicate my life to the Roman Catholic Church and the People of God. On the day that I was ordained, I vowed to live a simple life of service.

Unlike those who join a religious community, I did not have to take the three traditional vows of Obedience, Celibacy and Poverty.

As a diocesan priest, I only had to promise to live a life of Obedience and Celibacy. When folks ask why we don't do poverty, I simply say, that after Obedience and Celibacy, y'all can't get the money, too!

As you know, the life of a priest can be filled with many trials and tribulations. From the rigors of being a pastor to the trials of dealing with Archdiocesan officials, it's not always easy to do what we do. But, I am happy to say that in the midst of it all, I have been truly blessed.

As the Gospel songs says,
"I've had some good days. I've had some hills to climb. I've had some weary days And lonely nights.

But when I look around, And I think things over. All of my good days They out weigh my bad days So I won't complain."

I can honestly say that I know that I've been blessed.

Blessed to sit in the presence of Popes and Presidents.

Blessed to pray with inmates and prisoners.

Blessed to preach before tens of thousands and to inspire them all with the Word of God.

Although I could list for you hundreds and hundreds of things that make being a priest tough, I'll just simply say, "Thank You, Lord... I won't complain!"

Many folks think that living a life of Obedience and Celibacy will drive a man crazy. Although you could argue that at times I can be a little nuts, I assure you that it's not because of my vows. It's because of my genetics. I come from a long line of crazy Black-Creole folks. It ain't from my vows. It's in my blood.

461

Today, I want to confess to you that although I have been pretty good with being Obedient to the Archbishop and his Successors, I haven't been as good when it comes to Celibacy.

Back in 2001, I fell in love with a beautiful female and actually allowed her to live with me in my rectory for more than 12 years. I know that it may be hard for you to believe. But, if you would've seen her, you would have fully understood why I fell in love with her. She had big beautiful brown eyes, a swagger in her walk and a heart that was filled with unconditional love. Of course, you know that I'm talking about the love of my life, Miss Pepper Louise, my beloved Rottweiler.

For twelve plus years, Pepper and I were inseparable. When I evacuated for Hurricane Katrina, my girl was at my side. When we returned home, we lived together in an RV and later in a gutted out rectory. Pepper was with me through the ups and downs of saving a parish from closing and when I decided to leave *Our Lady Star of the Sea* to work full-time at St. Augustine High School.

Pepper was the love of my life. And, Everybody knew it.

Well, on December 11, 2013, Pepper moved to Doggie Heaven. Although it's been a while since she passed in her sleep, I still think about my girl and the love we still share. God used her on many occasions to be my calm in the storm and my comfort on what could have been lonely nights.

A few months after Pepper moved to Heaven, I decided to welcome a new dog into my home.

In February of 2014, I worked with the New Orleans Bulldog Rescue to find an English Bulldog that could come and live with me.

On March 18, 2014, Tooka Rochelle Ricard, moved into the Old St. Raymond's Rectory and became my new friend. Although she has many enduring qualities, I can honestly say that Tooka is no Pepper.

Pepper was the sweetest dog on Earth. Everybody loved her. But Tooka, on the other hand, is as crazy as crazy can be.

One minute, she's the most loving dog on Earth and the next minute she's ready to attack anybody whom dares rings the door bell. I honestly think that she's bipolar. She ought to be on medications or something. Cuz, she really is nuts!

462

Although my boys keep saying that maybe I should trade her for another Bulldog, I kinda like her. So, I'm not ready to give up on her yet no matter how nuts she might be.

Luckily, when I travel, my boy Chris is willing to watch after my crazy dog. I don't know what I would do with her if Chris couldn't handle her whenever I have to travel to preach. Although she sometimes looks at him crazily, she knows that he's the Alpha Dog and won't cross that line of dominance. All he has to do is raise his voice and she seems to obey his commands. (Unlike with me and the Archbishop, Tooka actually listens to and obeys Chris' commands.) But, even Chris knows that Tooka is crazy. So, he watches himself around her and knows that her bipolar side can surface at any minute.

Back in June of 2014, Chris found out just how crazy Tooka could be.

It was then that Chris graciously took care of Tooka while I traveled to Chicago and later was a presenter for the Archbishop Lyke Conference that was held in downtown New Orleans. While I was gone, he made sure she was well fed and that she was let out into the backyard to "*handle her business*" on a regular basis. He really does a great job in taking care of our crazy friend.

On the Sunday that the Lyke's Conference ended, I wanted to treat Chris to something nice since he had taken such good care of a dog with split personalities. So, I brought him home a delicious Seafood Platter from Landry's Seafood. In addition to french fries, his platter included tender fish, seafood-stuffed shrimp, stuffed crab, and crispy fried shrimp & oysters.

All the way home, that platter was talking to me in the car. Man, it smelled good. And, I knew that Chris was going to love it.

When I got home, I handed Chris the bag from Landry's and headed to my room to change. About 10 minutes later, all I heard was Chris' yelling for me to come get my crazy dog. I could only imagine what Tooka was doing.

When I got to the den, Chris was furious and Tooka knew that she was in trouble. You see, Chris had put his delicious plate of Landry's Seafood on the coffee table. When he got up to run to the restroom, Tooka decided to help herself to everything that Landry's had to offer.

She ate the shrimp. She ate the stuffed crabs. She ate the fried oysters. She even ate all of the french fries. The only thing left was one stuffed shrimp and a whole lot of dog slobber.

Although she tried to pretend that she didn't do it, the slobber gave it away.

Needles to say, Chris was furious. I don't think that he talked to her for at least two weeks. His heart was set on devouring that seafood platter and ended-up with nothing but disappointment and a well-fed dog.

Not too long ago, I thought about Tooka and Chris' Seafood Platter when I was reading through the Gospel of our Brother Matthew. The 15th Chapter of Matthew's work talks about a dog and the Master's table. But, unlike Tooka, this dog is only given the scraps and not the whole meal.

In Matthew 15:21-28, we hear,

> At that time, Jesus withdrew to the region of Tyre and Sidon. And behold, a Canaanite woman of that district came and called out, "Have pity on me, Lord, Son of David! My daughter is tormented by a demon." But Jesus did not say a word in answer to her.
>
> Jesus' disciples came and asked him, "Send her away, for she keeps calling out after us." He said in reply, "I was sent only to the lost sheep of the house of Israel."
>
> But the woman came and did Jesus homage, saying, "Lord, help me."
>
> He said in reply, "It is not right to take the food of the children and throw it to the dogs."
>
> She said, "Please, Lord, for even the dogs eat the scraps that fall from the table of their masters."
>
> Then Jesus said to her in reply, "O woman, great is your faith! Let it be done for you as you wish."
>
> And the woman's daughter was healed from that hour.

In this Gospel episode, we hear the story of a Canaanite woman who went to Jesus to seek his help in curing her daughter. You see, her daughter was being tormented by demons and the woman knew that only Jesus could set her free from this torment. When she approached Jesus, she begged Him to come and heal her daughter. But, initially, Jesus refused to help her. In fact, he didn't even respond to her pleas.

Now, the Jesus we encounter in this episode is not the Jesus that we are used to. Normally, Jesus responds immediately to the cry of the poor or lame. But for whatever reason, he chose not to even acknowledge her at all.

That is why his disciples said to him, "Send her away, for she keeps calling out after us." They probably thought that Jesus just didn't feel like being bothered by this foreigner.

Seeing that his disciples were bothered, Jesus replied to the woman by saying, "I was sent only to the lost sheep of the house of Israel." In this, he was telling her that He was sent first to save the people of Israel. After they have heard the Word and believed that He was the Messiah, He would then save the rest of the world.

Although the woman understood what Jesus was telling her, she also knew that her daughter would not be healed if she did not persist in her begging. So, she replied to Jesus by saying, "Lord, help me." And then He said in reply, "It is not right to take the food of the children and throw it to the dogs."

But, this persistent momma replied to Jesus by saying, "Please, Lord, for even the dogs eat the scraps that fall from the table of their masters." In other words, "Lord, we don't need much. Just one word from You and we will be good!" It was then that Jesus recognized her faith and told her that her prayer would be answered. At that moment, her daughter was healed.

At first, this Gospel reading can be confusing.

How is it possible that Jesus could initially tell someone that He was not going to answer their pleas?

How is it possible that the Lord of Lords would not take care of the needs of someone who came to Him in great desperation?

How is it possible that Jesus would not help a mother in need?

Part of why this episode was written was to show us that Jesus did indeed come to save the People of Israel. But, it also shows us that even Jesus realized that He would not only save the people of his Ancestral lines, He would also take care of the needs of others.

One of the big things that jumped out to me in this passage, was the rich image of feeding scraps from the table of Christ to the dogs. It is Jesus who initially said, "It is not right to take the food of the children and throw it to the dogs."

465

But, the Canaanite women reminded Him that "even the dogs eat the scraps that fall from the table of their masters."

This is a very profound statement of faith.

She fully believed that just an itty-bitty crumb from the table of Christ could not only heal her daughter. A crumb from Christ could also heal the world.

You know, it's too bad that most of the people in our world can't recognize just how powerful the crumbs from the Table of Christ can be.

Just a morsel of Jesus could change anybody's life. All you need to do is "Come to the Table of Mercy prepared with the wine and the bread. All who are hungry and thirsty, come and your soul will be fed."

Today, as we reflect on the power of Crumbs from Jesus, we must also reflect on how often we may be turning away folks that we see as dogs from the table of the Lord.

Who do we treat as if they are not worthy of the love of Christ?

Who in our minds is undeserving of the Graces offered by our Lord, our Church and even this Sacramental Feast?

Who are the people that we have consciously and unconsciously tried to deny access to the Lord because we don't believe that they are worthy of even a crumb that just might fall from the Table of Sacrifice?

If we are truly honest, we all have to admit that we have that list of "Known Sinners" that we would readily deny entrance to this Banquet.

For some, it's the folks that have hurt us through the years. For others, it's the folks who have hurt our community. While for others, it's the folks that we perceive as possibly being able to hurt us or our families.

No matter what, we all could come up with a list of folks that we would deny the chance to be feed by Jesus, the Bread of Life.

In reflecting on this we must then ask ourselves, who am I that I would have the audacity to tell someone else that they don't deserve a chance to know, love and serve Jesus as their Lord and Savior?

Who am I that I could possibly believe that I have the right to turn another person away from the Lord or the Church?

Who am I to deny anyone a chance at being fed by the Lord?

Just who am I?

No one has the right to turn even the dogs of the world away from the table of Christ. Neither I, the Archbishop or the Pope can claim that right. So, I warn you to be careful. By trying to deny someone access to Jesus, you are actually denying Jesus himself. And in doing so, you are teetering at the gates of Satan.

Today, we must call on Jesus to allow even the dogs of society to have a chance to eat some of the scraps at His table. For, it will be those scraps that just might save them.

Sometimes, I wish that we all had faith like that Canaanite Woman. Can you imagine what our lives would be like if we truly believed that even a crumb from this table could fulfill our every need?

Just a Crumb from His Table could bring about the very healing that we have been longing for.

A Crumb from His Table could strengthen our battle against the devil.

A Crumb from His Table could touch whatever ails us.

All that we need is just
     a Crumb from His Table and our lives would be made whole.

Well, I don't know about you.
     I can only speak for myself.....

But, I truly believe in the power of those Jesus crumbs.

I've seen with my own eyes how some Jesus Crumbs have fixed the troubles of hurting families.

I've seen how some Jesus Crumbs helped save a troubled marriage and helped a husband and wife renew their commitment to one another.

I've seen how some Jesus Crumbs have touched troubled youth and lead them to become evangelists, teachers and preachers of His Word.

467

I have even seen with my own eyes how Jesus Crumbs have turned a young murderer into a repentant Child of God.

My brothers and sisters,
I'm not telling you something that I've heard or read in some book. I'm telling you about something that I have seen with my own eyes and not another's.

So, today, rather than focusing on folks whom we might deny a seat at this Eucharistic Feast, why don't we focus on what we need to get from His Table?

Is there something going on in your life that you really need Jesus to stop what He's doing right now and come to heal?

Is there something in your body or in your heart that you need the Lord to touch and nourish in a miraculous way?

What is it that you need from Jesus today?

Like that Canaanite Woman, today is the day for you to say to the Lord,

"Have pity on me, Lord, Son of David! - My daughter, my son, my husband, my wife, my mother, my father, my grandchild, my friend, my coworker, my student, my teacher, my boss, my preacher, my deacon, my Bishop, my priest, and even myself are tormented by some demons."

"Have pity on us, Lord, Son of David!" "Have pity on me!"

Today, we all need to come to Table of Mercy and finally get rid of whatever demons that might be tormenting us.

Even if you only walk away with just a Scrap from this table, I assure you that just a Crumb of Jesus is all that you will need.

You know, when I look back at my 20 years of being a priest, I assure you that I could pinpoint at least 10 times when I could have just walked away and given up on the Church and all its peoples. Although I have been truly blessed by the life that I get to live, it hasn't always been easy.

There have been times when either the people in the pews, the pastors in the churches and even the bishops in the cathedral have made me want to just give up on the very thing that God called me to do when He knit me in my mother's womb.

468

But, thanks be to God, it has been in those very moments of anger, disappointment and despair that I have truly come to believe in the healing power that comes from His Table.

People of God, there ain't nothing going on in your life that a Crumb from Jesus' Table can't fix!

It's up to you as to whether or not you are willing to cry out to Jesus and simply say, "Have pity on me, Lord, Son of David!"

You know, when Tooka ate Chris' feast from Landry's Seafood, she definitely needed Chris to have pity on her. It was hard for him not to kill her as he gazed upon an empty plate where his delicious Seafood Platter once stood.

But, maybe God was using Tooka to teach Chris and me some valuable lessons:

First, be thankful for all that you receive because you never know when it could be taken away.

Second, even a dog deserves a scrap from a table at Landry's Seafood hence the name "doggie bag".

And finally, if you really want to enjoy your seafood platter, never put it within the reach of a bipolar Bulldog!

Today, my brothers and sisters, Jesus invites us to come to His Table with our hands and our hearts open to receive the Crumbs that He has prepared for us. I challenge you to approach The Table of Grace with the same faith that brought that Canaanite Woman to Jesus.

Also, come with that same innocence that Tooka approached that table of Seafood.

With innocent faith, you just might leave as blessed as that woman's daughter and as full as my bipolar Bulldog!

Amen